Reminisce

BY

CONSTANCE BATTERSEA

MACMILLAN AND CO., LIMITED
ST. MARTIN'S STREET, LONDON
1922

COPYRIGHT

Printing Statement:

Due to the very old age and scarcity of this book,
many of the pages may be hard to read due to the
blurring of the original text, possible missing pages,
missing text and other issues beyond our control.

Because this is such an important and rare work, we
believe it is best to reproduce this book regardless of
its original condition.

Thank you for your understanding.

Frontispiece.

MACMILLAN AND CO., Limited
LONDON · BOMBAY · CALCUTTA · MADRAS
MELBOURNE

THE MACMILLAN COMPANY
NEW YORK · BOSTON · CHICAGO
DALLAS · SAN FRANCISCO

THE MACMILLAN CO. OF CANADA, Ltd.
TORONTO

REMINISCENCES

Ere the parting hour go by,
Quick, thy tablets, Memory!

MATTHEW ARNOLD.

TO

ANNIE YORKE

MY DEAR SISTER

"A BOOK OF REMEMBRANCE"

Some said, " John, print it " ; others said, " Not so."
Some said, " It might do good " ; others said, " No."

JOHN BUNYAN.

PREFACE

I BEGAN writing these Reminiscences in December 1917, whilst I was spending a few weeks at Bath, and continued them when recovering from an attack of diphtheria at my dear sister's house, Hamble Cliff, early in the following year. I started boldly on my self-imposed task, without any fixed plan, trusting blindly to my memory, for I had neither diaries nor old letters at hand to assist me. I fully believe that my recovery to health was hastened by this work, which both interested and fascinated me. But how little did I then realise what it would entail in the way of patient research and the unearthing of old documents, often a painful, nearly always a pathetic task. Indeed, I was anxious from the beginning to give some distinct picture of the many members of my family, scattered as they are amongst the great capitals of Europe. In doing this I found that the complications arising from the Rothschild marriages and intermarriages would prove puzzling, not only to the writer, but even more so to the reader. In fact, in mastering all their ramifications I felt the same pleasurable excitement as might be experienced by one who not only successfully arrives at the heart of an old-fashioned garden maze, but also finds her way safely out again.

Recalling the years of a singularly happy childhood

and youth seemed to give me a re-taste of some of the
joys of early spring; there was no discordant note to
distress me, only one of sadness when I recognised that
some great opportunity had perhaps been missed, or
that some wonderful blessing had not been sufficiently
appreciated at the time.

I have lived under three reigns, and have had the
inestimable advantage of seeing and knowing many
distinguished men and women. Our social life was
not confined to any special groove, and our education
and upbringing had a cosmopolitan colour that fitted
us to enjoy foreign travel and foreign modes of thought.

My dear mother's liberal yet deeply spiritual nature
influenced us in learning to respect those of other creeds
and other churches, and my father taught us, by his
example, to associate ourselves with philanthropic work
that did not necessarily emanate from those of his own
Faith.

These Reminiscences will have neither political nor
historical value, but they are faithful annals of a happy
and not uneventful life. I had, indeed, no thought of
publishing, but have at last yielded to the advice of
my kind publisher and many friends. Thus I crave
the indulgence of my readers, to whom I now, although
with many misgivings, offer these pages, written in the
hope that they may prove of interest to some of the
members of my own family and my husband's, recording such facts on both sides as affectionate hearts might
wish to preserve, though not necessarily such as would
easily have found a chronicler.

I am anxious to offer my grateful thanks to all those
whose valuable advice and criticism have so materially
helped me in writing these Reminiscences; also to the

authors and publishers who have given me permission
to quote from their books, papers, and correspondence;
to Mr. Colyer Fergusson, to whom I am indebted for the
carefully drawn Tables of the Rothschild and Montefiore
families, and to my secretary for her devoted work and
assistance; whilst the memory of those no longer with
us, who encouraged me by their warm sympathy and ever
ready help, is very present with me to-day, when I pen
the last words of these pages.

Constance Battersea

October

1922

CONTENTS

CHAPTER I

CHAPTER XVI

CHAPTER XVII

CHAPTER XVIII

CHAPTER XIX

CHAPTER XX

CHAPTER XXI

CHAPTER XXII

ILLUSTRATIONS

CHAPTER I

THE FIVE ARROWS AND THEIR DESCENDANTS

" CONCORDIA, INTEGRITAS, INDUSTRIA "

MY great-grandfather, Mayer Amschel, had always been somewhat of a mythical personality to me, but I gathered that he was born in 1744 in Frankfort-on-the-Main, the son of a merchant and money-changer, that he started business for himself in 1760, and that he was well gifted with those qualities that ensured success in a life of financial enterprise, and also with great knowledge and love of art. I was particularly attracted by a well-known anecdote in connection with him, how the Elector of Hesse-Cassel (William IX.) placed his money and his treasures in the keeping of my great-grandfather, about the year 1800, when the spirit of revolutionary upheaval was sweeping through the world, to the destruction of property, of art, and of beauty; and how in after years, when peace had been restored, the Elector received back from the hands of the Jewish merchant's sons his treasures intact. These facts have been successfully illustrated by Moritz Oppenheim, the well-known Jewish artist, in his own romantic way.

I once visited my great-grandfather's grave in the Jewish cemetery at Frankfort, and could hardly believe that the date 1812 on the tombstone referred to one whose widow I had actually seen; yet so it was. Mayer Amschel's wife, my great-grandmother, Frau Rothschild as she was always called—Gudela Schnapper by birth —died on the verge of her 96th year in 1849.

1

B

As a very young child I was staying at Frankfort-on-the-Main with my parents a few months before her death, and was taken to see, or be seen by, my venerable relative. I remember being ushered into a room by two maids, who led me up to a couch on which reposed the tiny form of a little old lady wearing a big cap that framed her face and hid her hair. She raised herself up a little and said some words to me in German. I shrank back somewhat alarmed, but the two maids proceeded to offer me cakes and fruit, after which I was led from the room.

Years afterwards I realised that I had been admitted into the presence of a remarkable personality, the mother of nineteen children, ten of whom had grown to adult estate. Born long before the French Revolution that convulsed and changed the face of Europe, my great-grandmother would never leave her old home in the Judengasse, the Jewish quarter of the town; no entreaties of her sons would ever induce her to move into a more modern and brighter district, or to accompany her youngest son James to Paris, where he was settling into his new home and taking his position as head of the Paris Banking House. She lived in the simplest conditions, constantly visited by her children and grandchildren, who were devoted to her.

Of my great-grandmother's five sons, Nathan came to England about the year 1798. He was sent to a cotton-broker—Mr. Behrens—in Manchester, where he lived for some years. He could speak no English at first, and wrote his home letters in the German language, but in what are called small Hebrew characters. He must have been extraordinarily shrewd, with a positive genius for business. I believe he migrated to London in 1803, where he married Hannah Cohen, a sister of Judith, wife of Sir Moses Montefiore. Whilst still quite young, he established the celebrated Banking House in New Court, St. Swithin's Lane.

The many transactions both at home and abroad in

THE ELECTOR OF HESSE-CASSEL ENTRUSTING HIS TREASURES TO MAYER
AMSCHEL ROTHSCHILD AT THE COMMENCEMENT OF THE NAPOLEONIC
WARS IN 1806.

THE ELECTOR OF HESSE-CASSEL RECEIVING HIS TREASURES FROM MAYER AMSCHEL ROTHSCHILD AT THE CLOSE OF THE NAPOLEONIC WARS IN 1814.

which he was engaged during years of anxiety, but also years rich in surprises, included the one connected with the never-to-be-forgotten battle of Waterloo, when the fate of Napoleon was for ever sealed. There are many different accounts of how the news of the victory of the Allies was brought at an early date to the knowledge of my grandfather. Some of these accounts are rejected as not being authentic. I like to think that a pigeon was the bearer of the glorious news, but I believe it came in a rather more prosaic fashion, through one of my grandfather's agents, who awaited the result of the battle at Ostend, came across the Channel in one of my grandfather's special boats, and was the first to bring the news to London.

CHAPTER
I.

Nathan Mayer hastened to acquaint the English Government with the information he had received, but no credence was given him in spite of his assurance that the almost unbelievable statement was true.

On the evening of that eventful day, when one of the members of the Government was driving out to dinner, his coach was stopped and surrounded in the streets by a cheering mob : they brought the confirmation of the news that the battle had been won by the Allies, and that Napoleon was a prisoner !

My dear maternal grandmother, Henrietta Rothschild, youngest daughter of Mayer Amschel, married a younger and very handsome brother of Sir Moses Montefiore, Abraham by name, who died at a very early age in 1824. She was closely connected with the years of our childhood and youth, was a devoted mother and grandmother, and credited her grandchildren with every kind of good quality and many talents that they may not have possessed. She was of a very bright and cheerful nature, and had a great fund of the racy old Jewish humour, which made her conversation most entertaining. She never became quite English, in spite of her long life being chiefly spent in this country, and never lost her German accent. She spent many weeks with

us at Aston Clinton every winter, until the year before
her death, which occurred in 1866. Her own country
home was Worth Park, a beautiful property in Sussex,
bought by her husband, which she gave to her eldest son
on his marriage. When in London she continued living
in Stanhope Street, where, in her younger days, she
entertained most hospitably. There also, on Saturday
evenings, all the members of her family assembled, such
gatherings being very much the fashion in those days.

I cannot omit the name of Sir Moses Montefiore in
this brief sketch of my mother's family, for he played
a prominent and distinguished part in the Jewish annals
of the early years of the last century.

As far as I, personally, was concerned, I saw but
little of my great-uncle, in spite of our double connection
with him, for not only was he the brother of my maternal
grandfather, but he had married Judith Cohen, a sister
of my father's mother, Mrs. N. M. Rothschild.

Sir Moses was one of the most orthodox members
of the Jewish Portuguese Synagogue, belonging to the
scholarly Sephardim, his ancestors having come from
Italy to England in the eighteenth century. The name
of his ancestor, Amadio Montefiore, registered his having
paid Town Taxes in Leghorn on May 19, 1661, as did
also that of Ismael Montefiore in 1697.

I have been told that a red silk curtain, belonging to
the Ark of the Synagogue, can still be seen preserved in
the city of Leghorn. It is embroidered with gold—in
the centre a Hebrew inscription, at the foot a lion on
a mount holding a bunch of flowers in its jaws (this
refers to the name of *Leoni*, lion; *Montefiore*, mount of
flowers). On the reverse side of the curtain is a dove
with an olive branch in its beak. This refers to the
family name of the wife of Leoni Montefiore—Rachel
Olivette—to whom the Synagogue was indebted for the
curtain and its design. The date is 1650.

Sir Moses was bitterly opposed to the part that his
brother Horatio took in espousing the cause of the

reformers, who had established a synagogue on new lines, where both worship and teaching were carried on more in accordance with Westernised views than with those of the old-established synagogues. The breach that this occasioned between the two brothers lasted during the greater part of their lives, many members of my mother's family supporting the reformers. Their synagogue has now, after seventy years, a very assured and definite position, its ministers being much respected for their learning as well as for their social work. But to return to Sir Moses: he was well known by his commanding presence, as well as for his very courteous manners and address, which stood him in good part in his interviews with Royal and other distinguished personages.

For thirteen years the brothers-in-law, Montefiore and Rothschild, lived in close proximity to one another in houses in New Court, St. Swithin's Lane, and there was much friendly intercourse between them. Later Sir Moses owned a house in Park Lane, and bought East Cliff, Ramsgate, as a country seat, where he spent the concluding years of his life.

In a diary[1] of Lady Montefiore we read how " Mon," as she called her husband, " took a steak at New Court," probably with N. M. Rothschild, for the lady—his wife —was dining at home that evening. We also learn how Lady Montefiore, after a visit to some seaside resort, accompanied " Mon " to town to inform Hannah (wife of N. M.) of the good state of the health of their children (Charlotte and Lionel), whom they had recently been seeing.

Again, looking into the diary, we read how " on one Sunday, December 25, 1825," Sir Moses and Lady Montefiore started from home at four o'clock in the morning, in their own chariot, which conveyed them " to the ' Spread Eagle,' Bishopsgate Street, where the stage started for Yarmouth, in which Mon had engaged

[1] From *The Jewish Chronicle*, June 20, 1902.

two places." " As usual, Mon was a quarter of an hour before his time." This matutinal start evidently did not upset the health or the tempers of the travellers, for on the following day Lady Montefiore was able to write :

Dec. 26.—I may class this as one of the happiest days of my life in the serene and obliging society of my dear Mon, and blessed with health and cheerfulness and an unremitting desire to please, for which I cannot sufficiently thank the Almighty.

It would be impossible for me to give a detailed account of the good and important work that Sir Moses succeeded in doing for his Community, in which he displayed great courage and zeal and tact, nor will I attempt to do so. But as these Reminiscences are specially personal, I feel drawn to record two occasions which I clearly remember, when I had the pleasure, a very rare one, of seeing and conversing with this venerable relative of mine.

The first was in the year 1865, when Sir Moses was visiting my grandmother in Great Stanhope Street, she being already stricken with an illness that led ultimately to her death. Sir Moses was eighty years of age at that time, and was contemplating his sixth visit to Jerusalem. He looked well and vigorous for his age, giving us a vivid account of what his journey to the East would be like, of the work that was awaiting him there, and of the reception that he looked forward to from his devoted co-religionists in Palestine. My sympathetic interest in his words must have been very evident, for turning to me Sir Moses asked, " Why not come with me ? You would enjoy the journey from beginning to end, and the experience." The wonderful old man would not have been astonished had I acquiesced, and now, years afterwards, I regret not having done so. I remember that one of his nieces proved to be his companion (his devoted wife was then no more),

THE MONTEFIORE FAMILY IN 1797.

On the left Abraham Montefiore, on the right Sir Moses Montefiore, with two of their sisters.

and that journey was not even the last he undertook, for he visited Jerusalem once again in his 91st year, when he smilingly reproved those who anxiously set the dangers of fatigue before him by saying, " I keep a Bath chair in Jerusalem."

When I next saw Sir Moses it was in his own house at East Cliff, Ramsgate, where my mother and I visited him during our few weeks' stay at Westgate. He was then on the verge of his 100th birthday ! He seemed shorter and smaller than on the former occasion, and the skin of his face was like parchment. He had returned from a short afternoon drive, but was quite active and ready for conversation. He received us in his room up-stairs, where I noticed a large Hebrew Bible lying on a high reading-desk, with its open page, suggesting, and rightly, as we were told afterwards, its daily use.

Sir Moses asked us a few questions, steering cleverly away from any dangerous topics that might arise in the shape of controversial matters, and, after signing with a trembling hand a photograph of himself for my mother, ended our interview by giving us both his blessing in the Hebrew tongue.

We left him, impressed as we were by that glimpse of one who represented a bygone generation, with its reverence for the orthodox Jewish Community, its grateful recognition of England's priceless gift of civil and religious freedom, but also with its narrow and somewhat hard estimate of those who were taking a broader but not less spiritual view of Judaism.

My paternal grandparents lived for a short time after their marriage at St. Helen's, near New Court, where my father was born in 1810 ; they moved later to a house on Stamford Hill, Stoke Newington. This house, with a spacious garden, was in close proximity to one inhabited by my maternal grandmother. Thus, as children, my parents were playmates for a short while in adjoining gardens. The one house passed long ago out of the family, but the other, now the property of my cousin, Claude Montefiore, has become a Reformatory Training School for Jewish Girls, and bears the appropriate name of " Montefiore House."

My paternal grandmother, Mrs. N. M. Rothschild, was a clever woman, authoritative and somewhat masterful ; she managed all the members of her family, even when they had attained to man's estate. She was striking in appearance, with very beautiful blue eyes, a fine brow, and a straight Grecian nose. Her husband died abroad in 1836, at Frankfort, where he had been attending his eldest son's wedding, leaving her the mother of four sons and three daughters. She continued to live in the homes he had given her, at 107 Piccadilly, and for a few weeks in the year at Gunnersbury Park, Acton. This truly beautiful mid-Victorian villa, a most suitable residence for a man whose daily duties took him to London, was within easy riding or driving distance of New Court. Once it had been a Royal residence, belonging to a daughter of George III. My grandfather, alas ! did not live to inhabit the home to which he had been looking forward with pleasurable impatience. He died before I was born, but I have a faint recollection of my grandmother. I remember being taken to see her on various Saturdays by my father, and always being smartly attired on these occasions. But she never entered into our lives, and I felt no special sorrow at her death in 1850.

My grandfather, Nathan, and his four brothers, Amschel, Solomon, Charles, and James, respectively founders and heads of the kindred Banking Houses in the cities of Frankfort, Vienna, Naples, and Paris, were raised to the Austrian nobility in 1822, but Nathan never assumed the title of " Baron," though he acted as Austrian Consul-General. Thus the five brothers were closely united in their financial business, which during the middle of the last century increased by leaps and bounds, and acquired a world-wide reputation and importance.

N. M. ROTHSCHILD.

In later life Nathan is reported to have said : " It
requires a great deal of boldness and a great deal of
caution to make a great fortune; but when you have
got it, it requires ten times as much wit to keep it."

My father, the second son of N. M. Rothschild, was
born in 1810, and married in 1840 Louisa Montefiore
(born 1821), his first cousin, grand-daughter of Mayer
Amschel of Frankfort.   The Baronetcy was conferred
upon him in 1846, his elder brother, Lionel, having
refused the honour in my father's favour.   But failing
any sons being born to my parents, the title was to
revert, as it did, to my Uncle Lionel's son, Nathaniel,
who later was raised to the Peerage.

My father was devoted to his mother ; indeed he had a
great idea of what filial affection should be, and claimed
the like from his children.   He had the kindest heart
and most generous nature of any one I have ever known,
and was extraordinarily unselfish.   His love for his
elder brother was indeed beautiful.   He was of a naturally bright and cheerful disposition, ready to make the
best of everything, satisfied with his round of daily
duties and the enjoyments that his love of social life
and his country pursuits brought him.

As children we were never allowed to grumble at
any little disappointment, and from an early age were
taught by my father to " be satisfied," which was his
motto for home life—he setting us a splendid example.
We were also never encouraged to make plans, so that
we should not worry our elders by constantly inquiring
whether these plans might be realised.   So when a trip
abroad was in prospect, my sister and I would call it by
some other name and thus mystify our relatives.

From 1847 we inhabited a beautiful house in London
—No. 2 Grosvenor Place Houses, as it was then called,
the middle one of the three houses built by the then
Marquis of Westminster in Grosvenor Place, on the
site of St. Anne's Hospital, which had recently been
pulled down.   My father took a long lease of the then

unbuilt house, and, as soon as it was completed, proceeded to have it carefully decorated by the most capable French artists. It was also exquisitely furnished according to my father's remarkably good taste, well known to all members of his family. Amongst other works of art, it contained one glorious picture by Van Dyck, a gift from my maternal grandmother.

As very young children we had lived for part of two or three years in Paris, but upon returning for good to England we spent the greater part of the year in London and the autumn months in Brighton. Once, indeed, my father rented Lord Darnley's house at Sandgate, which suited us all so well that he wanted to purchase it; but this he was unable to do, so he turned his attention to the county of Bucks, where his two brothers were already in possession of considerable property. My father, being very fond of shooting and hunting, was fortunate in finding in that county a small house lying just outside the Vale of Aylesbury — that splendid hunting ground—and under the beech woods of the Chiltern Hills, where he had good pheasant-shooting. There we settled down in 1853, spending six months of each year at Aston Clinton.

My dear father's death occurred in 1876, but my mother continued during her long widowhood to make Aston Clinton her principal home, where she died in 1910. My sister and I, loath to cut ourselves off completely from our old home, still retain the house and grounds, where we spend a few weeks each year amongst the surroundings of our youth (1922).

During the early months of the Great War, in 1914–15, Aston Clinton House, our old home, was given over to the Commanding Officer of the Twenty-first Division, then encamped on the Halton estate. It was there that first Sir Edward Hutton and later General Forestier - Walker was quartered with his staff. I spent many week-ends with my military tenants, and made some good friends amongst them.

SIR ANTHONY DE ROTHSCHILD.

One fine summer's day I stood at the crossing of the
roads, near the town of Missenden, watching the departure of the Division, marching off to join the army abroad. With the deepest regret I heard, as time went on, that some whom I had known well and learnt to look upon as friends could never be welcomed back again by me, as they had laid down their lives for their country.

To return to the 'fifties. The house was unpretentious at first, but comfortable; as time went on, however, it was enlarged and re-enlarged, finally covering quite a substantial piece of ground.

As usual, my father was most particular in furnishing according to the prevailing enthusiasm for French art; indeed, in this case it was most successful. Without having any executive artistic power himself, he had most unerring good taste, and people said he never bought or praised anything that had not reached a high standard. With him it amounted to intuition. The house, however, remained, even when enlarged, too small for my father's hospitable proclivities; he loved seeing guests round his table, and was always asking friends to join his shooting parties. He had great family feeling, also strong racial attachment. The Rothschilds were, in his eyes, people apart from all others, and he kept up a close connection with the foreign members of his family. His Jewish proclivities brought him into touch with the philanthropic and educational work of his race, who at that time were only just beginning to emerge from their life of separation. In my childhood the Jews were still suffering from civil and religious disabilities; they had no very assured social standing, and there was in many quarters a deep-seated prejudice against them. My family, whilst remaining true to their religion, established a firm footing in the social and political life of their country, and beyond that were recognised as being some of the best landlords that the county of Bucks had ever seen.

Their sporting tastes made them popular amongst their country friends and neighbours, and my parents' genuine charity and kindness of heart endeared them to the clergy in their villages and to all those who were working for the welfare of the people.

I find it almost impossible to describe my dear mother. She was " unique." It would indeed be difficult to meet with a mind as distinguished, a manner as refined and dignified, and an appearance as attractive as she possessed. Without having any real pretensions to perfect beauty, she had a great deal about her that was beautiful—large, blue, expressive, searching eyes, a noble brow, the most delicate pink and white skin, and a wealth of glorious rich auburn hair that in her youth and middle life fell below her waist in waves. After her marriage, which took place in 1840, she wore her hair parted carefully above the forehead, and drawn in bands close to the well-shaped head, the little straggling curls escaping from her comb in beautiful profusion. But at an early age she adopted the matronly cap, which for the last forty years of her life became merged into the widow's head-dress, now so consistently discarded. When old age asserted its claims, her hair, silky and wavy as ever, became as white as snow. She was small and slight in stature, with much natural dignity that gave her an air of aloofness; indeed, some found her difficult of approach. This was partly due to her shyness and low estimate of her own power. Her inborn distinction forbade the approach of anything low-toned or vulgar. She had a very real and unusual charm. She was a profound reader and a very independent thinker, not easily to be moved from any conclusion at which she had arrived after due and careful consideration. Hers was a fine spiritual nature, rising above all sectarianism, even above racial bias, and claiming affinity with the noblest minds of every creed. She read with pleasure Martineau, Parker, and Robertson's sermons, feeling some kinship with

LADY DE ROTHSCHILD.

Unitarianism, but she was also much attracted by the Society of Friends—by their philanthropy, the simplicity of their lives, the quiet dress of their women folk, and their dislike for merely fashionable or frivolous pursuits. She never cared much for social enjoyments (this probably because she had been very delicate in her youth and middle life, and was never able to bear much fatigue), although she was admirably fitted for the pleasures of conversation, and immensely popular amongst friends and acquaintances. But her own people were certainly not forgotten. Profoundly anxious to help them spiritually and ethically, she started, with some Jewish friends, devotional Sabbath classes for the benefit of the Jewish working girls. Some mention of her indefatigable activities in connection with these classes and other branches of her communal work will occur later in these Reminiscences; suffice it to say here that in all her works of charity she was closely associated with her sister-in-law, the wife of my uncle, Lionel de Rothschild.

It was partly the result of a foreign bringing up, and also of her own delicate health, that my dear mother was never able to indulge in any very strenuous out-of-door exercise, nor did she ever attempt to learn any of the games so much appreciated and indulged in by the modern girl. But she loved the country for its peace and calm beauty, and simply delighted in the homely surroundings of her house in Buckinghamshire. Her affection for her beloved companions—her dogs— was very touching, and never waned; until the end of her days she was never without one of her favourites, and the little faithful animals were not slow to repay the love bestowed upon them. She was deeply interested in village life and all its concerns. Country life, carried on as it was in our hospitable house, meant frequent visits from relatives and friends; thus my mother became more easily acquainted with men and women of literary, political, and social standing than

she might otherwise have done. Those who knew her
well loved to be with her, not only on account of her
interesting and inspiring conversation, but for her
keen sense of humour and her quick response to pleasant
and suggestive talk.

My mother was always deeply appreciative of the
society of young people, with whom she had often more
in common than with their elders, for she remained
young in heart, young in hopeful belief, young in
sympathy all her life. She was full of pluck and
generally optimistic. Fearlessly she looked forward
and trusted the people; thus, in politics, she was a
faithful Liberal. She never wavered in support of
Liberalism, *as she read it*, but she was on the happiest
terms with Lord Beaconsfield (a friend of her youth),
and had other acquaintances in the Conservative camp
whose friendship she appreciated. Her quick insight
into difficult questions, her extraordinary grasp of mind,
combined with her extreme modesty, made her an
interesting and uncommon personality; but owing to
this very modesty she did not always do herself justice,
and it was difficult to make her believe how much she
was beloved. She could not endure conceit or swagger
in any one, and was also a little severe upon stupidity;
indeed, she did not " suffer fools gladly." From
childhood she had shown great talent for drawing and
painting, working for many hours daily in her youth
and middle life, continuing into old age—first at portrait-
painting, working both in oils and water-colours, then
at flower-painting in water-colour and pastel. Her
touch was quite beautiful, and her eye for colour exquisite. She wrote remarkably well, but always shrank
from the ordeal of publication.

I was born in London in 1843, and as there were
only twenty months between the ages of my sister
and myself, we were from our earliest days, in all
things, closely connected : together in the nursery
and in the schoolroom, watched over by the same

nurses and attendants, trained by the same teachers, following the same pursuits, sharing the same amusements. And here I cannot resist inserting a really touching and beautiful letter, written to my sister on her fourteenth birthday by our nurse Mrs. Spearing, who came into my mother's service on the very day that I was born, remaining until my tenth year. She was a tall handsome woman, with a commanding presence and pleasant bearing, a widow of recent date, with two sons.

" December 9.

" I cannot allow this day to pass," she wrote, "without writing to congratulate you on your 14th Birthday. May you live to enjoy many, very many in health and happiness.

" I remember it was a lovely moonlight night on the 9th of December when you were born. Dear Miss Constance was sweetly sleeping in her little cot, and the waits were playing just under the window ; the music was very pretty. As we expected a distinguished visitor, Jane and I were sitting up, waiting the arrival, when, to our great joy, other music was heard in the *house*, much more agreeable than that which was under the window ; and presently one of the prettiest little faces I ever saw came peeping from underneath a flannel mantle."

I distinctly remember Mrs. Spearing reading *Line upon Line* in turn with the newspapers, and I think she must have been a devoted member of some very evangelical church. I can recall an alarming description she once gave me of eternal punishment for those who resented the true teaching, but, seeing my shocked expression of countenance, she assured me that we and our parents would in all likelihood find ourselves amongst the saved. I never repeated these theological remarks at the time, rightly conjecturing that they would have led to the expulsion of Mrs. Spearing from our terrestrial heaven—the nursery. Her absorbing affection for us, grafted upon a naturally jealous disposition, made her resent the attendance of others about us, and with the

CHAPTER
I.

exception of Jane, mentioned in the letter, her temper did not contribute to the comfort or happiness of those who came for a short time under her sway. She lived to a good old age, as a pensioner of my mother's, and ended her days at Southampton, where an occasional visit from Canon Wilberforce greatly pleased her.

Perhaps it would not be out of place were I to state here that in those old days domestic service bore no stigma, as, unfortunately, some think it does now, but was an honourable, even an enviable, calling. From an early age village youths and maidens would aspire to serve in the " big house " connected with the soil of their own county, and considered it a matter of justifiable pride to remain *a lifetime* with one employer, thus helping to carry on the traditions of that house, keeping warm the name it might have acquired for generosity and hospitality. I can speak, indeed, with grateful recollection of the many devoted men and women in my parents' household, whose excellent service was deeply appreciated. If, unhappily, there was a failure amongst them, the cause could generally have been ascribed to over-indulgence in the matter of drink, which in those days was not unknown in other grades of society.

My dear father, having lived abroad for some years, introduced into our establishment the novelty of a French manservant, who acted as butler, valet, and confectioner. Désprès belonged, indeed, to the old order of retainers; his very appearance gave a patent of distinction to the house. His sonorous voice in recommending some specially well-cooked dish to the guests at our dinner-table, and the way in which he would whisper into their ears the year of vintage of our much-prized French wines, could never be forgotten and has never been equalled. He would spend hours in arranging the dessert for the dinner-table, and stand in his white jacket with his arms crossed, smiling at the giant peaches and grapes that he had been buying in

Covent Garden for the festive board. He cherished a Chapter romantic attachment for some of the older members I. of the French family, and rejoiced in our frequent visits to Paris, where he was always sure of a kindly welcome, especially from my aunt, Baroness James de Rothschild. Déspr<u>ès</u> loved big cities and grand country seats, but Aston Clinton in those days was not to his taste, and he begged to be left in London when we migrated into Bucks. This wish was readily granted, until ill-health and advancing years drove him at length into well-earned retirement, which he found in France with his own people.

Among the pictures that memory conjures up of past years I can see that of a stately French coachman, Gentil by name ; he was a very fine driver, with an imposing seat on the box of one of the old-fashioned carriages of the day, where, in wig and livery, he let his driving do full justice to a pair of strikingly beautiful horses. He died from an accident whilst still in our employ. Personally, I wish I could enumerate all those, past and present, to whose good and faithful service I am indebted, whether under our parents' roof or in our own household, for have they not smoothed the paths of life for us, and brought a great measure of comfort and happiness into the home ?

My dear mother found much happiness in bestowing gifts of fruit and flowers on friends and neighbours, whilst later my husband loved opening The Pleasaunce gardens to the many who sought rest and change at Overstrand. But fruit and flowers and luxuriant gardens are not evolved by the waving of a magician's wand ; they all need long and careful preparation, and to the gardeners who have produced these happy results, both in Bucks and in Norfolk, my thanks are due.

It is strange, yet not strange, to recognise how social life resembles a web of many threads, all depending one upon another, and so intimately connected that, if but one strand be cut, the complete fabric may be

C

Déspes — butler to Anthony.

injured. Thus, rulers and subjects, employers and employees, masters and servants, should on both sides conduce to one harmonious whole, of which they can ensure the safety by banishing from their midst feelings of distrust and by encouraging those of active sympathy.

Let me revert to the members of my mother's family, especially to one who was universally beloved by all who knew her or came into touch with her, my mother's only and dearly-loved sister, Charlotte, who married Horatio Montefiore, her relative—a widower with twelve children—at a comparatively early age, and died in giving birth to her second child, a son. She had been delighted on hearing that her child was a boy, for she had destined him for the Jewish ministry, and she was spared the grief of ever knowing that he was of weak intellect. At the same time she had not the happiness of living to realise that her eldest child, Helen, had inherited many of her own fine and noble qualities and intellectual tastes.

Always of a delicate constitution, but with a strong purpose and will, she possessed an unusual character. My aunt had all the instincts and making of a great social worker, also a certain romantic element in her nature, which influenced all the actions of her life. Her husband belonged to the reformed Jewish Community, and she heartily endorsed and accepted his views, thus incurring the displeasure of Sir Moses Montefiore, whose orthodoxy was unimpeachable.

My mother had idolised her sister, to whom she looked up as to a superior being. The death of that dear sister was the first awful grief she had ever experienced, and it left its trace upon her for many a long year.

My two uncles, brothers of my mother, were considered by us as delightful playmates. They were closely in touch with us, and often stayed in our country home. Joseph, the elder one, was in many respects an interesting man, with a considerable gift for writing and

Charlotte

MRS. HORATIO MONTEFIORE.

= Horatio - widower with 12 kids
Montefiore

Sister of Louisa M.R.

an extraordinary sense of humour. He might have
gone far, had he taken the trouble to study or work for
any one aim, but he was of a careless, somewhat lazy,
disposition, with no ambition or any calling for public
work. He had a very kind heart and an affectionate
nature, but as a boy he had been spoilt, and I often
felt that he was a failure, although a very lovable one.
He had high spirits as a youth, and even as a man
would romp with us and amuse us in many ways, but
he did not shine in general society and was absurdly
shy. He married in middle life Henrietta Sichel, a
relative, and had two sons, one of them being the
present Sir Francis Montefiore. His younger brother,
Nathaniel, was a very different character. Less attractive in appearance, in buoyancy of spirits, and elasticity
of mind than his brother Joseph, he was a man who
gained enormously upon further acquaintance. Less
spoilt and petted as a youth, with a more concentrated
nature, he made up his mind at an early age as to
his aims in life. He was fond of travel and of study,
particularly of chemistry and of medicine, and determined when quite young to work for the medical
profession. He went through his hospital training at
Guy's, but he never really practised, although his skill
and knowledge were constantly placed at the service
of the poor or helpless. He took a kind and generous
interest in the Jewish Infant School, of which he was
President, and where he was idolised by teachers and
children. In 1856 he married Emma Goldsmid,
daughter of Sir Isaac Goldsmid, who most happily
was able to supply the very qualities in which he was
perhaps weakest, being a very practical, clever woman,
with a strong will and much determination of character.

They had two sons and two daughters, who were all
very dear to us. It was sad that their eldest son,
Leonard, should have died at an early age; he was
brilliantly gifted, and would assuredly have made his
mark. When at Oxford, he joined an Ultra-Radical

group of students, his democratic views being extremely pronounced. He thus offended some people by what they deemed his Radical pose, and by the censure that he was in the habit of meting out to men and women whom he thought fashionable and frivolous. And here I feel that I cannot do better than quote some lines from the eloquent pen of one of his greatest friends, Lord Milner, to whom we are indebted for a touching memoir, as a preface to a volume of Collected Essays and Letters by L. Montefiore, privately printed and produced in 1881. Lord Milner tells us of L. M.'s "deep and wide sympathy for the labouring class, and his strong interest in all that could make their lives more human as well as more comfortable. He was naturally a great advocate of Workmen's Clubs, and of every means of promoting healthy social intercourse among the poor."

He gave his services freely, and they were much appreciated by the late Canon and Mrs. Barnett, who were at that time starting their great campaign of social reform in Whitechapel. " He was ever ready," continues Lord Milner, " to lend his help to make the social meetings of working people a success, either by conversation, by reading, or by simple entertaining lectures, in giving which he had a happy facility. With his fluency, his plain language, and his genius for vivid description, he could interest audiences to whom lectures on any subject were only too likely to be dull and incomprehensible. He was by nature rather a thoughtful man of action than a man of thought. All his interests lay on the side of the human and the real. Speculative doubts troubled him but little . . . a simple belief in goodness, a reverent delight in all that was bright and beautiful in the world, and a deep love of his fellow-men—these were his religion."

His younger brother, Claude, gifted with an exceptionally fine intellect, and an intensely spiritual nature, has attained a very high position as a Hebrew scholar

and as a theological student and writer. He is deservedly respected and loved far and wide. His genial
simplicity he inherits from his father, also his modesty
and quaint humour, whilst the reforming spirit that in
his grandfather's case produced a revolt against some
aspects of orthodoxy and bondage to Talmudical pre-
cepts, reappears in the grandson, and has caused him to
found a synagogue of so-called Liberal Judaism, where
he himself officiates in turn with the minister, Rabbi
Mattuck, a very talented American co-religionist.

Of the two daughters, the one is Alice Lucas, widow
of the late Henry Lucas, an excellent Hebrew scholar,
who has translated into English verse with much success
a volume of fine Hebrew hymns, besides being the
author of some attractive English poems. The younger
daughter, a warm-hearted, lovable woman, married the
late Sir Lewis M'Iver, to whom she proved the most
affectionate and devoted of wives.

All the branches of my family used to keep the
ordinances of our religion in a greater or less degree of
strictness, and although my sister and I were not
brought up in a strictly orthodox Jewish manner, our
religious education was a very thorough and careful
one. We kept the Sabbath day in practice as well as
in spirit, beginning after breakfast by reading parts of
the Sabbath Service, and continuing by receiving Bible
instruction from our mother. We never wrote nor did
any lessons on Saturday, nor did we drive or ride, no
horses being taken out on that day. When in London
we generally paid family visits with our father, who
always walked with us on the Saturday.

My dear mother never cared for the long interminable
Synagogue services, which she did not find devotional
or inspiring (they have much improved since then),
and the fact that driving on the Sabbath was strictly
prohibited made it almost impossible for her to have
attended Synagogue, even if she had wished to do so.
But on most of the Jewish holy days we were to

be found in our seats in the gallery of the Orthodox
Synagogue, and as children we enjoyed following the
Hebrew words of the chants and portions of the Bible.
We all fasted on the Day of Atonement, but, with the
exception of my father, spent this, the greatest holy day,
at home and not in Synagogue.

The Seder or Passover evenings were festivals which
we greatly enjoyed. For these, we all assembled at my
Uncle Lionel de Rothschild's house in Piccadilly, and
our friend and Hebrew master, Dr. Kalisch, read the
service. We looked forward to joining in the choruses
of the cheery hymns, and every one was supposed to be
very jolly on these occasions.

It was our custom to spend the Jewish holy days
that fell in the autumn at Gunnersbury Park, where at
first we were the guests of my paternal grandmother.
This was an annual treat that we greatly enjoyed. My
cousins were five in number, two daughters and three
sons. The elder daughter, Leonora, already distinguished for her charm and beauty, never cared for
childish games, but walked soberly about with her
elders ; we saw but little of her at that time. On
the other hand we found a genial and lively companion
in the second daughter, Evelina. The eldest son,
Nathaniel, was rather stiff and stand-offish when we were
children, but we admired him for his good looks, and I
used to think his knowledge on many subjects very
wonderful even at that early age. Alfred and Leopold
were our dear and devoted playmates, ready to share
our games, and to make our stay very delightful, and
in a measure exciting, as we got into all manner of
scrapes under their guidance. We were not a little
alarmed of my Uncle Lionel in those days, but knew
how devoted our father was to his brother, whom he
used affectionately to call " Rabbi Lev," so we wanted
him to like us. My aunt (his wife and cousin), Charlotte
Rothschild, had married at the age of seventeen, and
had arrived in England from Frankfort as a young

and beautiful bride. She was very accomplished and a CHAPTER
brilliant linguist, with great social charm and power.   I.

At my uncle's house distinguished political guests
were constantly to be found. He and my aunt entertained enormously between the 'fifties and 'seventies, and
were I to give a list of their frequent guests, I should
mention nearly all the most remarkable men of the
day, particularly those in the political world, as well as
the most beautiful and fashionable women. As we
grew older we were included in the invitations. I
seem to have developed a love of society at a very
early age, if I may judge by the following extract from
a letter written to my mother by her sister :

. . . Mamma wrote to me she accompanied you and
Connie to Mrs. L.'s, and she was delighted with her pet,
thought her the best dressed child there. She seems to take
after me, in her early love of dancing and society ; may
she in other and more important respects be in every way
better than her aunt, may her energy be better employed,
and may a far greater share of perseverance make her activity
far more useful to herself and others. Dear child ! I have
many hopes for her . . .

I am now anxious to devote some more of my recollections to the years of my childhood, before attempting
any account of the many interesting people I have met
and known during a long lifetime.

CHAPTER II

Oh ! talk not to me of a name great in story,
The days of our youth are the days of our glory,
And the myrtle and ivy of sweet two-and-twenty
Are worth all your laurels though ever so plenty !
BYRON.

CHAPTER II.

WE loved our country home, and speedily made ourselves acquainted with the village folk, who were quite ready to receive us in their cottages, to entertain us by their chatter, and to cater for our special tastes. As they knew my absorbing love for and interest in very young infants, I was allowed to hold and dandle every child I could lay my hands upon, always hoping that I might some day find an abandoned baby in a hedge and take it home, to keep for my very own. My mother begged me not to express this wish in public, or it might have been realised all too soon.

There was one very peculiar and amusing old woman in our village who used to keep us in fits of laughter by her extraordinary stories of the doings in the household of Lord Lake, our predecessor at Aston Clinton, in whose service the narrator had lived. The grand words she used in speaking, her performances on the tambourine, her dancing, her singing, her antics, all in her tiny room—her apartment, as she called it—had a most comical effect. Another dear old lady, who looked as if she had stepped out of one of the nursery picture-books, received us with an old-fashioned curtsey, and spoke in language far above her station in life.

24

CONSTANCE AND ANNIE DE ROTHSCHILD AS CHILDREN.

There was a farmer, and his wife and family, who
entertained us with elderberry wine and home-made
bread; and there was a gamekeeper's wife with an
unfailing flow of conversation and much talk of dogs
and their extraordinary feats of intelligence, which
specially appealed to my sister.

At that time, in the 'fifties, the only day-school in
Aston Clinton was kept by a drunken schoolmaster,
who had about thirty miserable dejected-looking male
scholars. This was the National School, under the
Rector's sway, and a disgracefully bad one it was.

During those years straw-plaiting was the staple
industry and main feature of the county. Schools for
teaching children to plait were held by a few old women
in the village. One of these schools at Aston Clinton
was presided over by a little cripple, deformed and
unable to stand or walk. She was carried into her
chair, and managed her classes like a queen from her
throne. She could only use two of her fingers, but would
grasp a little stick or birch, with which she threatened
any lazy pupils. She also succeeded in working some very
wonderful samplers. The atmosphere was asphyxiating.

At the early age of eleven I developed a passion for
teaching, and, my sister obediently conforming to my
wishes, we both resolved, if permitted, to introduce some
measure of education into the school of our friend the
dame. We explained our wishes and designs to the
accommodating dame, and, armed with some lesson-
books, we proceeded to instruct the little " plaiters."
They were delightfully ignorant, and we enjoyed ourselves extremely, and were even encouraged to go further
afield to another school of the same sort in our village.

On one damp, warm afternoon in autumn our mother
found us immersed in this, our favourite occupation,
and was so horrified at the atmosphere she encountered
upon entering the room that she forbade us to continue
our self-imposed work. Great distress resulted on our
part, but we were not to be beaten.

The boys did not attend their school on Saturdays; why not beg for the use of their building for our purposes? No sooner said than done. We appealed to the Rector of the day, and he, although an anti-educationist, granted us this favour, and we boldly issued invitations to the girls frequenting the dame's school to attend our classes on the following Saturday afternoon. It was a bold venture, but when my mother came to inspect us in our new and airy premises, she found us surrounded by a number of very eager pupils, who were being taught reading and writing by my sister and myself, and arithmetic by our competent German companion, Miss Morck. Our mother soon felt that our youthful attempts at instruction should give place to some method of real education, so my kind and ever-generous father, obedient to her desire, built a beautiful girls' school for the village of Aston Clinton. Never has the building of any edifice been so carefully and affectionately watched as this was by our young selves. I even tested the growth of the walls by going each day to jump over them, until my efforts were out-distanced by the masons' work. In an early diary of that date I find: " The wish of my heart is now granted, we have a school of our own at Aston Clinton." Then we canvassed the village most diligently to secure pupils for the opening day, and proudly counted fifteen girls whose parents were anxious to see their children properly educated. The Rector was most discouraging. He feared that in time many would be lured away from the plaiting schools, which would ruin the old dames, and he would not even be pacified by my mother's assurance that the old dames should be pensioned for the rest of their lives. He did not see the use of education for girls, and thought the Sunday School (which was a very bad one) gave them all the teaching they required. We listened, but inwardly triumphed. Education was at a low ebb in the 'fifties in England, but we can now congratulate ourselves that Aston Clinton led the way to a better state of things, at all events in Buckinghamshire. We really loved that little school, and some of the happiest hours of our lives were spent there. When a few years later it had become too small for the number of scholars, my dear father enlarged it, and later again he was faced by the fact that it could not contain the infants—boys and girls—who were then becoming eligible for school attendance.

It was about that time that, my father asking me what I should like to have for a birthday present, I boldly answered, " An Infants' School." My request was granted, and I was allowed to lay the first stone of the new building. I must add that the capital teaching in this school, with the songs and recitations of the infants, greatly entertained my dear father for many years. It is not a little interesting to record here that Matthew Arnold was our first Inspector, and became one of our greatest friends.

Besides our many village interests and occupations, my sister was extremely fond of open-air sports, especially of riding across country. After a series of nice little ponies, we had two of the very best and fleetest horses in the stables, particularly one called " Lancer," a chestnut, famous for the way in which he took leaps.

My paternal grandmother, a far-seeing and clever woman, felt that her sons could not get enough healthy exercise whilst leading their busy city life, so she strongly advocated their owning some land in the country and hunting during the winter months. This they agreed to, and began by following the " Old Berkeley " foxhounds, the kennels being in the neighbourhood of Tring. But fox-hunting did not always provide a run, it often meant a blank day, and as my uncles and father could only spare one day in each week for their sport, they resorted to stag-hunting, such as was then the fashion at Windsor, which in all probability ensured a run. My grandmother had purchased a few fields in the village of Mentmore, in the very centre of the best hunting ground in Buckinghamshire, where finally the stables and kennels were built, my youngest uncle, Mayer de Rothschild, taking as residence a small house on the property, used afterwards as the laundry. The Hunt was entirely financed by the brothers, and became extremely popular in the Vale, attracting to the meets, which took place on Mondays and Thursdays, large numbers of people mounted on every style of palfrey, and driving every sort of vehicle from an elegant phaeton to a coster's cart. The farmers, *à tour de rôle*, entertained the sportsmen with copious refreshments before the stag was turned out, and as any loss that they might sustain in the field was handsomely covered, the sport was much encouraged.

I always shrank from every kind of cruelty, and, not possessing my sister's fine courageous spirit, I did not feel as enamoured of the sport as she did, although I loved no less the early ride or drive in the fresh air.

The celebrated author, Whyte-Melville, began by being one of our hunting acquaintances, and became one of our friends. He was extremely amusing and easy to entertain. It was after hunting with the Rothschild hounds that he wrote one of his popular poems, " The Lord of the Vale " (The Stag).

It was later, after my Uncle Mayer's marriage to Juliana Cohen, that he added to his property and built a beautiful house on the Mentmore heights, commanding a glorious view of the Vale. It was designed by Sir Joseph Paxton, of Crystal Palace fame, whilst Mr. Barker, a great collector of fine art, well known in the 'fifties, helped to furnish and decorate the interior.

My uncle and his young wife lived in the cottage during the building of the big house, of which the first stone was laid by Hannah, the little daughter of nine months old. It was finished in 1853, but my grandmother did not live to see it ; she died whilst my uncle and aunt were on their wedding tour in 1850.

Next to the horses, or rather long before them, came the dogs in our family history. We had many beloved companions, who gave us their affection and their faithful adherence from the day when they were introduced to us until the sad end of their short lives. As we were excellent walkers, they accompanied us daily over the hills and among the beech woods, where we loved to wander : black and tan terriers, a faithful Skye, a wonderfully intelligent pug, Blenheim spaniels of unimpeachable descent and aristocratic ways, dachshunds, most loving and lovable, little Yorkshire terriers, etc., etc., were amongst the beloved companions of childhood and youth. Many pages could be written concerning our favourites, for they had, each one, their own individuality and characteristics; my sister was their best friend in the house, and she gave them her most devoted and unselfish care, even stealing down in her nightdress in the early hours of the morning to let into the house one of her favourites who might have been shut out for the night. The dogs sat to her for their portraits, and had their histories told in prose and in verse, and now their resting-place may be seen under one of the yew trees on our lawn.

We spent quiet and happy evenings at Aston Clinton after our busy days. When my father was at home we played whist, which he taught us carefully ; when he was in town our mother would read to us, introducing us in this easy and pleasant manner to some of our best authors. I can never forget *Ivanhoe*, *The Abbot*, *Kenilworth*, *David Copperfield*, *Oliver Twist*, and other classic novels, after hearing them read evening after evening ; and my earliest acquaintance with some of Shakespeare's finest plays dates from that period.

Perhaps this would be the place to speak of our studies, which were very seriously carried on between the years of ten and eighteen. Indeed they made us very happy, and also unhappy, for I was desperately conscientious, and in my youth I fear I was a horrid prig, also somewhat of a tyrant over my kind and unselfish sister. I insisted upon imparting my newly-won knowledge to her, and tried to instruct her during our walks —until I hope she rebelled. Some brotherly chaff and indignation would have speedily corrected me of my absurdities.

My dear mother, who loved book-learning, and who longed to have well-educated and seriously-minded daughters, encouraged us in our studies, and perhaps did not enter enough into the modern craze for games and outdoor pursuits ; but knowing her wishes, we put the steam on and worked with a will. I should like to describe one or two of my masters. To begin with, there was Dr. Kalisch, a German and a Jew, a very fine Hebrew scholar, and an exceedingly able man. His father brought him up in extreme orthodoxy, hoping that he might take his place in the Jewish ministry. In the revolutionary years of 1848 the young student, with others of republican tendencies, had to flee from Germany and seek a safe refuge in England, where he had introductions to the then Chief Rabbi, Dr. Nathan Adler, who soon recognised his abilities. Dr. Kalisch was but twenty-one when he started giving lessons in Hebrew and German to my cousins, the children of Baron Lionel de Rothschild, and was able, at my mother's request, to spare some of his valuable time to devote to our studies. Undaunted by our extreme youth—I was about eight, my sister under seven—our preceptor undertook the task and proceeded to teach us the Hebrew alphabet. I can remember our sitting on the ground and writing out Hebrew verbs on large sheets of paper. We learnt not only Hebrew, but a great many other things besides from this extraordinary young student, all aflame with his passion for political and religious freedom and the love of fine literature. His services were greatly valued by my aunt, Baroness Lionel de Rothschild, as well as by my mother ; the two sets of cousins became his very devoted pupils, particularly my cousin Alfred and ourselves. Ours was a lasting and warm friendship until his death, which occurred in the 'eighties. Many cherished memories of old days are connected with his name. Owing to his influence a book was written by my sister and myself that occupied us for more than three years, and had a certain success. With Dr. Kalisch we read many works of Schiller and Goethe and learnt a number of poems by heart; I tried my hand at translating some of these into English verse, which both interested and amused me.

Dr. Kalisch married the daughter of Rabbi Stern of Frankfort, and we speedily made friends with that lady, and have always retained a warm interest in their family, particularly in the very talented and energetic daughter, Mrs. Hoster, well known as an authority on foreign languages and a splendid teacher of stenography and typewriting. Her offices in the City and classes for instruction in the West End are justly celebrated.

Our master of English literature, Professor Brewer, connected with the Record Office, librarian to the then Lord Salisbury, was also one of the lecturers at King's College. We enjoyed our delightful lessons with him enormously, and the notes I made at the time were most useful to me many years later, when I held a Shakespeare Class for pupil teachers. I think it was Professor Brewer who first awakened my taste for good English literature. And here I cannot refrain from quoting the following encouraging sentences from two of his letters, addressed to me after many years of fruitful study with this inspiring master:

MY DEAR MISS DE ROTHSCHILD.— . . . I must thank you for the charming little epilogue you sent, of which I beg to keep a copy. With so much of the true feeling of poetry in you I wish you would cultivate poetry, and make yourself master (mistress, if you please) of the resources and depths of English versification. I would recommend

for this purpose a careful study of Tennyson, or some of
the extracts published by Palgrave, of which I saw a copy in
your room at Aston Clinton : only that I do not like extracts,
as it is not easy to arrive at the master-principles of any
writer by such short specimens. As you are reading Italian
you are in the way of this study. So far as I know the
greatest masters of English versification have begun with a
full preparation of Italian. You have the minor poems of
Milton and Spenser's *Faery Queen* to help you.

I am glad you are getting on with your translation of
Gervinus.[1] It will assist you in many ways to improve your
English. But you must not pin your faith to Gervinus. As
I have told you before, I expect better things from you even
than this. People that can walk—which I hope you will be
able to do soon, in more ways than one—have no right to
crutches. . . .

Very many thanks for your kind letter. As you are
reading Ariosto, let me ask you to compare him with
Spenser, and bear in mind his wonderful popularity during
the sixteenth and seventeenth centuries—and how it was he
exactly hit the taste of the times. Cannot you put down a
few memoranda on paper to that effect, and allow me the
pleasure of reading them ? I hope you do not throw away
your papers, especially those which you have written of late
for me. That would be a great pity. I do not mean to
flatter you ; but a series of papers written connectedly on
English literature is more wanted than anything else, and I
think *you* might do much towards this. . . .

Dr. Brewer ended his days as Rector of a small parish
in Essex, where I do not think he ever felt quite at
home, for he more than once told me that he greatly
preferred old MSS. to old women !

Our French master, M. Le Brun, was a very ardent
grammarian, and took enormous pains in teaching us to
write correctly and to build up our knowledge of the
French language on a sure foundation. Perhaps he
lacked the idealism of our dear English and German

[1] *A History of Rome*, in German, by Gervinus.

masters, but he was a most careful and conscientious
teacher.

He was fond of repeating the saying of another distinguished French grammarian, who, when dying, feebly gasped, " Je meurs," then struggled to add, " Et on peut aussi dire, Je me meurs."

My sister, who had a very pronounced talent for drawing, worked under an old and clever master of my dear mother's, Mr. Shepperson, a charming, lovable man, devoted to her and kind to her daughters. Annie had an extraordinarily correct eye for portraiture; with one or two strokes of her pen she was able to produce a vivid and strikingly characteristic likeness, and she had also much talent for grouping and composition. In looking through a little book of my sister's drawings in pen and ink, I am struck anew with the accuracy of her portraits; one drawing, where I am depicted suffering from a nightmare of my many masters, is excellent and most amusing.

Besides having a very decided gift for drawing, my sister had also much epistolary talent, and from a very early age wrote most entertaining letters. This power has been hers throughout her life, and her numerous and detailed epistles to my mother and myself have always been looked forward to and read with great pleasure and amusement.

I cannot resist including a letter from her pen, written at the age of ten :

FOLKESTONE PAVILION HOTEL,
August 6.

DEAR MAMMA—We are very comfortable here and arrived at 4½ o'clock. Papa did not like *his* room much, and we took a nice drive to Sandgate, to see if we could find better apartments than his ; we went to Mrs. Robert's Inn. She informed us that there was a Camp on the hill of German soldiers—two thousand. It would not be pleasant to meet these gentlemen in our walks and they make such a noise. Papa said *no* to Sandgate. When we came home we found

D

capital rooms awaiting us. Papa's scolding did good, I think; it chased an old gentleman out of a nice room which is now your dear Husband's.

We have had a nice walk; old Folkestone is very amusing with its tumbling-down houses and little streets.

I have observed that all the ladies wear hats from 50 to 3 years of age.

Mr. Shepperson came this morning before we left London, dear old man. He was so hot when he came that I inquired if he had not walked very fast: "Yes, I did," he answered; "there was a gentleman in front of me walking very fast indeed with his pocket-handkerchief hanging out of his pocket. I knew that I would not like to have lost mine, so I ran after him. I got very hot, walking so fast."

Was it not good of him?

He begged of me to draw upon the beach; there are some pretty groups, I remarked.

Adieu, my own Mamma, remember your affectionate and loving chick,   ANNIE.

The late Sir Frank Crisp of Friar Park, Henley-on-Thames, who was a nephew of Mr. Shepperson, wrote to me about sixty years after the early days of our drawing lessons, that he used to walk down Grosvenor Place with his uncle, who pointed out to him the house where we, his pupils, lived. As Sir Frank Crisp wrote to me, he little thought then that in future years he would, as a baronet, have the honour of entertaining Queen Alexandra in a beautiful and perfect garden of his own creation. In his letter he sent me an invitation to the said famous garden, but, unfortunately, I was never able to accept it.

My sister and I both loved music and enjoyed the pleasant fortnightly concerts of the Musical Union of those days, which we were allowed to attend. Without having any very decided talent, we both played quite well enough to amuse ourselves and others also in those ante-critical days, when great excellence was not demanded of amateurs. We read well at sight, and had, at times, the rare good fortune of accompanying on the piano such great artists as Joachim, Bernard Molique, Lady Hallé, and Piatti. Herr Pauer was one of our masters, a kind and jovial German, who played better than he taught. We had also the good fortune to come under the tuition of a first-rate pianist and splendid teacher, Anna Molique, the daughter of Bernard Molique. This lady first came to stay with us at Aston Clinton whilst we were all young people, and she speedily became a great favourite. My dear father christened her " Molico," and Molico, or Molly, she remains until this day. She had a rare genius for teaching, and succeeded, moreover, in whatever she took in hand. During the many years that she has lived at Aston Clinton, she has taken a very vivid interest in village life. Thus she started and carried on singing classes for men and women, an evening school for boys, sewing classes for girls, and meetings for mothers, all eminently useful and popular, besides which she arranged brilliantly successful concerts and dramatic performances, eagerly looked forward to and much appreciated. In addition " Molico " endeavoured to establish a straw-mat industry in the village, which attained a remarkable measure of prosperity. Besides these achievements, she trained many little village girls for domestic service, of whom at least one hundred must have passed through her hands. Warm as was her affection for all the members of my family, she showed a special devotion to my dear mother, and was the prime mover in the village for raising a beautiful drinking-fountain to her memory.

To continue the account of our schoolroom days, I was always fond of scribbling, and began to compose so-called poetry almost before I could hold a pen. In this I was much encouraged by my mother and her sister, and as I grew older I indulged in dreams of becoming an authoress. Thus many of my lessons gave me intense pleasure—such as composition, essay-

writing, attempts at fiction, whether in English, French,
or German, and I could and did learn poetry by heart
quite easily; on the other hand, I remembered very
few historical dates, and was also a very indifferent
arithmetician.

I regret very much that we were not taught botany
and that we had no experience in practical gardening,
but, indeed, what I may call practical education was not
then much sought after. We had no lessons in needlework, dressmaking, or cookery, and were not taught
to dispense with the services of a maid. We were
brought up in some respects according to mid-Victorian
ideas ; we never walked alone, or rode without a groom,
or went to parties without our constant chaperon—my
dear mother. We were also very simply dressed, and
we never thought of coming in to luncheon after a walk
without removing our hats and smoothing our hair.
It was strange that my mother could not accustom
herself to a hat, but clung to the old-fashioned bonnet
(that useless headgear in wind or sunshine !) both in
town and country, and crowned her glorious hair with
a cap whilst still a very young matron. Her long and
voluminous skirts were not modified, even for a country
walk, and became often on very close terms with
Buckinghamshire mud. She also followed the custom
of the day by coming down to breakfast with her
gloves, which were carefully drawn on at the close of the
meal. In the evening we, as children, later on as girls,
were supposed to take part in any social amusements
that might be going on, and we knew that it was our
duty to make ourselves pleasant and agreeable to our
elders. Sitting round a centre table, talking whilst at
work, was the fashion of the day for old and young.

How different are the manners, customs, amusements, and dress of the young girls of the present day,
probably as different as were ours from those of the
early Victorians ! In spite of some things that occasionally shock my old-fashioned ideas and prejudices, I

feel that the greater freedom granted in these days to young girls of the upper classes has brought with it many advantages, and we of the older generation, when we occasionally feel inclined to shake our heads over some outrageous toilette, some careless manner of speech or act of discourtesy to their elders, should also recognise and rejoice that increased independence has brought into many lives a wider sphere of usefulness, a further possibility of development for mind and character, and therefore a surer prospect of well-earned happiness.

CHAPTER III

CHAPTER III. THE three brothers, Nathaniel, Alfred, and Leopold—
sons of my Uncle Lionel de Rothschild—were curiously
unlike in character and in tastes. Natty, as we always
called him, was the quietest, the most taciturn, the
shyest. He was the most English in his habits and
favourite pursuits. He was a less good linguist than
his brothers. His generosity was simply superb, only
to be equalled by his modesty, and very few knew
what a kind warm heart beat under that somewhat
reserved exterior. He never talked of what he did,
and it was only after his death that the wide scope of
his charity became known to the public.

Cottage-building was one of his hobbies, and very
comfortable and well-constructed his cottages are, with
a low rental to recommend them. His wife, my dear
cousin Emma, was heart and soul with him in this
excellent work. He built four hundred at the very least
on his estate.

Of course it goes without saying that he was a great
financier, and much thought of in the City. But not
in the City alone, for his advice was often sought and
followed by men of the highest position in the State.
He represented the Borough of Aylesbury as a Liberal
in the House of Commons for twenty years, and in
1885 he was raised to the Peerage by Mr. Gladstone

38

LORD ROTHSCHILD.

and sat in the House of Lords as the first Jewish Peer. Further, he was appointed Lord Lieutenant of the County of Bucks. This, however, is not a detailed memoir of his life, only a very sketchy little account, so I must confine myself to a few traits that may not have been known to the world at large. All the county appreciated the great agricultural shows at Tring Park, where the Shire horses and Jersey cattle were bred. This beautiful Hertfordshire estate, bordering on Bucks, had acquired historical fame from its having been the gift of Charles II. to Nell Gwynne. Part of the house is old, and had been left in much of its original condition until my Uncle Lionel purchased it in the 'seventies. But Nathaniel altered and added to it very considerably, and to its advantage. The gardens and hothouses were also cultivated with care and became widely known. As a very young man he evinced much love for and interest in botany, this taste for natural science descending in still greater measure to his sons. He loved children, and children loved him ; he always drank tea with his grandchildren in the nursery when they were staying with him at Tring Park, and utterly unbent in their society.

He played a very great part in connection with his own Community, of which he was recognised as the lay Head, and as such was constantly consulted by the Chief Rabbi, who told me that he looked upon my cousin as a perfect model in his punctual and careful attention to all matters of detail in business. When he was a young man he was very fond of history, and I remember Lord Beaconsfield saying once, when dining at 148 Piccadilly, " When I want to know an historical fact, I always ask Natty." (As is well known, Lord Beaconsfield left his mass of correspondence to the care of my cousin and Lord Rowton.) Nathaniel was a great reader, but only in special fields, and I never heard him quote a line of poetry, nor did he give me the idea of a man who took any special interest in literature.

Of his dear wife I have, I think, written elsewhere in these chronicles; she has been, and is, one of the very dearest friends that my sister and I have ever had, and has shared to the full many of our joys and griefs.

Walter, the eldest son, the present Lord Rothschild, unmarried, is a very competent student of natural science. It was he who founded the splendid Natural History Museum at Tring, containing one of the most complete collections of birds and butterflies in existence, besides many cases full of mammals; and there he is generally to be seen hard at work. He is one of the trustees of the Natural History Section of the British Museum. He is extraordinarily modest about his own acquirements, and added to his modesty has a charmingly unselfish and unworldly disposition.

Charles, his brother, has the same very marked turn for natural science, in his case chiefly directed to the study of the insect world, in which he has long been recognised as an expert. He was consulted some years ago by our Government as to the origin of the bubonic plague, said to have been imported into Europe through the parasites of rats; this has been engrossing his careful attention for some time. Charles is also much occupied with the culture of certain bulbs, growing them with care in his own very beautiful gardens at Ashton Wold. He is one of the three—alas, only three!—members now left of the New Court firm. He has married Roszika, a Hungarian, who will, I think, play a very prominent part in the family history, as she is a very remarkable woman, with much nobility and strength of character; they have three daughters and a son.

Evelina, the only and well-beloved daughter of Nathaniel and Emma, married Clive Behrens, the great-grandson of the Behrens to whom my grandfather, Nathan Mayer, was sent in Manchester, when he came over as a mere youth to England. Their family consists of two sons and a daughter.

LADY ROTHSCHILD.

It will be very difficult for me to describe at all adequately my dear cousin Alfred, to whom ever since my girlhood I had been warmly attached. His devotion to my dear mother strengthened the tie between us. *Alfred* He said on one occasion to my husband, " I believe that, with the exception of her own daughters, no one cares for my aunt as I do." And, indeed, he gave many a practical proof of this affection. As a youth, hardly grown out of boyhood, he was in the habit of coming to Aston Clinton to shoot with my father. I remember the first time that he appeared, in a suit of brown velveteen, we were all struck by his good looks, and my mother said to me, " What a charming picture of youth and good spirits he would make ! " He had a warm affectionate heart and a generous nature. He was also highly gifted, and had a great flair for financial operations, especially such as had to be conducted with promptitude and secrecy. His very considerable talent for languages stood him here in good stead : German and French he spoke like his mother tongue. He was no reader, but had the art of picking the brains of clever men, and in this way acquired a great deal of information concerning many subjects. He had a genuine love for and appreciation of the arts of music and painting, with a very thorough knowledge of pictures (principally of the French, English, and Dutch Schools), of china, and other objects of art. It was owing to this, and to his natural intuition for all that was rare and beautiful, that he was elected one of the trustees of the National Gallery, and also of the Wallace Collection. His musical bent found expression in a fine orchestra, of which he was patron, and it greatly enlivened his visits to Halton.

After his father's death, when the Bucks estates were partitioned by the three brothers, Halton, once the possession of the Dashwood family, from whom it had been purchased by my Uncle Lionel, with its pretty village and its glorious beech woods, was the object of his choice, and there he built his very un-English mansion.

To him the country, and country life, represented a rest from New Court, and the possibility of entertaining more completely and more lavishly than in London. But he never became the typical English landlord as his brothers had been. To him the village was an unknown entity, and he never tried to understand the lives and conditions of the inhabitants ; it was all a closed book to him, in which he took no individual interest, although his generous instincts led him to perform over and over again the kindliest actions. His heart always responded to the call of physical suffering and distress. I am tempted to quote the following :

It is absolutely impossible for me to tell you how many times I have appealed to Mr. Alfred in the pathetic cause of Charity ; but I can truthfully say that never once during the many years I had the privilege to know him did he ever fail in responding most lavishly to my requests. . . .

No visitor ever went empty away from Mr. Alfred's home in the country. Giant boxes of hothouse flowers and great baskets of luxurious fruits, delicious cakes and chocolates were packed into every carriage with the departing friend. The gifts were endless, but were part and parcel of the visit. Every one was treated alike, from a Grand Duchess to a simple Madame.[1]

He had a cosmopolitan mind, certainly not a parochial one. Being unmarried, and rather at the mercy of doctors, secretaries, and dependants, whom he alternately liked and distrusted, he occasionally failed to see the true proportion of things, and did not always obtain a fair ungarbled version of facts.

His mansion was completed in 1884; it was built on modern French château lines. The view over the Vale is simply glorious, but the approach and grounds might have been more advantageously laid out. The collection

---

[1] *Old Days in Bohemian London*, by Mrs. Clement Scott.

of pictures and *objets d'art*, to which he was continually adding, was, I believe, unique.

In the autumn of 1884 there was a grand opening ceremony, the Prince of Wales (Edward VII.) being the first Royal guest to be entertained at Halton, and I can well remember that evening, when a celebrated conjurer from Paris gave an entertainment, witnessed by many of the most beautiful women of that year.

It was all very perfect, very smart, very up-to-date, and Alfred took his place at once as a kind and liberal host. As time went on, week after week the band would play, the funny little circus of performing ponies, dogs, birds, etc., would exhibit their tricks, whilst Alfred, as conductor of his orchestra and as master of his troupe, would excite sometimes the admiration, and occasionally the good-natured sarcasm, of those admitted to his circle. It was a very unusual, un-English course of things, and, as such, was not always appreciated. But I was sincerely grateful to my cousin when the band was allowed to play at my request, once in the Convict Prison at Aylesbury, and upon another occasion at Aston Clinton, for an audience who could not otherwise have had such a treat.

His patriotism and eagerness to work heart and soul for his country's sake induced him, during the autumn of 1913, to offer his grounds for the manœuvres, and to entertain most royally the officers and men of the different regiments. Further, it led to his placing his estate (ill-fitted as it is for the purpose) at the disposal of the military authorities at the beginning of the Great War, and also to his giving his glorious beech woods unreservedly to the Government. This last may have been a patriotic action, but it is one that has filled the hearts of those who knew and loved the Halton woods as they were in old days with sadness. The Halton estate is now converted into one of the chief centres of training for the Royal Air Force. A huge aerodrome, innumerable workshops, and all the paraphernalia of a very large camp, thrust themselves into one's vision

CHAPTER III.

at every point, whilst the throbbing of the aeroplane engines overhead is hardly ever silent during the daytime.

Alfred's health was never of the strongest; towards middle life he developed heart trouble, which occasioned him much nervousness and anxiety.

Alfred resembled some of the older members of our family in his shrewd Jewish wit, his frequent *bons mots*, his love of good-humoured chaff, his quick sense of the ridiculous, and his social talents. He had a great admiration for the Rothschild family as such, although he may not have always cared for each individual member; he was very much alive to the necessity of their keeping strictly to the family motto, and keenly jealous for their good renown in all parts of the world. I think the sadness occasioned by the long war hastened the death of my dear cousin; he seemed very hopeless and dejected almost from the first, and the fact of the cleavage that it necessarily caused in our once so united family must have caused poignant grief to his affectionate heart. He died in January 1918, and I, ill myself, and full of sadness, could do nothing to ease my mind but write the few lines with which I am ending this little sketch :

IN MEMORIAM—A. DE R.

Adieu ! dear friend, 'tis hard to see thee go,
To see thee quit thy beauteous home on earth.
Beloved and loving here, e'en since thy birth,
To many a heart thy going forth brings woe.
What happiness didst thou not erst bestow !
What times of gladsome cheeriness and mirth !
When thou wast host there never was a dearth
Of kindly hospitality and cheer, a flow
Of gracious courtesy, a welcome kind
To all alike whom e'er thou claim'dst as guest.
How keen of wit thou wast, how shrewd of mind !
How quick to know whatever Art held best !
How truly generous to search and find
The word and gift to set a heart at rest !

February 1918.

N. M. ROTHSCHILD AND HIS WIFE, HANNAH, WITH THEIR CHILDREN.

From left to right, Mayer, Louisa, Charlotte, Lionel, Nathaniel, Anthony, and Hannah Mayer
seated at their feet on the ground.

From a Picture at Gunnersbury Park.   Date about 1822.

Leopold, the youngest of my Uncle Lionel's sons, was a great favourite, and the spoilt child of an adoring mother. He was named after Leopold, King of the Belgians, Queen Victoria's uncle. Soon after his birth, Mrs. Disraeli, visiting my aunt, had said to her, " My dear, that beautiful baby may be the future Messiah, whom we are led to expect—who knows ? And you will be the most favoured of women." This story has been often repeated to us, and when Leo was a young child I believe he had been called the " Little Messiah." He had a very careful home education, never being sent either to a private or to a public school. He spent three very happy years at Cambridge, where he soon made many friends. I have some interesting copies of letters given me by Lady Jebb, from her husband, Sir Richard Jebb, to his mother, in which Leo's name appears, as well as that of my husband, affectionately mentioned.

Leo may possibly not have been as much to the fore in the world of finance or of diplomacy as his two elder brothers, but he was really gifted and a most interesting and pleasant companion. He was a delightful host, and never happier than when entertaining his numerous guests and members of his family. His generosity was quite extraordinary. He had very pronounced country tastes, and these, added to sporting proclivities, made him select Ascott and Newmarket as his favourite residences. But he was also very partial to Gunnersbury, which had none of the defects of villadom and many of the advantages.

Once, when we were all young and spending a happy holiday at Gunnersbury, it occurred to my aunt that she would like to show us the inside of a convent at Hammersmith, where she was much liked and respected. Carriages were ordered, and we were told to be ready at a certain hour. Punctually we appeared — besides our mother and ourselves, my cousin Evelina and her friend Miss Probyn, a very witty and amusing sister of

Leopold

Sir Dighton Probyn, also a *young lady* who had not
been seen by us before. She had large dark eyes, and
walked very bashfully, holding her skirts rather tightly
round her knees. Who could this be ? Tishy Probyn
was giggling, so was Evelina—the *young lady* was Leo
in feminine attire. " She " got into one of the carriages,
to our astonishment, and off we all drove to the said
convent. There we dismounted and were very kindly
received by the Mother Superior, who took us over her
domain, not having an idea that we were not all of the
feminine sex. I remember one awful moment when
Leo caught his skirt on a banister, and a good-natured
nun stooped down to set it right for him, and another
still worse time when Father Heneage, priest and
confessor at the convent, insisted upon receiving us in
his parlour. He had been a very gay man of the world
before taking the vows, and had known my uncle and
father intimately, as attaché in Paris, so he was much
interested in making our acquaintance. As he passed
us in review, he said to my aunt : " And this a niece,
and this another niece, daughters of dear Anthony ? "
and then, pointing at Leo : " And this yet another
niece ? "

Oh ! how relieved we were when we got safely back
into the carriage, and how my aunt scolded and cried,
and said she never thought that Leo would have followed
us into the convent ! It was a plot got up and carried
out by Evelina and her friend, but as he was only
nine years of age no great harm had been done.

I can remember another time when, aided and
abetted by Alfred and Leo, my sister climbed through
the open window of one of the glass-houses at Gunnersbury and came out with a good provision of peaches.
These would have been very delicious, but by some sad
stroke of fate we kept them too carefully in our pockets,
and they arrived in a pulpy condition that evening in
London. I once incurred disgrace at Gunnersbury
by putting a poor little kitten on to a hot stove to

LEOPOLD DE ROTHSCHILD.

warm its feet (as I thought they were cold), and I can
also remember how we all acted charades and dressed up
and entertained ourselves and one another most happily
time after time, until Aston Clinton became too dear
to us, and we would not leave it, even for the pleasures of
Gunnersbury.

Adjoining the Bucks estates, within two miles of
Leighton Buzzard, surrounded by property belonging
to the then Lord Overstone, stood a charming old farmhouse of the eighteenth century, in the very centre of
the hunting country. This was acquired by my Uncle
Lionel, and after his death became the property of
his son Leopold. In time the old farmhouse blossomed
out into a picturesque, very original, many - roomed,
glorified cottage, with a beautiful garden that was
evolved from the fields ; the view over the Vale being a
very extensive one, including an enchanting glimpse of
the Mentmore towers. Leopold acquired by degrees
most of the land round the place, and it was a happy
day for Wing and the neighbouring villages when he
became landlord. The adjoining fields of Southcote
proved very valuable as nurseries for baby race-horses,
whilst the kennels for the staghounds and the very
spacious stables made the whole property an ideal
residence for a man of sporting tastes and most hospitable
intents. Who would be the fortunate lady to reign as
Queen over this little Paradise ? There were several
conjectures that all proved without foundation. When
we were in Vienna in the year 1873 we were told of
a beautiful young bride, Mrs. Arthur Sassoon (Louise
Perugia), connected with many of the Austrian Jewish
families, who had just arrived in London, and was then
making her début in society. Accounts of her great
beauty made me anxious to see this lady, and upon my
return to London I was told that my cousin Hannah
had been much impressed, not only by her good looks,
but also by the charm of her personality. The husband,
Arthur Sassoon, was a scion of a celebrated Jewish

Persian family, who had settled in India, where, besides acquiring great wealth, they had proved generous benefactors. Louise and Hannah became close friends, and Leo's happy marriage was to some extent the result of this friendship. Louise had a young sister, her junior by several years, who, as time went on, came to London and was introduced to the family. I had the honour of meeting her upon her first visit to Ascott, and remember seeing an elegant, rather delicate-looking girl, somewhat shy and retiring, simply but very becomingly attired in a dark green cloth dress. I can recall that she was mounted on one of Leo's perfect hunters and rode to the meet with her sister ; this was a kind of *baptême de sport* which must have been successful, for within the next few days we were told that Marie Perugia was the fiancée of Leopold. He was eighteen years her senior, but young in heart and fresh in his spirit of enjoyment and love of life.

Many were the messages of congratulation that poured in upon the bridegroom, amongst them a letter from Lord Beaconsfield, who wrote : "I have always been of opinion that there cannot be too many Rothschilds." The marriage took place in 1881, and the day proved a memorable one. It was the 19th of January, following upon a terrific snowstorm and blizzard, which prevented some of the guests from attending the wedding. Amongst those, however, who did was the Prince of Wales, who seemed much impressed with the Jewish marriage ceremony, and had his place, I remember, opposite the Ark between two of my cousins. From this happy marriage sprang three sons : Lionel, Evelyn, and Anthony—the second son, most charming and well-beloved, doomed, alas, to the great grief of his family, to fall in Palestine during the Great War, in November 1917 !

My dear cousin Leopold died in the month of May of the same year, deeply and universally regretted. He was always the kindest of friends to me and to my sister.

MRS. LEOPOLD DE ROTHSCHILD.

I learnt to know Marie and to appreciate her many
good qualities of head and heart on two trips that I
took with her to Bayreuth, in 1892 and 1897. We had
much conversation at all hours of the night and morning, and such bright talk added greatly to the pleasure
of these expeditions.

Ascott became well known as a perfect week-end
house for tired statesmen and men of business, and my
cousins were the very centre of much pleasant and varied
society during the whole of their married lives. But
I rejoiced particularly in the fact that there the old
Rothschild traditions were well maintained, and that the
relation between landlord and tenants was so perfect.

One of the great charms of the view from the terrace
at Ascott is the glimpse it affords of the towers
of Mentmore—a truly beautiful edifice of Italian-
Elizabethan architecture. It was greatly to the credit
of my Uncle Mayer that, whilst still a comparatively
young man, he should have conceived the idea of devot-
ing so much of his fortune to the creation of so perfect
a hunting seat, and it spoke well for his perspicacity
that he should have placed himself in the hands of those
competent to give him good advice. He had neither
the perfectly correct taste of my dear father, nor the
knowledge of his elder brother, but he was determined
upon making his home at Mentmore into a veritable
palace of fine art, and he succeeded.

Mentmore was not only a centre for many members
of the hunting and racing world, but also—and this
greatly owing to the ambition and energy of his wife—
a rendezvous for many of the political, literary, and
musical stars of that age.[1] My aunt was a very clever
woman, with a quick mental grasp and much power of
expression, lacking somewhat in idealism and imagination;

[1] The Rt. Hon. Robert Lowe, Mr. Bernal Osborne, Mr. Hayward,
Mr. Delane, etc., etc., were amongst her constant visitors, whilst Lord
Houghton, Thackeray, Matthew Arnold, Whyte-Melville, etc., were
amongst her occasional guests.

E

her talents seemed to me always more of a masculine than of a feminine order. For many years she was very active in mind and in body, when suddenly she was overtaken by serious illness, from the effects of which she never quite recovered. From that time she lost much physical power, and lived rather an invalid life, although, fortunately for herself and others, she retained to the end the perfect use of her keen intellect.

The only child, Hannah, was adored by both parents, but being more of a Rothschild in her nature than a Cohen, I think my cousin's affection for her father was the closer. I was first introduced to her by her aunt, Lucy Cohen, her mother's sister. Hannah, aged two weeks, was lying in her cradle, and I was called upon to admire the beautifully-shaped hands of the infant, which I cordially did. It was one of those little hands that held the trowel which laid the first stone of Mentmore. An only child, be it boy or girl, has a somewhat lonely and unnatural life to face, more so, necessarily, in the case of a girl than of a boy. Hannah's was no exception to the rule, and this in spite of her parents' great affection and admiration for their child. From the first she took her part in the pleasures of the chase. She was intimately acquainted with the denizens of the kennel, knowing each one by name, and mounted on a perfect pony she followed in many a good run, to the pride and delight of her father. Unfortunately the violent exercise was too much for so young and tender a frame, and for one year of her life the active little girl had to give up all exercise and lie on her back, just at an age when most children are either at lessons or at vigorous play. The mischief had been discovered in time, mercifully, by my uncle Nathaniel Montefiore (my mother's doctor-brother), and this in spite of a contrary medical diagnosis; further advice was sought, which only confirmed my uncle's words.

Hannah had but little training of the regular schoolroom order; as a very young child, however, she was

HANNAH DE ROTHSCHILD, 1875.
(COUNTESS OF ROSEBERY.)
From the Painting by G. F. Watts, R.A.

admitted to her mother's drawing-room, and there introduced to a brilliant social circle. Thus she heard much of interest, and had an education of a sort beyond her years. She had a very decided gift for music, inherited from her mother, also a beautiful singing voice. I believe she showed a taste for drawing when she was young, but this had not been encouraged. Surrounded as she had been from her earliest years by the choicest works of art, she learnt what to admire and what to reject, and gained a sound knowledge of the subject. Her father acquired many more precious objects than my father did, but knew less about their history and value, whilst Hannah was better trained as a connoisseur than we were.

My uncle predeceased both his brothers, in the year 1874, and my aunt, after a long and painful illness, died on her yacht in the Mediterranean waters in 1877, leaving her daughter mistress of Mentmore and of all that pertained thereto. It was fortunate that she had an excellent head for business and thus was able to manage her large property exceedingly well. But the cares that her estate entailed upon her came to an end in 1878, the year of her marriage.

When we were children it had been our habit to take early morning walks in Rotten Row, Hyde Park, where we used to meet two little girls about our own age, with whom we struck up a childish friendship. We did not know one another's names, but amongst other things gravely discussed our lessons for the day. To the astonishment of our friends, we once revealed the fact that we were actually learning Hebrew; on the following morning, resolved not to be outdone, they solemnly informed us that their brothers were students of the Greek language! These same brothers, in Highland dress, became realities to us, a few months later, when we saw them standing on the balcony of the house next to ours, the residence of the Duke of Cleveland, who had married Lady Dalmeny, the mother of Mary and

Constance Primrose—our friends of Hyde Park.   And
some years later the elder brother of the same two
playmates became, much to our delight, connected
with us by his marriage with our cousin Hannah.

On one cold dark day, in the December of 1874, my
cousins, Ferdinand and Alice, son and daughter of
Anselm de Rothschild of Vienna, invited me to drive
with them to Lodge Hill, six miles beyond Aylesbury,
a steep eminence about 600 feet above the level of the
sea—really at that time a bare wilderness, where a
farmhouse, a few miserable cottages, and some hedge-
row trees were standing.   The place under that grey
wintry sky did not look attractive, and the roads were
certainly not adapted for wheel travelling, excepting
for that of farm carts.   As we began to mount the hill
our horse felt what would be required of him and
sagaciously slackened speed, at last refusing to go any
further; and this was not astonishing, as the wheels of
the carriage were sticking fast in the mud.   So we
dismounted, and, youth being on our side, we managed
to struggle on for a while, gaining some idea of the view
to be obtained from the top of the hill, without actually
arriving at its summit.   Tired and somewhat disappointed, I exclaimed at last, " And is it here, Ferdie,
that you intend building your palace ?   Is this to be the
site of your future park ? "   For it was to show me the
ground that he had purchased from the Duke of Marlborough that I had been invited by my cousin to take
that drive on that memorable winter's day.   And it
was actually there on that bare hill-top that in 1880
the palace stood, in its park and grounds of over
3000 acres, dominating a wide stretch of country,
overlooking vast pasture-land and wooded heights.
What labour, ingenuity, patience, long-suffering on the
parts of owner, architect, builder, landscape gardener,
that creation demanded it is not in my province here
to relate, but I have gained some knowledge of the
task from a privately printed description of Waddesdon,

by the pen of my cousin himself. Suffice it here to say that the services of a very distinguished French architect, Déstailleur, were retained, who at my cousin's request drew the plans for a château of the Renaissance period, whilst the very ornate and carefully considered garden was designed by Lainé, who also hailed from the land of France.

A French château placed amongst the rural surroundings of an English county awoke the curiosity and interest not only in the whole neighbourhood, but farther afield, and there in his Buckinghamshire home my cousin entertained largely. In the visitors' book occur names most distinguished in art, literature, and politics in the social world of that time, whilst Queen Victoria, to the delight of her loyal subjects, spent one beautiful and never-to-be-forgotten day in the month of May 1890 at Waddesdon. I enjoyed that event as much as any of Her Majesty's subjects. Numerous other members of the Royal Family were at different times my cousin's guests, amongst them the Empress Frederick, who, in relating her impressions of that visit, said, " The host was as delightful as the place was beautiful."

Ferdinand was indeed a delightful host and gifted with much social talent. He was extremely cultivated and well-read, an able and refined writer both in English and in German. Politics, rather to the astonishment of his friends, claimed his attention in middle life ; he succeeded Lord Rothschild as one of the Liberal Members of Parliament for the Aylesbury or Mid-Bucks Division.

I am tempted to close this short account of Waddesdon with the following pathetic words by Ferdinand himself : " May the day be yet distant when weeds will spread over the gardens, the terraces crumble into dust, the pictures and cabinets cross the Channel or the Atlantic, and the melancholy cry of the nightjar sound from the deserted towers ! "

This is, indeed, prophetic of the doom that is over-

CHAPTER taking many of the most glorious country homes of
III. England. Mercifully, this sad picture has not been
realised in respect to Waddesdon, for, in spite of
the unexpected death of its well-beloved owner in
1898, the place has prospered under the tender and
unremitting care of his devoted sister Alice,[1] to whom he
left his Buckinghamshire estate.

My father's second sister, Hannah Mayer by name, had
married in 1839 Henry FitzRoy, brother of the then
Lord Southampton ; he was a young man of talent and
great promise. My aunt was a beautiful girl with a fair
skin, blue eyes, a small but graceful figure. She was
very musical, had a sweet singing voice, and played
the harp exquisitely. Her disposition, however, was
less pleasing than that of her sister Louisa ; she was
easily ruffled in temper, and could make herself and
others also most uncomfortable by fits of jealousy.
She was never much in sympathy with the members of
her own Community, and after two or three years of
social life ended by defying the traditions of her family,
not only in marrying one outside the Faith, but also
in adopting her husband's religion. Her widowed
mother, violently opposed at first, ended by giving a
kind of tacit consent to the marriage, and, won over by
the charm and goodness of her prospective son-in-law,
actually facilitated a kind of runaway match, accompanying the beautiful bride in a four-wheeler to the
church door. The marriage was a happy one, at all
events for the first years, and might have been still
happier had it not been for my aunt's somewhat jealous
temperament. But, indeed, Mr. FitzRoy gave her no
occasion for alarm on that score ; he proved a devoted
husband, and a no less kind and tender father to the two
children born of this marriage. Arthur, the eldest, was
a very promising boy, singularly gifted ; he died at
the age of fifteen, after a long and trying illness, the
result of a fall from his pony.

[1] My cousin's fine and noble life on earth ended on May 3, 1922.

His sister, Blanche FitzRoy, one of my most beloved
playfellows and companions, outlived that dear brother
for many a long year. We were, indeed, great friends
from childhood. After her husband's death, my aunt,
fearing that her young daughter might suffer from the
gloom and depression of her home life, used to invite
my sister and myself very frequently to spend an
afternoon with Blanche, then a denizen of the schoolroom, a most industrious and eager young scholar.
Of course we discussed our studies, and as we were
much interested at that time in English history, we
ranged ourselves on opposite sides ; thus Blanche
was the Cavalier and I the Roundhead, and many a
fierce battle we waged. At one time, overcome by my
feelings, I actually seized upon a bottle of ink as a
weapon and was about to fling it at the Cavalier across
the schoolroom table, when my arm was arrested by
the poor governess who was listening with alarm to
our heated argument.

Everything that we learnt was very real to us, and
we felt that life, as lived by my cousin, alone with
her sad, invalid mother, could only be brightened and
cheered by excursions into poetry and romance. We
both used our pens very freely, but added to the gift of
composition Blanche, like my sister, had a remarkable
talent for drawing.

My aunt's health grew steadily worse until her
daughter was about to make her entry into society,
when for a very short while she revived sufficiently to
take Blanche to a limited number of dances, relapsing,
however, very soon into complete invalidism. It was
then that Blanche followed her own inclinations, made
her own friends, and met the man with whom she
fell desperately in love, who was eventually to be her
husband. Thus she gave her heart irrevocably at the
age of twenty to Sir Coutts Lindsay, clever and fascinating, but twenty years her senior, and, in spite of
some objections on the part of her uncle and trustee,

she insisted upon marrying him. The ceremony took place in the drawing-room of the home of her girlhood, her mother lying sick unto death in the room above.

Sir Coutts was a good artist himself, and his wife helped him materially with his art. The Grosvenor Gallery, which was their creation, was a notable and original venture in the 'seventies. In its fine spaces pictures were exhibited to the very best advantage, beautifully hung with an artistic background, never overcrowded or badly placed. Watts, Burne-Jones, and others of well-earned fame sent the best specimens of their work to this gallery, which came to an untimely end after the separation of husband and wife. There were a few years of brilliant happiness, followed by a shock that ended the dream. Blanche was cast in heroic mould. She was firm of purpose, relentless where wrong had been inflicted, very generous, but also determined.

The promises of her husband proved unreliable, so the final parting came, and Blanche started life anew with her two devoted daughters, Effie and Nellie. The beautiful Scottish home, Balcarres, had to be abandoned, and the large London house in Cromwell Place, with its comfortable studio, became a grave of past happy and unhappy memories. Blanche was indeed wonderfully gifted. She wrote much in verse and in prose. I have a list of her publications before me; amongst them I see the following titles : *Lyrics, The King's Last Vigil, The Apostle of the Ardennes, The Flower-Seller, The Prayer of St. Scholastica, Poems of Love and Death*, and many others. In her prose writings—essays, short stories, and novels—she evinced a real sense of humour as well as pathos. Her daughter writes :

They are brightened as by sunlight, with many a flash of wit and pure fun, for she loved to " play," as she herself called it, and through the indulgence of that sense of fun and humour her powerful intellect found its ready re-creation.

She knew and had many interesting friends, prominent members of the artistic and literary world, who were often to be seen at her house. As a young married woman she had a good studio, where she spent many hours diligently painting, both portraits and copies of well-known pictures. In the latter she excelled, her copies being executed in masterly style and with great care.

Her leaflets, " Green Leaves," which appeared four times in the year, and are, to my mind, most charming literary treasures, contained much from her own pen, and also valuable and appropriate quotations, some of them but little known, which well deserve being read and remembered. The leaflets were not for publication, but were given away, not only in England, but also in some of the colonies, to very eager and grateful recipients. A poem called " For England," written at the time of the Boer War, was sold in leaflets for the benefit of the Red Cross, and at that period brought in a sum of £300.

She loved music well enough to enter the ranks of pianists and violinists, but she had hardly time or strength for her many different pursuits, and would probably have attained to greater perfection had she contented herself with one, or at most two, of her favourite studies; but her mental activity was great and undaunted.

For the last years of her life Blanche Lindsay was fighting an unequal battle with ill-health. In 1913 she had a seizure from which she did not recover. Her daughter Helen, who with her sister Effie[1] had been her mother's devoted nurse and companion, wrote as a postscript to the last of the " Green Leaves " that ever made its appearance a beautiful little notice from which I am transcribing the following :

No strange voice called her, but the voice of a Friend. For her there was no pain of parting, and we, who love her, rejoice because we know that although the great change stole upon her suddenly, it came not unawares.

---

[1] Wife of the Rev. S. Henrey, Rector of St. George's, Brentford.

CHAPTER IV

There is, perhaps, no act of memory so profoundly interesting as to recall the careless mood and moment in which we have entered a town, a house, a chamber, on the eve of an acquaintance or an event that has given a colour to our future life.—LORD BEACONSFIELD.

CHAPTER IV. My sister and I inherited from both parents a very marked appreciation of fine natural scenery ; thus we prized and loved above everything our own beech woods, with their glorious autumn colouring, and the extensive views over the Vale of Aylesbury.

This love of scenery, amounting in my sister to a passion, led to an amusing little incident when she could not have been more than seven years old.

We were taken by our parents for a little tour in England, and were looking forward with some excitement to visiting Matlock in Derbyshire, of which place we had been told that it was singularly attractive and beautiful. We had, unexpectedly, to sleep one night at Derby on our way, the trains not being convenient for the longer journey. We retired to our beds under the fond belief that we were at Matlock. On the following morning my sister, expecting to see a mountain and a river, rushed to the window and looked across a busy street straight into a butcher's shop, which sent her into a paroxysm of surprised anger. My mother came running into our room to find out the meaning of the sounds she had heard, and was greeted by my sister exclaiming piteously, " And is this what

58

you call romantic? and is this what you call beautiful?" After this outburst she flung herself sobbing and furious upon her bed, and so great was her disappointment and anger that it was difficult to pacify her. With such a temperament one can well imagine the frantic delight that it gave my sister, and I may add myself, to visit the most beautiful scenery in Switzerland and in Italy, as well as the interesting towns of Germany.

I was a very young child, not two years old, when I first was taken abroad to be introduced to foreign relatives, but my mother told me that I gave great promise of becoming a good traveller even at that early age.

In those mid-Victorian days, people travelling in comfort or luxury were always accompanied by a courier (we had a foreign servant) and took their own carriage with them. I can recollect quite well sitting with our nurse in our large and comfortable travelling carriage that was strapped upon a railway truck, and thus going down to Dover; the carriages and horses were then shipped across the Channel and again required for our stay in Paris. In those days there were no sleeping-cars on the trains, no expresses that carried you straight from London to Vienna, or Rome, or any other great capital. Trains were slower and stopped more frequently, adventures whilst travelling more looked forward to, new acquaintances made more easily; there was indeed less hurry about everything than there is now. Thus it was that on one of our homeward journeys, travelling on a Rhine steamer, I was made aware of the presence of a very tall stranger, wearing glasses, speaking English, and evidently anxious to elicit from me some response to his many questions. I remember staring at him as if I could not quite place him in my category of friends. I was then about six years old, and was startled when he took me in his arms, poised me upon one of his shoulders, walked up and down the deck of the steamer with me, and began to tell me

fairy stories about the Rhine. I became deeply impressed by this new playmate, and was very sorry to
say good-bye at the end of our journey. The giant
came to see us in London, and finally brought with
him two daughters, older than ourselves, but still quite
willing to be playmates. The giant was no other than
the author, Thackeray, and his daughters were the future
gifted writer, Lady Ritchie, and her sister, Mrs. Leslie
Stephen. My mother greatly valued the friendship
thus begun on the Rhine steamer, and here I include
two letters from Thackeray:

KENSINGTON, *December* 28.

DEAR LADY DE ROTHSCHILD—It has not been Annie's
fault but mine that the two most beautiful bon-bon baskets
I ever saw have come into the house and given the greatest
delight to the children whom you remembered so kindly,
and that you have had no word of acknowledgment for
such a charming present. Annie brought me a letter ten
days ago which has grown dingy already in among my papers.
I wanted to write myself and thank you for your remembrance of us, but waited until my work should be done for
the month before I began to pay my debt of gratitude.
The printer's devil has only bid farewell to the house an
hour ago. I had hardly time to think about kindness or
gratitude or Xmas until he was gone, and now he is quit
of the premises. I hope it's not too late to tell you that I
was very pleased when your presents came to think that you
were so good as to remember the children. It would have
pleased you to have seen their pleasure : and what further
pleased me in this pleasant transaction was that the young
ones, who thought the two baskets the most beautiful and
splendid treasures they ever had in their lives, nevertheless,
and with a severe pang, resolved to give one of them away
to some little friends of their own who had been very kind
to them. This act of self-denial rejoiced the paternal heart,
and I like to tell it in confidence to your ladyship, so you see
you have made a great number of young folk and a middle-
aged gentleman happy. Could bon-bons ever be expected

to do more ? Who, if one could but be sure that they would
always bring the same result about, wouldn't one be eating
pralines and chocolate all day ? This, however, reads like
a remark out of *Pendennis* or some such book, and I don't
wish to figure in that as an author any more now the month's
work is done ; or only as the author of the two children to
whom you have been so kind.

Dear Lady Rothschild, accept my thanks and best wishes
for the New Year for you and your family, and believe me,
ever most faithfully yours,

W. M. THACKERAY.

ABERDEEN, March 17, 1857.

DEAR LADY ROTHSCHILD—I hope you know that I am
murdering the 4 Georges in Scotland and never heard of
your beautiful party till the flowers were all dead, the
dancers all in bed, the candles all out, the supper all eaten,
the ices all melted, and the plate all locked up.

How long this business of George-killing is to last I don't
know, but I have months yet of the House of Brunswick
before me. Heaven bless them ! I never thought my late
gracious Sovereign would put so many 100£ in the pockets of
—Yours always to command,

W. M. THACKERAY.

What a fine wedding you have had in your family ! What
a parasol ! What a pretty bride ![1]—we met them all at Aix-
la-Chapelle last autumn, and I think we all liked each other.
I know I did.

She often spoke of him with happy pride, and she
would read and re-read *The Newcomes, Pendennis,* and
Vanity Fair, always finding fresh interest in their pages.
In *Pendennis* there occurs the following beautiful and
touching passage, which the great author wrote as a
picture of my mother :

What one sees symbolised in the Roman Churches in the

---

[1] Leonora, daughter of Baron Lionel de Rothschild. The bridegroom
was Alphonse, eldest son of Baron James de Rothschild.

image of the Virgin Mother, with a bosom bleeding with love, I think one may witness (and admire the Almighty bounty for) every day.   I saw a Jewish lady only yesterday with a child at her knee, and from whose face towards the child there shone a sweetness so angelical that it seemed to form a sort of glory round both.   I protest I could have knelt before her too, and adored in her the Divine beneficence in endowing us with the maternal " storgé " which began with our race and sanctifies the history of mankind.

I never had the good fortune to know Charles Dickens personally, but once heard him read in public, with wonderful effect, some chapters from *Nicholas Nickleby*.   I remember his pathos in describing Squeers's terrible school, also the humour with which he seemed to overflow in the funny passages of the story.   And I was present in June 1870 at Westminster Abbey when Dean Stanley preached a funeral sermon, to an enormous congregation, on the death of one of England's greatest novelists.

Whilst still in our early childhood we spent part of two to three years in Paris, my father's help being required in the Banking House of our family in that city. During one winter we inhabited one of the spacious apartments in the house of my uncle, Baron Solomon de Rothschild, one of the sons of the founder of our family.   He had lived for some time in Vienna, but towards the end of his life had left his business in that city to his only son Anselm, and migrated with his wife to Paris—this partly to be near his only and most beloved daughter, Betty, who had married her uncle, James de Rothschild, the youngest son of the old Frau Rothschild, and partly on account of the failing health of his wife, who, I believe, had never appreciated a residence in Austria.

Whilst we lived in our Uncle Solomon's house we talked German to him and his wife—he calling out " Gute Nacht, Kinderchen " every night when we went

to our beds. He was not long in following us, for his
strange habits led him to retire at 8 o'clock in the
evening, to go out driving at 5 A.M. in the summer, and
at 7 A.M. in the winter. He died in 1855, having outlived
his wife by one year.

It was during a walk in the gardens of the Tuileries,
when I was about five years old, that I was presented
to the celebrated General Changarnier, a great friend of
my aunt's and a zealous supporter of the Orleans branch
of the French Royal Family. He noticed that one of
the buttons on my gaiters had become unfastened, and,
placing himself on a seat, he drew me on to his knee, and
to my astonishment put the offending button back into
its place. After our return to England he wrote me a
letter, which I still possess, addressing me as if I were
a grown-up girl, when I was still a child, much to the
amusement of my mother.

Having relations in Paris, Frankfort, and Vienna,
and being always most kindly received and entertained
by all of them, we felt very much at home in any one of
those cities.

Thus an account of our foreign trips would necessarily
include an account of many members of our family,
whom we were, from very early days, in the habit
of visiting. Frankfort being the old home of the
Rothschilds, it is only natural that I should speak
of that city to begin with, and also because some
of my earliest recollections are indissolubly connected
with it.

Frankfort had its own peculiar position. In those
days (the middle of the nineteenth century) it was
still one of the four free German cities belonging to the
Hanseatic group — the others being Lübeck, Bremen,
and Hamburg.

Frankfort was the capital of a small republic, the
seat of the German Diet. Representatives of foreign
and of German Courts and States were accredited to
this small but important capital, which thus acquired

no inconsiderable social importance.   It really had
some of the setting of a metropolis.

The old town, with its narrow streets and gabled
houses, pointed roofs, and four old towers guarding
four of the principal roads from the town into the
country, produced a mediaeval effect and was ever
interesting to our childish eyes.

The Judengasse, which my great-grandmother never
left, was an extraordinarily narrow and tortuous street.
It was crowded with memories of the past; also it could
tell of the origin of our family.   It stood in striking
contrast to the modern town of Frankfort, with its
elegant streets and lofty residences, where lived many
of our co-religionists, notably members of our own
family.   But I think that the romance and history that
clung to the Judengasse made it very attractive to me.

The first two visits we paid to Frankfort, when I
was hardly more than a baby, were undertaken in
company with my grandmother, who used regularly to
visit our aged relative, her own mother; later on these
were repeated, when some of the English members of
our family had, on their marriage, returned to live in
the old city.

I will try and give some short account of some of my
relatives.

To begin with, there was a very old uncle; he must
have been my great-grandmother's eldest son, Amschel
by name, whose wife was called Eve (I remember her
as a stout, rubicund lady).   He lived in a pretty villa-like
house, I think on the Bockenheimer Chaussée, which
stands out in my memory for one particular incident.

We happened to be staying at Frankfort for the
Jewish holy days that fall in the autumn months.   I
was allowed to accompany my parents to the evening
meal served in my Uncle Amschel's " Succoth " or
garden-house, where he and his wife, with others of
his family, were celebrating the incoming festival, the
Feast of *Succoth* or *Booths* (Feast of Tabernacles).

Seated at a table gay with fruit and flowers, where
the red wine was passed from one guest to another, my
uncle bade us welcome and proceeded to say a long
grace in Hebrew before we tasted our first dish. I
rather think that a handsome youth, one of our cousins,
was present, helping his uncle in his ministrations.
The garden-house was decorated to look like a bower;
small open spaces were left in the roof through which
we were able to see the heavens, on that night bright with
stars—this to remind us of the Israelites living in booths
or tents during their forty years of wandering.

Besides this old uncle of mine, who died when we
children were still quite young, there was at one time
living in Frankfort an only son of Solomon de
Rothschild—it was Solomon, one of the original " five
brothers," who founded the Banking House in Vienna.
This son, Anselm, married the eldest sister of my
father, Charlotte, a tall and handsome woman, remarkable for her brilliant colouring and fine presence.
He had a very charming villa residence, the " Grüne-
burg," on the outskirts of Frankfort, where for a
time he lived with his family, but later on he made
his home in Vienna, and there he remained at the
head of the Austrian branch of the great Banking
House. Besides this he acquired a large property
in Silesia—" Schillersdorf "—which was celebrated for
the varied and wonderful amount of game it afforded
to the sportsman. I think this was specially designed
for the benefit of his sons; his own tastes were
very simple, and he used to live in his hunting lodge in
the latter years of his life, leaving his grand country
house to his children. He was a very witty and
amusing man, with marked literary tastes. For a time
he corresponded in verse with Count Beust, then the
Ambassador at our Court, an intimate friend of my
uncle's ; he was also much attached to a cousin, George
Samuel by name, an intelligent and interesting personage,
with whom he used to have endless games of chess.

F

My uncle and aunt's family consisted of seven children—four daughters and three sons. Julia and Matilda, the two elder ones, had very graceful, beautiful figures, and were of most distinguished appearance. They were very much attached to my dear mother, whom they looked upon almost as a playmate. They were both well gifted. Julia was a true artist in the widest meaning of the word, and Matilda a brilliant pianist and charming composer. The two sisters were the first female smokers that I had ever come across, and my youthful eyes gazed with astonishment at this masculine indulgence—the ladies were smoking cigars, not even cigarettes. The sisters married brothers, Adolphe and Willy de Rothschild, sons of the head of the Naples house.

And here I should like to say a word concerning these intermarriages in my family that were the custom during the two generations of which I am writing.

At that time the Rothschild family had attained a very remarkable position in England, France, Germany, Austria, and Italy. This they owed to their genius for finance, to their strict businesslike habits, and to the family feeling that made the interests of one branch common to all. They certainly carried out in their lives the family motto: " Concordia, Integritas, Industria." Their vast financial undertakings in the five European capitals brought them into close touch with the rulers and statesmen of those countries; no other Jewish financiers had before that time attained to such a position, or if they had, they had ceased to be Jews. But the Rothschilds were strict adherents to their Faith and deeply interested in the affairs of their Community. They were looked upon as the leaders of the Jews wherever they lived, and deserved such appreciation. From all these causes they were on a different social plane from their co-religionists, and gradually became habitués of a world still closed to many of their own Jewish friends and connections. But as orthodox

Jews they were strongly opposed to mixed marriages; thus the frequent intermarriages amongst relations became the only way out of a difficulty which was the result of circumstances.

Julia's husband, Adolphe, was a fair-haired, handsome, cheery youth; he loved the world and delighted in entertaining his friends. He had a very great opinion of his wife's taste and knowledge, and allowed her a free hand in making what proved to be a wonderful collection of *objets d'art*. These priceless articles were in time placed in my cousin's beautiful house in Paris. They had also a charming rural abode on the outskirts of Geneva—" Prégny " by name—where as young girls we were most kindly entertained, and enjoyed ourselves greatly.

Matilda's husband, Willy, whilst still a very young man, became extremely orthodox in his views. Before he married, he made his bride promise to respect them implicitly. The promise was given and faithfully kept for fifty years of married life. The young bride, on becoming a matron, tied her brown locks under a close-fitting cap, never rode or drove on a Sabbath, never ate Talmudically-forbidden food, never dined out, or was served upon dishes other than those that were specially kept for herself and family, and never travelled without the killer or purveyor of food, who was in her husband's service. The home of the newly-married pair was in Frankfort, where Willy took his place in the family Banking House.[1] They had three daughters, one of whom is Baroness Edmond de Rothschild, living in Paris.

The third sister, Louisa, in her young days a pretty girl with large, blue, sentimental eyes, had two or three years of social life in Vienna, and married a Baron Franchetti from Turin in 1858.

---

[1] Matilda, Baroness Willy, attained the age of 90 on the 5th of March 1922, when, surrounded by the members of her family, she gave a dinner-party in celebration of the event. She is in full possession of all her faculties.

My Uncle Anselm had three sons : Nathaniel, Ferdinand, and Solomon — or Albert, as he was called. We were on terms of great intimacy with Ferdinand, the second son, who finally settled in England, and became a naturalised English subject. He married an English cousin, Evelina, my Uncle Lionel de Rothschild's second daughter, the brilliant and beautiful girl who, alas ! only lived for two years after their marriage ; but in spite of his great loss, Ferdinand remained true to his English home. He took to hunting and to all manner of country pursuits, even to English politics, becoming an M.P. for the County of Bucks, in which county his Waddesdon estate was situated. After Evelina's untimely death, Ferdinand's youngest sister, Alice, who had been left in a very solitary position by the death of her mother in 1859, came to England and shared her brother's homes. She had known something of Buckinghamshire before then, having been our guest at Aston Clinton, with her talented governess, Mademoiselle Hofer, for four years consecutively, when we welcomed her amongst us as one of ourselves. It was then that she entered fully into our simple schoolroom life ; we had lessons together, and we scampered about on horseback together. In the evening we devoted ourselves to whist and halma, Alice being most proficient in all games, and invariably the winner. She was a very fine rider, and soon outgrew the ponies or hacks that were our palfreys at that time, becoming later a well-known figure in the hunting field. We were, indeed, the fastest of friends, and Alice learned to love and revere my mother as if she had been her own child.

After some years Alice bought a house in London, 142 Piccadilly, next door to her brother's, and also an estate in Buckinghamshire, Eythrope, adjoining Waddesdon, where she had full scope for her love of flowers and landscape gardening. As she grew older she felt the longing for more sunshine than England gives us in the winter, so she purchased a charming roadside villa, close to the town of Grasse in the Department of Les Alpes Maritimes, South of France. Here she acquired ground and laid out a most beautiful and attractive garden, that ultimately traversed the road and crept up the side of a mountain, ending in a Belvedere commanding an extensive view of land and sea. There I had the pleasure of spending some weeks with her at various times. One of those visits in 1891 was notable, owing to the fact that I was in attendance on H.R.H. Princess Louise, and that Queen Victoria was staying at the Royal Hotel in the town of Grasse, with her suite. My cousin gave her villa the name of Victoria, as a memento of Her Majesty's visit. But of this later, for I hope to be able to give some account of the few brief interviews that I had the honour of having with our Queen.

My mother's sister-in-law and namesake, Louisa de Rothschild, the greatest friend she ever had, was my dear father's youngest sister. A very bright, taking creature she was ; her pleasant voice, her ringing laugh, her genial manner, and above all her *joie de vivre*, made her a great favourite in society. At the age of twenty-two she married her cousin, Charles de Rothschild, a man of great ability, the brother of the Italian bride whom my uncle, Lionel de Rothschild, had brought to England from her home in Naples.

When Charles came to London to claim his bride, Louisa, he took her to live with him in the old town of Frankfort-on-the-Main, their future home, he being one of the chief members of the Rothschild Banking House. There my aunt spent her married life, an Englishwoman in heart and soul, never loving her adopted country, never speaking the German tongue with great ease or fluency.

My uncle and aunt lived in a very cosmopolitan set, and their house became the centre of much pleasant society. Seven daughters were born to them, between

the years of 1843 and 1862. There was, I believe, some
disappointment at the absence of a son in this large
family, but it was a short-lived disappointment, and
we, the cousins, felt that no improvement could have
been possible where all in those early days were so
bright, so beautiful, and so lovable. We were never
happier than with those cousins. The two elder ones
were our special friends : Adela, the future wife of
Solomon de Rothschild, with whom her brief married
life was spent in Paris; Emma, the future wife of
Nathaniel de Rothschild, the first Jewish peer in Great
Britain. The third daughter, Clementina, called after
Lady Clementina Villiers, was radiantly lovely, but her
life was ended after twenty-one years, during which
time she had given promise of other gifts besides those
of personal beauty. The fourth daughter, Thérèse, with
her dark handsome face and loving generous nature,
became the wife of James de Rothschild, and thus joined
the Rothschild family in Paris. Hannah Louisa died
unmarried, whilst the two younger daughters, Margaret
and Bertha, broke with all family traditions and became
respectively the Duchesse de Gramont and the Princesse
de Wagram. Assimilating very easily French customs
and habits, they both became thorough Frenchwomen.
Alas, they both died during middle life, leaving children
to mourn them! Prince Wagram never got over his
beloved wife's death, but the more volatile Duc de
Gramont, a widower when he married, took to himself
a third wife, an Italian.

In the years 1855 and 1859 we spent some weeks at
the Günthersburg, and they were very happy weeks for us.
They stand out distinctly in my memory. The Günthersburg was an ideal home about a couple of miles from
the town of Frankfort ; it stood in a beautiful garden,
with a large farm attached to it, of which Göbels
was bailiff, a fine stout German, always ready to aid
and abet us in our amusements. We drove about
in a delightfully primitive farm-cart, taking the roads

that led through fields bordered on either side with well-covered fruit trees, and we drank coffee and ate black bread and butter (ambrosial fare it seemed to us) in the farm itself. There also we were present one day at a merry-making of farm hands, real *bona fide* German peasants, who began dancing in the afternoon, going steadily on until midnight.

It was at Frankfort that we had our first lessons in swimming. The teaching was admirable, far better than anything in England, and although my courage often failed me, yet I learned to swim quite respectably before leaving Frankfort.

We lived with our cousins in their schoolroom; we worked together and played together and became the fastest of friends. That friendship, thank God, has never waned.

In 1864 we took a further trip into Germany, which we enjoyed enormously, and made acquaintance with Dresden, Saxon Switzerland, Prague, and Nüremberg. I can remember it all distinctly. We were very eager to see as much as we could of the old German cities, and studied our guide-books assiduously. We were really capital sightseers, kept up to the mark by both parents, and were taught to take an intelligent interest in pictures and monuments. So eager was our mother not to miss anything that we often travelled by night, and went sightseeing by day.

On that tour we were joined by Alfred Seymour, a very agreeable fellow-traveller, who did not accompany us merely for the pleasure of the trip.

I am now anxious to give a short account of the French members of the Rothschild family, as I knew them when I was a child and later as a young girl.

As I have already stated, we used very frequently to visit Paris, where indeed my parents had had some idea of settling in the 'forties; but as things turned out, my father's younger brother, Nathaniel, owing to his marriage with his cousin Charlotte, daughter of Baron

James, took the place in the French Banking House that my father would have filled.

Paris in the 'forties was politically in a very unsettled condition, as I was often told by my mother, and as I have since learnt from the many gossipy memoirs of the times; but in one way it had become a very stronghold for our family. The French Rothschilds were ardent supporters of the Orleanists, and my aunt became the warm admirer, and indeed devoted friend, of Queen Marie Amélie, wife of Louis Philippe, the Bourgeois King. The Jews were indeed well treated at that time in France by the reigning family, and my relatives were quick to show their gratitude by their devotion to the Royal House. Indeed, my aunt would never recognise any other dynasty, refused to be presented to the Prince President, and even later, when Napoleon became Emperor, still clung loyally to her old friends of the House of Orleans, and never made her curtsey to the reigning Imperial couple. But the Emperor was shrewd enough to know that the clever Jewish financier would be most useful to him, and my uncle carried out to the letter his favourite maxim that financiers should have no politics, so that he was not only cordially received at the Tuileries, but was also asked to act as host to His Imperial Majesty, who proposed himself as guest at Ferrières, the magnificent château that my uncle had built.

The invitation was given, and the wily monarch, on presenting his arm to my aunt when the banquet was announced, said, with a smile, " Madame, you would not visit me, so, as I much wished to make your acquaintance, I have been obliged (happily for myself) to be your guest." The Empress did not accompany the Emperor on that occasion, nor do I think that my aunt ever met that high-spirited and unfortunate lady, but she knew and liked Princess Mathilde, with whom she had many literary and artistic friends in common.

And here I must give a picture, however slight, of

that very remarkable woman, known to us children as Aunt Betty, and to the world in general as Baroness James de Rothschild, who came from Vienna at the early age of seventeen to settle in Paris as a married woman in the 'twenties. I remember coming across a passage relating to my aunt in Lady Granville's correspondence with her sister Lady Carlisle (Lady Granville was our Ambassadress in Paris in the 'thirties), saying:

On Saturday we dined at a sumptuous feast at Rothschild's. He has married his niece, a pretty little Jewess, *née coiffée*, a very good thing at Paris, for just out of her nursery she does the honours of her house as if she never had done anything else. (*Letters of Harriet Countess Granville.* The Hon. F. Leveson-Gower.)[1]

Her eldest son, Alphonse, was born in 1827. Although German was her native tongue, and she never acquired a true Parisian accent, she could and did converse easily and brilliantly in French, whilst her letters in that language were marvels of epistolary power and grace. Her many gifts enabled her not only to start, but successfully to hold, a " Salon," which in those years proved to be much valued and appreciated. It was a great time of reconstruction in Paris, an apparent calm after many storms. In my aunt's Salon many of the foremost men in politics and in literature were habitually to be found. She proved invaluable to her husband, my great-uncle James, for the social support she gave him in the influential position that he owed to his financial genius. Besides these qualities, she was generous and warm-hearted. Her love for her own people, the deep interest that she took in the welfare of the Community, never left her. As a young woman she started her benevolent schemes for the poor of her race in Paris, and it was greatly owing to her influence that the excellent Jewish schools and hospital were founded. She was very Jewish at heart, knew the old

[1] By permission of Sir George Leveson-Gower.

Hebrew tongue very well, could write German in the small Hebrew characters, and clung with affection and devotion to all the observances of her religion. Her husband, in talking of her to her English relatives, would call her "my good lady"—a title she richly deserved; and when the business of the day did not square with his religious observances, he would say, "My good lady never drives on Sabbath," or "My good lady would not go out to-day, but I must do such-and-such things," thus sheltering himself behind her adherence to old forms and customs. She was in every way a noble woman.

My uncle purchased his charming estate, Ferrières (in the Department of Seine et Marne), some time in the 'thirties. The château of those days, I believe, was comfortable and roomy, but very different from the present magnificent building that rose in its place some twenty or more years later, which was planned to provide suites of rooms for every member of my uncle's family and their possible families to come. Needless to say, such arrangements were more theoretical than practical. People prefer living under their own roof-tree, however humble it may be, and "in-laws" are generally better friends when they do not spend weeks in too intimate a proximity to one another.

Ferrières stands in the midst of a large wooded estate, where the shooting used to be kept up in magnificent style. But a second historic event was to make it famous. In 1870, the year of the Franco-German war, the château was taken possession of by the King of Prussia and his son, the Crown Prince Frederick, who used it as their headquarters. The visitors' book bears the names of the Royal Prussian Family, of Moltke and of Bismarck, also of some three or four hundred German officers.

Let it be stated at once that during *that* war French property was respected by the enemy, and no harm was done to the château, except for the wholesale destruction of the game in the park and the emptying of the cellar, where, however, the best wine was no longer to be found. I remember the communiqués appearing daily in the papers, with " Ferrières " under Royal or martial signature. My uncle had died in 1868, and all his sons were fighting for their country.

Returning to 1848, I can dimly remember an incident connected with my French relatives. One evening—it seemed to me the dead of night—I was carried downstairs in our house at Grosvenor Place to see my aunt, her daughter, and youngest son, who had fled from Paris at the outbreak of the Revolution (when their beloved Orleans dynasty had been overthrown), and when the French Royal Family were also seeking refuge in England. My aunt and family had arrived in a sad state of misery and depression ; I believe that my hospitable parents were providing rooms and beds hastily to receive them, and that even our nursery was being invaded.

In 1870, as a parallel to this picture, when the Commune had brought mob-rule to dominate Paris, my aunt would not leave her house in the metropolis, the courtyard of which had been transformed into a hospital. One afternoon, returning from some charitable errand in her carriage and pair, she was stopped by an angry crowd in the Bois de Boulogne, and asked how she could dare to drive when people were starving and wanting horseflesh for food. The mob were about to unharness her horses when she, rising in her carriage, confronted the crowd and said, " Yes, take my horses if you will have them, but I am as good a patriot as any of you. Come and see my hospital in my own house ; and do you not know that I have three sons who are all bearing arms and fighting for our country ? " The mob cheered, and, forming themselves into a bodyguard, marched by the side of the carriage, accompanying my aunt triumphantly to the gates of her house.

Her family consisted of four sons and one daughter.

Alphonse

Leonora

The three elder sons and the daughter came in quick succession between the 'twenties and early 'thirties, the youngest son not until the 'forties. Alphonse, the eldest son, was a very remarkable man, not only brilliantly gifted for his work as a financier, but also fond of culture and greatly interested in politics and world history. He visited America as a young man— a trip not often taken in those days—and made acquaintance with the leading men of the New World. He was devoted to my mother, a few years his senior, with whom he kept up an affectionate correspondence, reading the books on philosophy and on history that she recommended. He used frequently to stay with my parents in London, affectionately calling us his young sisters. He married Leonora, eldest daughter of my Uncle Lionel de Rothschild, distinguished for her great beauty. Although she lived her life from the age of nineteen in Paris, where she was immensely popular, she remained English at heart, visited England regularly once or twice a year, kept up with all her English friends, and never lost her taste for sport. Every winter she spent some weeks in England hunting in the Vale of Aylesbury. She was a very plucky horsewoman until quite late in life, and actually started a Stag Hunt at her French country seat, taking over an English huntsman and a pack of hounds. She gave proof of her lasting affection for her own country by a request in her will that she might be buried in English soil, and this was faithfully carried out, although she died in Paris.

Alphonse and his brothers were passionately devoted to their mother, who lived to the age of eighty-one, and not a day passed without their spending some portion of it with her.

I must here mention an incident that revealed conspicuously the fine elements in the character of my cousin Alphonse. It happened one day in Ferrières that, while shooting his coverts with a party of friends, he received,

accidentally, a shot in the face from a somewhat un-
practised gun. In the confusion that ensued it seemed
impossible to single out the offender, and although my
cousin was shrewdly aware of the gun that had given him
the wound, which eventually caused him to lose one of
his eyes, he would never disclose the name of the unhappy man, even to his intimates or to members of his
family, and always kept on friendly terms with him.

On another occasion some dastardly ruffian sent an
explosive parcel to his banking office, addressed to
" Baron Alphonse de Rothschild." Fortunately for
himself, my cousin was far away at the time, drinking
waters at a health resort. One of his most trusted
subordinates unfastened the parcel and received the
contents in his face, producing the most agonizing
wounds and a threatened loss of sight. The news
being telegraphed to Alphonse, he returned immediately
to Paris and gave the most unremitting and generous
care to the unfortunate man, telling him over and
over again that he, his chief, ought to have been in
his place.

Alphonse was not only head of the Banking House
in Paris, but also President of the Chemin de Fer
du Nord, and to his great delight, when already an
elderly man, was elected one of the forty members
of the French Academy. His opinion was greatly
sought after by men of all shades and classes, and
his knowledge of art and of literature caused him to
be well received and much appreciated in many circles.

Of his three brothers, Gustave, only a year his junior,
very good-looking as a young man, married Cécile
Anspach, the daughter of a clever French barrister,
who played her part well as one of the acknowledged
beauties and clever women under the Third Empire.

Solomon, the second brother, brilliantly gifted, but
less addicted to steady work and habits of business
than his brothers, married Adela, the eldest daughter
of my Uncle Charles of the Frankfort House, the most

charming and fascinating of women. Alas, after a
very short married life he died, leaving her a young
widow with an only daughter!

Edmond, the youngest, married Adelheid, daughter
of Willy de Rothschild, also of the Frankfort House.
Husband and wife have always been deeply interested
in everything connected with the Jewish Community
in France; schools, hospitals, and dwelling-houses for
the Jewish poor have been their special care. They
have visited Palestine more than once, and the great
Jewish colonies in that country owe their existence
principally to their generosity.

Alphonse's only son, Edouard, now the head of the
French Banking House, married Germaine Halphen,
and has two sons and two daughters. He is now
the owner of the beautiful and historic Château de
Ferrières. Alphonse's eldest daughter, Bettina, married
Albert de Rothschild, late head of the Vienna Banking
House, and had five sons and two daughters, of whom
the third son succeeded his father in the firm, the
second son being the husband of Clarice Sebag Montefiore. Alphonse's second daughter, Beatrice, married
Maurice Ephrussi.

Gustave's only son, Robert, married Nellie Beer,
elder sister of Lionel de Rothschild's wife in London,
and has two sons and two daughters. Gustave's three
daughters married respectively — Lucie, the eldest,
Baron Leon Lambert; Aline, Sir Edward Sassoon;
Juliette, Baron Emanuel Leonino.

Edmond's eldest son, James, is now a naturalised
Englishman, and has lately inherited the fine property
of Waddesdon from his aunt, Alice de Rothschild. He
has a charming English wife, Dorothy Pinto.

Baron James de Rothschild's only daughter,
Charlotte, who, as I have already stated, married my
father's brother, Nathaniel, in the 'forties, inherited
some of her mother's gifts; added to these she had very
considerable talent both for music and for drawing.

Owing to an accident in the hunting field my uncle was, at a comparatively early age, attacked with partial paralysis, increasing until he was totally blind and unable to use his limbs. His very active brain, however, was not affected, and he was acquainted with all the political, social, and family gossip of the day. He was extraordinarily patient, and one never heard a complaint pass his lips. My father used to pay him regularly one or two visits each year, and we could thus look forward to seeing our French relatives more frequently than we should otherwise have done. Both my uncle and his wife always received us very kindly; and my aunt, when we found her in Paris, would take us to see some of the best plays, which were admirably acted, ending up with an ice at Tortoni's (the famous restaurant), thus giving us an evening of unqualified delight. Of the four children born to my uncle and aunt, two died in infancy, whilst the other two, both sons, grew to man's estate. The elder, James, was remarkably able, a student, taking a deep interest in French mediaeval literature, collecting rare books on the subject, and editing and writing others himself. His wife is Thérèse, familiarly called " Thésie," the fourth daughter of my Uncle Charles of Frankfort, well known in Paris, where she has spent the years of her widowhood, as well as her married life, in countless works of benevolence. Her son, Henri, took his degree as Doctor in the French School of Medicine, and has worked very assiduously ever since. He founded a hospital for mothers and infants in Paris, also a free dispensary which he superintended himself, and during the war was instrumental in providing ambulances with doctors and nurses for the French Army, often accompanying them himself to their destination. Since then he has become a most successful playwright for the French stage. In 1895 he married Mathilde Weisweiller, and has two sons and a daughter. He has one sister, Jeanne de Leonino, who, like the rest of her family, is busily

engaged in works of charity, chiefly for her own Community.

The old Rothschild dwelling-house in the Rue Lafitte
has now been incorporated with the banking offices.
As the years crept on, my cousins all acquired beautiful
mansions (" Hôtels," as the French call them) in various
districts of Paris, the present taste for the site of dwelling-
houses taking them farther and farther away from the
commercial part of the city.

Besides their town residences they all have country
places; but the real spirit and genius for country life is
not, I think, inherent in the French nation, and there is
much suspicion on the part of the peasantry in their
dealings with a class other than their own.

In the winter of 1864 I had the great good fortune,
whilst staying in Paris, to be present at a Court Ball.
I was immensely pleased when the invitation was pro-
cured for me. One memorable evening in January of
that year, I drove, garbed in clouds of white tulle and
speechless with excitement, in the company of two of
my cousins to the Palace of the Tuileries. The great gates
of the " Cours d'Honneur " being flung open, we entered
the Palace. As we walked up the steps to the Ballroom
I noticed the gigantic men of the Emperor's guard, one
upon each stair, standing in most impressive array. A
fine orchestra was playing, when suddenly it was silenced,
and a voice called out " Leurs Majestés ! " We, who
were grouped at the foot of a dais, were aware that a
short thick-set figure of a man clad in uniform, leading
by the hand one of the most graceful and beautiful
apparitions I had ever seen, had entered from the back
on to the platform. The Empress Eugénie, then about
thirty-eight years of age, exquisitely attired in white
satin and tulle, curtsied as I have never seen any one
curtsey before nor since, to the right, to the left, and to
the ladies facing her. Then she and the Emperor
descended from their platform, and danced, or walked
through some dances, after which they entered into

conversation with their guests, sending, I remember
to my great delight, for my cousin Leonora, Baroness
Alphonse, to whom they must have made some pretty
speeches, for she returned to us blushing and smiling.
Some of the great beauties of the Imperial Court were
pointed out to me, but no one, to my mind, could vie
that evening in grace and charm with the Empress
Eugénie. I had the rare pleasure of seeing Her Majesty
again a few days later, when during a hard frost I
was taken to the frozen lake in the Bois de Boulogne.
There the Empress, clad in black velvet and sables,
was skimming lightly over the ice, giving a hand on
either side to an attendant cavalier. A small velvet
hat was poised on her fair hair, and her complexion,
more radiant than ever, did not belie her semi-Northern
origin. I believe that the Emperor was also to be seen
on the ice that day, but I did not recognise him amongst
the skaters. When next I had the pleasure of seeing
the Empress, it was many years later (1883) in Italy.
The beautiful Empress had become a grey-haired widow
by that time, but she still bore traces of her former
beauty, and her figure had become more commanding
than purely graceful. We had been staying in the
same hotel at Perugia, where, however, we had not
met, the Empress having kept her rooms owing to a
severe chill. My sister was allowed to prescribe homoeo-
pathic globules for Her Majesty without seeing her, and
the Empress declared that they had had a very good
effect. Her lady-in-waiting, Madame d'Arcos, an old
friend of ours, spent an hour or two in the evenings with
us, giving us much gossipy news of her Royal mistress.

My husband and I met Her Majesty at the railway
station the morning we left Perugia—we being bound
for Orvieto, and the Empress for Siena. No first-class
carriage having been retained, we proposed giving up
the places that we had already secured to the Royal
party, and finding others elsewhere; but this the
Empress would not allow, and with her lady-in-waiting

G

joined our little party. Mr. Story, the sculptor, and his wife being already installed in the compartment, presentations rapidly followed, and our short journey was made under very pleasant conditions, the Empress talking unrestrainedly in very fair English.

I have a distinct and charming recollection of a little " escapade " to Paris, and a stay of a fortnight in that brilliant city in the month of May of the year 1879. The present Dowager Duchess of Abercorn, then Marchioness of Hamilton, was my companion, and we had the jolliest time imaginable. It would have been impossible to find a brighter or more congenial fellow-traveller than the Mary Hamilton of those days, gifted with a keen sense of humour and an inexhaustible power of enjoyment. My companion found unlimited interest as well as pleasure in her shopping and exploring expeditions, which took her alternately to the tempting shops in the Rue de la Paix and elsewhere, to the picture-galleries in the Louvre, to the cell of the unfortunate Marie Antoinette in the Temple, even to the gruesome Morgue. And the thrilling accounts she gave of her day's adventures astonished, but also attracted in no small degree, those to whom she related them, generally members of my French family, Mary Hamilton having always been a warmly-welcomed guest in their houses. It is a pleasure in touching upon those days to feel that, in spite of the lapse of years, the friendship between those two visitors to the French capital remains unbroken.

It was always a matter of surprise to me, when we visited Paris during the Second Empire, how seldom we met any well-known men or women of artistic or literary fame at the pleasant but informal dinner-parties and evening gatherings that took place at my relatives' houses. It is true that I can remember being introduced, as a very young girl, to the great composer Rossini by my aunt, Baroness James, and I met Béranger, the old philanthropist, at dinner in one of my cousins' houses by my special desire, when I was no longer a young woman. But these were solitary cases, and when I ventured to question those I knew best in Paris on the subject, I was told that there existed an immense cleavage in France between what they call the Bohemian world and Society. Politicians, since the Republic, were for many reasons tabooed. The Faubourg St. Germain, closely allied to the Clerical party, had for years kept severely to itself and did not smile upon non-Catholic houses.

Artistic and literary men and women liked their own free-and-easy form of social intercourse; they were frankly bored with the ladies and gentlemen of that period, and they liked to meet one another unrestrained by the question of evening dress, indulging in unconventional supper-parties, where smoking by both sexes was unrestricted. Conversation was, I believe, most animated and amusing at these Bohemian gatherings, where it was no uncommon habit to discuss moral questions in a very open and audacious manner, the mantle of decent hypocrisy being ignored; it was also well known that the private lives of many members of the company would hardly pass muster, even judged by the somewhat lax moral standard of those days. On the other hand, I was frequently condemned to listen, in the more fashionable circles, to endless talk on " sport " or to Parisian gossip, not always in the best taste, knowing all the while that many of the company were not more respectable than their brothers and sisters of Bohemia.

The philanthropic world, again, had its own frequenters, for, except at the periodical smart bazaars, the Parisian women of fashion, since the old Royalist days, seldom were seen elbowing their somewhat dowdy sisters on their errands of mercy. Of course there were brilliant exceptions, especially amongst my own family, who generally felt themselves bound to offer personal as well as financial help to the members of their own Community.

CHAPTER V

CHAPTER
V.

I SHOULD like to dwell a little upon some of the pleasant and amusing continental journeys that we used to take, also upon the impressions made upon me by the interesting or original people whom we had the good fortune to meet.

I remember 1862 very distinctly. It had long been a promise of my father's that we should make acquaintance with North Italy, and in March of that year we had the opportunity of so doing. My cousin and most intimate friend, Adela, the eldest of the Frankfort cousins, was to be married in the early days of March to Solomon, the genial, brilliant, somewhat dare-devil son of my great-uncle James. We were bidden to attend the wedding at Frankfort—one of those celebrated family gatherings at which we met a whole concourse of relations. My aunt's seven daughters, from the handsome bride-elect down to the little girl of a year old, formed a goodly assembly when they were all congregated in the fine reception-rooms of the Günthersburg. There the marriage ceremony took place, and, after spending a few more days in the company of our relatives, we set off for our Italian tour in a state of pleasurable excitement. We had with us a dear, delightful Italian lady—Signora Galimberti—who had spent a few weeks with us at Aston Clinton, during the previous two winters, for Italian and singing lessons, and to

84

whom we had taken a very great fancy. She was a Milanese, and had often talked to us of the beauty of her native country, Italy. We travelled on the old Mont Cenis route, by *vetturino*, a novelty not without charm for us. No one in those days was in a hurry, and the leisurely gait of the horses as we climbed up the winding paths enabled us to get out whenever we chose to walk and make closer acquaintance with the road. But we galloped down in good style from the summit of the Pass into one of the little border towns at its base, and awoke on the following morning to the delightful fact that we were close to, if not already in, Italy. My great and curious desire had always been to see one of those unfortunate creatures disfigured by a goitre, and very soon that wish was to be gratified. A poor beggar, who could hardly speak, and on whose long loose neck an excrescence, almost long enough to throw over his shoulder, was growing, came up to the carriage, thrusting out his hand for alms. That one specimen was enough for me, and I am sure that I never wished to see another poor idiot afflicted with one of those terrible deformities. But the goitre meant Italy, or at all events the approach to it, for I believe that we were then at Sion in the Valais. Turin was too modern and northern a city for our taste, but Genoa, the first truly Italian town that our eyes beheld, bathed, as it were, in sunshine, and full of noise and colour, gave us a thrill.

At that time the Genoese women still wore the charming head-dress of soft and beautifully-coloured material, in which they could drape the figure as well as the head, and which was handed down from mother to daughter. Like most Italians, when young, they were very graceful, and carried their gold bead necklaces and ornaments with distinction. Genoa on that day was gay with flags : Garibaldi had been in the town, but had gone, or was going, to Milan. So were we. Genoa had lost its charm for us—we must hasten on. So we took the afternoon train on a glorious day in March, and found

ourselves in a city mad with delight, and bedizened
with flags and colours. We were about to drive up to
the hotel when a great shout of welcome resounded in
our rear, our coachman pulled up, and an open carriage
passed us, quickly turning into the courtyard, already
thronged with people. We followed and sprang out of
our vehicle, as Garibaldi, surrounded by a welcoming
crowd, was alighting from his conveyance. I remember
making him a low curtsey; he acknowledged our salute,
and, as he walked into the hotel with his own special
grace, I thought what a fine head his was, and how
superb he looked in his red shirt and grey cloak. Our
rooms in the hotel were just above his; and the fact of
his having a balcony on which he could appear induced
the crowds to spend hours in front of his windows
shouting for him to come out.

In the evening we all went to a gala performance of
the ballet *Flick and Flock* at the Opera, and there
witnessed a rousing scene. The place was packed,
Garibaldi and his suite in the big box facing the stage.
Upon his entry the people rose and sang the Garibaldian
hymn, " Italia una." In those days poor Italy was
not " una," the Quadrilateral being still held by the
Austrians. This gave the Milanese an idea for that
special performance.

A scene depicting Venice under Austrian rule was
shown on the stage, when suddenly martial music
was heard, and in rushed a regiment of Bersaglieri,
storming Venice and taking the city from the foreign
ruler. The whole house rose, the people cheered like
mad—so did we. All sang the Garibaldian hymn, women
laughed and wept, wreaths of laurel were handed up
to the hero of Italy, and the Bersaglieri were recalled
again and again. What a night to remember! The
streets were alive until two o'clock in the morning.

The following day we got Garibaldi to sign his
photograph for us, then, after watching his departure,
we applied ourselves seriously to sight-seeing in the

town. We were much attracted by the Milanese ladies
in their black veils, which they wore instead of the
French bonnet ; whilst the peasants from the country-
side, who thronged the Cathedral (for we were there
on a festival day), looked charming to my un-
accustomed eye.

We saw everything that " Murray " told us we
ought to see and a great deal more, and then continued
on our way to Venice and Verona.

The first four days at Venice were a terrible disappointment—it rained continuously—but suddenly the
skies cleared, the rain ceased, and delight followed upon
delight. It was an unforgettable time, all the more
delightful because we met the newly-married couple
(my cousins) on their honeymoon, and spent some
pleasant days in their company.

My mother enjoyed this Italian trip as greatly as
we did; she loved Italy, where she had spent some
happy years in her girlhood ; she was also keenly
interested in its splendid works of art, as well as in the
historical memories that cling to that country.

We revelled in our gondola, and when the sad day
of departure approached, not the least trying incident
was our farewell to the two magnificent gondoliers,
Pietro and Pieretto, who accompanied us to the station,
and to whom we repeated, over and over again, " A
rivederci."

Venice was at that time under Austrian rule, which
was much resented by the Italians, who showed their
resentment by keeping sternly aloof from their favourite
and attractive haunts when the superb Austrian band
played in the Piazza. On other days the Italians were
to be seen enjoying themselves at the countless cafés in
this unique meeting-place, where the pigeons congregate,
within a few minutes' stroll from some of the greatest
wonders of the world.

I have revisited Venice and have seen her free,
under the Italian flag, but in spite of this, and in spite

of my ardent feelings for Garibaldi and political liberty, I have never enjoyed a subsequent visit as much as I did that first one of heavenly memories. Perhaps this may be explained by the fact that on subsequent visits illness dogged my footsteps when they turned Venice-wards. During one autumn my father suffered from a severe attack of gout, whilst on two other occasions I was a victim, first of measles and then of chicken-pox, being laid up with the former illness in the historic Hotel Danieli, and during my second time of isolation on my sister's yacht, the *Garland*, which was lying in the Grand Canal. But I look back with grateful recollection to the attack of measles, for I feel that I owed my acquaintance and friendship with Robert Browning to that contretemps. The poet, whom I had met in London, but knew only slightly, came to see us at Venice, where he was living with his son. He was much attracted by my husband, pitied him for his lonely condition during my captivity, accompanied him daily on expeditions by land and by water (he knew every street and bridge in Venice), and finally, when I was convalescent, called and entertained me most gloriously. Mr. Browning did not look like a poet, but he was a poet to the heart's core.

Strange to say, when I was recovering from chicken-pox, I had visits from another delightful author—Henry James; also from Dr. Münthe, the extraordinarily agree-able Swedish doctor and clever writer.

The last time that I saw Venice was in 1913, but the place I had once loved so well was too full of the ghosts of other days to bring me unqualified joy. I am sure that it is unwise to revisit scenes that remind one too vividly of a happy past, for the ghosts that crowded round me prevented me from enjoying the beautiful City of Dreams as I had done before, and as I had hoped to do again !—the city rising out of the waters, the city of visions and of romance, since then mercifully saved from the bombs of the enemy !

Upon starting from Venice in 1862, with tearful eyes and aching hearts, on a long night and day journey across the Semmering Pass to Vienna, I can remember how we gradually revived and cheered up, for by some lucky chance we were given a wonderful railway carriage, most luxuriously fitted, belonging, I believe, to an Austrian Archduchess. In spite, however, of the delicious comfort of a real bed in the train, I managed to wake up during a brilliant starlight night when passing the fortress where Silvio Pellico had been immured for years. If I did not actually see the fortress, I felt that it was there close by, and even the name of the station, now forgotten, was to me full of romance and poetry.

We were not inclined to admire or to appreciate Vienna as a city, after Venice, but we found kind relatives who made our visit enjoyable, and we young ones were of course always ready for fresh impressions. Our sight-seeing ardour had to be satisfied as usual, but besides that we were to have some social pleasures. My uncle, Anselm de Rothschild, gave one or two dinner-parties in our honour. I can remember sitting next to the French Ambassador, the Duc de Gramont, a very magnificent gentleman, of whom I felt in great awe, and upon another occasion being seated by a far more interesting and delightful individual, Julian Fane, of the British Embassy.

I saw Vienna again in 1873, when my father was one of the British Commissioners for the International Exhibition held in that city. My mother and I accompanied him, and greatly enjoyed our visit, in spite of the following drawbacks : it was the month of May, but the weather was far from May-like ; we had repeated storms of snow and hail, which interfered with the success of the Exhibition ; also, Vienna was passing at the time through a financial crisis not conducive to a peaceful frame of mind amongst its financiers, represented principally by members of my family.

It was then that we saw much of and made friends with Lord and Lady Dudley. She was in all the resplendent beauty of her youth, added to which her charm and simplicity of manner made her a great favourite in Viennese society.

Lord Dudley, meeting me one day in the gallery of the British exhibits, asked me to point out any object that I specially admired. I unhesitatingly pointed to a truly magnificent bracelet of diamonds and cat's-eyes. What was my astonishment when, on the following morning, the bracelet was brought to me with a few kind words from the donor. I wanted to return it—in fact my mother encouraged me to do so—but a letter from Lady Dudley stopped me, and I accepted the gift with much confusion of spirit. As if to prevent me from feeling shy, Lady Dudley showed me a perfectly glorious diadem in emeralds and diamonds which her husband had given her at the same time.

One morning, when we were returning from the Exhibition, we were told in a solemn whisper by the hotel porter that the Kaiserin had been calling upon some Royalty who had just arrived, and that we should very likely meet H.I.M. on the stairs. The man was right; as we turned to go to our rooms, we saw standing on one of the landings the most graceful, attractive vision that eyes could desire to rest upon. The Empress Elizabeth, for she it was, had at that time a very youthful gipsy-like expression, with brown laughing eyes and rather a roguish smile on her lips. She was very tall and graceful, and I remember remarking her long flowing dress, like a train, and her small, rather coquettish bonnet. I saw the Empress again, riding in the Prater, in a dark blue habit, with her long glorious plaits hanging down to her waist. She sat her horse well, and was a fine and intrepid rider.

Another time we were bidden to an evening party at Court and duly presented to their Majesties. The

Empress was all in white, with great gleaming knots of emeralds in her wonderful hair. During the evening, whilst she and Lady Dudley were seated together on a sofa, Lord Dudley said to me, " There are the two most beautiful women in the world." And I thought he was right. Poor Empress, her life was a sad one, but not so abnormally sad as that of the Emperor !

We were introduced to another Royal pair whilst at Vienna, to whom we gave our hearts at once—the Crown Prince and Crown Princess of Germany. She was our own Princess Royal, not beautiful or stately, but with a distinction all her own, brilliantly clever, and anxious to make herself agreeable to the English visitors. She entertained us most kindly one afternoon, and chatted away very pleasantly on all chance meetings. As for the Crown Prince, we English ladies all behaved disgracefully in running after him most persistently, and were jealous of the one he might sit next to and converse with. And to think that he could be *the father of the Kaiser* !

> How clearly on my inner sense is borne
> The fair, fresh beauty of the mountain morn,
> And cries of flocks afar, and mixed with these
> The green, delightful tumult of the trees.
> (From " Ammergau," by FREDERIC MYERS.)

Another foreign trip of most delightful memories was to Ober Ammergau in 1871. We arrived at our destination late one afternoon in August, in the gathering shades of evening. We found ourselves instantly in the scene of happy preparation and cheerful bustle.

Travelling vehicles of all shapes and conditions were lining the single village street, whilst long rows of peasants from the adjacent countryside were coming in, often carrying their simple supply of provisions with them. The hotel where we were most comfortably lodged was kept by the excellent Georg Lang, who was ready to give us all information concerning the play and the performers. The weather looked somewhat threatening ; we were alarmed for the morrow ; even now I can remember G. Lang saying, " Better a somewhat grey sky than too hot a sun." But the morrow proved all that could be desired. At six o'clock the firing of the guns awoke those who were not already awake with excitement, as we were ! Soon afterwards the peal of church bells announced the first celebration of Mass. Our breakfast awaited us at 7.30, and at 8.30 we were asked to be in our places. A very orderly quiet crowd was making its way into the theatre. At that date this building was only partly roofed in, whilst the natural hill scenery made a beautiful background to the stage, where the members of the chorus, already grouped, were faced by the orchestra. Early as it was, the Prince and Princess of Wales came punctually into their places, exactly in front of ours, with a few English friends of their party, and from first to last gave their most undivided and reverent attention to the performance. We sat absorbed and motionless from 8.30 to 11.30, then went home to a frugal meal and rest, to return to our seats from 1.30 to 4.30. The afternoon portion must have been most trying and exhausting to the principal actors, and there was a kind of murmur and sigh of relief at the close ; of course, all applause was forbidden. Silently we went on our homeward way, our thoughts dwelling upon the wonderfully beautiful and touching performance it had been our privilege to witness.

On the ground floor of the hotel there was a display of beautifully carved wooden objects, which visitors bought as souvenirs of the place, all made during the winter months by the inhabitants of the mountain villages. And here, after their evening meal, came our English Royalties to make their purchases. We could not resist going down to salute them, and I remember how attractive the Princess of Wales looked in a green Tyrolese hat. Both she and the Prince were seemingly

delighted with their visit, and spoke with much appreciation of the Passion Play.

We stayed for another day to explore the village, and were rewarded for so doing by a visit in the evening from no less a personage than Joseph Meir, who had played the principal part on the day before with great dignity and pathos. He told us that he had had a year's preparation, during which time he had never entered a " Gasthaus," or attended any convivial gathering ; indeed the players all looked upon their performance as a sacred duty. Meir was touched by the kindness of the Prince and Princess of Wales, who had sent for him to express their admiration for the Passion Play, and especially for his fine personification of so difficult a part. The Princess at the close of the interview had presented him with a diamond ring, which he was wearing that evening. He said he hardly believed that he would play the same part again, but he did so once, or even twice, and ended his career, I believe, by taking the character of Pontius Pilate. He told us that it was generally the rule that the part of Judas Iscariot should be given to some blameless inhabitant of the village, so that no onus could possibly be attached to the man who portrayed so unpopular a personage. The performances take place at intervals of ten years, every Sunday during four months of the year, and the rehearsals and preparation begin a full year in advance.

The date of these performances has only been altered twice : once in 1870, during the Franco-German War, when it was postponed to 1871 ; the second time in 1920 (deferred until 1922) on account of the Great War, which had prevented the necessary preparations and rehearsals.

Ever since the Middle Ages these plays have been given in solemn remembrance of the miraculous arrest of an epidemic of the plague, which had devastated the surrounding country.

I feel that it would not be inappropriate were I to give

here (although the events to which I shall allude occurred many years later) a short account of two visits to Bayreuth, where I was once more brought into touch with German histrionic art, and was again made aware of the faithfulness to detail shown by actors and singers, and the great care bestowed upon every part of the musical performance.

It was in the month of August 1892 that my first memorable visit to Bayreuth took place. I recall setting off in great spirits with my two very pleasant travelling companions, Marie de Rothschild and the present Lady Derby, then Lady Alice Stanley. They were both great adepts at discussion, and I can remember how we kept ourselves awake on one night journey, when we could not secure sleeping cars, by embarking upon some controversial subject that was provocative of interesting talk.

We arrived at Bayreuth full of delightful expectation, and settled ourselves in a small and homely inn, where we obtained much information concerning the celebrated performances. During our stay I was present at the representations of *Tannhäuser*, *Die Meistersinger*, *Lohengrin*, and last, but certainly not least, *Parsifal*. I was much struck by the darkened house, with all the light concentrated on the stage, and by the extraordinarily quiet attitude and behaviour of the audience : no applause allowed during the performance, not a whisper heard ; no disturbance from rustling sheets of programmes or books of words, but complete and reverent silence.

The *Parsifal* day passed like a long service in a place of worship. In spite of the great heat and some measure of fatigue, the performance gave me the keenest sense of real enjoyment. How little could any of us, who were only acquainted with these masterpieces in their English setting, have had a conception of what their singular and unique charm would be in their appropriate surroundings at Bayreuth ! The entire place seemed only to exist for the sake of these beautiful

representations, and so complete and harmonious were
they that even the grotesque and somewhat childish
features—such as the realistic dragon in one piece, and
the rather coarse scene of the Venusberg in another
—were unable to destroy the perfection of the whole
staging.

Parsifal was certainly a wonderful experience.
Dreary as it was in some very long scenes, it was
surpassingly grand in others ; this one performance
dominated, as it were, all Bayreuth. I can remember
carefully recording my impressions at the time, and
feeling then, as I do now, how difficult it would be
successfully to transplant such an extraordinary operatic
production to a London stage, and retain anything of
the original atmosphere.

I paid a second visit to Bayreuth two or three years
later, and my impressions remained the same. It was
then that my acquaintance commenced with Lady
Gosford, a most interesting and agreeable companion,
with a truly original mind and a great sense of humour.
I have one of her notes still by me inviting me to meet
her at the Waldhütte, an hour's excursion from Bayreuth.
One of our friends had been giving me lurid accounts
of the moral condition of smart London society, and
upon my expressing much horror at the same, I had to
undergo a vast amount of teasing from the lively
narrator, who was determined upon shocking me.
Lady Gosford declared that as a result of these revela-
tions I should suffer from nightmare, and urged me to
write a book with a detailed account of my outraged
feelings. I promised that I would do so with a dedication to herself. The following words occur in a letter I
received on the next morning :

You were quite right to rest, so as to gain strength
for your nightly contest with the peerage. I accept with
pleasure the dedication of your book. Will it be called
" A Soul tortured by the British Aristocracy " ? What a
sale it would have !

On that visit we were bidden to a very grand evening party at Frau Wagner's house. I recollect the crowded drawing-room, containing many photographs of Mr. Arthur Balfour; the tightly-closed windows, in spite of a stifling atmosphere on the night in question ; a tall majestic lady, dressed in black, walking to and fro, welcoming her guests and enforcing silence before the commencement of each musical performance. I can remember the hum of French, English, German, and Italian voices during the intervals of songs and piano recitals. I can still see myself surreptitiously opening a chink in a window and letting a little fresh air into the rooms, hiding myself discreetly afterwards in the folds of the curtain, so that I might escape the wrathful and watchful eye of Frau Wagner. I can also recollect trying to quench my thirst with what I thought was a harmless and delicious beverage, which turned out to be an intoxicating " Mai-trank " that almost sent me staggering home.

The memory of Germany, as I once knew that country, with its music and its poetry, its old cities full of romance, its good-hearted people living their simple industrious lives—that memory, alas ! is now over-shadowed by the curse of the terrible war that so cruelly disturbed the peace of the world for many a long year.

In the Spring of 1869 we determined upon visiting Rome during the Easter Festival. Our dear mother was only too happy to renew her past memories, and so our desire was carried into effect. Our Italian friend, Signora Galimberti (or " Gari " for short), was again one of our party, and we had as well the signal good fortune of chaperoning to Rome a most charming woman, the late Lady Ritchie, then still Annie Thackeray, daughter of my mother's early friend, the great novelist. Never was there a more unpunctual, inconsequent, amusing, attractive, delightful travelling

companion than Miss Thackeray, and her society added
greatly to the pleasure of the first part of our trip.
She had been invited to spend a few weeks with her
friends, the Storys, in their beautiful apartment high
up in the Barberini Palace at Rome, where they entertained largely both Americans and English, in addition
to those Romans who cared for semi-Bohemian as well
as fashionable society.

Mr. Story, the son of the American judge of that
name, whose fine work as a sculptor was universally
recognised, was a very interesting, cultured, and agreeable man, whilst his wife was known to be most hospitable and kindly ; their daughter, Edith, an attractive
young girl, was gifted with a fine voice and considerable
musical talent. Later she married Simone Peruzzi,
Marchese dei Medici, but at that time she contributed
to the pleasant social atmosphere of the home. The
sons, both distinguished as they grew to manhood, were
at school in England.

But to return to our journey. We drove by *vetturino*
on the beautiful Riviera road, from Cannes to a few
miles short of Genoa, and enjoyed this so much that,
had it not been for the prospect of Rome, we might
have been tempted to linger longer on the way. However, we gave ourselves time to renew acquaintance
with Genoa, and to make acquaintance with Florence,
and then, rapidly passing on to Cremona and Bologna,
went joyfully on our way to Rome.

And here let it be mentioned that our powers of endurance as travellers were being well put to the proof.
At that time the now fashionable *coupé-lit* did not
exist, so that we had to sleep sitting up in the not
uncomfortable but not too luxurious railway compart-
ments; on the other hand we had the opportunity of
seeing many more interesting places than we could have
done in later years, when the *train de luxe* carries the
traveller like a parcel or letter from the point of departure
to that of final arrival, without any break on the way.

H

On one clear beautiful morning in March I was awakened after a night's journey in the train, and suddenly saw what looked like a phantom building floating in the sky: it was the cupola of St. Peter's. Then followed a swift run through the Campagna and we were *in Rome*! The wonderful church of San Paolo fuori le Mura, with its lofty statues extending their hands, seemed to give us a welcome and a benediction as we steamed into the station. How curiously the present and the past met in those days! I remember my sister observing that in Rome in the year '69 " there were a few shops, one omnibus, and quantities of fleas," and, I should like to add, scores of beggars. Well, in spite of the two latter plagues, it was a very enjoyable Rome, and I shall always be grateful for having had the privilege of seeing it under the picturesque old Papal régime, which, however, has been so often described that I will only mention the two glimpses I had of the Pope (Pio Nono), whose movements were still unfettered, and who said Mass openly and publicly in St. Peter's, blessed the faithful from the balcony of the Basilica on Easter Sunday, and was to be seen on other occasions actually walking in the open country, surrounded by members of his Court. The spectacle that struck me most forcibly was the scene on Easter Sunday. My mother and I had not attempted to attend the Easter ceremony in the great church itself, but when we arrived on the Piazza San Pietro the open space was filling quickly. As noon struck the bells pealed, the cannon fired, the regiments of soldiers presented arms, and most of that mighty concourse threw themselves on their knees.

Many anecdotes have been told of Pio Nono, the liberal-minded Pope, on whom liberal-minded Italians had built fond hopes at the beginning of his reign.

Lord Odo Russell,[1] the British representative at the Papal Court, where he was a very great favourite, one

---

[1] Later Lord Ampthill.

day made the following remark to the Pope: " I wonder how it is that Your Holiness can be so good and amiable to me, a Protestant."

" You are a Protestant, it is true, my dear Russell," was the rejoinder, " but such a very indifferent one." Which reply amused Lord Odo immensely.

Alas ! when I next visited Rome the Pope was no longer to be seen on the balcony of St. Peter's or on the roadside, blessing his people; and gone was the splendour of the old Papal Court, with its mediaeval setting, its wealth of colour, its grand carriages and prancing horses, carrying the magnificently-robed Cardinals on their daily drives in and out of the Papal city. " Italia una " was growing and the Papal States were shrinking.

Besides the many books that we were reading concerning Rome and its wonders, we had also the advantage of being personally conducted round the galleries, churches, and ruins by a remarkably clever and very cultivated man—the Marchese de Vitelleschi.

From Rome we travelled to Naples, where we spent a very delightful time, although we still kept true to our allegiance to Rome. I know that Pompeii stands out most clearly in my remembrance of those years. We had a glorious day for our visit to the excavated city, and were entertained at a charming luncheon in this strange spot by a connection of ours—the Comtesse de Montfort and her Italian husband, she being a cousin of my mother, Lydia Helbert by name. We ate macaroni in true Neapolitan style, and, not being a teetotaller at that time, I believe that I drank the toast of our return in Neapolitan wine.

My mother was enormously interested in our visit to Naples in '69. She had known and had loved the place in her youth, and amongst other well-remembered spots she pointed out to us the beautiful mansion on the Chiaja which had once belonged to my Uncle Charles, the founder of the Italian Banking House, and where his brilliant daughter, Charlotte, had spent her youthful years.

I returned more than once to Rome and Naples, once in company with my husband, who was greatly in sympathy with and a devoted student of Italian art, and on other occasions in my sister's yacht, the *Garland*. On one of these yachting expeditions we spent a few days in Rome with the Storys in the Palazzo Barberini. It was there that I met, and was greatly taken by, Lord Dufferin, who at a luncheon given by our hostess suddenly asked if any one could give a satisfactory answer to the following question : " Who were Jachin and Boaz ? " I remember that Mr. Nevin, the minister of the American Church, was amongst the guests, and he answered boldly, as did Mr. Story : " Boaz ? why, of course, the husband of Ruth, but who or what was Jachin ? " I knew, or thought I knew, but felt that I could not show my superior knowledge in such company. Profound silence. Then I whispered to Lord Dufferin, who was my neighbour : " Pillars of the Temple, on which nothing rested." But I was not allowed to keep this to myself. " Go up to the top," called out Lord Dufferin ; " you are the first one I have ever met who has answered this poser." I felt rather ashamed of myself, because I knew well that had I not been reading with great care Stanley's delightful book on the Jewish Church, I should most probably not have been able to answer the question.

It was also in Mr. Story's hospitable house that I made the acquaintance of Mr. Newton, of British Museum fame, who was deeply interested in excavations, and who on our first visit had been so attentive to Annie Thackeray that the Storys were building up a romance in connection with their two friends. It was also at the Barberini that I met the authoress of the famous " Battle-Hymn of the Republic," Mrs. Julia Ward Howe, who herself related to me the origin of her thrilling lines.

At the commencement of the war between the North Chapter
and South in 1862, Julia Howe awoke one morning   V.
at 5 o'clock to the sound of the tramp of many feet,
and to the spirited singing of

> John Brown's body lies mouldering in the grave,
> But his soul goes marching on.

She flung on her wrapper, as she expressed it, and,
looking out of the window, saw a regiment of the
Northern Army on the march to join the fighting
forces. She listened with enthusiasm to the music
and returned to her bed thinking, " The song is fine,
I appreciate those martial strains, but the words
revolt me—could there not be better ones ? " There
and then the inspiration came to her, and she wrote
without hesitating the fine hymn that America has
adopted :

> Mine eyes have seen the glory of the coming of the Lord.

Years afterwards, in 1910, when Mrs. Ward Howe had
attained the age of 91, she received the degree of
Doctor of Humanities at Boston. When she was wheeled
into the theatre on this occasion, the entire audience,
numbering about 3000, rose to their feet and burst
into singing the Battle-Hymn. Mrs. Howe was a very
amusing woman, with a great deal of natural humour
and ready wit ; she had a very handsome daughter,
Maud, who came and spent a few days with us at Aston
Clinton some years after we had met her mother, and
who ended by marrying a man many years younger than
herself.

When we were young, and still in the schoolroom,
we were great romanticists and ardent devotees of Sir
Walter Scott. We had been introduced to some of
his finest works by my mother, to whose inimitable
reading aloud we owed many an exciting and interesting
evening. Perhaps our desire to cross the Border, and
become acquainted with Scottish places of romantic

fame, was first kindled by the perusal of Scott's novels. I can remember the thrill with which I approached Holyrood, and my delight at being taken to see Abbotsford and Melrose Abbey. Several times did we repeat our visits to Scotland, and perhaps the trip to the Isle of Skye, planned with much care and excitement, remains the most clearly defined in my memory of old days. Skye seemed at that time to be far removed from the ordinary traveller's beat, remote from the civilisation of the nineteenth century. Besides our four selves, my aunt, Baroness Charles de Rothschild, and her daughter Emma were of the party who invaded Skye, and we were further enlivened by the cheery companionship of Lord John Hay, son of the then Lord Tweeddale.

Our ride to the Cuchullin Hills on little mountain ponies accompanied by a guide who spoke an incomprehensible lingo, and the drive that our mothers took that same afternoon on an accommodating postman's cart, provided talk and merriment for many a long day to come. I remember the beautiful manners of the ferryman, who, upon running our boat into harbour on arrival, announced with a graceful bow, as he removed his bonnet, " Isle of Skye, ladies and gentlemen." The hotel was as unlike the modern hotel as might have been expected, and could easily have served for a romantic scene of fiction. All would have been perfect had not my father been suffering from a slight gouty attack, and the possibility of his being laid up in those uncivilised regions was not a pleasant one ; but enforced quiet restored him to health, and we bade adieu to Skye with some emotion. Scotland still remains to me a country of much charm and of great beauty.

Alas ! my happy days of travel are now at an end. I can only unlock the cells of my memory and bring forth some of its treasured pictures for my delectation.

Besides our interesting trips abroad, we spent some

weeks of the summer months in the 'sixties both in
Ireland and in Scotland. These first visits were succeeded by others at different periods, but I think it was
our first acquaintance with Ireland that offered us a rare
field of delightful adventure, such as we never forgot,
and which left an unrivalled impression upon our
minds and hearts. Our visits to Newtown Anner, the
beautiful home of our friends, Mr. and Mrs. Bernal
Osborne and their daughters; to Shanbally Castle, the
romantic abode of the Lismores; to Bessborough,
Curraghmore, Woodstock, were accurately described by
my sister and myself in the daily letters that we wrote
to my dear mother, who had been detained in London
by *her* mother's serious illness.

" I cannot give you any idea of the brilliancy of an
Irish landscape," my sister wrote in one of her home
letters; " everything is so atmospheric that it has
almost an unreal appearance." We visited Lord Fer-
moy's estate from Cork, travelling by water. " The
banks of the river are very pretty and the Cork Harbour
magnificent. The broad river, the innumerable stations,
the town slightly lit up, the *Gemüthlichkeit* of the people,
reminded us very much of our expedition to Saxon
Switzerland " (which had taken place in the preceding
year). We were greatly interested in the Irish peasantry
and enjoyed visiting those of the Newtown Anner
estate, so different in speech, appearance, and dress
from the villagers of our own home. The pretty little
speeches and well-turned compliments, the ready wit
of the Irish men and women of the soil, were very
pronounced and pleasing to the English visitors. We
watched the dancing one Sunday afternoon at the
four cross roads, and were much flattered when one
young Irishman after another came up shyly but
civilly inviting us to dance. Upon my saying that I
had never learnt the steps of a jig, I was told in the
most delightful brogue that I could soon be taught, and
that it would be an honour to teach me. I think my

CHAPTER
V.

sister and I both wept when the ship carried us back to the shores of England, so successful had been our little trip, and so much had my dear father enjoyed himself, not only with his own friends, but also with the genial Irish whom he met. I paid several other visits in later years to the Emerald Isle, but I do not think that any of these left such vivid and pleasant memories as did that first one when we were both young and ardent sight-seers. However, I feel I cannot omit the mention of a visit to Dublin in the 'nineties, comprising, as it did, a warm reception from the students of Alexandra College, where, by the invitation of Miss White, the kind and cultured head, I gave an address to a fine band of young scholars. Miss White had been for some time a vice-president of our N.U.W.W.

CHAPTER VI

SOCIAL LIFE

I feel like one
Who treads alone
Some banquet-hall deserted ;
Whose lights are fled,
Whose garlands dead,
And all but *she* departed.
                    THOMAS MOORE.

OUR dear mother had never looked with an eye of favour, even of indulgence, upon children's balls and parties during the years of our schoolroom existence. She was determined that we should lead simple and healthy lives. We were, however, not by any means banished to the precincts of the schoolroom, but were encouraged to join our elders, and to take part in the pleasant talk that had a way of running on uninterruptedly between our parents and their guests, and did not cease suddenly on our entrance into the room. Life, for us, was not run on lines too frivolous or too studious ; the lessons we learnt, and from which I trust we profited, were culled from people as well as from books. And we had many kind grown-up friends before we, as it were, came out. There was, indeed, no great cleavage between the years before we entered what is called the world, and the early years after we had done so. I was considered by some people to be very grown up when a child, and by others childish when I came out. I know that in my heart,

nly I hardly dared to say so, I thought the young
men with whom I habitually danced rather silly and
often dull in comparison with the friends of our schoolroom days—such as Mr. John Abel Smith, Sir John
Hippesley, Mr. Bernal Osborne, and Mr. Delane,
the famous editor of *The Times*, and others. With
Mr. Delane we rode daily in Rotten Row, and were
much flattered when that gentleman expressed his
annoyance at our having once changed the hour of our
equestrian exercise from 6 o'clock in the evening to
8 or 8.30 A.M.

On one occasion I remember being asked by some
acquaintance for the latest news, and at my look of
bewilderment my questioner remarked, " Well, *you*
ought to know, as I see you daily riding with Delane."
As it happened, on that very day Mr. Delane, who took,
or pretended to take, a great interest in our studies,
had been asking me how much I knew of mathematics,
and had enjoined upon my sister and myself the study
of Euclid, which advice, I believe, we followed conscientiously. Mr. Delane became a dear friend, and we
rode with him not only in Rotten Row, but also in the
muddy lanes and over the grassy fields of Bucks. It
was very sad to see him when he began to fail in
health, and seemed hardly able to take any interest
in the talk that went on around him, but dropped
asleep at the dinner-table. He died in 1879.

John Abel Smith, a fine specimen of the English
gentleman of the last century, with his beautiful manners
and gentle courtesy, was a warm friend of our family.
A convinced Liberal, he had stood by my uncle time
after time during his many contested elections, and
none rejoiced more than Mr. Smith when the Jews
were at last given their Parliamentary rights and
privileges. How often he came to stay with us at
Aston Clinton, and what delightful rides we used to
take with him ! his first words on arrival always
being, " Where are the young ladies going to take

me to-morrow ? " I am happy to say that the friendship commenced with the father continued to a second
and third generation. Sir John Hippesley, another
gentleman of the old school, full of pleasant talk and
ready to be amused and to amuse, very cultured and
artistic, was often shocked by the manners of the
young men of the present day, and said that they
ought to listen respectfully whilst their elders held
forth ; he also regretted the fact that they ceased to
use the word " sir " when addressing their seniors.

My dear father seldom if ever rode with us ; he said
it made him too nervous. He hunted once a week, on
Mondays, and went out shooting with one or two friends
about once a fortnight during the autumn months. In
those early days there were not the great " battues "
that we have grown accustomed to as the years have
gone by, but friends and country neighbours were asked
for a day's sport and were quite content with small bags.

Bernal Osborne, whom we as children called " The
Prophète " (he gave himself that name when we persistently asked who he was), was a much appreciated
member of our circle of friends. Some people thought
him captious, and were afraid of his witty but biting
tongue. But to us he was always kind and friendly, and
showed his very best side when in the company of my
parents. He was extraordinarily original and brilliant,
and could keep a whole room full of people amused
by his chaff and fun.

Mr. Osborne's apt wit was of so evanescent a
character, and depended so much upon his facial
expression and also upon the environment of the
moment, that I find it difficult, almost impossible, to
give a satisfactory instance of its readiness. But I can
recall one notable occasion at Aston Clinton, in 1873,
when Mr. Osborne, seated at the card table, was playing
whist, his partner being no other than H.R.H. the
Prince of Wales. Upon the Prince's asking whether
the stakes should be half-crowns, Mr. Osborne answered

quickly, " Certainly, sir, we could hardly play for
crowns."

It was somewhat late in life that he became appreciated, and almost taken possession of, by some members
of what was popularly called " The Marlborough House
Set," and by them introduced to the Prince and Princess
of Wales (Edward VII. and Queen Alexandra). He
became a firm friend of their Royal Highnesses, but was
never obsequious or untrue to his own convictions. He
married Miss Osborne, an Irish heiress, and added her
name to his own, Bernal. She was a clever and original
woman, but of very dissimilar views to her brilliant
husband. She owned a lovely estate in Co. Tipperary,
which we visited in 1864. The two daughters of Mr.
and Mrs. Osborne, Lady Blake and the Duchess of St.
Albans, were friends of ours from a very early age.

I do not think that, in spite of my love of dancing,
I was very eager to leave my happy schoolroom life,
and make my appearance as a young lady in society,
particularly as my sister and I, who had always been
such close companions, were not going to make our
presentation curtsies on the same day of the same year.
I had the precedence of age. I remember being first
amused at the idea of a Court train and feathers, and
then thinking that we were all wasting much time
over a good deal of nonsense ; but when the great day
actually arrived, I imagine that my feelings were not
unlike those of most nervous débutantes. It was to
be a Drawing-room in black and white (Court mourning
for the Duchess of Kent) held by Queen Victoria,
and I have a dim recollection that it took place in
St. James's Palace.

After being well looked at, perhaps openly admired
and inwardly criticised by kind relatives and friends,
and by all the members of the household gathered for
that purpose in the hall of our house, my mother and I
prepared to start. I remember that my dear father

came back purposely early from the City on that day,
to see that I was properly equipped, and that I was
wearing a beautiful string of pearls, his gift, which he
had had collected for me, together with a similar one
for my sister, during all the years of our childhood.   We
had the grand chariot out on that occasion.   It was
drawn by a splendid pair of dark-brown horses that
tossed up their heads most proudly, as if well aware of
their importance.   The said carriage had an uncomfortable fashion of swaying backwards and forwards,
which was somewhat conducive to sea-sickness.   Our
French coachman, well bewigged and in Court array,
sat on the ponderous hammer-cloth of the huge box
seat, whilst the two footmen in State liveries, with
staves in their hands, stood at the back of the chariot,
holding on by straps arranged for that purpose.   The
streets seemed teeming with life, and I felt as if I were
the central object of attention.   I was undeceived
when I became aware that many smart carriages of all
sorts and sizes, filled with men in uniform and women
in gala dress, were speeding along the same road that
we were taking, and falling at last at a walking
pace into long lines, until our arrival at St. James's
Palace.   I thought we got quite quickly enough to
our destination.   There we found ourselves amongst a
number of mothers and débutantes, the latter looking
rather like a flock of sheep—most of us may have been
as timid.   After awaiting our turn, and nervously secur-
ing our veils, we all moved on together, nearer and
nearer to our place of execution (as it seemed to me),
and then we knew that we were on the threshold of the
Throne Room.   I begged of my mother to go first so
that she should not see my curtsey, and obeyed her
mandate of pulling off the glove from my right hand,
which was to touch that of H.M.   As I passed through
the doorway I felt my train being removed from my
arm and drawn away from my waist.   Then suddenly
I heard our names shouted out, and knew that I was

standing before a group of personages in the midst of whom I could distinguish a small lady in black, wearing her crown of diamonds and her ribbon of the Garter— small, but immensely dignified. She seemed to me to be constantly in the act of bowing. A hand, which was a very beautiful one, was extended towards me; I took it in my ungloved one, and kissed it, curtseying down to the ground. I then passed on with more curtsies, still longing to get another look at the bevy of princes, princesses, and grandees grouped round H.M., but I was not allowed to pause. I was ignominiously, as I thought, hurried on, my train hastily gathered up and thrust under my unwilling arm, and so I rejoined my mother and left the Palace in a somewhat exhausted condition.

When I got home I was cross-questioned by my sister as to my experiences, and felt that I could not tell her half of what she wanted to know. However, in the month of May in the following year she had the same ordeal to go through, after which we attended many Drawing-rooms together.

But it was my privilege to meet Queen Victoria in a far less formal manner than on the day of my presentation at Court. Through the kindness of Princess Louise, the Queen's daughter, I spent Sunday the 23rd of May in the year 1886 at Windsor Castle, going down with H.R.H. on the Saturday and returning on the Monday. The weather was glorious, the chestnuts in Windsor Park in full and magnificent bloom, and the whole place redolent of Spring.

I had an early breakfast on Sunday morning with the household, and then betook myself, being unemployed and alone, to the long corridor, where I amused myself by a study of the interesting portraits and pictures that hung on the walls.

In the afternoon I was taken by my kind Princess, at my own desire, to see the Wolsey Chapel, where the body of the Duke of Albany was entombed. I was

told that this request of mine had given Her Majesty
satisfaction.   Later in the day, after calling upon Lady
Ponsonby, I was informed that I was to dine with the
Queen.   So my low-necked evening gown had to appear,
as well as my emerald and diamond ornaments, and in
gala dress I awaited with others the appearance of Her
Majesty in the long corridor.   I remember some functionary calling out in a loud voice, " The Queen ! ", the
door opening, and a short but stately figure in black
advancing towards me with the greatest dignity and
solemnity.   I curtsied down into the ground, and felt
as if the carpet were going to swallow me up.   The
Queen walked into the dining-room between her two
daughters, Princess Louise and Princess Beatrice, but
the minister in attendance that evening sat on one
side of his Royal mistress and one of the Princesses on
the other.   Conversation was carried on in a very low
key, so low that once or twice I felt much inclined to
scream.   After dinner we repaired again to the corridor,
when the Queen beckoned for me to come to her.   Her
Majesty's voice was very pleasant, and her manner most
kind.   She began by telling me that she had once seen
my great-grandfather at Frankfort and had never
forgotten him.   I ventured to dispute the fact, reminding Her Majesty that the gentleman in question had died
in 1812, before her own birth.

" But I did see a very remarkable man of the name
of Rothschild when I was a child and visiting Frankfort
with the Duchess of Kent," maintained Her Majesty,
ignoring my remark as to the date of her birth; " it
surely must have been the husband of that wonderful
old Frau Rothschild."   " No, ma'am," I resolutely
insisted on my side, " it was not possible.   Your
Majesty must have seen my great-grandfather's eldest
son, Amschel," which answer hardly seemed to satisfy
the Queen.   Then followed inquiries after many
members of my family, and a few gracious words about
my dear mother—much treasured and appreciated as

coming from the lips of one who evidently possessed great discernment of character. The Queen then spoke to me in terms of admiration of my mother's uncle, Sir Moses Montefiore, who had died the previous year (1885) at the age of 101. Her Majesty remembered that when, as a child, she spent a few weeks one summer with the Duchess of Kent at Ramsgate, she was warmly welcomed by Sir Moses, whose residence, East Cliff, was situated in that pretty seaside place. The Queen went on to relate how Sir Moses had presented her with a little gold key that unlocked his garden gate, and had begged of her to make use of it during her stay. " And, indeed, we did," continued the Queen, " and I still possess the key."

Then I ventured to recount to Her Majesty how my venerable uncle used to drink her health every day in a glass of port, removing the small skull-cap which he habitually wore, and saying most fervently, " God bless the Queen." This little anecdote seemed to please Her Majesty very much, for she esteemed and respected my uncle greatly ; in fact, the Queen had shown her appreciation of him as soon as it was in her power to do so, by giving him a knighthood upon her accession.

My next visit to Windsor was in the May of 1890, when I was again in the company of H.R.H. Princess Louise and Lord Lorne were returning on that day (May 7) from Torquay, where they had been inspecting and opening a very charming Art Exhibition and where I had had the honour of accompanying them. A Royal command from Windsor to meet the celebrated explorer, Stanley, then just returned from Central Africa, was the cause of our stopping on the homeward route. I first met the distinguished traveller (who did not look at all distinguished) at dinner with the household, and was present when he was introduced to Her Majesty. We were all invited to take our places behind the Royal Family in one of the spacious and beautiful

rooms, where a map of Africa, illustrating Stanley's
perilous journeys, was exposed for our view. A very
interesting lecture was given by the traveller, the
details of which have now, I regret to say, escaped
my memory. At the close, a little coal-black youth
was taken up to the Queen by the lecturer and formally
presented. Her Majesty smiled graciously and extended
her hand; the boy grasped it and wrung it warmly,
perhaps rather severely, for I noticed that the Queen
seemed not merely astonished, but uncomfortably so, at
this action. But the boy went smilingly and serenely
away from the dignified presence of Her Majesty, not
knowing how he had transgressed the ordinary conven-
tions of Court etiquette.

Again I had the pleasure of meeting the Queen at
Grasse, on the French Riviera, in the year 1891, when
Princess Louise and I were the guests of my cousin,
Alice de Rothschild, in her beautiful villa, which, after
H.M.'s visit to Grasse, was named Villa Victoria. Her
Majesty, with Prince and Princess Henry of Battenberg
and their suite, was settled in the Grand Hotel in the
town, but within a few minutes' walk of the Villa.
Thus it was almost daily that I had the privilege of
seeing, and often of speaking with, the Queen, who
seemed to be fully enjoying the beauties of the South.
Her tall majestic Indian attendants, headed by the
" Munshi " (as he was called), and the picturesque
Scottish servants in their Highland dress, added to the
romance of the scene.

One evening the Queen sent for my cousin and
myself. We found Her Majesty sitting in a small room
at the hotel, listening, whilst at work, to Princess
Beatrice, who was playing duets on the piano with the
Queen's maid-of-honour and private secretary for the
time being, Marie Adeane, H.M. beating time with her
crochet needle. She made us be seated, one on each
side of her, and we had quite a pleasant informal talk.
The Queen expressed her delight at all the arrangements

I

that had been so carefully made for her comfort and privacy; she was astonished at Alice's energy and capability, and called her, in speaking privately of her, " the All-Powerful."

We had sunshine and also grey weather, both literally and metaphorically, during that visit, for illness seemed to haunt our footsteps. To begin with, Prince Henry of Battenberg was only just recovering from an attack of measles contracted at Grasse. Then, owing to an epidemic of smallpox in the town, we were all vaccinated by the Queen's command. The Indians, who had never gone through this process before, suffered considerably. Besides this, many of the suite complained of bad sore throats—it was thought owing to the recklessness of those who walked out at sunset, this being specially dangerous in southern lands. Saddest of all, one of the Queen's housemaids, who had been sent in advance to prepare for Her Majesty's arrival, developed blood-poisoning from the prick of a needle, to which, after some days of great suffering, she finally succumbed. The Queen was most kind and sympathetic throughout the illness, and later to the relatives of the poor girl, who came out to Grasse at Her Majesty's request. We attended the funeral service, which was held in the hotel, the Queen and all her suite being present.

On most days, even when the wind was cold and sharp, Her Majesty would take her daily drive, always in an open carriage, often in the direction of the Alpine passes. On other days the favourite donkey-chair might have been in request, as I described in one of my home letters.

VILLA VICTORIA, GRASSE,
ALPES MARITIMES, *April* 1, 1891.

. . . We had had a delicious morning, with air like crystal; part of it I spent on the mountain side, *panting* after H.M.'s donkey chair. Off goes the donkey at a good firm pace, led by the groom, Randall. H.M. in a grey shawl, with a mushroom hat, a large white sunshade, sits comfortably installed in a donkey chair; then come the two Princesses close behind, walking like troopers; the two Scottish servants not quite so active; beside them romps the collie " Roy," Lady Churchill and I close up the procession, and the little pug belonging to Princess Beatrice toddles last of all. The Queen never stops, but goes steadily on to the end of Alice's delightful mountain drive, and then into the gardens of a villa belonging to a great perfume manufacturer. At the entrance of this garden Alice is continuing her road as a surprise to the Queen; but Her Majesty's keen eyes discovered signs and tokens of the new road and she was informed of Alice's plans. I told Her Majesty that it was a state secret, and begged of her not to appear as if she knew anything about it when Alice will conduct her for the first time on the road, which is being levelled, widened, and straightened by about fifty stalwart Provençal peasants. " It is a secret, a secret," said H.M. with a smile and a twinkle, like a child who thinks that the great fun of a secret is in divulging it.

The Maharajah Duleep Singh drove all the way from Nice to lunch with the Queen, and to beg forgiveness for his disloyal conduct. He is in a crippled condition and dying. Princess Louise was present when he arrived and was much touched, for the poor man sobbed and cried bitterly. The Queen, who had always taken a deep and affectionate interest in the Maharajah when he came to England as a boy, said, " I forget the past ; it does not exist."

The Carnival week was duly kept at Grasse, and the " Battle of Flowers " was the occasion of much fun and merriment.

The Queen took her station upon the balcony of the hotel with the Princesses and suite. I stood behind Her Majesty, holding a huge basket filled with beautiful flowers sent from the Villa, with which I supplied the Queen, who flung them down to the gaily-dressed populace crowding the pathway below. Some daring masqueraders, disguised as pierrots, climbed up to the balcony, holding out money - boxes, and were duly pelted by Royal hands with sweet-smelling blossoms, whilst from Sir Henry Ponsonby they received more lasting tokens of favour. It was a very gay scene, and afforded much amusement to the Queen, who demanded more and more flowers, until at last we had to resort to the trick of having them picked up and brought back from the street only to be flung down again. I could not help expressing my amusement at this scene by frank laughter, which was checked by one of those present. Later in the day I was cheered by hearing that Her Majesty had said, "I did enjoy hearing Mrs. Flower laugh."

There were some pleasant visitors at Grasse during our stay there, amongst others Sir Mackenzie Wallace, the interesting author, and Lord Lytton, then our Ambassador in Paris. I had a long chat with the latter, whilst he was awaiting Her Majesty's summons, and found him most entertaining and delightful. I met him again when I had the honour of dining with the Queen, who, I remember, on that occasion talked to me of her daily lessons in Hindustani with the " Munshi," asking me several questions concerning the Hebrew alphabet, which she was anxious to compare with those of other Oriental languages. I was indeed sorry when Princess Louise reminded Her Majesty that it was growing late, and that she ought to take her well-merited rest before the heavy work that awaited her on the morrow, and thus ended that interesting interview.

I had the pleasure of seeing Her Majesty several times after her visit to Grasse, but never in so informal and pleasant a manner. Indeed I am most grateful for these more intimate glimpses of a Queen whose personality, if I may say so, had always greatly attracted me, and whose influence on the political and social life of the nineteenth century was so remarkable.

After this lengthy digression, which is concerned with many later incidents in my life, I will return to my earliest social experiences. These do not hold the most attractive memories, and this for several reasons.

I had no girl friends with whom to compare impressions.
Our mother had never encouraged such friendships,
and my sister and I had led lives of sheltered childhood
and girlhood, somewhat aloof from others of our own
age.   Then our mother from the first resolutely set her
face against what she called day-time dissipation,
conducive, she considered, to over-fatigue of mind and
body.   We were never taken, therefore, to the fashionable breakfasts—really garden - parties—river excursions, picnics, race-meetings, etc., etc., which were
much loved by other girls.   My mother, not being
very strong, and not allowing us any other chaperonage
than her own, found that her strength would only be equal
to attending evening festivities, without the added toil
of day functions; besides which, she could ill bear the
idea of our suddenly and entirely discontinuing our
studies.   Indeed, we were allowed only a limited
number of entertainments in the week—this to ensure us
against over-fatigue—but on the other hand we were
not permitted to recoup our strength by lengthy morning slumbers.   I remember going to many rather
solemn dinner-parties during this my first year, and
also to a number of enjoyable dances.   This was before
the days when married women began to compete most
unfairly in the ballroom with young girls, and therefore
the girls had a very good time.

In my young days the balls were always opened
with a stately quadrille, followed by a waltz, a polka,
a polka-mazurka, or lancers, whilst at Court balls and
in some private houses the Scottish reels were vigorously
danced.   At Holkham I had the honour of being introduced to an Irish jig by H.R.H. the Prince of Wales,
later our gracious sovereign, Edward VII.   Bunny
Hugs, Turkey Trots, Jazz and other innovations were
unknown then.   There was a great deal of innocent fun
in those days, it seems to me now; Society did its best
to attract the young and the fresh of both sexes, and
Society received a very satisfactory response.   Indeed

everything was simpler, less extravagant, less complicated than it became later on, and I am grateful to say
that I saw, and can recall, the very happy days of the
best of the Victorian epoch. Of course Society, or what
was acknowledged as Society, was far more exclusive
than it is now, therefore easier to manage. A comparatively small number of people were in the habit of
meeting continually in each other's houses, and
rarely was an outsider expected or admitted, unless
perhaps in the person of a male genius or a female
beauty. The fast set was far removed from our orbit
at that time, and the professional beauty had not yet
emerged from the seclusion where she was maturing.
The young people loved a good dance on a well-polished
floor with a fine rousing band, and did not expect to
see the rooms with which they were acquainted transformed for the one night into bowers of roses, or to be
regaled at a supper with the finest wines and most
expensive viands. These were to come later. But for
all that, the London Season was a serious matter, with
few or no week-ends as a distraction from the main
business ; on the other hand, there were the Saturday
evening parties given by the Prime Minister, Lord
Palmerston, and his wife, which it was considered quite
the right thing to attend. Marriages were looked
forward to as the result of a busy and satisfactory
season, extending from May, or even earlier, to the
end of July, a really successful maiden hardly ever
going unmarried through more than three seasons.

In those days the Park and Rotten Row were in
their glory. It was the fashion to ride either before
breakfast, or else between 12 and 2 o'clock, or after
6 o'clock in the afternoon. The early equestrians were
dubbed " the liver brigade," as they rode at a fine
pace for exercise, whilst many of those who appeared
during the later hours of the morning were politicians
and fashionables of both sexes, the evening riders
including men whose business kept them occupied during

the greater part of the day. Women wore habits fitting
closely to the waist, very long skirts, top hats with
ample veils, and white kid gloves, their saddles always
having three pommels. The men were very carefully
attired, as if for an afternoon town call; no bowler
hat was ever seen in the Park, and smoking was not
tolerated.

Besides equestrians, during the afternoon there was
a wonderful display of carriages. The old-fashioned
barouche, often drawn by splendid horses, the newly
invented light Victoria, and the phaeton with its quick-
paced cobs or ponies, were all to be seen near the
Serpentine, or between Hyde Park Corner and Albert
Gate. It was the fashion in those days for men to
drive a smart prancing horse in what was called a cab,
with a small groom clinging on behind in a very alarming-
looking position. Women in their carriages were
becomingly and elegantly attired ; the audaciously
short walking skirt, the loosely-fitting blouse and low-
necked bodice were unknown in those more punctilious
days. Bonnets, becoming to some faces, especially so to
the radiantly beautiful Princess of Wales, were always
worn, and the sensible hat, a protection against sun
and storm, relegated to country wear ; in fact, in cases
where the bonnet was not discarded, the wearer would
occasionally, especially at the seaside, attach to its rim
a green silk shade called " an ugly," immortalised by
Punch in the 'fifties and 'sixties. Comfort is now the
order of the day; then the conventionalities ruled
supreme.

Hardly any carriages were to be seen in the Park
on Sundays, the only equestrians being a few men
who took their exercise at a very early hour of the
morning, but between 5 and 7 o'clock on Sunday afternoons, and, indeed, on other days in the summer months,
numbers of pedestrians sat and walked in Hyde Park.
Church Parade was hardly in vogue before the 'seventies.
Different parts of the Park and of Kensington Gardens

came into fashion in different years; thus it often
happened that people were inconveniently crowded by
their own choice into a small space, leaving other
beautiful and shady walks practically empty. Many
customs owed their disuse to the advent of the
bicycle and the motor-car, amongst them the regular
attendances at church services. I can remember
Sundays spent in friends' country houses, when hosts
and guests alike were always present at the morning
service in the parish church; but of late years this
has changed. Few of the guests, or even of the house
party, are now seen amongst the congregation, and it
is not unnatural that many of the household follow the
example of their employers. In time, from loss of habit,
the old and good fashion of regular attendance at a
place of worship, good alike for master and servant,
mistress and maid, has become a matter of choice, not
of duty.

My sister and I, although we loved riding in Rotten
Row and walking in the Park, did not much appreciate
driving about the London streets for the purpose of
leaving and returning cards, which was considered one
of the duties of grown-up young ladies. Besides dinner-
parties and balls, we greatly enjoyed the concerts that
we regularly attended, also our visits to the opera and
theatre. We knew personally a few of the foremost
actors and actresses, amongst others the Alfred Wigans,
Sir Squire and Lady Bancroft, Ellen Terry, Sir Henry
Irving, Sir John Hare, and Coquelin, the great French
actor, who once invited my sister and myself on the
stage between two acts of *Cyrano de Bergerac*, taking
off his huge sham nose to show us how cleverly it
had been constructed and fastened on for that famous
performance.

Our mother, besides her duties as a chaperon,
devoted herself as before to her painting and her books;
and even in the busiest of seasons she never neglected
the philanthropic work that took her to the crowded

streets and narrow courts of the East End, and regularly
to the Jews' Free School. She was always very much
afraid that we might become too fond of a frivolous
existence and too much captivated by worldly amusements, so she fostered in all ways, not only our love of
country pursuits and devotion to our country home,
but also a serious outlook on life and its duties. Now,
although I had to a great extent the *joie de vivre*, I
found my mother's society so stimulating and fascinating, and my sister's so witty and amusing, that I really
never craved for the excitement of a London season,
as other girls may have done whose home life was laid
on less pleasant lines.

Possibly such a bringing-up may have made us somewhat severe in our judgment of contemporaries, and
perhaps we were led to set too much store by literary
or intellectual acquirements, and too little by those of
a practical nature. My mother hated any kind of
showing off, and deprecated the then still existing habit
of producing portfolios of drawings to outwardly admiring
friends, and giving performances on the piano in the
drawing-room, where the visitors were supposed to listen
to and be charmed by the young people's music. My dear
father, who had a most exalted opinion of my mother's
intellect, gave her a perfectly free hand in her rule of
the schoolroom. He was of a truly amiable nature,
loved society, and proved himself to be an excellent
host. He enjoyed taking us out, as well as entertaining
at home. My parents gave some very pleasant dinner-
parties in London, whilst in the country my father's
hospitable disposition led him often to invite more guests
to our house than it could conveniently hold. A warm
welcome always awaited our visitors, and they liked
coming where they knew that their company was so
much appreciated. As my father was fluent in French
and German, it amused him to receive foreigners, and
as he was for some years Austrian Consul, this became a
duty at times as well as a pleasure ; thus in 1862, when

the second great International Exhibition was held in London, he kept open house for the Austrian visitors.

Many acquaintances that we made in those early years grew into friends. A country house can be a splendid place either for arresting or for developing friendships, its close proximities revealing so much that would remain otherwise hidden or only guessed at. My mother was not quick at taking fancies, but she never forgot or threw over old friends for new ones; and if she was somewhat critical in her judgments, she had also a generous appreciation of fine moral and mental qualities. But it was easy to see that she revolted against wasting her time upon those entirely unsympathetic to her, whose moral standard was utterly different from her own, and she would fly, when she could do so, to her beloved books—those ever-suggestive (if silent) friends and companions. And in reading, she chose authors whose note was sobriety, and whose pages demanded concentrated thought on the part of their readers. Thus she loved the poetry of Matthew Arnold, whilst that of Swinburne never appealed to her. As a young woman she greatly enjoyed the works of Dickens, Thackeray, and Anthony Trollope in the way of fiction, and in later years she read with discrimination and much pleasure the novels of George Eliot, never changing her first opinion of them, namely, that both in conception and in language the earlier productions, such as *Adam Bede, The Mill on the Floss*, and *Silas Marner*, were the greatest and would be the most abiding of them all.

I conclude this chapter with the following interesting letter from Matthew Arnold to my mother, and a quotation from a letter to his own mother:

2 CHESTER SQUARE,
December 28th, 1861.

MY DEAR LADY DE ROTHSCHILD—A thousand thanks for your most kind remembrance of my little boy. He is better, and enchanted with the beautiful box you have sent him—

poor little fellow, as he is condemned to the house for the CHAPTER
whole winter, he will have plenty of time to admire it. VI.
Some day in the spring or early summer I shall bring him
to thank you.

However much I may like Paris I seem destined to see
very little of it at present.   But I have been living the last
month with that for which I like Paris best, by reading a
new book of Sainte-Beuve—*Chateaubriand et son groupe
littéraire.*   I got it because Sainte-Beuve wrote me word
he had quoted a poem of mine in it, but got quite fascinated
as I went on.   It is little known in England, because it goes
too much into details about French Society and French
Literature for common English readers ; but the literature
and society are those of Chateaubriand, Madame de Staël,
and their contemporaries : the most interesting company
possible.   The book has made a scandal in Paris, because
of the havoc it makes of Chateaubriand's reputation for
good Catholicism—but it is well worth reading apart from
the interest of this scandal, and I recommend you, who are
one of the few people who still read anything, by all means
to get it.

My compliments to Sir Anthony and your daughters—
and with my renewed warmest thanks, I am always, dear
Lady de Rothschild, most truly yours,

MATTHEW ARNOLD.

November 13th, 1861.

. . . I had a very pleasant day at Aston Clinton with
the Rothschilds last Friday, and a superb game of croquet
with the girls.   Such a lawn, tell Fan ! perfectly smooth,
yet so wide that in no direction could you croquet to the
end of it.   Their croquet things were very grand, and much
heavier than ours.   At first this put me out, but it is an
advantage when you get used to it, and you have infinitely
more power with heavy mallets.   Afterwards I had a long
walk with the girls in the woods of the Chilterns.   They are
all great favourites of mine, the mother particularly. . . .

CHAPTER VII

This is the place.   Stand still, my steed,
Let me review the scene,
And summon from the shadowy past
The forms that once have been.
LONGFELLOW.

CHAPTER VII. WE had some good friends amongst the clergy in our county of Bucks.   To begin with, Maynard Currie, rector of Mentmore.   The living was in the gift of my uncle, Baron Mayer de Rothschild, and Mr. Currie had been warmly recommended to him by our mutual friend, Mr. John Abel Smith.   Maynard Currie, who came to his incumbency as quite a young man in 1858, was cultivated and agreeable, a Whig in politics, and certainly not extreme in his religious views.   My uncle and aunt were both sincerely fond of him ; his social gifts and ready wit appealed specially to the latter, and he was constantly dining and spending the evening with them and their guests.   Thus he made the acquaintance of many distinguished men and women of that day. My uncle affirmed that there was no clergyman in the neighbourhood to be compared to him.   Unfortunately, after some years, a trivial event was the cause of a serious break in his friendship with the Mentmore family.   Their daughter Hannah, then emerging from the schoolroom, had expressed a wish that a child about

124

to be born in their village, of parents to whom she was very partial (they had both been in my uncle's service), should be called after her. But it happened to be a little boy, and not the expected girl, that made his appearance in this wicked world, and there was no male equivalent to the name of Hannah. What was to be done ? My uncle and family were in London. An anxious and perplexed telegram was sent by the parents ; my cousin Hannah's reply was awaited with impatience. The answer came : " Why not Hannibal ? " Why not, indeed ? Because the rector refused to christen the new-born child with so pagan a name ; entreaties were in vain—his " No ! " was final. Hannah was very angry, Maynard Currie very obdurate, my aunt sad, my uncle disturbed, the parents of the child tearful. At last the christening day came ; Mr. Currie repeated his objection, and said, moreover, that were he to give way in the matter the child would be known by his playmates as " Animal." So he received quite an ordinary appellation, but it was an understood thing that at the mansion he would always be known as " Hannibal " and that he was still to be regarded as Hannah's namesake.

Mr. Currie used frequently to visit us at Aston Clinton and was inseparably connected with our happy days there. He took immense interest in our schools (he was one of the Inspectors for the Bishop) and helped us with our Penny Readings, for he was a capital reciter, and a still better actor, and he enjoyed to the full all the winter gaieties in which we took part. But he had also a very serious and earnest side to his character, for which some people did not give him credit, and his sermons never failed to appeal to his parishioners as well as to a more cultivated congregation. We were truly grieved when he left Mentmore for the Norfolk living, given him by his cousin, the then Lord Kimberley, where he finally settled, having married the only daughter of Lord Cadogan.

Lionel Dawson Damer, rector of Cheddington in the 'sixties, was another great favourite of ours. Very musical, and gifted with a pleasant singing voice, he was immensely interested in his choir, training the boys of the parish himself. He was very fond of helping in village concerts, and most kindly came several times to Aston Clinton for that purpose. He was much beloved by his parishioners, whose lives he was always anxious to brighten. During the years of his ministry at Cheddington he had occasionally house pupils, whom he introduced to us; thus we became acquainted with the young Lord Huntly, then a most engaging youth, with a bright open countenance and a strong Scottish brogue; also with Lord Randolph Churchill, who gave promise of unusual intelligence and originality. I remember upon one occasion, when my father had asked him to spend a couple of days at Aston Clinton and to go out shooting with a few friends, Lord Randolph, then a youth of seventeen, was not forthcoming at the hour of the start. He had ensconced himself in his room with a volume of Macaulay, had carefully locked the door, and was indulging in a morning with his books. Mr. Damer was very fond of his pupil, and used often to be a guest at Blenheim, where he was always welcome. Ultimately he left Cheddington for a living near Bournemouth, married a sister of Maynard Currie, finally retired on account of ill-health, and led a very quiet secluded existence, devotedly nursed by his wife until his death, which took place at a comparatively early age.

The Rev. Augustus Birch, rector of Northchurch, whose brother Henry had been private tutor to King Edward VII., was another of our clerical friends. He happened to be an excellent shot, and had many pleasant days out shooting with my father. He was a pre-eminently social man, and enjoyed conversation that entailed bright repartee, give and take, thrust and parry. I was told that he was a very impressive preacher, but I never heard him in the pulpit. I knew that he was an excellent letter-writer, and I remember seeing some very clever verses from his pen. He was brother to John Birch, also a friend of my father's, some time Governor of the Bank of England.

Harper Crewe, a near neighbour of ours and rector of Drayton Beauchamp, was a very good botanist, and well known to all the members of the scientific flori-cultural world. He had some rare and curious plants in his garden, and was in correspondence with many of the great botanists, both in England and abroad. He was an uncompromising Evangelical in his Church views, as he was an uncompromising Tory in politics. Indeed, his political feelings urged him to have his church bells rung upon one occasion when Mr. Gladstone had been defeated at the polls. I teased him by telling him that I had related this to a daughter of Mr. Gladstone's, who had attended his church whilst she was our guest, which fact rather upset his equanimity. Besides his love of botany, he was a scientific collector of butterflies and moths, and could show countless specimens to his visitors. He had one of the tiniest of parishes, and ample time to follow his bent for natural science.

Not many miles from Aylesbury lived a strange old rector, the Rev. —— Earle, generous and good-hearted, but much addicted to the pleasures of the bottle. He knew his failing and kept a curate, especially for his Sunday ministrations, which he seldom felt able to conduct. But all the same he was beloved by his parishioners, to whose temporal needs he attended most faithfully. He was also appreciated by some of his neighbours for his scholarly attainments and love of the classics. We met him once or twice on Sunday mornings in the train returning from London, and he told us frankly that he went to town on Saturdays, not wishing to meet his parishioners until after the morning service was well over. I heard that he was buried with a volume of Greek poetry in his folded hands.

We were often chaffed about our numerous friends amongst the clergy, and upon some one's saying that we knew as many in Bucks as there were letters in the alphabet, my sister and I composed the following rhymes, which were duly written out and illustrated by Annie's clever pen :

" A " is the Archdeacon at the top of the tree ;
" B " is for Bonus, the Buckland bee.
" C " is for Currie, so wise and so witty ;
" D " is for Damer composing a ditty.
" E " is for Eaton, so crabbed and cold ;
" F " is for Ferres, who owns a small fold.
" G " is the glebe land that makes them grow fat,
" H " is for Hutchinson—already that.
" I " is for Isham, of stateliest mien ;
" J " is for Jeston, whom we've never seen.
" K " is the kettle for clerical tea ;
" L " is the handsomest Lane you can see.
" M " is for Mason, alone and forlorn ;
" N " is for North, who is happily gone.
" O " is for Ouvry, settled at Wing,
" P " is for Partington—queer little thing !
" Q " is the quarrel between High and Low,
" R " is the Rubric from whence it does flow.
" S " is for Seymour, a chatterbox truly ;
" T " is for Turner with a parish unruly.
" U " is the unwary one whom they are teaching ;
" V " is for vanity 'gainst which they are preaching.
" W " is for Wharton, fled from the Vale ;
" X " is for Christmas with pudding and ale.
" Y " is the youth who takes Holy Orders ;
" Z " is for zeal—may it shine on our borders !

KEY TO CLERICAL ALPHABET

A—Archdeacon Bickersteth.
B—Rev. Edward Bonus, rector of Buckland.
C—Rev. Maynard Currie, rector of Mentmore.
D—Rev. Dawson Damer, rector of Cheddington.
E—Rev. Wynne Eaton, rector of Aston Clinton.
F—Rev. —— Ferres, rector of Hulcot.
H—Rev. —— Hutchinson, rector of Pitstone.
I—Rev. —— Isham, rector of Weston Turville.
J—Rev. —— Jeston, rector of Cholesbury (too far from Aston Clinton to visit).

L—Rev. —— Lane, rector of Little Gaddesdon.

M—Rev. —— Mason, rector of Wiggington (at that time a lonely parish).

N—Rev. —— North, rector of Mentmore (succeeded by Mr. Currie).

O—Rev. —— Ouvry, rector of Wing.

P—Rev. —— Partington, rector of Stoke Mandeville.

S—Rev. —— Seymour, rector of Northchurch (prior to Rev. Augustus Birch).

T—Rev. —— Turner, rector of Whitchurch.

W—Rev. —— Wharton, rector of Bierton.

This masterpiece enchanted Mr. Currie, who quoted it upon all occasions and finally insisted upon showing the original copy to the Bishop of Oxford—none other than the great Wilberforce.

What pleasant visits that genial Bishop paid us, and how much he appreciated my dear mother ! I remember how on one occasion he ran a race with me, and how we both arrived at the goal at the same moment, to his great amusement. The very first time that I saw the Bishop, and also heard him, was at a Confirmation in the village, which we were allowed to attend (I being about twelve years old at the time). I was deeply impressed by the Bishop's wonderful voice, and can still recall some words that he said to the candidates. He was speaking of the Divine Spirit, which in Hebrew we should call " Ruah ha-Kodesh," and he said : " The Spirit is invisible, we cannot see it, but we can feel its influence; it is there. Think of the waters of a lake, calm and placid; suddenly they are stirred, ripples arise upon the surface. What has caused them ? A breath of wind which touches them without being seen. And so the Divine Spirit may touch our hearts; we feel it, but cannot see it." I went home and repeated nearly the whole of the episcopal address to my mother, word for word. I remember hearing him again at Aylesbury, in a crowded church, upon the occasion of a Hospital Collection, and I can recall his description of a patient, sick unto death, but tenderly and kindly

K

nursed, within a hospital ward ; also a truly awful
delineation that he gave of a lost soul, although I do
not know what the connection between the two could
have been. A poor man in a labourer's smock was
sitting near us, with his eyes fixed upon the Bishop,
following every word that was said with the deepest
interest and feeling.

There is mention made in one of Matthew Arnold's
letters to his mother in the year 1864 (these letters were
collected and edited by the late G. W. E. Russell) of a
sermon preached by the Bishop at Buckland, on the
occasion of a school-opening in that village. Mr. Arnold
and the Bishop, with several others, were our guests
for that ceremony. The reference was not very
complimentary to the preacher, but " there were
many extenuating circumstances," as the Chaplain
explained to Mr. Arnold, " the Bishop preaching under
some constraint, so many not of his own faith being
present."

" Some of the thinking—or pretended thinking—in
his sermon," wrote Mr. Arnold, " was sophistical and
hollow beyond belief. I was interested in finding how
instinctively Lady de Rothschild had seized upon this.
. . . Where he was excellent was in his speeches at
luncheon afterwards : gay, easy, cordial, and wonderfully happy."

Our dear Bishop, we always found him " gay, easy,
cordial, and happy," and were quite ready to mingle
our tears with those of the wives of the clergy
when His Lordship was translated from Oxford to
Winchester.

And here I should like to insert the following letter
addressed to my mother in the 'sixties by Bishop
Wilberforce, on the occasion of a Confirmation that he
held in the beautiful little village of Halton. The letter
is both interesting and amusing, referring, as it does, to
the customs of the day.

January 31.

MY DEAR LADY DE ROTHSCHILD—I am very much
obliged by your kindness, and shall hope, as you are so good
as to wish to have me, to come on from Halton to dine
and sleep.

Are you aware that I travel on these occasions with a
Chaplain, and my own horses, and must ask you to be
troubled with these also if you kindly receive me?—I am,
most truly yours,   S. OXON.

I remember another event that brought the Bishop
to Aston Clinton: it was the Halton Industrial
Exhibition, planned by our four selves in 1868, and
splendidly carried out by enthusiastic and willing
helpers.   Mr. Disraeli, then Premier, opened the Exhibition—almost the first of its sort to be held in a purely
agricultural district.   As I may have occasion to return
to this later on, I shall not dilate upon it here.

I think it was very liberal-minded of our parents,
especially of our dear father, to have kept open house,
as it were, at Aston Clinton for our clerical neighbours.
Before they settled at Aston Clinton, clergymen as
individuals were practically unknown to them; but
when once we were in possession of our Buckinghamshire home our parents took them upon trust, offering
them not only very kindly hospitality, but also their
friendship, which was in most cases cordially accepted
and reciprocated.

Mr. Bonus, who came originally from Cuddesdon,
recommended and sent by the Bishop of Oxford to
the little village of Buckland, had lodgings in our
village, and was frequently to be seen at our house.
He had his Sunday mid-day meal regularly with us,
and my father, hearing upon one of these occasions
that he had had the misfortune to lose an old and
much-valued watch, replaced it by another and far
more valuable one.   He married our clever village school-
mistress, Miss Deneulain, much to the surprise of his
colleagues.

Another of our clerical neighbours, but of a different date, for I only knew him in the 'nineties, was the Rev. —— Ragg, Rector of Marsworth, a scholar and an artist, most enthusiastic in any work that appealed to his imagination. He was a most original man. His church being in a dilapidated condition, and the tower showing signs of falling in, he determined upon restoring the building, but instead of an appeal for funds, made an appeal for labour ; he himself led the way, and in a workman's dress proceeded, with a few others, to erect the scaffolding from which the work could be commenced. In fact, he had to be his own architect, builder, mason, labourer, and sculptor. Lady Rothschild at Tring Park took great interest in this unique restoration, and it occurred to me one day, whilst being shown the corbels in the church, that Mr. Ragg, in carving the features of the corbels representing Faith, Hope, Charity, Purity, must have had the noble and fine profile of my cousin in mind.

The advowson of the parish of Aston Clinton is in the gift of Jesus College, Oxford, and, as in the early days it was a valuable one, it was for many generations given to the oldest Fellow of that College, invariably a Welshman, who, when he exchanged University existence for parochial work, would take to himself a wife.

When we first settled in Aston Clinton, in the 'fifties, we found as rector the Rev. Charles Wynne Eaton, who, aided by Queen Anne's Bounty, had built the charming existing Rectory. Mr. Eaton was a very fine scholar, but had no knowledge or appreciation of village life and its requirements. His influence was nil. His wife, whom he had married as a widow, was still less suited to her environment, and horrified my mother one day by telling her that she would like to flog all the schoolboys, and that the drunken master, who, in our opinion, ought to have been sent about his business, was far too good to them. There were two daughters by Mrs. Eaton's first marriage, who, to our young eyes, seemed rather terrible spinsters. The three ladies could be met taking their daily constitutional on the high road to the top of the Tring hill and back again.

One circumstance connected with Mr. Eaton was exceedingly touching. He had a favourite white short-haired terrier, without which he was never seen. After the rector's death the little creature found its way to his master's grave, from which post no one could move him. He lay there for two days and a night, and was finally found dead on the spot, not having touched food since the rector's life had ended. When we were told of this by the kindly curate, Mr. Welburn, we felt that there must have been some latent good in Mr. Eaton which we had not discovered, and were somewhat penitent at our non-appreciation of him. But the family departed, and we saw no more of them.

They were succeeded by another somewhat curious couple, the Rev. Charles Heaton, also a Welshman, a kindly, very silent man, and his most voluble but good-hearted wife, startling in her remarks, and always most unexpected, not only in what she said but in what she did. Mrs. Heaton was very friendly and hospitable, but she was less suited to village life than to a garrison town, or some gossipy seaside place. She was the daughter of an admiral, and Southsea was the spot of her predilection. How she detested the Aston Clinton mud, and declared that she could not abide the poor old women's long stories ! But for all that, she was very kind to many who were ill or in trouble. Mr. Heaton, a book-lover, was, I believe, not happy in the pulpit; his voice could hardly be heard, and his sermons were therefore not impressive or enlivening.

After the death of Mr. Heaton, in 1881, another Welshman, the Rev. Thomas Williams, came into possession of the Aston Clinton living, his family consisting of his wife, five daughters, and three sons. The spell was now broken, and it was, from the first

day, evident that the rector and all those belonging
to him were fully cognisant of village work and of all
that it comprised. Mr. Williams was, moreover, of
scholarly mind, a great reader, especially of history,
and, like all Welshmen, a student of genealogies. He
was a determined Conservative in politics, and therefore strongly opposed to Mr. Gladstone's Government.
However, on one occasion, when the rector came under
the direct charm of the great statesman and Churchman,
he was not proof against his personal attraction. Mr.
Gladstone and Mr. Williams walked home together from
the Aston Clinton church one Easter Sunday morning,
and were soon engaged in deep conversation, evidently
to their mutual satisfaction, the statesman addressing to
the rector some very complimentary remarks concerning
his sermon.

Mr. Williams was not much in sympathy with many
of the movements of the day ; for example, he did not
encourage temperance societies, although his own household was practically run on temperance lines. Nor did he
believe in county or parish councils ; nor did he care for
the many educational innovations that were coming in
rather too hastily during the 'eighties and 'nineties. He
was a very consistent Churchman, with no great sympathy, theologically, for dissenters, although his kindness of heart led him to treat all his parishioners with
consideration and courtesy. His letters were charmingly written, and he could be very pleasant in conversation. My dear mother much enjoyed her talks with
him. His wife and his daughters were extraordinarily
active in the parish, and the many entertainments
that they organised, with much skill and patience, were
wonderfully successful. Their Sunday School did them
great credit and grew to very respectable dimensions ;
indeed they proved themselves most capable, and
therefore most fortunate, in all the parish work that they
undertook.

Mr. Williams was succeeded in 1903 by the Rev.

J. R. Cohu, who brought a new element into the parish. For the first time in its history Aston Clinton has a rector of non-Welsh birth and antecedents, claiming the Isle of Guernsey as his natal place. From his partly French origin his personality bears characteristics, both mental and physical, different from those of the purely British subject. Mr. Cohu is an untiring student as well as an active parish priest, and his theological writings, from a Modernist point of view, have taken a deservedly prominent place amongst such works. His wife, a clever artist in water colour, the daughter of the artist N. E. Green, is an ardent worker in her husband's parish.

I feel that I cannot omit some mention of our Nonconformist friends, who held in many cases a very honourable position in the county. For political reasons my uncles had for many years selected as their tenants men of Liberal views in politics, and they generally proved to be dissenters. This was the rule before the days of the ballot. The Whig tenants, naturally anxious to be on friendly terms with their landlords, the members of my family, and aware of their sporting tastes, opened their gates freely to the hounds and their masters. Even the introduction of the ballot did not change any of these time-honoured customs.

The Nonconformists were to the fore in matters educational and social, and proved at the beginning of the temperance crusade to be our very best supporters and co-workers. They also fully appreciated my mother's efforts in regard to the education of the villagers; their own Bible teaching was so thorough that, by a strange irony of circumstances, the prize, a Prayer Book from the Bishop of the diocese, generally fell to the children of Nonconformist parents.

When I used to attend the temperance meetings throughout the county, I was in most cases invited to gatherings held in chapels—this not only in Buckinghamshire, but also in Norfolk and in other parts of England. The temperance cause would never have prospered as it has done had it not been for the unselfish and generous help of the Nonconformist bodies. But when the Church gradually came in and gave her encouragement to temperance teaching, she brought with it new elements of gaiety and of beauty, which introduced, as it were, side-shows to the temperance movement, such as mild theatricals, posing in tableaux, dressing up, etc., sometimes tabooed by the more austere chapel-goer. I can remember the remonstrances addressed to us on one occasion because at one of our Penny Readings the audience had been convulsed with laughter at listening to the inimitable scene between Mrs. Nickleby and the mad suitor, wonderfully well rendered by our friend Mr. Damer. That a clergyman should have kept his audience amused by what was a pure invention was indeed a serious and unpardonable offence. " Would it have been better to have made them cry ? " I asked tentatively. It would not have shocked our friends in the same way. But in spite of some eccentricities, all honour to those who were, for so many years, well to the fore in matters of educational and social reform, who made themselves responsible for maintaining without State help their ministers and their places of worship.

In the roll of our many acquaintances in the county of Bucks occurs the name of Mrs. Acton Tindal, whose husband was a solicitor in Aylesbury. Mrs. Tindal, a daughter of the Rev. John Harrison, rector of Dinton, was quite an original personality ; tall, and dressed like an early Victorian picture, with her full and trailing skirts, her shawl pinned across her shoulders, her poke-bonnet and long drooping veil, her fair curls falling in profusion on each side of her face, she invariably attracted attention. She spoke very slowly, choosing her words with the greatest care and precision, underlining, as it were, what she was saying by a nod of her head that gave a waving movement to her curls. She had large blue eyes, and a fair beautiful skin ;

moreover, she was a poetess. Her husband was a more ordinary personage. I remember that at a dance we gave in 1873, when the Prince of Wales (Edward VII.) honoured our house at Aston Clinton with a visit, Mrs. Acton Tindal was much in evidence. H.R.H. asked me who that very remarkable and peculiar-looking lady could be. The lady in question noticed that she was being observed, and her curtsey was a performance to be remembered. I am afraid that her poetical powers were not always as much appreciated as they ought to have been by her friends in Bucks—but no one is a prophet in his own country !

I will briefly mention other friends once identified with our happy country home, whose names should not be omitted from these pages.

Mr. and Mrs. Bright, owners of Stocks, a charming little estate nestling under the Ashridge woods, were very much connected with our life in Buckinghamshire. Mr. Bright was his wife's second husband. She had first married, almost out of the schoolroom, a Mr. Gordon, some twenty or more years her senior. He was a literary man, and had acquired a certain celebrity through having been a friend of Sir Walter Scott's. It was related to me that the great author, upon a visit to Stocks, during a drive with his host, had inquired the name of the village through which they were passing. " Ivinghoe," was the reply. This romantic name appealed strongly to Sir Walter, and he gave it, slightly altered, to the hero of one of his earliest and finest novels, *Ivanhoe*.

Mrs. Bright was a very pleasant neighbour, warm-hearted, friendly, and full of talk, ready to entertain and be entertained. We saw much of her and of Mr. Bright, who often joined my father's shooting parties in the days between the 'fifties and 'seventies. She outlived her second husband by thirteen years, and died at a somewhat advanced age in 1891. Stocks was hers for her life. By Mr. Gordon's will she was empowered to leave it to one of seven persons. Most of these predeceased her ; but, in order to make sure of her successor, and being anxious concerning the future of her beloved Stocks, she determined upon presenting her property during her lifetime, instead of bequeathing it after her death, to one of the few remaining possible heirs. Accordingly she settled it upon Sir George Grey, the grandfather of the present Viscount Grey of Fallodon (1922), to whom the estate would naturally come. Sir George, already an old man (having lost his son, equerry to the Prince of Wales), came to Stocks with the said youth, who instantly won the heart of Mrs. Bright. The place was made over to the two, grandfather and grandson, in succession—Mrs. Bright remaining tenant for life. When a few years later, after his grandfather's death, the young Sir Edward appeared, fresh from his parliamentary victory, with his newly-married and handsome wife, Mrs. Bright congratulated herself upon her discernment, and upon her choice of the future owners of Stocks. But alas for human wishes and plans, so often brought to naught ! Sir Edward Grey loved fishing best of all sports, and there was no river or stream in the neighbourhood of Stocks—it lacked the charm of water. Later, when he was not engaged in parliamentary work, his duties took him to Northumberland, where his chief property lay, and he went to Hampshire for pleasure, so after the death of our dear old friend, Mrs. Bright, Stocks was sold to Mrs. Humphry Ward, the distinguished author, and niece of Matthew Arnold, who with her husband and children spent many happy days there.

Before I bid farewell to Stocks, I should like to add that the house was greatly altered and improved by the Wards, and the grounds very attractively laid out. When Mrs. Ward first appeared on the scene, there was much perturbation amongst her country neighbours and the inhabitants of Aldbury village, who looked upon her as one antagonistic to the Church and its human representatives. But all fears were soon allayed. Mr. and Mrs. Ward and their family, especially their eldest daughter Dorothy, became most popular in the county, because of the good work they were untiring in doing, and for the interest they took in the village of Aldbury.

Since I wrote the above, we have had to mourn the death of Mrs. Humphry Ward, who died in March 1920. Her family have left Stocks, the beautiful home in its woodland setting, for ever.

The following letter, the contents of which deeply touched me, may, I feel, be included in these memoirs :

STOCKS, 1918.

I dreadfully want you to join the Joint Parliamentary Advisory Committee—to which, as you know, dear Mrs. Yorke already belongs—and to help us in the work we are at present engaged on—viz. the endeavour to add two Women Commissioners to the Prison Commission. . . . As you know, it is not my subject at all, but some of our members are very keen and know a great deal about it. I need not say how grateful we should be for your opinion and advice.

I send you our Blue Paper and a copy of the Cripple Children's Report, by which we really succeeded in adding a new Clause to the Education Bill. I want you so much to join us !—Your affectionate MARY WARD.

Hartwell House was an attraction to us in our young years, and we used periodically to visit its strange old owner, the learned Dr. Lee. He would take us into his wonderful and crowded museum, where on one occasion he presented me with a little stuffed bird, hoping that it might prove the forerunner of a collection of my own, for he said that the pleasure of collecting, no matter what, was one of the chief roads that led to a happy life.

On one unforgettable starlight night we were admitted to his famous observatory, and invited to look through the telescope, receiving much valuable information at the time. To us the astronomer seemed a very old man, and when, in company with one of his own years, he came to dine at Aston Clinton, we were not astonished at seeing the two aged guests of my parents dropping placidly off to sleep after their repast.

The Hartwell estate has been in the possession of one family—the Lees—for seven hundred years. Part of the house is of very old date, but I believe it was almost entirely rebuilt in the seventeenth century. One fact will always add greatly to its interest: from 1809 to 1814 Hartwell was the abode of Louis XVIII., the exiled King of France, and his Queen, who died there; with them came about 180 persons belonging to their household and Court. Many distinguished names, such as those of the Royal Dukes of Berri and of Angoulême, also those of Duras, de Gramont, de Servant, de Blacas, that of the Archbishop of Rheims, etc., became well known in the neighbourhood. Indeed, several of the monarch's companions died at Hartwell and are interred in the little churchyard belonging to the place.

I have read in Ditchfield's *Memories of Old Buckinghamshire* how " the halls, gallery, and larger apartments were often divided and subdivided into suites of rooms for the use of the members of the French Court and household, in some instances to the great disorder and confusion of the mansion. Every outhouse and each of the ornamental buildings in the park that could be rendered capable of decent shelter was densely occupied. It was curious to see how some of the occupants stowed themselves away in the attics of the house, converting one room into several by the adaptation of light partitions." Moreover, I have been told that a garden was laid out upon the roof, where, besides shrubs and flowers, vegetables were grown for the use of the inmates.

After the death of Dr. Lee, Hartwell came into possession of his nephew, Edward Lee, who with his mother and sisters took up his abode in the fine old house. There he continued to live after his marriage until his death in 1909. The place is now let to Lord Leith of Fyvie.

One of Mr. Lee's sisters married Colonel Goodall, the owner of another historic place in the vicinity of Hartwell. Dinton Hall is a picturesque house with a beautiful view of the Chiltern Hills. Part of the edifice is of very remote date, whilst, according to an article by the Rev. C. Lowndes in the *Records of Buckinghamshire*, " the north front indicates the date of its erection as being about the time of James."

Colonel and Mrs. Goodall had always been warm friends of ours, and I had constant opportunities of seeing the former ; for many years we both attended the Board of Visitors in the Female Convict Prison, Aylesbury, Colonel Goodall being our chairman, until his last severe illness compelled him to resign.

Colonel Goodall died in 1918 at Dinton, and was followed in January 1920 by his wife, leaving no direct heirs.

Chequers Court is another delightful house, which was very dear to us from earliest days. The owner, when we first saw her, was a very old lady, a descendant of the fifth generation from Oliver Cromwell, Lady Frankland Russell by name. Her daughter and heir married a Colonel Astley, whom my father used to meet at shooting parties in Norfolk. In time Colonel Astley and his wife came to live at Chequers, where the Colonel died in the 'sixties, at a comparatively early age. His widow, Mrs. Frankland Russell Astley, a bright and clever woman, with much talent for drawing and a great love of nature, to whom Chequers belonged, lived on with her three sons and her mother in the beautiful old place. We used often to drive over from Aston Clinton. The grounds are charming and as romantic as the names given to parts of the property : " Velvet Lawn," " Silver Spring," " Happy Valley." What grand picnics we have had at Velvet Lawn !

The house, which replaced one of older date, had been built in 1566 and had been very beautiful, but, in the early years of the last century, when taste and knowledge in connection with architecture were at a low ebb, it had been restored and modernised and much disfigured ; ugly stucco covered and hid the fine red brick walls, whilst gables, a clock-tower, and other added excrescences were not conducive to beauty or elegance. Fortunately a further restoration in 1896, when the stucco was removed, revealed once more the old and fine colour of the brick, and a still later restoration, made by Sir Arthur Lee, now Lord Lee of Fareham, added materially to the comfort and beauty of the house.

As I am not attempting to write a detailed account of Chequers, I cannot go into the complicated history of its various possessors, but of course I do not wish to omit the fact of its owing much of its prestige to the great figure of the Protector, Oliver Cromwell, who used to visit his daughter, Frances Russell, the wife of Sir John Russell, then owner of Chequers. Up and down the long gallery, to me full of romance and interest, Cromwell is said to have paced, and there, we are told, he received the men of Bucks who came to consult their great leader and patriot, to receive instructions concerning the difficult work that lay before them, or to pay homage to the man who believed that in all he undertook he was obeying a Divine command.

The relics of Cromwell, which were religiously kept under glass in the great gallery, and the sword which he wielded at Naseby in 1645, were objects of awe and interest to one who had a great veneration for the Roundheads and their leaders.

In 1831 Chequers Court was the property of a Sir Richard Greenhill, who was able, through some connecting links, to assume the name of Russell. A curious incident is connected with this owner of Chequers. Having no lineal descendant, he bethought himself of bequeathing his historic property to the Duke of Bedford's son, Lord John Russell, whose politics he shared. So one fine day, with the title-deeds in his pocket, he went off on a thirty-six mile ride across the Vale to Woburn Abbey, the princely abode of the Duke of Bedford. The reception he met with was less cordial than what he had expected ; no refreshments were offered to the hungry man, the would-be benefactor of his host's son, so, without disclosing the purport of his visit, he bade the Duke farewell, bestrode his horse, and rode back to Chequers with the title-deeds in his pocket. He lost no time then in making his will and leaving his property to his cousin, Sir Robert Frankland, who assumed the name of Russell, which the testator bore. The lady, whom I remember in my childhood as extraordinarily old, who had been in her youth a celebrated beauty, was the widow of that same Sir Robert, and it was their daughter, Rosalind Alicia, who married, in 1854, Francis L'Estrange Astley, my father's friend of shooting days. Colonel Astley was a descendant of Sir Jacob Astley, who had fought in the Civil Wars on the side of the Royalists ; thus, by a strange stroke of fate, the two descendants of the two rival parties were united, not only as man and wife, but also as owners of the Chequers estate.

My parents' friendship for the Astley couple was extended to their children, who often came to our house as little boys, and who, when they grew to man's estate, were no less welcome. Bertie, the eldest son, married Lady Florence Conyngham, and had one son and one daughter. Hubert, the next brother, became the husband of Lady Sutton, the young and beautiful widow of Sir Richard Sutton. Reggie, third and youngest, married in middle age Lady Corbett, a widowed sister-in-law of Lady Sutton. Bertie died, as his father did, at an early age, leaving the estate to his only son, who married at twenty-three and met with his death in a flying accident before he was thirty.

From his widow, now re-married, the beautiful property
was bought by Lord and Lady Lee and finally presented
to the nation (1921) for the use of future Prime Ministers.
Thus the names of Astley and Frankland Russell can
no longer be associated with that of Chequers!

Within a few miles of Chequers stands Hampden
House, once the home of the Patriot Hampden, cousin
of Oliver Cromwell. It is now occupied by the Earl of
Buckinghamshire, who married a Scottish heiress, Miss
Mercer-Henderson; he is the present representative of
the family through the female line of the Hampdens.
(The estate has changed hands often through heiresses.)

John Hampden, the Patriot, was born in 1604. He
was the Member of Parliament for the Borough of
Wendover in 1625. He received his death-wound at
Chalgrove Field in 1643, fighting against the Royalists,
dying at Thame in Oxfordshire, within a few miles of his
old home. He was buried in the Parish Church of
Hampden. And here I may insert the following fine
passage from Lord Macaulay's pen :

His soldiers, bare-headed, with reversed arms and muffled
drums and colours, escorted his body to the grave, singing
as they marched that lofty and melancholy Psalm (xc.) in
which the fragility of human life is contrasted with the
immutability of Him to whom a thousand years are as
yesterday when it is past and as a watch in the night.

A life-size bronze statue of Hampden is erected to
his memory in the Market Square of Aylesbury, and
from a long inscription on one of the panels I quote
the two following lines :

> Against my King I do not fight,
> But for my King and Kingdom's right.

The statue of another patriot and great statesman,
that of Benjamin Disraeli, Earl of Beaconsfield, is about
to be erected in the same Square (1921).

Ashridge, well beloved by me, principally on account
of its beautiful mistress, Lady Brownlow, one of three

very interesting and attractive sisters, all personal friends of mine, has its own special charm.   The house, a some- what modern Gothic erection, built on the site of an old abbey, is not equal in beauty to, and is hardly worthy of, the glorious park in which it stands.   This is a bit of true forest land, with great sweeping beech trees, stretching far away on the one side to the gorse-covered common of Berkhampstead, and on the other to the pasture-fields of the Vale of Aylesbury.

It is said that when Queen Elizabeth was a young girl, in the reign of her sister Queen Mary, she spent some time at Ashridge, in a kind of semi-imprisonment, walking in the beautiful trim garden that already existed there, and sitting in the shade of the ash trees, of which one single specimen still remains, and from which the name of " Ashridge " is derived.   The interior of the modern house owes its charm to the fine Italian pictures that hang on its walls, to the stately furniture and gorgeous colouring of the rooms, and to the atmosphere of true artistic refinement that meets you as you enter the building; although, unhappily, she who was the very centre of all that was distinguished and beautiful is no longer there (1921).

I can never forget the days that I have spent at Ashridge, some of the happiest in my life : I owe many real friends to these visits.   Had it not been for Ash- ridge I might possibly never have known Wilton, the delightful home of Lord and Lady Pembroke; although it is more than probable that my settling in Norfolk would have admitted me sooner or later to Blickling Hall, one of the most beautiful Tudor residences in England, with its then peerless owner, Lady Lothian. At all events, the three sisters became three of my closest friends.

At Ashridge, as a girl, I was much impressed by the stately figure of Lady Marian Alford, the mother of Lord Brownlow—a true lady of the old school, a staunch Tory and Churchwoman, to whom the words " Liberal "

L

and " Dissenter " were anathema. I rather think that she had some prejudice against our family on religious and political grounds ; but to me she was invariably gracious, and even friendly. I admired her for her grand personality and her artistic sense. The latter found full play in the care she bestowed upon the wardrobe of her beautiful daughter-in-law, in the early years of Adelaide Brownlow's married life, when Lady Marian's advice was freely given and gratefully taken.

Amongst a crowd of very distinguished guests whom I was privileged to meet at Ashridge, were Sir Alfred Lyall, Henry Cowper, Arthur Balfour, Alfred Lyttelton, the Holman Hunts, and Percy Wyndhams.

Fond as the Brownlows were of their Ashridge property, much of their affection was given to Belton, their estate in Lincolnshire, of which county Lord Brownlow was Lord-Lieutenant. This is a perfect William and Mary manor, standing in very beautiful grounds.

The following lines were written by Princess Mary, Duchess of Teck, after a very happy visit that Her Royal Highness paid to Lady Marian Alford at Ashridge in the year 1861 :

ODE TO LADY MARIAN ALFORD

While Ashridge Halls still beam with light
And revels gay awake the night,
Our hearts' best homage we would pay
To her who now inspires our lay.
With courteous grace and gentle hand
Dispensing gifts throughout this land,
The poor man's friend, the rich man's joy,
In her we find without alloy
Whate'er can charm and raise the mind,
For she is *noble* as she's kind.

MARY ADELAIDE.[1]

The Duke and Duchess of Teck spent the early days of their honeymoon at Ashridge in 1866.

[1] From *A Memoir of H.R.H. Princess Mary, Duchess of Teck*, by Sir Clement Kinloch-Cooke, K.B.E., M.P.

Since I wrote this short and incomplete little sketch of Ashridge, Lord Brownlow too, the husband of my dear friend, has passed away, and their house stands lonely and empty, its treasures, like those of so many others of England's stately homes, offered for sale. I went over it in its present deserted condition with many a heart-pang, re-peopling it, by memory's aid, with some of those bright and beautiful beings who made it so dear to me in my youthful years.

CHAPTER VIII

THE HARDWICKE FAMILY AND ELIOT YORKE

I've wandered east, I've wandered west,
Through many a weary way,
But never, never can forget
The love of life's young day.

WM. MOTHERWELL.

IT must have been in the 'sixties, when my cousin Evelina was in the habit of going into society under the chaperonage of my mother, that upon one occasion, at a ball given by Mrs. Washington Hibbert, Evelina, after an inspiriting waltz, informed me that her partner had been one of the most amusing and delightful of young men. I was eager, of course, to make his acquaintance, and when I did so (he was introduced to me that evening) I saw standing before me a very handsome youth, with fair hair, bright blue eyes that twinkled with fun, and fine delicate features. It was only an introduction and a talk of five minutes' duration, or even less, during which time I learnt that Eliot Yorke—for it was he—equerry to Prince Alfred (afterwards Duke of Edinburgh), was about to accompany his Royal master to the Antipodes. My cousin declared that he was the most agreeable young man she had met for a long while, and I was quite ready to subscribe to her dictum, little thinking of what the future held in store for all of us. I did not meet him again until the year 1872, but meanwhile I had made life-long friends with many members of his family, whom I met on the occasion of some very

148

delightful visits that we paid to Lord and Lady Hardwicke at Wimpole, their fine country seat in Cambridgeshire.

In the year 1867 we took our first trip to Switzerland
with our parents, and it was there that we made the
acquaintance of Victor Yorke, the third son of the
Hardwickes, and one of the most accomplished and
delightful of human beings. On our return journey I
remember remarking and then listening to the performance of a few rustic-looking musicians at the station,
whilst near by stood a young Englishman, his gaze fixed
upon the violinist of the party and his foot keeping time
with the music. He was in company with an older
man; they both belonged to our Horse Artillery, and,
as it happened, were going to stay not only at Lucerne,
but also at our hotel.

We travelled back together and we began to talk in
the train; we talked on at dinner at the table d'hôte,
and we talked on during a very cheerful evening—so
cheerful that we all agreed to ascend the Rigi in each
other's company on the following morning.

Victor Yorke was at that time twenty-six years old,
good-looking, and very attractive. Like all the Yorkes,
he had much taste for music, a charming voice, a very
good ear, and was also a violinist of some ability. He
had besides marked talent for drawing and sketching.
Apart from his many accomplishments, he possessed a
serious side to his character, with a fine conception of
conduct and duty. I remember asking him which he
liked best, drawing or music. He answered, " Drawing, because I can sing whilst I draw, but I cannot
sketch whilst I am at the piano or playing the violin."
Then he added, " And I love sketching from Nature,
because I am all the while admiring and loving the
beautiful and perfect works of the Creator."

Those words still haunt me, as well as the remembrance of that radiant figure, so happy in himself and
conferring so much happiness on others, alas ! destined

so soon to end his bright existence on earth. What fun we had on the Rigi! what a cheery evening we spent there! —thanks to Victor Yorke, who even executed a kind of war-dance in our rooms, singing the liveliest songs whilst he touched up some sketches in his note-book. Before the dawn broke on the morrow we all met on the mountain-top. Victor Yorke still stands out clearly in my memory, sketch-book in hand, painting with extraordinary rapidity the delicate tints of the first flush of day. He was entranced by the view, a very wonderful one on that particular morning, for the clouds had gathered below us in what is called a " Nebelmeer," looking like pink sea-waves, hiding for the time being the snowy peaks of the Bernese Oberland.

The acquaintance thus begun did not come to an end with that happy little excursion in Switzerland. Victor Yorke and his military friend visited us at Aston Clinton in the autumn, and the former proved to be one of the brightest guests we had ever entertained. I remember that he and his friend told us how they had been present at the German manœuvres of that year, and how impressed they had been by the extraordinary development and improvement that had taken place in the German forces, especially in the Prussian army, a fact soon to be made manifest to the world at large in the Franco-German War of 1870.

Victor Yorke went out shooting with my father, and riding with us, and finally left with a promise to return very shortly and help us with a Penny Reading that we were getting up in the village.

The promise was duly kept, and once more, in December 1867, the bright and happy youth was added to our little circle of friends. He stayed on after they had all left us, to sing and play at our village gathering. He had somewhat alarmed us during his visit by telling us he had been suffering from violent pains in his head and had had a kind of seizure, but that one of the great London doctors had assured him he might safely pay us his promised visit, for the change might prove beneficial, provided that he was not over-fatigued. Meanwhile he was in the highest of spirits, and we all went forward with gay and happy hearts with our preparations for the evening festivity. On the night of the performance the village schoolroom was packed with people. Victor Yorke ascended the platform, and to my sister's accompaniment sang, most beautifully and dramatically, a ballad, the subject of which was the entry of a soul into Paradise, his clear voice ringing out almost triumphantly, "Adonai, Adonai, Thy children come."

After a chorus sung by the school children, a reading from *The Grandmother* by Tennyson was announced, and Victor again took his place on the platform. He did not look quite comfortable, and I feared that the lamp had been put at a wrong angle, but he read on to the following verse :

" Willy, my beauty, my eldest-born, the flower of the flock ;
Never a man could fling him : for Willy stood like a rock."

As he said these words he fell forwards off the plat-form at my feet, and there was complete silence for the moment amongst the awed and terrified audience, then a rush forward. Willing arms carried him into the teacher's house, and two doctors, hastily summoned, arrived within a very short time. But no earthly help was of avail ! Victor never spoke again, and died that night without regaining consciousness. A bad accident in Canada was supposed to have left some injury to the spine.

It was a terrible time for us all, rendered all the sadder as the fatal stroke took place within two days of Christmas, which increased the difficulties of travelling and transmission of news. However, in spite of this, the bereaved parents came to Aston Clinton to look once more upon the beloved features of their son.

Lord and Lady Hardwicke from that moment

entered so fully into our lives that I feel I should like to give a short description of them and their family as I knew them in the late 'sixties, before the tie became yet closer through the marriage of my sister with Eliot Yorke, their fourth son.

When I first saw Lord Hardwicke he must have been about sixty-eight years of age ; he always brought a picture of the sea before me, his fine healthy colour, his brilliant dark eyes with their quick glance, his language, racy, to the point, original, direct—all seeming to belong to the old seafaring world. He had no time to waste on useless, tiresome trappings of speech, but knew what friends he cared to have and what kind of things he thought worth caring about. He knew for a fact that he was averse to Liberal politics and that even the word " reform " had an offensive sound to his ears, and he never would believe in the integrity of a Liberal Government.

Lord and Lady Hardwicke had such a proper sense of the duties of landlords that until their eldest daughter, Elizabeth, had attained the age of sixteen, they all made their country seat, Wimpole, in Cambridgeshire, their home for the whole year, looking after their property and caring for their tenants and villagers, spending their income upon the estate, which was left in a perfect condition upon the death of Lord Hardwicke in 1873. Only a few weeks in the summer were spent at Sydney Lodge in Hampshire, near Netley, and it was whilst staying in this latter charming abode that Lord Hardwicke took to the pleasures of yachting, shared by all the members of his family, who proved to be excellent sailors.

Lady Hardwicke was a true and good helpmeet to her husband and enjoyed her life, spent, as those of so many of England's best women have been spent, in devotion to her family, her home, and her village. She was a brilliant musician, and sang with unusual taste, as Lord Beaconsfield writes to Mrs. Wyndham Lewis in 1838 :

Lady Hardwicke is without exception the most dramatic singer I ever listened to ; her voice is most sweet and powerful, and she is so unaffected that she actually sang without stopping for so long a time that it was near one when our *petit comité* broke up.

I never met persons who seemed to enjoy life more, or who seemed fonder of each other than the Hardwickes.[1]

Lord Royston, the eldest son, an easy-going, happy-go-lucky, brilliant member of the social world in the 'sixties and 'seventies, known for a time as " Champagne Charlie," was not slow in dissipating the fortune that his father had been at great pains to build up for him. When I first knew him he was an entertaining talker and an agreeable companion, not devoid of talent, and with much kindliness of heart. I can see him now in faultless attire, with his carefully arranged black satin tie, his beautiful pearl pin, his lustrous hat balanced at a certain angle upon his well-brushed hair, his coat sleeves always showing precisely the same amount of white cuff, his pleased-with-himself-and-the-world expression. As a young man he was considered a success, but as an older one perhaps a disappointment. His wife was the younger daughter of Lord Cowley, our Ambassador in Paris, Lady Sophie Wellesley, a singularly beautiful woman. Their only son died unmarried after inheriting the title, which reverted to his uncle, John Yorke.

Of John Yorke's brothers, the next was Victor, of whom I have already written in detail ; my brother-in-law Eliot followed him in age, whilst Alick was the youngest of the family. There were three daughters— Elizabeth, Mary, and Agneta.

Elizabeth, or " Libbet," as she was always affectionately called by friends and intimates, was a remarkable and very attractive woman. When I first met her in the year 1863 she was a striking personality : tall, with a fine figure, a noble presence, a bright, intellectual,

---

[1] From *The Life of Benjamin Disraeli*, by Monypenny and Buckle.

CHAPTER
VIII.

handsome face, she could not easily have passed unnoticed. She had great distinction of manner and voice,
was very ready in conversation, and could show herself an
excellent *raconteuse*. Like the rest of her family, Libbet
was gifted with great histrionic power, and at the annual
performances at Wimpole during the Christmas holiday
would take to perfection the comic parts.

In those days the late Duchess of Teck, mother of
Queen Mary, was closely drawn towards the brilliant
young girl, and this friendship only ceased with the life
of the Duchess.

" In 1855 " (so writes Lady Biddulph in the Memoir of
her father) " *Personation* and *Popping the Question* were
given before their Royal Highnesses the Duchess of
Cambridge and Princess Mary. A very small party
was invited to meet their Royal Highnesses, and a
great deal of merriment was our reward.

" On one great occasion we had Frank Matthews as
prompter, and we none of us forget seeing him initiate
Lady Agneta in the art of making a stage kiss. Oh,
how we laughed! He cried so much during the performance that he prompted badly ; but perhaps the dear
man was touched by the family talent." [1]

Lady Elizabeth was a good French scholar and spoke
and wrote the French language with very great ease ;
one of her dearest friends was Lady Ashburton, a sister
of the Duc de Bassano, who held high office at the Court
of Napoleon III. It was probably as a result of this
friendship that Lady Elizabeth, in later years, had many
opportunities of intimate conversation with the Empress
Eugénie, whose beauty, distinction, and misfortune
greatly attracted her. As a girl, Lady Elizabeth naturally professed the politics of her family, and was proud to
call herself an ardent Tory ; but after her marriage with
Mr. Adeane, one of the leading Liberals of her county,
she gradually accepted the Liberal principles of that

[1] From *Charles Philip, Fourth Earl of Hardwicke*, by Lady Biddulph of Ledbury.

day, and became a strenuous supporter of many a Liberal CHAPTER
measure.   Her husband's long and trying illness, fol-   VIII.
lowed by her early widowhood, withdrew her for some
time into inevitable seclusion, when the care of her three
children proved her most engrossing occupation.   From
this, however, she emerged when a mandate came from
Queen Victoria appointing her to be one of her Women
of the Bedchamber.   It was an office she appreciated,
for she had a loyal heart; moreover, nearly every
member of her family had held, or was holding, a post
connected with the Royal Family.

Lady Elizabeth enjoyed her return to a larger and
a fuller life, restricted though it was by the Queen's
determination, after the death of the Prince Consort,
not to resume her former social duties.   She only left
Her Majesty's service upon the occasion of her second
marriage with Mr. Biddulph, then Liberal Member of
Parliament for S. Herefordshire, later raised to the
Peerage as Lord Biddulph of Ledbury, the owner of a
beautiful estate in the romantic old town of that name.

Lady Biddulph naturally felt some grief at leaving
the service of her Royal mistress, but this was partly
assuaged by the fact that her eldest daughter, Marie,
now the Hon. Lady Mallet, in a way succeeded her
mother in the Royal household, first as Maid-of-Honour,
and later, when married, as Woman of the Bedchamber,
and then as Secretary to the Queen, a very important
post.   Sir Bernard Mallet, her husband, Registrar-
General 1909–1920, is also well known as a man of
letters, whilst his very capable wife has been for many
years both actively and efficiently engaged in municipal
and philanthropic work.   Their two sons, Victor and
Arthur, served their country well during the Great War,
the one in the Army, the other in the Navy.

Lady Biddulph's second daughter, Maud, married
Mr. John Cator, of Woodbastwick in the county of
Norfolk, where both husband and wife won golden
opinions for their patriotic conduct during the war.

Their house was turned into a Red Cross Hospital, some 400 sick and wounded passing through it, Mrs. Cator herself acting as the very efficient Commandant.

Charles Adeane, Lady Biddulph's only son, is a well-known figure in Cambridgeshire, of which county he is now Lord-Lieutenant, and where his excellent work as a practical authority on agricultural matters had long been known and much appreciated. His wife, Madeline, a sister of the late George Wyndham, once the versatile and brilliant Secretary for Ireland under the Premiership of Arthur Balfour, now Earl of Balfour, is the mother of several charming daughters and one precious son.

Lady Biddulph's love of beautiful surroundings never left her, and she devoted much time and attention to the care of her garden and the arrangement of her flowers. As she grew older she became very infirm and somewhat helpless, but her nobility of expression remained with her to the last. Her hair retained much of its early golden tint, her face was always fresh and charming in colour, her eyes bright and expressive.

Occasionally she would speak of the flight of time and of a hand that seemed beckoning to her from the shadows, but she did not repine or complain ; she had a child-like beautiful faith that had never wavered in spite of many trials and of the sorrow inseparable from the toll of years ; she retained to the last the warm and loving heart that found its greatest joy in the society and the happiness of those she loved best.[1]

Mary, Lord Hardwicke's second daughter, was a singularly beautiful woman, and she had a singularly unhappy fate. Upon her appearance in Society she was instantly acclaimed as one of the most distinguished beauties of that year, her dazzling presence, her brilliant spirit, and her love of enjoyment bringing her many admirers. When quite young, she married Mr. William Craven, a cousin of Lord Craven, who, as the possessor of a

---

[1] From *Wings*, the official organ of the Women's Total Abstinence Union, " In Memoriam " notice, contributed March 1916, by C. B.

beautiful country home, an ample fortune, and a pleasing personality, was considered an excellent match. But both husband and wife had no well-defined sense of duty. Their fortune was soon dissipated, their country estate put up for sale, and all semblance of home life at an end. After this Mr. Craven and his wife were seldom seen together, and finally separated, in spite of the fact that they had a young family of four children ; and at last, Mary Craven, brilliant and fascinating, clever and attractive as she had once been, after living abroad for many years, came to the close of her life in sad, I may say tragic, circumstances.

Agneta, the third daughter, was neither as beautiful as Mary nor as brilliant as Libbet, but she was a very pretty and attractive young girl, and an accomplished pianist, with a fine mezzo-soprano voice. Her sterling qualities, her deeply religious nature, her affectionate heart, her loyal and unselfish character, brought her many life-long friends. Agneta married Victor Montagu, Lord Sandwich's second son, a naval officer, a gallant, breezy, cheery sailor, who had already made his mark in the service. They spent some time together in foreign ports, Victor being a great favourite wherever he found himself, especially with the King of Greece and Queen Olga, as well as at the Court of Berlin. Agneta, like the rest of her family, was singled out to be the friend and companion of Royalty, acting for some time as lady-in-waiting to Princess Christian of Schleswig-Holstein—our Princess Helena.

Victor and his great friend, Lord Brassey, were present at Kiel on the occasion of the opening of the Canal. They were both well known to, and their society much appreciated by, the Kaiser, as Victor relates in the interesting reminiscences written with his bright and fluent pen, which are well worth reading, and give one a good picture of life in the Navy during the middle and closing years of the last century. He not only distinguished himself in the service, but also excelled as a sportsman, being very expert with the gun and the fishing-rod. He died an Admiral in 1916, without having inherited the title, that of the Earldom of Sandwich, from his elder brother. He left a son, the present Earl of Sandwich, and three daughters. His wife, Agneta Montagu, died in February 1919.

Before speaking of Eliot, my brother-in-law, I will dwell for a little upon the youngest of Lord and Lady Hardwicke's children.

Alick Yorke had many social gifts and various well-defined tastes, none of them leading, however, to the career his parents had fondly planned for him, which would eventually have landed him in the Wimpole Vicarage as successor to the Hon. and Rev. Archdeacon Yorke, Canon of Ely. Alick did certainly try his best to qualify himself for becoming a clergyman, but he was not fitted for the calling, and wisely gave it up before it was too late. He could sing and act like a professional, he wrote remarkably well, and had inborn taste for all that was beautiful and choice in art. His histrionic performances were really first-rate —there he shone with undisputed excellence, much appreciated by Queen Victoria, for whose amusement he got up very elaborate entertainments at Osborne. He was for some years equerry-in-waiting to the Duke of Albany, with whom he had formed a fast friendship at Oxford. He was a kind friend, always anxious to please those whom he cared for. Although he was fond of every comfort, and had even some luxurious tastes, he could deny himself much, and lead a really simple life when it was for the benefit of others. He was a thorough-going Tory and an ardent Churchman. He talked some-what wildly about politics, especially Liberal politics, and did not try to understand them. He was rather short and unmanly-looking, but he had a very bright mobile expression of countenance, fine dark eyes, brilliant teeth, and a kindly smile. He suffered a good deal during the last year or two of his life, and died very suddenly in

Sicily in 1911. He never married. In old days Alick would always prophesy that if we were fortunate enough to make his brother Eliot's acquaintance, that brother would supplant him in our affections.

At last the day came when we were to meet Eliot. It was in 1870 at a pleasant gathering at Wimpole. I do not remember any guests besides ourselves. There were, however, several members of the family, the two married daughters, Libbet and Nety, with three of the brothers, making a very cheery party. Eliot had just returned from the Antipodes with the Duke of Edinburgh, and had brought with him as his personal attendant, to his father's horror and disgust, a Chinaman, who in his gorgeous dress, with his long pig-tail and his solemn, inexpressive face, aroused a good deal of attention. (He turned out to be a most reliable servant.)

The members of Lord Hardwicke's family and his guests sat during the Sunday church services in a gallery at the west end of the beautiful chapel close to Wimpole House. This was very comfortably furnished like a room. Suddenly, in the middle of the proceedings, Lord Hardwicke would rise from his seat, walk to a small fireplace, and poke the fire into a fine blaze. No one seemed to be astonished at this, for all knew that whenever the preacher's sermon attained what Lord Hardwicke considered undue length he would show his disapproval by a vigorous thrust of the poker. What a clever, cheery family they were, with their many gifts, especially those connected with the drama ! As Lady Biddulph wrote, when describing the Wimpole evenings :

If anything pleasant or amusing was on hand, such as a dance or our "private theatricals," my father would wave his hand and say, "Clear the decks ! Clear the decks !" We often used to " clear the decks " for games of Post or Magical Music. Evenings at Wimpole were never dull. . . . Histrionic art also was much cultivated in the holidays under the able management of Uncle Eliot Yorke, M.P.

All these performances were strictly confined to the family, including the painting of the scenery and the composition of Prologues, Epilogues, etc. As we said in one of these compositions, " We are no London Stars, we're all of York(e)."

On that memorable visit we young ones had a picnic luncheon in the park and were waited upon by the solemn Chinaman. Eliot was full of fun, and kept us all happy and laughing at his jokes. He told us many anecdotes about his Royal master, and was interesting as well as amusing. Lord Hardwicke showed us over Wimpole House on one of the days of our visit, and explained all the improvements and alterations that he had made. Naturally he was proud of them ; he had spent £100,000 on completing this work. Alas, that Wimpole House, so beautiful, so cared for, with its fine park, its prosperous farms, its charming village, should have passed out of the family for ever !

My dear sister had been much attracted from the first by Eliot Yorke, and on his second visit to Aston Clinton, in the winter of 1872, she became engaged to him.

This engagement was contracted on both sides under very unusual circumstances. It was the first time that any member of our family had married outside her own Faith, without entering her husband's Community. It was also the first time that any English peer's son had become connected with a Jewish family, where the wife remained true to her own persuasion. It was a bold thing to do, and at the time it produced a great sensation. The difficulties appeared insurmountable. My sister was very patient, and my father was moved to give a reluctant consent to so unusual a proceeding. The weeks of their engagement were spent at Aston Clinton. Concessions had to be agreed to on both sides, and had it not been for Eliot's sterling qualities, his confidence in my sister, and her devotion to him, the marriage would probably

THE HONOURABLE ELIOT YORKE.

never have been solemnised, as it was in the month of February 1873, the legal ceremony taking place in the Registry Office situated in the workhouse of our Parish of St. George's, London, in the presence of some members of our family and some of that of the bridegroom. I remember the Dowager Lady Barrington, Eliot's aunt, being present, and saying afterwards (she was an old lady at the time) that, should she ever make a second marriage, she would like it celebrated in the same way, she thought it so *homely* and *comfortable*. The religious ceremony was held in the chapel of Wimpole House.

Eliot's Royal friends had all shown much interest in his engagement. I remember that when we had the honour of entertaining the Prince of Wales at Aston Clinton in January 1873, H.R.H. brought a present for my sister from the Princess and himself, and wished to give it to her on his arrival. At that moment, as it was late in the day, she was already dressing for dinner, but as he insisted upon seeing her, she was fetched down in a white *peignoir*, with her hair hanging down her back, to receive the bridal gift of a bracelet. The members of the Royal Family never relaxed in their friendship for my brother-in-law, and were always most gracious and kindly to his wife.

It was a very happy union, only marred by Eliot's too delicate health, which was a constant source of anxiety to his devoted wife. A charming house in Curzon Street, No. 17, was purchased for them by my father, and there they spent a few months of each year during the short period of their married life, the rest being divided between Netley Fort and their beloved yacht, the *Garland*. Netley Fort was in the near neighbourhood of Sydney Lodge, and was besides admirably fitted to be a convenient yachting station. It was rented by Eliot, and it was only after his death that my sister took possession of Hamble Cliff, which had been left to her husband by his father.

M

Netley Fort, or Castle, as it is called, is now (1921) owned by Colonel the Hon. Sir Harry and Lady Emma Crichton.[1]

In the autumn of 1873, when Lord Royston, M.P. for Cambridgeshire, succeeded to the title of Hardwicke, Eliot was returned as Conservative Member in his place, but he never took any pronounced part in politics; in fact, his heart was not in his work. The long debates in the House of Commons struck him as being a terrible waste of time; political methods he found wearisome, and he had not gone through the mill which might have led to political distinction. It was a very great pity (at least so it appeared to me) that Eliot never had the chance of becoming Governor of one of our Colonies. As such he might have made his mark; I feel sure that in governing he would have been both just and humane. He had the rare genius of knowing how to get into touch with different classes, and of making friends amongst all sorts and conditions of human beings. This was probably the result of his having travelled extensively, and thus seen and learned to appreciate people of many different nationalities. His distinguished and really beautiful face captivated all at first sight; added to this, his charming and very unusual gift of song gained him a ready welcome in many different circles. Can I ever forget his rendering of " O rest in the Lord " ? His own true child-like faith responded warmly to the words into which he put all his loving heart. Eliot had also the divine gift of humour to a very marked extent, and would pass from grave to gay, from sentiment to arrant nonsense, without hesitation or warning; but, like his sentiment, his nonsense was absolutely pure and never descended to anything of questionable taste, or touched the profane. He loved fun, and wholesome laughter, and was a past-master in comic acting, and in the impersonation of striking characters.

[1] Sir Harry Crichton died in May 1922.

It was after a heated and crowded political meeting in Cambridge that he caught the chill that eventually proved fatal to him. This chill developed into pneumonia, and after but a few days' illness he died on one cold foggy morning in the December of 1878. No one who had known him in his days of exuberant spirits and radiant happiness but felt the cruel tragedy of that early death, and deplored the dark shadow that fell upon one of the happiest of homes. It was then, after five years of her perfect married life, that my dear sister accepted her widowhood as bravely and unselfishly as she had entered upon every other difficult phase in her life. Her loss only made her the more ready to sympathise with others, and her desire to be actively employed in philanthropic work filled her days more and more with such occupations as have brought her, and are bringing her, into close contact with those who strive and with those who suffer.

To me and to my husband (I had only been married one year at the time of Eliot's death) he was a very great loss. We both looked upon him in the light of a dear brother, and although Cyril and he had agreed to scowl upon one another from their opposite seats across the floor of the House of Commons—for Cyril was going to stand at the next General Election—they had also determined that no political controversies should ever disturb their friendship. Strange to say, they had been together as schoolboys at Cheam under the well-known master, Mr. Tabor, and after dear Eliot's death my sister found, amongst a little collection of childish books, a small Bible, with an inscription in a youthful hand, "To my dear Eliot, from his friend Cyril." One cannot but lament that friendship such as theirs, from which both might have culled many a fragrant blossom, should have ended so swiftly, when all seemed bright and full of promise.

My dear brother-in-law rests in the pretty and peaceful churchyard of the village of Hamble, where

also are the graves of his two brothers, John and
Alick.

My sister inherited through her husband the charming property of Hamble Cliff, on Southampton Water.
It is a very original, picturesque domain, of no great
acreage, adjoining the grounds of Sydney Lodge. It is
also in close proximity to the Royal Victoria Hospital,
Netley, which, with the British Red Cross and Welsh
Hospitals, sheltered during the Great War as many as
3500 wounded soldiers at one time.

The house, Hamble Cliff, built by Sir Arthur Paget,
father of Sir Augustus, our Ambassador in Rome in
the 'seventies, though small, has many attributes of
a larger one, and the grounds, shelving down to the
water-side, are well planted with fine trees, revealing
glimpses of the distant shore and the busy water-way.

From the *N. B. R. C.* (Netley British Red Cross)
Magazine, September 1918, where an appreciative little
account of Hamble Cliff and its mistress appears, I
transcribe the following :

There are many points of interest in the Hamble Cliff
garden. The glory of the place in the summer months is
its wonderful wealth of roses. . . . Many of the trees deserve
more than a casual glance. There is a fine specimen of the
Cedar of Lebanon. Near this stands an Australian tree—
Sequoia Wellingtonia; the Cork Tree, the Japanese Cedar,
and the Arbutus are an interesting trio. Nor should we
pass by the Pyrus Aria, with its wondrous twisted stem,
white flowers in the Spring and red berries in the Autumn.

These grounds proved an immense boon to the staff
and inmates of the hospitals during the war, when they
were much frequented and appreciated by nurses and
patients.

Hamble Cliff is greatly beloved by my sister. There
she finds herself the very centre of endless objects of
interest, all claiming her care and attention. Readily
does she respond to the numerous calls upon her time

THE HONOURABLE MRS ELIOT YORKE.

and her strength. They come from many different sources and entail much work. Amongst other things she has become a great authority on primary education, having had much experience as manager of elementary schools. She is a member of the Education Committee of the County Council for Hampshire, and was for some time the only lady on the Council of the University College of Southampton. In addition to this, she is a very devoted worker for the Temperance cause, President of the Band of Hope Union, and late President of the Women's Total Abstinence Union and of several other societies. Her old and faithful friend, Archdeacon Wilberforce, used to call her the Archbishop of Southampton; indeed, when I think of the radius that her activities cover, and of the way she has always inspired and is still inspiring other workers, whilst keeping herself modestly in the background, I can but recognise that the quaint name given to her, half in joke, half in earnest, describes, fancifully if one likes, but truly, the position she fills. At all events she holds many threads in her capable hands.

She is a well-known personality in her neighbourhood, trotting about from morning until evening, often accompanied by her beloved dogs, regardless of the toll of years, alert, unwearied, helpful, bright and humorous.

CHAPTER IX

CYRIL

And manhood fused with female grace
In such a sort, the child would twine
A trustful hand, unask'd, in thine,
And find his comfort in thy face.

In Memoriam.

I THINK it was in the year 1864, on a bright day in December at Aston Clinton, that I saw Cyril Flower for the first time. He came with my cousin, Leopold de Rothschild, one of his most intimate College friends, both young men having ridden over from Mentmore. After a little chat we adjourned to the billiard-room and played, or pretended to play, a game of billiards, knocking the balls about, laughing and chaffing until the short hours of daylight warned the riders that they should start on their homeward gallop.

I can remember that we were much struck by the remarkably good looks of Leo's friend : his fine features, bright dancing eyes, mass of waving golden hair and ruddy complexion produced a picture of youth, vigorous health, and bright activity such as one seldom sees. He was bubbling over with fun and nonsense, and yet, at that early stage of his life, had the eye to notice and the knowledge to appreciate much of the artistic furniture in our house, so carefully selected by my father.

Fate did not bring him into our orbit again for some time, but we often heard his name affectionately mentioned by my cousin. Years after that first meeting

166

CYRIL FLOWER
(LORD BATTERSEA).

Cyril would talk to me, not only of his University life, but also of his happy school life at Harrow, where he had been especially drawn towards his master, Dr. Farrar, later Dean of Canterbury, who fully reciprocated the boy's affectionate devotion, often corresponding with him during the holidays, and even introducing him as the hero in one of his well-known books, *Eric, or Little by Little.*

Many letters that I have in my possession from Dr. Farrar to Cyril are a touching witness to the warmth of that affection. Of his many Cambridge friends Cyril never tired of speaking, and soon after our engagement I became familiar with the names of G. O. Trevelyan, Lord John Hervey, the Hon. Arthur Strutt, J. W. Clark, Frederic Myers, Sir Richard Jebb, etc., etc.

Sir Richard Jebb was evidently deeply impressed by the extraordinary popularity amongst all sorts and conditions of men that his undergraduate contemporary and friend, somewhat his junior, had acquired, for in one of his frequent letters to his mother in 1865[1] he writes :

The more I see of Flower, the more interesting he becomes as a psychological study. He is the only instance with which I am acquainted of a man whom the whole world has agreed, with one consent, to pet, from Whewell (Master of Trinity) to the white-aproned men who carry the baked meats from the kitchens on their heads ; nobody can resist him. The most dyspeptic and fastidious dons ask him to dinner. Professors write him notes and send him books. Scarcely a man of his set who has left the University for the last two years but has correspondence with him. Artists are perpetually painting him. Bootmakers call to borrow his boots as models. I have constantly come into his rooms with him when he has found anonymous presents on his table. In short, he is the irresistible man. I think he is a very dear boy and too good to be spoilt, but I sometimes

---

[1] *Life and Letters of Sir Richard Jebb*, published by his Wife. By permission of the University Press, Cambridge.

fear that when he leaves Cambridge for London he will find the change rather trying. Here he is the sovereign master of the situation.

And again :

I like Flower so very much, though, indeed, I should be a singular exception if I did not. He is the only man I ever met who has some of the qualities of a charming woman also, and that without a shade of effeminacy ! . . . We furtively reconnoitred my future habitation. Flower, from whose taste I consider there is no appeal, liked the rooms, and suggested several little things that might be done to make them comfortable by and by.

After such a testimony from the youthful pen of one of his most brilliant College friends, I will add the following by the latter's widow, Lady Jebb :

Sir Richard Jebb was buried in St. Giles' Cemetery on the 13th December 1905. The funeral cortège met in Trinity College. . . . Amongst the Pall Bearers were Lord Reay and Lord Battersea. . . .

My dear husband, suffering at the time from what proved to be the commencement of his last illness, came home complaining of chill and fatigue, but he said : " I was glad to have been able to respond to Lady Jebb's wishes, and to have personally received her grateful and friendly thanks."

But to go back.

Cyril ended his happy University life by taking his B.A. degree in 1867 and his M.A. in 1870, and was then " called to the Bar," showing a genuine inclination for the legal profession. He read under the guidance of a barrister, who became Mr. Justice Day, and there was much promise of his future success. But his father's death changed his whole career. A growing estate in a suburb of London, bequeathed to him and his brothers, demanded intelligent management and supervision, and to such work, very congenial as it proved to him, Cyril devoted his time and energy. He had a great love of bricks and mortar, an innate sense of architectural beauty and comfort, and a happy temperament that enabled him to mix in good fellowship with all sorts and conditions of human beings, such as he came into contact with in Battersea.

His father had married twice and had left two large families. Of the first family Cyril was the eldest and in closest companionship with Arthur, the brother next in age to himself, his partner in the estate management ; whilst his only sister, Clara, his dearest and most intimate friend, was married to W. T. Brand in 1871. The marriage has been one of great happiness. The fiftieth anniversary was appropriately celebrated in July 1921, at a gathering of devoted friends. Of Clara I can only speak in terms of the greatest affection ; her unselfishness, her faithful friendship, her strong sense of duty awaken my deep admiration. Her only child, Dorothy, is one of my most dearly-loved companions ; she was a great favourite of Cyril's and has always been intimately connected with our Overstrand life.

Early in life, Arthur married Isabel Duncombe, the daughter of Sir Philip and Lady Duncombe, of Brickhill, Bedfordshire, and had a numerous family—five sons and four daughters. Parents and children have always shown me the greatest affection, and many of my happiest days have been spent in their company.

From middle life Arthur's days were full of suffering ; he bore his trial with rare fortitude and patience, greatly helped by his love of reading and the keen interest he took in many subjects, his wife being from first to last the ministering angel, who never left his side and who forestalled all his wishes. He died in 1911.

Of my husband's three remaining brothers, Herbert was exceedingly good-looking, a very fine rider, and a great favourite with my sex—perhaps unfortunately so for himself, for when only a youth he proved very attractive to older women of the world, whose influence was not of the best. In 1876 he married Viscountess

Dupplin (formerly Lady Agnes Duff), their short but happy wedded life only lasting for a few years, for Herbert died at the early age of twenty-seven in 1880.

Horace, kindly and good-natured, was also devoted to sport of all kinds, but owing to a bad fall out hunting he became an invalid for some time before he died at the age of thirty-four in 1885. He showed much patience and courage during his days of suffering, and was greatly beloved by all the members of his family, particularly by his sister Clara, his devoted companion and nurse.

"Peter," so-called, whose real name was Lewis, acquired an immense reputation as one of the boldest riders in the hunting field. He was well known in the Shires, and became very popular with all lovers of sport. His seat on horseback was very graceful, and he had a wonderful power over his horse, but I do not feel that I ever became truly acquainted with the real " Peter "—the man of many adventures, whose name figured not only in the sporting papers of the 'eighties, but also in a recently-published, much-discussed book (1920) recording other adventurous exploits, which were, to say the least of them, most original. Peter was not over-strong and did not spare himself. His doctors warned him of the dangers of our climate in winter, and obedient to their words he sought warmth and safety more than once in India. But he fell a victim, at last, to a chill, and died, aged forty-six, in the November of 1902, much regretted by numbers of friends.

I was married to Cyril in November 1877, Canon Farrar performing the ceremony.

We both determined upon making Aston Clinton our home during the autumn and winter months, so that my dear mother, then a widow, should not have the spectre of loneliness to apprehend. I think the charm of her society appealed greatly to my husband in his choice of a country home, at all events for the first years of our married life. He and my mother had many tastes and interests in common; her strong Liberal bent; her outlook upon all matters connected with the upraising, the comfort, the happiness of the people ; her love of fine literature, her knowledge of art, and above all her pleasure in the companionship of the young, endeared her to my husband, who would often tell me, half in joke, half in earnest, that I was not as good a Liberal as she was, and that I had not her remarkable quickness of intellect or her penetration into character—which was quite true. I was only too pleased with the conclusions he arrived at, as well as with his genuine affection for my dear sister and her fascinating husband. Unfortunately, the happiness afforded us by Eliot's dear presence was of very brief duration, as we lost him in 1878.

Aston Clinton, being within easy reach of London, was most conveniently situated for Cyril. He could attend to his town duties on some days in the week, hunt on others, and also entertain mutual friends in our country home. Thus during those years some pleasant acquaintances ripened into friends, and my mother learned to know and to appreciate many whose names have since then become famous ; besides which, the fact that many members of my family were living on their estates in Buckinghamshire added a pleasing variety to our social life.

For instance, it was at Mentmore that we first met Mr. Gladstone off his pedestal, as it were, and at his very best. At Tring Park we made closer acquaintance with Lord Morley, Lord Haldane, Lord Goschen, Mr. Balfour, etc., etc. At Halton we once actually lunched in company with the Shah of Persia. At Waddesdon we were of those assembled one May day in 1890 to greet H.M. Queen Victoria. Ascott, the beloved country home of my cousins, the Leo Rothschilds, opened its hospitable doors to many and various guests from November to May. There the company often included —to go back to the 'eighties—Sir Henry Calcroft, Lord Hardwicke, Lord and Lady Farquhar, Lord Hartington, the Duchess of Manchester, Sir Edward Hamilton,

Lord and Lady Derby, Count Mensdorff, the Austrian Ambassador, and above all Mr. Balfour.

Happily for me, I was able for many years of my married life to continue following my old and favourite pursuits. In this my mother encouraged me; she was always to the fore in all that she thought might benefit the people, and to the very last year of her life she was actively employed in her care for her poorer friends and neighbours. She also showed an interest in the working-men's houses which my husband was building on his Battersea estate, and which she visited in his company. She was much amused and pleased at his choice of names for some of the newly-planned streets, such as Dickens and Thackeray Streets, and Montefiore Street in honour of her uncle, Sir Moses Montefiore, the philanthropist.

At the beginning of my married life I was disappointed that we did not settle down in Battersea amongst the working classes. I suggested making a " House Beautiful " in that region, allowing of closer intercourse with and better knowledge of the men and women whose paths were so different from mine, and consequently so imperfectly understood by me. It would have been a splendid experience. I know I should have liked it. But it was not to be.

Cyril was much attracted by a house on the Portman estate, standing on high ground, at the extreme end of Oxford Street, where it merges into the Edgware Road, the house being a part of the old mansion once belonging to, and inhabited by, the Dukes of Norfolk ; and there we finally came (1879) with our Lares and Penates.

In some respects Surrey House was admirably situated. From the windows of the upper stories, when the horizon was clear and bright, an uninterrupted view across Hyde Park revealed the outlines of the Crystal Palace, with a distant glimpse of the Surrey Hills; whilst the space at the back of the house, unusual in a London building, allowed the necessary scope for the many additions—not always improvements—which it gave my husband the most intense satisfaction to invent and construct. His ideas on architecture were always too big for the spaces where we made our homes. A fine park instead of the modest Overstrand acreage, or a site on an open heath, would have suited him best for the creation of his country residence. But, as fate would have it, we pitched our tent in cramped or populous places, and wherever we chose to live he added and built, to accommodate furniture, statuary, pictures and books, of which we had a goodly collection. The effect was generally admirable, but whilst the work of altering and enlarging may have been delightful in itself, it proved to be a very expensive amusement. However, a London house, with fine reception-rooms and a broad and easy staircase, was not to be despised at a time when the Liberal party demanded social functions. I think I may say that we did our duty well. The entertainments that we gave were of a varied description and attracted a variety of guests. They were of all sorts and conditions. Cyril was a capital host, and the welcome that he extended to those who honoured and cheered us by their presence, both in town and country, was a very true one. I think many, old and young, went away cheered by the heartfelt kindness of his receptions.

In a charming letter addressed to me by that brilliant author, George Meredith, occur these words : " Give my love to him who is the brother of his guest "—a subtle and a well-deserved compliment. And Lord Morley in 1914, writing and thinking of Cyril and of my dear mother, said :

The happiest days of my life were passed in the early times of The Pleasaunce, delightful days of friendship, gaiety, reading, and talks of serious things.

(By the bye, it was Lord Morley who gave the name to our seaside cottage.)

Cyril's great love of art brought him into close touch with painters and sculptors, such men as George Watts, Burne-Jones, Millais, Sandys, Tissot, Whistler, Story, Gilbert, and others; he simply delighted in their company. He always deplored the fact that he had never been taught to use either pencil or brush, but his inborn taste was excellent. His natural *flair* for what was first-rate never deserted him; I can remember that he was much taken by, and bought, one of the first beautiful pictures ever exhibited by Lawson, when that clever artist was still unknown to the public. It was always the very best that he cared for; he was never contented with anything short of that.

Italy, that land of natural beauty and of artistic and historical interest, allured and enchanted him from the first. He would have loved to own a villa on the heights overlooking the lovely city of Florence, and he seriously contemplated taking a lease of Desdemona's Palace, on the waters of the Grand Canal in Venice. But when common sense, in the shape of his wife, made him turn his back on the attractions of Italy, he did his best at any cost to transplant Italian colouring and Italian designs into his London and Norfolk homes.

In all these matters he never waited for the world's verdict, but showed independence of thought and originality in taste. I believe it was owing to his suggestion that when the great pictures of the Blenheim Collection—amongst which is the famous equestrian portrait by Vandyck of Charles I.—came into the market, they were secured to the nation by Mr. Gladstone.

When young and remarkably good-looking, with a picturesque face and figure, Cyril had been repeatedly asked by artists to sit for his portrait. Watts made a sketch of his head, which, unfortunately, I do not possess; Sandys a three-quarter-length portrait in

crayons, and Gilbert the sculptor a fine bust in bronze.
But I regret that there should never have been a really
noble picture of him at his best, such a one as Watts
or Millais would have given us. His taste for art was
not limited to pictures, statuary, and architecture.
He had also a genuine love for music, and although he
was, unhappily, no executant, he could listen with true
and intelligent enjoyment to the performance of instru-
mentalists and singers.

On one occasion at Surrey House, when the Hungarian
Gypsy Band had given us a fine performance, Lady Hallé,
taking the violin from their leader, suddenly struck up
in inimitable fashion the " Radetzky " March, the whole
band joining in by ear and raising at the close of the
piece frantic cheers for the lady who had wielded the
bow with such magic skill.

If Cyril was a devotee of the pictorial arts, he loved
literature no less, especially poetry. He was a great
reader, and, fortunately for himself, had a most retentive
and literal memory. Thus, on occasions of illness and
convalescence, when reading was difficult or impossible,
he lightened the dreariness of many a weary hour by
repeating word for word some favourite lines he knew,
and knew well, by heart. He did not care for reading
aloud, nor for being read to—a source of regret to me—
but he could recite most beautifully; indeed, I have
never heard fine passages of the Scriptures more
impressively and more dramatically given than by
Cyril. He had a very real love for the Bible, in which
as a boy he had been well instructed, and I found
amongst his papers a number of favourite texts, written
in pencil, probably during his last long illness.

He had many friends and acquaintances amongst
authors, both men and women ; as a very young man
he had been introduced to Lord Tennyson by Mr.
Frederick Locker, and ever after bore the Laureate
unquestioning devotion. Frederic Myers was one of
his most intimate College friends, and later in life he

took trouble to meet and to know other distinguished writers.

I cannot resist quoting from a letter written to him in 1898 by the brilliant American novelist, Henry James ; it is of twofold interest, as it touches upon my husband's proficiency as a photographer [1] as well as upon his gifts as a host :

March 1898.

MY DEAR CYRIL—The photographs are magnificent and I am devotedly grateful. There is plenty of my substantial self in them, Heaven knows, but what I succeed in seeing to an exclusion of that, is *you* and *yours.* Your generous hand and hospitality . . . the sweet old Aston Clinton and our long and unclouded friendship, and so a massive monument to all which the two uncompromising images shall ever be tenderly cherished by—Yours most constantly,

HENRY JAMES.

Another reference occurs in a letter from the late Mrs. Humphry Ward to me :

November 1918.

. . . I was indeed grateful for your charming letter about the Recollections. Did you realise that the portrait of me in 1888 was from a photograph that Lord Battersea took of me at Aston Clinton ? How well I remember that visit !

And, as I am alluding to Cyril's success as a photographer, perhaps I may mention that the great historian, Stubbs, when Bishop of Oxford, staying with us at Aston Clinton, asked to sit to my husband, telling me in a playful aside that he had ordered his lawn sleeves to be most carefully washed for that occasion.

Further, amongst kind and friendly notes in recognition of hospitality joyfully given, I would quote this from Lady Ritchie, the daughter of Thackeray, one of our life-long friends, who, with Mrs. Cornish from

[1] Later in life he became a very painstaking and successful photographer, and has left many specimens of his industry in that direction.

Eton, had been spending an afternoon with us at The
Pleasaunce :

DEAREST CONSTANCE— . . . Cromer and Overstrand
really do rhyme to " happy land " for us. Hester enjoyed
her kind visit to you so much, and so did I, and my sight of
you all again with my *past* eyes (and my present eyes too),
while she looks on with her present ones.—Yours affectionately always,   A. T. R.

There is also the following from wonderful old Mrs.
Procter, widow of the poet Barry Cornwall, when she
was well over eighty. She declared that my husband
did not know his way to the Albert Hall Mansions, where
she lived, as he had never called upon her, so sent him
some directions :

I have made out a tour for your husband. He will leave
cards at Lady Ashburton's, then on Mrs. Butler at Rutland
Lodge, then on Mrs. Lowther, Lowther Lodge, then reward
himself by coming to see Mrs. Procter. I say " reward,"
because we are always the happiest when we are most liked
and appreciated. I am not afraid to take the field amongst
those ladies.

And this from Mary Cholmondeley, the gifted
novelist, in 1902 :

. . . My love to Lord Battersea. He was always so kind
during my long visit ; such a long visit is a test of friendship,
and he stood it nobly.

This from the Hon. Emily Lawless :

September 1906.

. . . I am so thankful to hear the improved account of
Lord Battersea's eyes. It was so good of him to send me
a little pencil letter about them in answer to my scrawl in
the train. Please tell him how grateful I am. It was the
first note, he told me, he had written since May. I have
felt very forlorn and like an *aged orphan* since I left your
sheltering wing. Nothing could have been kinder than they
were at B——, but still it was different; the sense of the
world as a happy and inspiring planet was gone.

N

The writers, often men and women of eminence, invariably spoke of my husband's genius for friendship and keen sense of what true hospitality should be. Indeed, I could not always keep pace with his views on the latter subject. At times I had to try and modify the warmth of his invitations, and to curtail, in as considerate a manner as was compatible with politeness, the length of a proposed visit that, beginning under a cloudless sky, threatened to end under a stormy one. I also felt, intuitively, that some of the very ardent and sudden likings he occasionally took to certain persons might lead to misplaced friendship, and that he might thus be preparing for himself hours and days of disappointment. But it was difficult to convince him of such possible pitfalls, and he went on trusting, caring, and taking endless pains in trying to help his friends, whenever they needed his help, to the very end. There were some friends, however, of whose affection he was perfectly secure, and in whom he could not be disappointed. " Where he was himself happiest was in the company of the little children, and no child but was happy with this careful guardian. Instinctively he knew the desire of the smallest heart, and no fairy Prince fulfilled those dreams more wisely. He loved them with an unselfish affection, and he made even the children selfless in his presence." These words occur in a beautiful and faithful tribute from the pen of an old friend, Lady Frances Balfour.

The ordinary school games had never taken very decided hold of Cyril, but in later years he evinced a liking for lawn-tennis, and still later developed a very true love for golf, probably fanned into flame by the fact of our living close to the beautiful Overstrand and Cromer Links, within view of the boundless ocean and within scent and taste of the invigorating North Sea breezes.

Hunting with fox- and stag-hounds over the pasture-land of Buckinghamshire had provided him for many

years with healthful exercise and great amusement ;
but, although a fearless rider, he was never, like his
brother Peter, in the first rank of horsemen. Racing
had no attraction for Cyril, nor indeed had any kind of
gambling. He never attended the popular race meetings, and would celebrate the great English holiday (the
Derby) by taking juvenile friends on that day to the
Zoological Gardens or the Crystal Palace.

His artistic nature found one of its best and most
delightful expressions in his pursuit of practical gardening, and, eager to understand fully what he was bent
upon accomplishing, he acquired at first hand scientific
knowledge of the subject. The garden at The Pleasaunce
was his creation, and a very extraordinary creation it is.

But before I can let myself speak of our Norfolk
home and of the happy years spent there, I must go
back to Cyril's introduction to political life and to our
first acquaintance with South Wales.

CHAPTER X

CYRIL AS MEMBER OF PARLIAMENT

BRECON—SOUTH BEDFORDSHIRE—SURREY HOUSE

You all did love him once, not without cause.
SHAKESPEARE.

CHAPTER X. I CAN remember that shortly after our marriage Cyril told me how he hoped, one day, to go through the magic doors of the House of Commons as M.P. His wishes were not unknown to some of our mutual friends, amongst others to Lady Elizabeth Biddulph, and it was her husband, then Mr. Biddulph, M.P. for S. Hereford-shire, who suggested that the Borough of Brecon in South Wales, until then looked upon as a safe Tory seat, might be successfully fought by a Liberal at the next General Election. Others confirmed this opinion, and thus advised we prepared to launch our bark upon unknown seas.

It was in the month of December 1878 that I had my first impression of the Brecon Borough. It was not a very cheerful one, and my heart sank within me. The journey from London seemed endless, the weather was cold and damp, the Wellington Hotel not attractive. I knew that Mr. Gwynne Holford, the sitting member, the owner of a beautiful estate in the county, had long been connected with the town, and was deservedly popular, also that our chance of victory was small, and that a gigantic task lay before us. The election

did not take place until April 1880. We knew instinctively that we should have the county people against
us, together with the representatives of the Army, and
probably the clergy of the Established Church.

Upon the first evening of our arrival the Liberal
agent, Mr. Bonnell Bishop, called upon us, and impressed
me by his quaint humour, his humorous advice most
amusingly tendered, and his evident desire to cheer me
up. My husband was very eager to make his acquaintance with the Liberal party in the town ; he was full of
courage, and looked forward with pleasurable excitement
to the canvass which he might have to undertake before
very long.

Scarcely had we left the station at Brecon when
Cyril was asked by the members of a Liberal caucus
to give them some of his views on the politics of the
hour. This he did in one of the largest public rooms of
the Wellington Hotel ; about thirty to forty were present
on that occasion, but not one of my sex, so that I,
who was anxious to hear the address, to have some idea
of the feeling amongst the Liberals for their future
candidate, was stowed away behind a screen, where I
could hear but was not visible. I do not remember
very much of that meeting, but recollect Cyril's ending
his little speech with the following two lines from
Addison, slightly altered :

> " 'Tis not in mortals to command success,
>   But we'll do more, *Breconians*,—we'll deserve it."

And we did !

We could count upon the support of the whole body
of Nonconformists : ministers, students of colleges,
also a fair number of the town folk and country people,
and of the not very reputable Irish contingent who
had settled, principally as miners, in the South of Wales.

We were advised to call upon a lady of the name of
Morgan, the widow of a clergyman, and whilst my
husband was interviewing some possible supporters, I

made my way to the home of that lady, and a charming and picturesque home it was. I was most kindly received, and within a few moments of my arrival her daughter Fanny appeared on the scene. I was attracted at once by a very striking personality, that of a young girl, whose fine brow, direct steady gaze, healthy complexion and golden hair made a pleasing picture on that snowy, dreary afternoon. Mrs. Morgan then and there promised her help in our difficult task, and was indeed true to her word, whilst her daughter seemed unaffectedly glad to make my acquaintance. My spirits rose accordingly.

It would be difficult for me to say how greatly I valued such friendship, or what a stand-by Fanny proved to me in those difficult times of my first acquaintance with the Brecon voters. Her younger sister, Nellie, whom I learned later to know and appreciate for her own fine qualities as well as for her unselfish devotion to her sister, became also a dear friend and a most enthusiastic supporter of my husband's.

I have a difficult task in trying to give in these pages any adequate account of Fanny Morgan. She is a very remarkable character. Her position in Brecon has for years been unique. Morally and intellectually she stands in the front rank of women — an honour to our sex. A convinced Liberal in politics; a supporter of Women's Rights from her earliest years; a devout Churchwoman, but trusted and beloved by her Nonconformist compatriots; a practical worker for years in matters connected with the welfare of the people; an earnest student of history and of antiquarian lore,— she fully deserved the honour that awaited her in the year 1910, when, after being the first lady Guardian in Brecon and the first woman Town Councillor in Wales, she became the Mayor of the Borough. As a tribute to Fanny's distinguished and all-denominational work, the chapels were closed on the first Sunday of her Mayoralty, and the ministers, with their congregations, accompanied

their beloved Mayor as she went in state to the Priory
Church. Surely such an unsolicited mark of respect and
affection was unprecedented! Fanny was always deeply
interested in matters connected with education, and is a
member of the Breconshire Education Committee and
of the Governing Body of the Brecon County Schools.
In the 'eighties the great work of Temperance Reform claimed her attention, and she was able to give
much valuable assistance to Lady Henry Somerset in
Herefordshire, besides being the moving power in her
own town.

In 1912, in spite of failing health that entailed much
suffering, she was appointed a member of the Joint and
Welsh Advisory Committee to the National Health Insurance Commission. Her advice was being constantly
sought, and she was always being pressed into more
and more active work. In recognition of what she had
accomplished and of the esteem in which she was held,
she was asked to accept from her grateful fellow-
townswomen and other friends (numbering more than
900) the gift of her portrait, painted by Mr. John Cooke,
in her Mayor's robes and chain of office. That portrait,
which she gave to the town, is now hanging on the walls
of the Brecon Guild Hall. I always have felt, and do
still feel, that Fanny was enormously helped by her
sister, whose bright temper and joyous sense of humour
made home life attractive and restful to the ardent
worker and student.

We spent part of the years 1878 and 1879 at Brecon,
and during that time Cyril became personally acquainted
with most of the voters, and certainly with every one
of his supporters. It was strange to see how sentiment
changed in regard to his candidature, how the Liberals
became strengthened in their allegiance, how the half-
hearted were won over, and how some of the bitterest
of his opponents were not only alarmed, but for the
time being disarmed.

From the first I had been advised not to appear on

the County Tennis Club ground, for no one there would have acknowledged my presence, and I was warned that at the ball held in connection with the Annual Agricultural Show no one would ask me to dance ; as it happened, one man was bold enough to do so, but he was an habitual drunkard, rather shunned by the ladies of Brecon, and quite tipsy on the night in question.

My husband had anonymous and threatening letters by the score, such as " Your Party is ruination to the country, Old Flower, and you want drumming to the Devil." Of course he disregarded them and only worked the harder. On April 1, 1880, he was rewarded by obtaining a majority of 59 votes in a constituency of 800 voters. I feel I may quote from a letter I wrote to my mother after the Election :

FFRWDGRECH, *April* 3, 1880.

And now, dearest Mother, I must give you a little account of Thursday, how the agitating hours passed, and how I got through the day. At 8.30 came a message from Cyril, begging us to come into Brecon at once. Behold me arrayed from head to foot in light blue, accompanied by Miss Morgan, driving down in the little brougham, with old Brown as a smart postillion riding on one of the dark greys and leading the other, and our little terrier wearing a large blue bow sitting beside the servant on the box. The day was lovely, bright and warm ; as we came to the first polling booth we met a crowd, on one side blue, on the other red ; we passed amidst cheering and *awful hooting*; then came a body of railway men, marching up to the poll, who recognised me and gave me a magnificent welcome. We dashed on through the little town, one mass of blue—500 bunches of artificial forget-me-nots had been sold in one morning!—and up to the Wellington Hotel, which was one mass of blue flags. All our vehicles and horses stood in a line before the door taking the voters up and down to the poll. We remained all day at the Wellington and looked at all the exciting scenes in the streets, sometimes venturing out for a little turn. Cyril drove and walked about all day. He was generally at the head of an immense crowd with his hat in his hand.

Mr. Holford passed our windows several times, once or twice at the head of all his labourers, who had walked over from Buckland. Fights went on under our windows, one fury of a woman dashing herself upon a man, knocking him down and trampling upon him. The Irish female " blues " were truly awful, offering to fight any male Tory who would like to have a turn. Our supporters came in from time to time very sanguine and hopeful, and Cyril was as self-possessed as if he were going out hunting.

After the close of the poll I became nervous and dispirited. Miss Morgan and I kept ourselves up by endless cups of tea, and visitors came dropping in one by one. Mr. Jones, the great temperance preacher, stood with me under the portico, and we begged of the people to go to the Coffee Tavern and not to the publics ; we entreated the respectable ones to keep the others in order if possible, but, alas, the drunkenness was awful ! I was in my little room at the back of the Inn at a quarter to seven, when I heard the tramp of feet. Cyril called out, " It is all right, we are in." I rushed out almost into the arms of the dissenting ministers, who stood there in a body. " But the poll is not declared," I gasped. " No," said they, " but your Agent turned his hat towards us from the window of the Town Hall—a preconcerted sign that you had polled enough votes to have won."

This seemed to me rather premature, but in another twenty minutes in dashes our Agent, screaming, " A majority of 59 ! " In dash the whole Committee, in rush all the ladies, and we all jump up and down as if we were mad. Then comes a roar of voices, the square is filling, the people stand in front of the house like a wall. Quantities of them rush in, and Abdul's[1] black face is the first I see. I went to the window and seized a flag and waved it enthusiastically, whilst cheer after cheer came ringing out. There were shouts for Cyril, who had to get out of the window and to stand on the sloping roof of the portico, grasping a point to keep himself steady ; a reporter hopped after him and one or two friends, whilst the little room was crowded to suffocation. The tipsiest people came pushing on me, and we quite panted

---

[1] Our African servant.

for breath. Cyril screamed out a little speech and then returned for more congratulations and handshaking. I was then conducted to the window, and silence was enforced by one of the ministers. I shouted out as loud as I could : " I must thank you for the great work you have done to-day, and will only say one word, but that shall be a Welsh one —' Buddigoliaeth ' (Victory)." They heard it and applauded vociferously. . . .

We settled for the time being in a pleasant country house, " Ffrwdgrech," the property of a Mr. Church. It was situated about two miles from the town, and was comfortable, though with no pretensions to beauty ; but the site was romantic. The lawn of the little garden disappeared into an attractive piece of woodland, where the birds sang merrily in the springtime, and through which ran the waters of a romantic stream, the wood climbing up a steep ascent and gradually losing itself on one of the turf-clad hills, so great a feature of Breconshire. How the west wind came sighing over that hill-top, and how the rain that it brought with it would beat, for days together, against our windows !

" Ffrwdgrech " was our Welsh home but for a short time ; later we settled down in Buckingham House, a delightful habitation in the town, the tiny and steep garden overlooking the river Usk—" King Arthur's Usk, which washes the very walls of Brecon," as an old seventeenth-century writer says, " on its way past Caerleon to the sea at Newport."

Buckingham House was part of an ancient and historic building supposed to have been connected with the old Brecon Castle by an underground passage. The town walls ran at the foot of a sloping bank in the garden of Buckingham House, which also contains one of the old towers of the wall. It owes its appellation to the Dukes of Buckingham, who had been lords of the Manor of Brecknock. Miss Morgan, in welcoming us there, said the name was of happy augury. The original building consisted of one house, now divided into three, of which ours was the centre house, whilst Mrs. Morgan and her daughters were our next - door neighbours, such close vicinity adding greatly to my comfort and happiness.

The town of Brecon has a picturesque setting. The beautiful Beacons frame it from the south, whilst life and freshness are brought into the streets by the waters of the winding Usk and the rushing Honddu. The Priory Church adds an historical interest to the little Welsh borough, and it was in that church on May 25, 1911 (in the year of Miss Morgan's Mayoralty), that in my presence and that of my husband's sister, Clara, a beautiful stained-glass window was dedicated, in fine and appropriate words, to the memory of my dear husband, by the then Archdeacon of Brecon, afterwards Bishop of Swansea. It was my gift in remembrance of Cyril, the last representative of the Borough of Brecon.

There were many delightful walks in the neighbourhood of Brecon, and charming expeditions for riders and pedestrians on the Beacons. It was prior to the days of motor-cars, but with fleet and sure-footed cobs, such as we possessed, we were soon acquainted with all parts of the country and made friends with many of the inhabitants. The people and the land were both attractive to us. Cyril made way very quickly with the Welsh folk. His task certainly had been no easy one. Still, in our favour came the great Liberal reaction and Mr. Gladstone's wonderful triumph in the Midlothian campaign, which affected many well-known Conservative constituencies. But, over and above all, Cyril had succeeded in capturing the imagination of the warm-hearted Celtic race : " he came as a complete stranger and he took them by storm." His good looks, his joyous spirits, his delight in poetry, his dramatic rendering of the same, his quickness of repartee, his successful platform oratory, and above all his sympathy with the people and his real kindness of heart, were the chief factors in his undoubted popularity.

In spite of the warning note that had been addressed to me on our first visit, I even came to be on good terms with some of our opponents! I was not so terrible a Radical as I had been painted, and the smartly-dressed county ladies were not so formidably hostile as I had been led to believe.

I did not visit the tennis ground, but I was present for the second time at the Annual Agricultural Ball and had more partners than I wanted, even dancing with Mr. Gwynne Holford! The young, pretty, and newly-married wife of the member for the county, Mrs. Fuller-Maitland, was going through my unpleasant experiences of the previous year, and came to me during the evening with appealing, tearful eyes, whilst I reassured her and bade her be of good heart for the future.

Amongst our Brecon friends were several of the Non-conformist ministers. One of these, Mr. J. B. Jones, became my teacher in the Welsh tongue, and it was he who instructed me in the pronunciation of the word " Buddigoliaeth."

My dear mother, when she was staying with us, de-termined upon also trying to learn that most difficult of languages, so we both set seriously to work with a Grammar and a Welsh and English Bible, and we proved very ardent, if not always very successful, pupils. I once managed to write a Welsh letter to my master, and for many years my mother and I were in the habit of adding a few words in Welsh to the letters that passed between us. Occasionally I attended a service in one of the numerous chapels — I believe there were eight or nine of these in Brecon, each denomination owning two places of worship, one for the services conducted in English and the other for those in Welsh. I was once taken to hear a most remarkable preacher, who came from a remote village on the hills. He spoke for nearly an hour in English with a delightful Welsh accent, in a melodious voice, with fine dramatic gestures, without a note ; he looked like an aged shepherd, and

his words were suggestive of solitary musings on the
lonely hillside.   He was most impressive.   The clergy
of the Church of England whom I met at that time
in Wales were neither eloquent nor impressive, nor did
they seem to be at all in touch with the people.

I attended a temperance meeting on one occasion
in a small village, when I spoke in a chapel.   It was a
beautiful frosty afternoon in December, and the women
came riding in from the mountain-side on their ponies.
To me it was a most picturesque experience to see the
snow-capped hills, the women in their high hats and
thick short skirts, the crowd gathered round the chapel
door, whilst the kind welcome that awaited me as I
walked up to the reading-desk made me feel at home
at once in those surroundings.   Temperance, or rather
total abstinence, had not been a very popular subject
in Wales; indeed, the moist atmosphere and prevalence
of rain were known to produce a certain amount of
mental depression that drove many to the dangerous
exhilaration of intoxicants.   I had been warned against
attacking this popular failing during the early years of
my husband's connection with the Borough, but towards
the end of our time at Brecon I had been asked, even
urged, to support temperance work, then in its infancy.

The personal interest that Cyril took in his supporters
was really very extraordinary, and often led to amusing
episodes.   Thus once amongst the crowds in Bond Street
he recognised a Brecon butcher, whom he stopped and
accosted by name, to the man's delight.   We had
frequent callers from the constituency when in London
—so many, in fact, that my sister re-named Surrey
House "New South Wales."   One evening, at a late
hour, my husband was startled by receiving a call
from a Brecon resident, who declared he must have
£10,000 immediately, or he might be led to commit
suicide.   The man was undoubtedly a citizen of Brecon,
but a very drunken one, and at that moment not
responsible for his words or actions.   He was given

some hot coffee, was locked into a spare bedroom for the night, and taken on the following morning, an abject and apologetic creature, to the railway station, his return ticket being presented to him in lieu of the £10,000 !

Another time, a most respectable-looking individual, with a printed Brecon address on his card, came to us at an early morning hour. His tale was a very plausible one, and he left our house with a sum of money that, had he been caught, would have lodged him in gaol— for he was a fraud, and his story purely imaginary.

Cyril took infinite trouble and pains in trying to place young men in fitting situations, and, I believe, actually helped over a hundred Breconians and found them posts where they were able to make a living.

Cyril was always deeply moved by the sight of suffering, particularly when a child was the victim. His heart opened out marvellously to the young and the tender. One instance has been recorded of how he obtained admission for a little invalid girl from Brecon into the Great Ormond Street Hospital, and how when her mother, who had left her in the hospital ward, returned on the following day to see her child, expecting to find her home-sick and lonely, she found my husband sitting beside her, the bed strewn with toys he had brought her, and the little girl radiant with smiles. Such an action would have seemed most natural to him, and I think he would have been greatly surprised had he known that it would ever be published.

Welsh carpenters and Welsh gardeners were imported from Brecon to Aston Clinton, and were often most ill-suited to English ways, but Cyril thought them all most delightful, and of course he became and remained the very idol of his constituents.

But at last the blow fell! In 1885, when the Redistribution Bill passed the House of Commons, the Borough, like many others of similar population, became disfranchised, and was merged into the County, of which

Mr. Fuller-Maitland was the sitting member. Thus the seat was lost, and our connection with Brecon came to an end.

At the public banquet given to us before we finally and regretfully bade adieu to Brecon and our many kind friends there, we were presented with a beautiful set of silver fruit dishes, many of the leading Conservatives being amongst the subscribers.

It was in that same autumn of 1885 that Cyril was invited to stand for the South Beds Division, comprising the towns of Luton, Dunstable, and Leighton Buzzard. Bedfordshire had been previously represented by Lord Tavistock, the son of the Duke of Bedford, who—in obedience, as he wrote to Cyril, " to his father's most strongly expressed wish " — retired from the contest, with no little personal regret.

The constituency was in most convenient proximity to our Buckinghamshire home—actually within driving distance of Aston Clinton. Cyril was not only known as a sportsman to his future constituents, but his fame as a platform orator had preceded him from Brecon. His adversary was Mr. Sydney Gedge, a strong Conservative. My husband's meetings were extremely well attended, and he had some very enthusiastic receptions during his campaign.

The polling at Luton took place on the 1st of December. My dear mother and Cyril's sister, Clara, were with me on that auspicious day, awaiting the result of the election in one of the large straw-hat factories of the town. We were in close vicinity to the Town Hall, and thus we spent an exciting morning watching the assembled crowds in the streets, men and women. Our friends were in capital spirits, and my husband's victory seemed assured. At one o'clock in the afternoon the High Sheriff, Mr. Hatfield - Harter, proclaimed the result, the Liberal majority having attained the overwhelming figure of 2209. It was a genuine victory, gained after a good honest fight, and naturally all the members of Cyril's Committee, who had worked most loyally for him, were wild with delight.

Early in 1886 my husband was given by Mr. Gladstone the appointment of Junior Lord of the Treasury, Whip to his party, and the letter that conveyed the offer, written by Mr. Gladstone's own pen, was seized upon by myself and carefully kept until this day. It ran as follows:

21 CARLTON HOUSE TERRACE, S.W.,
February 4, '86.

DEAR MR. CYRIL FLOWER—Pray give me the pleasure of receiving your permission to submit your name to the Queen as a Lord of the Treasury (my colleague) in the new Administration.—Believe me, sincerely yours,

W. E. GLADSTONE.

Cyril had, therefore, to seek re-election, but happily was not opposed. It was a position that suited him exactly. "He was one of the most popular Whips," wrote an old friend, "that ever guarded the doors; he knew the constituencies, and he knew the members, and as he did his own work with all his might, no member resented his request that the best his party had to give should be always on duty." He was indeed one of the most satisfactory of Whips. Members would say, when pressed into staying for a division, "We have not the heart to refuse Flower"; whilst Cyril, in speaking of his important divisions, would declare that he could account for every man on his side. I often heard it stated that he showed remarkable tact and patience in dealing with men, and unflagging enthusiasm for his work. He made no enemies, and had friends on both sides of the House. He continued as Whip when his party went into Opposition. It is rather a curious fact that he and the Hon. Sydney Herbert, the Conservative Whip during the same period, should have been considered the two best-looking men in Parliament.

South Beds was chiefly an agricultural constituency, and it happened that some of its wealthiest landowners, such, for example, as the Duke of Bedford at Woburn Abbey, Lord Cowper at Wrest, and members of my family in the near neighbourhood of Leighton Buzzard, had been for years past, and were still, Liberals in politics.

In 1885 the agricultural labourers were in possession of the franchise, and there was much discussion as to how they would use the vote. I agree with the late Mr. George Russell, who wrote in one of his delightful volumes of retrospect : " To those who, like myself, were brought up in agricultural districts, the notion that the labourer was a revolutionary seemed strangely unreal ; but it was a haunting obsession in the minds of clubmen and town dwellers."

It was in 1886 that Mr. Gladstone attempted to introduce a Home Rule Bill for Ireland into the Commons. He was defeated on the 8th of June by a majority of thirty votes, Cyril having foretold to a man the fatal result of this division. Again there was a dissolution, followed by a General Election, and again Cyril stood for the South Beds constituency. The fight was much harder than it had been on the previous occasion. The cause was a most unpopular one, and many old Liberals went over to the other side and voted for Mr. Bartlett, Cyril's opponent. However, by dint of hard work and any number of speeches in and visits to small villages, as well as towns, Cyril won again, but with a lowered majority of 673.

When Parliament reassembled a great change was apparent in the atmosphere of the old political world. Indeed, an overwhelming element of bitterness had been introduced, not only into the Houses of Parliament, but also into social life. Society was rapidly entering upon a new and difficult phase. It soon became apparent that the prominent men on either side could no longer be

O

asked, as they had been before that date, to meet one
another indiscriminately in the drawing-rooms of London
hostesses.   Cyril still acted as Whip for his party during
the Tory administration, which came to an end in
June 1892.   There was again a dissolution and General
Election.   Cyril worked like a Trojan, and his help all
over the country was enormously in demand.   He stood
once more for the same constituency, and was opposed
by Colonel Duke, whom he defeated, winning the seat
by the increased majority of 1019.   It was Mr. Gladstone's third administration, and it was the end of
Cyril's House of Commons career.   In the August of
the same year, when new posts and new honours were
being given to the old and trusted supporters of the
aged statesman, Cyril was offered and accepted a
peerage, leaving his constituents of South Beds much
disappointed and somewhat chagrined at his resignation.
His successor was a charming man, Mr. Howard Whitbread, son of one of the most popular and respected
landowners of the county, and a well-known public
character.

Before I follow Cyril any further on the new path
that lay before him, which, to my mind, was not half
so attractive as the old one, let me say a few words
about our life during the thirteen years he sat in the
House of Commons—I would even say our home-life,
because this is no attempt at a political history, over
which my pen would stumble.   I should like to linger
a little over some of the names that meant so much
to us in those old days, and that seem gradually to
be fading away into the mists of the past.   To begin
with, I think I may here put into words what I often
felt, namely, that although Cyril was deeply interested
in the House of Commons, and although he was a most
popular member both there and in his constituency,
his special talents did not lie in political work.   His
were not so much the attributes of the statesman as
they were those of the man of artistic taste.   Thus

Surrey House had to be beautiful and attractive as well as spacious, and Cyril spared no pains in its decoration, hoping that the contemplation of the glorious old marbles, fine colouring, and artistic designs would, if only for a short space of time, arouse and satisfy the sense of beauty in his many and varied guests. And varied, indeed, they were ; of this there could be no doubt. Surrey House was not only a meeting-ground for the Liberal party, but it opened its doors to musicians, artists, writers, philanthropists, as well as to many unknown to fame, and sometimes unknown to the hostess herself. Thus on one occasion, in the middle of an evening party, I was greatly puzzled by the appearance of a guest whom I could not place anywhere in my recollection, nor could any one else assist me in cataloguing the newcomer. I called my husband aside, and told him in hushed tones that I thought a burglar had crept into the house, and pointed to the individual in question. Cyril could hardly contain his amusement, but, reassuring me quickly upon the respectability of our guest, waited until the early hours of the morning to explain that the said gentleman, whom we none of us knew, had been asked at the request of a young lady with whom my husband had been riding in the Row, the lady being very anxious to meet the gentleman in the house of a third party. A proposal and an acceptance took place that very evening, followed by a happy marriage.

We entertained many Liberals both of London and South Beds, and we always tried to secure some leading members of the party for such evenings ; thus Sir William Harcourt, with his striking and stalwart figure, might have been seen elbowing his way through the rooms, whilst Lord Rosebery, Mr. Asquith, Lord Morley, Lord Haldane, etc., would occasionally give intense satisfaction to their devoted followers by appearing amongst them, if only for a short time. Wives and sisters of members of Liberal Associations, who perhaps were spending a short holiday in London, were frequently to be seen at such gatherings, and long afterwards would tell me of the enjoyment they had derived from them.

During our thirty years of residence Surrey House was the scene of many receptions in connection with societies such as the Union of London School Teachers, the Association of Working Girls' Clubs, the Children's Country Holiday Fund, and many others. It also provided the adequate space and fine setting for lectures and addresses given by such men as Sir Richard Jebb, Canon Ainger, Canon Scott Holland, Professor Drummond, Mr. Story, Mr. Zangwill, etc.; for concerts where famous artists performed in the cause of charity or for their own benefit; for sales of work that were more or less profitable, but all very amusing; for more than one exhibition of the Amateur Art Society, also of the Buckinghamshire Lace Industry, always extremely attractive. Here I must add that the Recreative Evening Schools Association also came into being in Surrey House. If the walls of that house could only speak, what wonderful and astonishing tales could they not tell! finishing up with perhaps the most unexpected of all, the transformation of the major part of the house and garage during the Great War into a vast receiving and distributing library for books by the million, sent through the Joint Societies of the British Red Cross and the Order of St. John of Jerusalem to the Military Hospitals in England and abroad; whilst the first floor and upper story were used as a centre for the reception of " comforts," packed and finally despatched in huge sacks to members of the Air Force. The names of Mrs. Gaskell, Hon. Secretary to the War Library, and of Lady Henderson, Hon. Organiser of the R.A.F. Comforts Fund, will thus be inseparably connected with Surrey House.

Cyril was indeed leading a very strenuous life during the years of his parliamentary career. He was

LORD AND LADY BATTERSEA.

assiduous in his duties as Whip, and, of course, had to
attend all meetings of the House, where he was frequently kept until the early hours of the morning.
But in spite of this he would drive down cheerfully in
the morning to his work at Battersea, or attend a
board meeting in the city, also visiting from time to
time one of the hospitals—the Metropolitan being the
one in which he took a vivid and special interest.

Quoting again from the pen of an old friend, I may
add :

Christie's was familiar with his presence, and his love for
the old Masters never blinded his eyes for the men of great-
ness of his own days. He was one of the very earliest to
recognise the genius of Burne-Jones and to become a close
friend of the artist. Some of the best-known of Sir Edward's
works were painted specially for this friend and patron of
all true art ; Gilbert, the sculptor, was another genius
whose first exhibited works were noticed by this keen eye,
and when he loved the art, he sought out the man who had
created it. He had the gifts of the architect and the eye
of the mason ; when his palaces of art were raised he loved
to deck them with colour and light.[1]

It was wonderful how he unearthed treasures hidden
away in little old shops and dark streets, both at home
and abroad ; for wherever he went he brought back
an extraordinary assortment of objects.

During the old House of Commons days, particularly
when Cyril was in office, we had very frequent and
pleasant luncheon-parties at Surrey House. These were
less formal and troublesome entertainments than set
dinners, which entailed much thought and arrangement
for at least a fortnight or three weeks beforehand. On
Government nights, or before some important division,
Cyril could not, of course, leave the House; he would
necessarily stay and dine there, and nothing amused
me more than joining him at these small and informal

[1] Lady Frances Balfour, *Westminster Gazette*, Nov. 28, 1907.

dinners, with the sure prospect of meeting some
agreeable Members of Parliament.

We often had great fun at those little gatherings,
and it was rather thrilling to hear the division bell
ringing, as it would do during our repast, and the cry
of " D'vision, d'vision ! " shouted along the stone
passages, then the rush of members up to the Lobbies,
leaving us quietly seated at the dinner-table awaiting
their return. We almost felt as if we were being let
into the secrets of Parliament, and taking part in the
government of the Empire. I remember once asking
a member (when the bell rang) what the division was
upon ; he replied that he did not know and did not
much care as long as he went into his right Lobby. On
fine warm evenings I have often sat on the Terrace
drinking after-dinner coffee, my attention being arrested
on one such occasion by a most instructive and interesting conversation—the subject that of German literature,
and one of the speakers the present Lord Haldane. I
begged later for an introduction, and I am happy to
recall that from that date I may claim the friendship
of a very remarkable man.

I have often had a seat in the Speaker's Gallery and
have greatly enjoyed listening to a fine speech or a
good debate. When Mr. Gladstone was Prime Minister
a chair was always retained for his wife in the right-
hand corner of that Gallery, where she would spend
many a long hour, constantly waiting to drive home
with her husband at the close of the sitting. I have
with interest watched Mr. Gladstone writing his daily
letter to the Queen, from his seat on the Government
Bench, intent on what he was doing, yet, as we all
knew, not missing any important point of the proceedings of the evening. I have also had the privilege of
hearing some fine speaking in the House of Lords, on
very notable occasions, though the more studied oratory
of the Peers, delivered in the quieter atmosphere of
their House, has never, to my mind, been as exciting

as that of "another place." But of "the Lords"
more hereafter.

Surrey House luncheons were very popular, I have been told, amongst our friends and acquaintances, although rather alarming to the mistress of the house, particularly when she was somewhat untried at her business.

When Cyril went out in the morning he would tell me to expect four or five guests, and often added : " Have something cold—but there is sure to be enough." In vain our much-tried cook would say that food must be hot before it is cold. On one occasion we were twelve at luncheon when half that number were expected, and I can remember whispering to my neighbour at the table, " Please only eat spinach, do not touch the cutlets." He looked very much astonished, and secretly wondered whether I had had intentions of poisoning my other guests, and was greatly relieved, and not a little amused, at my explaining matters to him when our meal had come to an end.

Very different in character and pursuits were the guests we entertained. My husband loved variety, and I was deeply interested in human beings of all sorts and conditions.

From the drawing-room gallery windows of Surrey House, which, as I said before, commanded an extensive and magnificent view, we have often witnessed interesting sights. There we have on certain occasions received friends and acquaintances. There, I recollect, we were assembled in 1887 to see Queen Victoria, as she drove from Paddington Station to the Guildhall, during her first Jubilee celebration, when many thousands of her loyal subjects turned out in the summer sunshine to do her honour. And there again we came in 1901 on an unforgettable day, a grey, cold, bleak day in February, when that same beloved Queen was being carried to her last rest. That scene will long remain in my memory. When I drew up the blinds of my bedroom at an early hour of the morning, I noted with astonishment the appearance of Oxford Street and the Park, where lines of black-clothed women had already taken up their places. Not a colour to be seen, whilst even the houses seemed to have put on mourning, and were draped with black or violet hangings. The great thoroughfare was very quiet; an extraordinary hush seemed to prevail. Our friends began to arrive early and took up their positions in the gallery; my husband left me to receive them, as his official duties took him to the station, there to await the arrival of the cortège.

We sat for some hours in a state of trembling excitement, until the booming of the guns came as the first herald of the approach. I seemed to feel the wind blow colder at that moment, whilst some black and threatening clouds looked like the harbingers of a nearing snowstorm.

Quietly the procession came into view. It was the mourning of the nation that perhaps struck the deepest note. I remember being much impressed by the silence of the streets, the absence of music, the continuous booming of the guns that had almost a fateful sound, then the noise of horses' hoofs striking the road, the rattle of swords, and the clatter of the stirrups. Then my eyes were arrested by the two principal figures of the day, our own King Edward, and the Kaiser Wilhelm, closely draped in his military coat, the collar of which almost hid his features. I remember remarking the deathly pallor of the German Emperor, and the way he seemed to be nervously evading the cold blast of the February wind. The coffin reposing on the gun-carriage and covered with the Union Jack looked strangely small and un-regal—yet it was a Queen-Empress being taken to her rest by her soldiers, and it was through the serried ranks of a stricken and orphaned people. The two monarchs rode close beside the coffin, members of our Royal house and foreign Royalties were in near proximity, whilst the carriages of princesses and high dignitaries followed in the long line of the cortège. But to me that small coffin and the two principal riders seemed to fill the whole canvas of that picture. When I talked over the events of the day with my dear mother, she told me how well she could recall standing in the gallery of St. James's Palace more than sixty years before that date, watching with many others the triumphal passing by of a radiantly happy young bride—beautiful from happiness—with her chivalrous and handsome husband, the man of her own choice. To my mother the close of that life seemed like a portentous pause in the history of our English nation, ominous of many changes to come.

From the windows of Surrey House in the November of 1907 I witnessed another historic sight : that of the German Emperor and the late Empress, then in all the prestige of their unique position, driving in semi-state in an open carriage on their way to the Guildhall, where His Imperial Majesty was to receive the Freedom of the City. The reception throughout was a hearty one, and the populace showed their appreciation of the Kaiserin's presence by a special cheer for Her Majesty, for, owing to the illness of one of the young German princes, it had not been the first intention of the Kaiserin to have accompanied the War Lord on his visit to England ; but upon hearing of the bitter disappointment that her absence on such a festive occasion would have caused, the Kaiserin resolved to be one of the party. Very smiling and delighted she looked, bowing right and left to those gathered in the roadway. I remember remarking that although she was not exactly handsome, she was gracious and attractive with her white hair, her fresh colouring, and her fine figure, set off by a becoming toilette and splendid pearl necklace. The Kaiser, as usual, looked rather fierce and forbidding. When I saw His Imperial Majesty again it was on his yacht, the *Hohenzollern*.

When our own gracious and well-beloved King Edward

CHAPTER VII. was taken to his rest in the spring of 1910 I had
  X.   left my old home, but living in Connaught Place, in very
       close proximity to Surrey House, I could still see the
       crowds massed in the Park, I could hear the sound of
       the guns, and I could note the approach of that sad
       and heart-stirring procession. But that, indeed, was
       enough for me. I could hardly have borne to witness,
       amongst a crowd of onlookers, the solemn passing of
       all that was earthly of that most genial and warm-
       hearted of monarchs, in the brilliant sunshine of a
       perfect May day.

       Thus sights, solemn, mournful, memorable, and re-
       markable in many ways, have become indissolubly
       connected in my mind with Surrey House, and crowds
       of human beings of all sorts and conditions have con-
       gregated in its vicinity, as we are told they did in days
       gone by, when flocking to the gruesome sights afforded
       them by Tyburn Gallows.

CHAPTER XI

Happy is the house that shelters a friend.—EMERSON.

RETURNING to the many friends and acquaintances who made that period of our lives so full of happy interests, I must note here that my dear mother was always ready to receive the guests whom Cyril was free to invite to Aston Clinton, and very pleasant those little parties proved. Without any of the popular aids to amusement now considered indispensable to a successful gathering, such as tennis or golf by day and card-playing by night, our parties were very happy ones. It is true that there was hunting in the Vale for the fortunate possessors of horses, and indeed one or two lovers of the sport kept their hunters in our stables during the winter months.

One of our best-beloved guests was Alfred Lyttelton, whose acquaintance, as an undergraduate, we made at Cambridge. My first glimpse of him was in the racquet-court, where he was playing in one of those games in which he revelled and excelled.

" One of the causes of Alfred's popularity, both at school and in after life, was his genius for companionship in all games, and perhaps specially in those where a steady nerve is essential. His generous delight in any good stroke of his companion made most people play their best when with him. And the same quality covered all his intercourse with others. He drew the best out of men, in play and talk and feeling, because

203

he never failed to discern it, and to welcome it with joy." He loved reading and music and pleasant talk. " Music stirred him more than any other form of art or beauty—it spoke in a language he understood." [1]

In reading an unpublished letter from Alfred to his cousin, Mary Drew, I came upon the following passage :

ASTON CLINTON, *December* 1880.

Sunday here has been delightful, plenty of reading, a very quiet, refined, and wholesome atmosphere ; Mrs. Flower in her most genial mood, full of the enjoyment, it seems to me, of life.

Alfred Lyttelton spent one or two Sundays with us in that and the succeeding year, then later again as a widower after his short period of heaven-sent happiness. Cyril urged him to bring his horse, and with Lord Minto and Ernest Crawley the friends had much enjoyment in the Vale, until A. L.'s hunting came to an end as far as we were concerned ; this when he married his second wife, Miss Balfour, known to her friends as " D.D.," who, without displacing the adored image of Laura Tennant from his heart, became a well-beloved and loving spouse.

Lord Minto, familiarly known to us as " Rowley," was a favourite habitué ; his splendid horsemanship made him a well-known character in the field, and his pleasant, easy ways caused him to be equally attractive when at home with us. He was very good-looking at that time, had beautiful expressive eyes with long curling lashes, and possessed much charm of manner. How little did we think, when we were entertaining him, that one day he would be Viceroy of India ! He was very fond of arguing on political matters with Cyril, whom he styled a dreadful Radical, whilst Lord Minto was himself, so he declared, an " old Whig." I think we were all pleased when he married Mary Grey, the youngest daughter of General Charles Grey, and thus

---

[1] *Alfred Lyttelton*, by Edith Lyttelton.

became the brother-in-law of another great friend of ours — no other than Albert Grey, later Earl Grey, Governor-General of Canada, who was one of the most attractive of men, an idealist whose heart and soul were bent upon social reform and the betterment of the people. He caught up others in the wave of his enthusiasm and carried them with him, whether they saw eye to eye with him or not. Alas, that a long and painful illness should have ended that valuable life—far too soon, as we poor mortals think ! CHAPTER XI.

Julian Sturgis, neither politician nor sportsman, enjoyed a little mild hunting one winter at Aston Clinton, and gave us much of his pleasant cultured society ; he was a good talker, and entered with zest into the pencil games then in vogue. Together with Frederic Myers, Edmund Gurney, and others, we composed sonnets, wrote questions and answers in verse, tried our hand at essays or stories in imitation of the style of known authors, and indulged in a variety of such-like amusements.

Mr. Myers had been for years an intimate friend of Cyril's, whom he had known at Cambridge, and for whose talents my husband had very great admiration. A poet when we first knew him, as the years went on he became an ardent Spiritualist, and one of the first members of the Society for Psychical Research. As a youth deeply moved and inspired by Mrs. Josephine Butler, he had been one of her most enthusiastic followers. It was then that he wrote his poem " St. Paul," which brought him instant recognition, and opened the way to the future favourable reception of his writings. I felt that both in his essays and poems the flow of words might almost overpower the ideas, but there occur very many fine and inspiring passages in his prose and verse. I remember being specially attracted by his *Wordsworth*, a book that appeared in the series of English Men of Letters edited by John Morley. Frederic Myers was a true lover of the poet, and very beautiful is this little eulogistic study from his pen.

Edmund Gurney and his wife were frequent guests of ours. We had first made their acquaintance at Pontresina in 1878, and had been much struck by the very able and original mind of Mr. Gurney and by the beauty and charm of his young wife. He was a musician *manqué*, who, after giving much time ,and thought to becoming a pianist, was told that he never could surmount the technical difficulties that the instrument offered. This made him very unhappy for a time, and he might possibly, had he sought other advice, have been encouraged to continue on the path he had chosen. But he submitted, and his pen came to the rescue. It was a serious pen, and he wrote seriously upon the theory of music in connection with the happiness of human life ; then being infected by the enthusiasm of his friends, Mr. Myers and Mr. Sidgwick, he gave himself unreservedly to the problems of psychical research, that perplexing and elusive subject, and devoted his time, his pen, and alas ! his strength, to that which seemed always evading his grasp. It was a sad ending to what had promised to be a fine career, for Edmund Gurney was one of the elect, both in mind and character ; those who knew him well admired and loved him. His wife had to encounter many dark days, also hours of unavoidable loneliness, in spite of which her devotion to her husband never flagged. She became on her second marriage the wife of Archibald Grove, who after some years of good journalistic work died in 1920 at the close of a long and painful illness.

Cyril's political friends would often come down for a week-end to Aston Clinton. I remember entertaining Sir William Harcourt, full of interesting and engaging talk ; with his fine memory for historical events and his racy anecdotes, he was indeed a much-coveted guest. I believe he could be severe and alarming, but to us he was always pleasant, and even forgave me upon one occasion at Surrey House when I forgot that he was a Privy

Councillor and sent him down to dinner in wrong
precedence.

I recall one morning in the smoking-room at Aston Clinton when he discoursed to me in a way that betrayed the Tory element in his character—he was really an aristocrat of the aristocrats, and would never have acquiesced in the politics of the present-day Liberals. We had known and loved Lady Harcourt, his second wife, as Lily Motley, daughter of the great American author and Ambassador to our Court, John Lothrop Motley, and have always been on terms of the most cordial friendship with her.

Lord Tweedmouth, as the Whip, Edward Marjoribanks, would often come and stay with us ; he was *persona grata* to Cyril, which I quite understood, but I was more attracted by his wife Fanny, daughter of the Duke of Marlborough, whose extraordinarily fine qualities greatly appealed to me.

Arnold Morley was another guest, an ardent Gladstonian, not particularly clever or fascinating, but quite pleasant-looking and pleasant-spoken, and very true to his colours.

Although Herbert Gladstone (the present Viscount Gladstone) spent a whole season with us in London, I cannot remember any special event connected with his visit ; we also entertained him several times at Aston Clinton. He was very good-looking as a young man, with quiet, easy manners, and is well known to all his friends as a most delightful letter-writer.

Lord Haldane came frequently to our Buckinghamshire home, where he would indulge in plentiful gossip that he called " biography." But it would be absurd to associate his name with the word " gossip," for he is one of the most remarkable men that it has been my good fortune to know, and the pleasing recollection of some interesting talks with him occurs to my mind whilst writing these words. In re-reading a little volume of Addresses that he delivered earlier in the present century,

I have been struck anew by his wide and profound views upon education, in regard not only to elementary education but also to secondary schools and university teaching. He had been a student himself in his young years at Göttingen, and his mind was deeply imbued with the German thoroughness and with the true love of learning inherent in that nation. I was also much attracted by the last address in the same book—" A Plea for Tolerance." " In view," writes the author, " of the fact that the majority of our fellow-subjects in the empire are of different religions to our own, a wide outlook among those who rule is essential here as elsewhere." But that wide outlook does not prevent him from saying, when speaking of the conflict between Science and Religion : " And yet, the advances of the last quarter of a century notwithstanding, religion remains a power as great and as living as at any time in the world's history." [1]

Besides his fine intellectual gifts Lord Haldane has always shown much and unusual kindness of heart. He never forgets old friends, and has indeed, even at much inconvenience to himself, done many a gracious act to give others pleasure. He has a student's pale colouring, rather heavy lids, and eyes that speak of close and tiring study.

On one occasion Lord, or as he was then, Mr. Haldane, having expressed a wish to meet Mary Cholmondeley the authoress, we had an appreciative and select little party, including Mr. Asquith, to enable him to do so.

Sir Charles Dilke stayed once or twice at Aston Clinton; he was a brilliant man, who could make himself very agreeable, but I never felt quite at ease with him. His second wife was Mrs. Mark Pattison, whom I knew intimately both before and after her marriage to Sir Charles. She was a woman of some talent and of forcible character, who rather favoured a special daintiness in dress and appearance, more French

[1] *Education and Empire.*

than English. Married at a very early age to the Rector of Lincoln College, Oxford, the fine scholar, Mark Pattison, greatly her senior, who died in 1884, she took a prominent place in the social life of the University, and was surrounded by a circle of men who were broad in matters of religion and of politics. Owing to delicate health, and perhaps in order to escape from the tedium of College life, she was in the habit of spending the winter at Draguignan, a town in the south of France. There she did much literary work in connection with French sixteenth and seventeenth-century art, of which she was a recognised critic ; she was also a regular contributor to the *Athenaeum*. She was a very well-informed woman, a persevering worker, a good French scholar, with great conversational and epistolary power. I shall never forget seeing her when her second marriage was in prospect. In spite of her deep mourning she was in exuberant spirits and could hardly contain her joy. Her championship of her husband, Sir Charles Dilke, through the hard times he had to encounter, was very fine, and was deeply appreciated by him. " We had planned everything " (he wrote to me after her death) " for my going first, as, tho' she was never well, she had, we thought, longevity. She had promised me to live on and do all the things that now I have to do— so ill—which she would have done so well."

A trio of friends often came to stay with us both at Aston Clinton and at Overstrand, sometimes separately, sometimes together, during the 'nineties and later.

To begin with, there was Spencer Lyttelton, an elder brother of Alfred's, for some time secretary to his uncle, Mr. Gladstone, and always the intimate friend and companion of his daughter Mary. He was a most delightful friend, and equally pleasant when alone with us or in society ; very good-looking, with a fine face and genial smile, he had nevertheless rather a gruff, unsympathetic manner, and sometimes a curt, ungracious way of answering questions that bored him, though in reality he had a

P

very tender heart and fully appreciated the affection of his friends. Why in that marrying family he had never married remained a mystery to those who knew and cared for him, particularly as he was very happy in female society! I think he was too diffident about himself, and he may have feared comparisons with a younger and more attractive brother. Spencer was an omnivorous reader and a good critic of literature, also an enthusiast for music. For many years he was a member of the Bach Choir, and rarely missed attending the Triennial Festivals. He had been a persistent traveller all his life, starting off for South America or New Zealand as if merely for a trip to Scotland, and with his knowledge and fine taste proved a most delightful companion on foreign tours. He was well acquainted with all the great picture-galleries of the world, as well as with the cathedrals and architectural treasures of most countries. He often joined my sister in her yachting trips, and was always welcome on the *Garland*. Like all his family he had been a fine cricketer when young, and took enthusiastically to golf later in life. He was very agreeable in daily intercourse, but unsociable as far as his own home-life was concerned, and even his intimate friends were not bidden, summer or winter, to his rooms. In spite of his reserve he was a welcome guest wherever he went, and none deplored his death in the December of 1913 more deeply than my sister and myself.

Colonel Collins, or Arthur Collins as all his friends called him, having been on the staff of Lord Lorne when the latter was Governor-General of Canada, continued as equerry to Princess Louise upon their return to England, and this was when we first made his acquaintance. He was a kind, genial, sensible man, with a quiet, unobtrusive manner, bright and witty in conversation. We often met when I had the honour of accompanying H.R.H. to functions in London or the country. The Princess had, on some occasions, a happy disregard of the exigencies of time, and I can remember how once, after visiting a hospital, I was being warmly pressed to return to tea by H.R.H., and how Colonel Collins remarked that the next meal would be an eight o'clock dinner, certainly *not* tea. "Impossible!" said the Princess. But my exhausted condition made me feel that the Colonel was right.

Colonel Collins was very fond of theatricals ; himself a good actor and first-rate stage-manager, he was proud at having been instrumental in getting up performances for Queen Victoria on several occasions, and in arranging matters for the actors and actresses who were summoned to the Royal residences. He and Alick Yorke found themselves on common ground there and worked in much sympathy when thus engaged.

I should like to record here the true kindness of heart and excellent judgment shown by Colonel Collins in his charitable work. He was deeply interested in the welfare of poor boys, taking a prominent part in the management of a club founded for their education and recreation, and being most successful in his dealings with them. The last years of his life were shadowed by much suffering, caused by an incurable illness borne with great patience and heroism.

The third of that trio of friends was Sir Algernon West, G.C.B., who was always a sincere and ardent supporter of Liberalism as it was known and practised in the days of Queen Victoria. A direct descendant from Sir Robert Walpole, he married a grand-daughter of the great Prime Minister, Lord Grey, was private secretary to Mr. Gladstone during the most wonderful years of his career, and Chairman of the Board of Inland Revenue. Sir Algernon West had been acquainted with all that was most attractive and interesting in the political and social world. His *Recollections* are very pleasant reading, giving us valuable pictures of an age that was distinguished not alone for talent and learning, but also for fine manners and gracious bearing ; indeed, for these last Sir Algernon West might well have served as model. "Sir Algy," as he was affectionately called by his friends, had always been a strict observer of proper and dignified etiquette. He was scrupulous in his dress and speech. Thus he marked his respect for the Army and Navy by using the word " sir " when in conversation with officers in uniform. Unlike many of the men of the present day he appeared in a black suit on Sunday mornings, and, whether in London or the country, was a regular attendant at church—not that sermons, even when preached by celebrated men, often attracted him, but he clung to the beautiful old words of the Bible and Prayer-book; he loved the old well-trodden ways, objecting to the many strange paths deviating from them. All his life he had been a devotee of Tennyson's poetry and of Thackeray's prose, and usually he had beside him some work by those fine Victorian writers, now so sadly neglected. He had a striking face and figure, and was a noble representative of the English gentleman. He passed away on March 21, 1921.

George Russell, son of Lord Charles Russell, and nephew of Lord John Russell the Prime Minister (1846), was an acquaintance of ours from the early 'eighties. As years went by he became an intimate and a well-beloved friend. He first came into our vision in April of the year 1880, when after a strenuous contest he was returned at the General Election as one of the two Liberal members for the Borough of Aylesbury, the other being my cousin Nathaniel de Rothschild. We had heard of George Russell in appreciative terms before then from Matthew Arnold, who had known him well from boyhood, and also from my brilliant cousin, Leonard Montefiore, his friend of University days, with whose Radical principles he was in sympathy, and we ought, under those conditions, to have given him a cordial welcome; but we were not at all forthcoming. His Election Speech did not attract us, and we were told and cautioned that his candidature would greatly imperil my cousin's chances ; at that time it was considered very doubtful that two Liberals could be returned for Aylesbury. But the young and daring aspirant for political honours went gaily on his way, proving successful in the end, and the Aylesbury constituency was duly represented in Parliament by two Liberal members.

In the last of Mr. Russell's literary works, published in 1918, I read the following :

The General Election of 1880 was, as nearly as our constitutional forms admit, a plebiscite on Foreign Policy, but to many a man who was then beginning public life the emancipation of the labourer was an object quite as dear as the dethronement of Lord Beaconsfield. It was not for nothing that he had read *Hodge and his Masters*, and we were resolved that henceforward "Hodge" should be not a serf or a cipher, but a free man and a self-governing citizen.

And this, I think, might be taken as the mainspring of Mr. Russell's political work. He was a convinced and thoroughgoing Liberal, and also a devoted follower of Mr. Gladstone.

George Russell was our frequent guest at Aston Clinton in the 'nineties, but he was never strong, and as the years went by he became a valetudinarian, and declared that he could not sleep unless in his own bed and under his own roof ; so he declined all country-house invitations. When with those who appreciated his company, and who were sympathetic to him, he could be the most delightful and entertaining of companions, and he was much sought after by hostesses who cared for a lively guest with a brilliant gift for conversation.

It is always very difficult to reproduce witty sayings, but I recollect that upon one occasion, when we were entertaining at Aston Clinton some noteworthy members of the House of Commons, amongst whom were aspirants to high political rank, Mr. Russell, turning to my mother, said, " I hope you have ordered Cabinet Pudding for dinner ! "

His comprehensive reading, his wonderful and accurate memory, and his taste for the best literature, with no distaste for gossip, made him as pleasant in society as he was *en tête-à-tête*. But he had, unluckily, a caustic tongue and a bitter pen ; he could not refrain from saying and from writing words that stung, and that often proved a terrible trial to the true and sincere friends he had gathered around him. Perhaps it was his delicate health as a youth, and also the fact of his lameness, which prevented him from taking his part in athletic and bracing sports and games, that caused him to be somewhat exacting and irritable ; he could not throw off worries as others could do by violent exercise and open-air pursuits, and this irritability of temper occasioned him, unfortunately, the loss of some friends. He himself wrote to me once, in an outburst of penitence, that his horrible temper had been the enemy of his life. Yet, in spite of all, he was blessed with some very devoted friends, and in return showed his devotion to them in many pleasant ways—for instance, the constant flow of amusing notes and letters in prose and in verse that came to them from his facile pen. His affectionate attention to a sick, ailing, or unhappy friend was quite beautiful, and his goodness of heart manifested itself in many an unexpected manner. In one of his bright little essays on Charles Dickens he writes : " Like all good men and great writers, Dickens had a friendly feeling towards food and drink " ; the same might have been said of George Russell, who was a decided *gourmet* and *gourmand*, and much appreciated the good things of the table. How he looked forward to the baskets of grapes and peaches that found their way from Aston Clinton to Wilton Street ! and many a funny and telling word of thanks came in return for these gifts.

I copy out one as a sample, written in 1887 and

addressed to my mother, Lady de Rothschild, and
myself :

> One in the unison of heart and heart,
> One in the joy your gentle lives impart,
> One in the equal love of fervent friends,
> One in all gracious deeds and worthy ends,
> Share, kindly souls, the thanks of him you feed,
> A friend in truth—perchance a friend in need,
> Who hails, as choicest boon of favouring fate,
> The sweet soft grace of charming chocolate.
> His frugal feast the dulcet dainties crown
> Like " Olga " [1] richly stuffed, like " Olga " russet brown.

George Russell had a fine gift of humour; it irradiated his conversation and his epistolary style. It never had a shadow of coarseness or irreverence, and, in spite of some occasional touches of bitterness or of irony, it had a very wholesome and manly tone. His respect for and attachment to the teachings of the advanced Church party (he was a devoted friend of Canon Scott Holland and Father Stanton) were not out of harmony with his keen sense of humour and enjoyment of pure fun. I feel that I cannot do better than close with the following lines by James Rhoades, which Mr. Russell quoted in the charming essay he wrote on Charles Dickens :

> Has he gone to a land of no laughter,
> The man who made mirth for us all ?
> Proves Death but a silent hereafter
> Where the echoes of Earth cannot fall?
>
> .   .   .   .
>
> Nay, if aught be sure, naught can be surer
> Than that earth's good decays not with earth,
> And of all the heart's springs none are purer
> Than the springs of the fountain of mirth.

Looking through the pages of an old and time-honoured visitors' book—always a trying and heart-stirring experience—the names of relatives, friends, and

[1] " Olga," a favourite dog—a little brown dachshund—belonging to my mother.

acquaintances, recurring as they often do in such a
volume, year after year, is like opening a window into
the past which reveals more than the mere signatures
would imply. I have copied a few, a very few of such
names, and would linger for a short space of time over
them—portraits I would call them, painted, as it were,
with ghostly brushes, and bringing back many precious
memories. The visitors' book stretches over a number
of years, from the 'sixties to the present date, and bears
witness to a varied selection of guests during so long a
period.

The name of Lyndhurst carries me back a number
of years. It gives me a thrill to remember that I have
seen and spoken with its distinguished bearer, whose
birth occurred in 1772. I can still see an old gentleman (very, very old he seemed to me then) in our
drawing-room at Grosvenor Place, seated there one
evening in a wheeled chair; it was on the occasion of a
dinner-party given by my parents, when my father
took me up and presented me to him. But Lord Lyndhurst never came to Aston Clinton. It was there, however, that his second wife came, a wonderful little old
lady, a very original personality, with her daughter,
Georgie Copley, now Lady Du Cane, a lively and
brilliant young girl, the intimate friend of my cousin,
Evelina de Rothschild. Georgie loved hunting and
dancing and acting and all the delights that this world
can afford; besides her social gifts she had great mental
power and a keen sense of enjoyment of intellectual
pursuits. She married Sir Charles Du Cane, at one
time Governor of Tasmania.

A dear old friend of the early days was George
Goldsmid, a man whose kind heart and genial manner
endeared him to many different kinds of human beings.
He was generous without ostentation, and always ready
to help any one in moral or physical distress. I
remember the wonderful assistance he gave us at our
Halton Exhibition, and how, to soothe the feelings of

an unfortunate exhibitor, who could not sell the piece
of furniture on which he had expended both time and
money, Mr. Goldsmid promised to take the matter into
his own hands and to raffle the *pièce de résistance*.
The object was sold, and well sold, but at the end of the
day we heard that Mr. Goldsmid had purchased nearly
all the lottery tickets himself. The people in our village
were devoted to him, he was an immense favourite in
our schools, and there was not a man on the estate nor
a servant in our household who would not willingly have
worked for him.

The visits of Sir George Trevelyan, politician and
author, nephew of the great Macaulay, were much appreciated by my dear mother and by ourselves; he was as
pleasant a companion as he was a fine writer; his
memory was excellent and his literary taste exceptional;
he cared much for pictures and natural scenery, and had
withal a simple homely way about him, which I found
very attractive.

I first saw George Trevelyan as a successful Cambridge
undergraduate, then as a politician—an ardent Liberal
and loyal Gladstonian, but later differing on the Home
Rule question from his great leader. The next time that
I met him he had joined the Chamberlain group, never
feeling very happy, however, in his somewhat uncon-
genial surroundings. In fact, it was not long before he
reverted to his former allegiance. I can still remember
a certain Sunday at Aston Clinton when, after a long
and earnest talk with Cyril and other Liberal friends,
George Trevelyan showed decided signs of unrest, and
soon afterwards we were told of his second *volte-face*.
My sister and I would point, years afterwards, to the sofa
where he and Cyril had sat that evening, calling it " the
field of battle " where our guest had been reconquered.

Of course it would be quite impossible for me to
attempt to give any complete or consecutive account of
the many guests who have passed through the doors of
our Buckinghamshire home during the years when first

our parents, and then my husband and I, gathered friends and acquaintances about us.

One figure is very distinct: that of Frances Balfour, now the widow of Eustace, a younger brother of Arthur Balfour. Daughter of the eighth Duke of Argyll, and personally resembling her distinguished father in her fair colouring and in the charm of her voice, I have always held her to be a remarkable woman. A telling speaker and a brilliant writer, she championed the cause of women's emancipation from an early day, and was a strong upholder of Mrs. Fawcett and her views, although opposed to the actions of the extreme suffragettes. Her sense of humour is very keen and adds a point to her speeches, whilst a somewhat combative disposition makes her enjoy a tussle of words. She excels in impromptu orations, is quick in argument and telling in retort, but she never descends to flippancy in order to be witty, nor is she ever superficial in her speeches, and one is always cognisant in hearing or in reading them of her strong religious belief, the foundation on which her work is built. She takes the deepest interest in all that goes on around her, living very fully in the present. She has the most remarkable pluck and force of will, which enables her to control bodily fatigue and discomfort, and to dispense, if need be, with many of the amenities of life. She is a very staunch friend, but her friendship never obscures her critical faculties. She is an unmistakable little personage, with her own peculiar style of attractive head-dress, copied from a picture of one of the Stuart princesses, which is becoming and characteristic.

Connected with her by marriage are Mr. Gerald and Lady Betty Balfour, both close friends of my husband and myself—as original, interesting, and delightful a couple as one can ever hope to entertain. They seem, however, to belong more exclusively to the Overstrand than to the Aston Clinton parties, and their names will occur again in connection with my Norfolk home.

Canon and Mrs. Barnett, a very remarkable couple,
have been guests of my mother's, and in the very
vivid Life of the Canon, edited and written by his wife,
that appeared in 1921, I note the following sentence from
his diary :

Drove over to Aston Clinton from Aylesbury, called upon
Lady de Rothschild—a very beautiful old lady.

I first made the acquaintance of Mrs. Barnett, then
a young and always a very lively personage, when we
were both on the Committee of the Metropolitan Association for Befriending Young Servants, in 1879. Mrs.
Barnett has an original mind and an original way of
expressing herself that might startle and even repel
some conventional people, but she is a remarkable
woman, and the work she has accomplished is extraordinary. The Canon was to me a most inspiring character, and I learnt much from him. He not only worked
for the people, the poorest and the most abject, but
he and his wife lived amongst them, and through their
influence many great movements have been set on foot,
and a thorough revolution in poor-law relief effected.
It was an education to be with Canon Barnett and to
hear him discuss big questions, although I could not
always agree with his views, and thought him occasionally
unfair to the more fortunate classes. I was, however,
greatly impressed by his spirit of religious tolerance to
all creeds, also by his desire to bring a sense of beauty
and refinement into his church and services, making
them attractive to those who only associated a day of
rest with an absence of life in the streets and abundant
potations of spirits and beer. In spite of some disappointments in his uphill work, he maintained a uniformly
cheerful disposition, and looked hopefully to the future
when many others despaired.

It was Canon Barnett who started the Toynbee
Hall Settlement in Whitechapel, of which he was the
first Warden. This Settlement is the centre of very

important educational and social work, and deserves the success it has attained. On one of the occasions when I was visiting him and his wife in the East End, and had to undergo a fire of rather violent criticism upon my outlook on life and daily occupations, I remarked to a friend later that " on all social reforms the Canon had depressed me and Mrs. Barnett had irritated me "— which criticism, being repeated to them, was often referred to with much hilarity.

It was owing to the Canon and Mrs. Barnett's efforts that the Whitechapel Art Gallery came into existence, where a very creditable collection of pictures is yearly exhibited to a large concourse of appreciative visitors.

Mrs. Barnett will long be remembered for her earnest work as a Poor Law Guardian, but principally as the originator of the Hampstead Garden Suburb, which very successful scheme is already serving as the model for other similar enterprises. Both Canon Barnett and his wife, in the undaunted courage with which they attacked many almost insoluble problems, seemed to have taken for their life's motto : " Where there is no vision, the people perish."

Sir Edward Hamilton, son of the then Bishop of Salisbury, private secretary for many years to Mr. Gladstone, and later Secretary to the Treasury, came for the first time to Aston Clinton, young and practically unknown. He was devoted to music ; I can remember playing duets with him in those days and thinking him kind and amiable, but with no very special characteristics. He was much liked by those with whom he worked in later life, and had a galaxy of friends, including my husband and myself, who deplored his last sad and long illness and his passing away before the appointed term of man's life.

Augustus Hare and Hamilton Aïdé, never seen together, but both somewhat similar in tastes and occupations, visited Aston Clinton from time to time. They were both writers, they both cared for society, they CHAPTER both had many friends and acquaintances in artistic, XI. literary, and fashionable circles; they could both paint with the brush as well as with the pen, and both made some clever sketches whilst they were our guests. They had both travelled somewhat extensively in Europe. Hamilton Aïdé was partly Greek, Augustus Hare had spent a great part of his youth in Rome, and they both had many friends in foreign capitals. Mr. Aïdé was an excellent French scholar, and liked receiving French writers in his rooms in London (it was there that I met the French novelist, Bourget). He had an attractive singing voice when young, and wrote the words of many songs which have been successfully set to music. Augustus Hare is well known by his admirable volumes, *Walks in London, Walks in Rome*; also by his biographical works, *The Gurneys of Earlham, The Lives of Two Sisters* (Lady Waterford and Lady Canning), but principally by *Memorials of a Quiet Life*—a beautiful account of the writer's kinswoman who had adopted him, and to whom he was devotedly attached. In speaking Augustus Hare had a very peculiar screeching voice in which he would occasionally tell ghost stories and other thrilling tales, whilst Hamilton Aïdé had rather a finicky *précieux* manner of speech, more like a woman's than a man's. However, both were very pleasant visitors and I enjoyed entertaining them.

Frederick Locker, another well-known writer of elegant verse and prose, was a dear friend and guest in both our country houses. His wife, Jane, daughter of Sir Curtis Lampson, was in some ways the very opposite of her husband, but she provided him with the happiest of homes. He was a widower with one daughter when she married him. She presented him with a family of two sons and two daughters, and also with a picturesque estate, "Rowfant" in Sussex, which she inherited from her father. Mrs. Locker-Lampson's name was immortalised in her own visitors' book, for a friend inscribed the following two lines, which she good-naturedly accepted as they were meant :

> As Delilah was to Samson,
> So is Jane to Locker-Lampson.

But she was a very generous, warm-hearted " Delilah," and " Samson " was, indeed, quite happy in his choice.

Mr. Locker's first wife was Lady Charlotte Bruce, and their daughter married, when very young, the second son of the Poet Laureate, Lionel Tennyson, after whose death she became the wife of Augustine Birrell. My husband and I were both intimate friends of the Lockers, and I am glad to say that the friendship continues to this generation. The two sons have what may be considered the unusual honour of both representing constituencies in the House of Commons (1922).

Frances Power Cobbe, who for many years had been one of my most honoured friends, spent some pleasant days with us at Aston Clinton, and greatly interested my mother by her originality and brilliant conversation. Her somewhat grotesque figure, surmounted by a fine intellectual head, made her a remarkable personality, one who could never have passed anywhere unnoticed. She brought her fine mental powers during the early years of her life to bear upon the religious controversies of the day, she herself emerging from a somewhat narrow Protestantism into Unitarianism, being much under the influence of Dr. Martineau, landing finally in a devout and very spiritual Theism. Writing, as she generally did, in passionate support of the redress of some social injustice, she devoted her very forcible and brilliant pen, first to the betterment of the laws as they affected women and children and those dependent upon charity, and then to combating the practice of vivisection by the medical profession. As the recognised leader of the Anti-Vivisection campaign, she encountered the hostility of men of science and of learning ; on the other hand she claimed as friends and coadjutors such personalities as Lord Coleridge, Archdeacon Wilberforce, Lord Shaftes-

bury, and Cardinal Manning. Strange co-workers,
united in thought and in action on this one point, who
would probably never have met under other conditions,
but who learned to appreciate and respect one another
whilst fighting an arduous and often a losing battle!

Naturally, the strength and depth of Miss Cobbe's
feelings led to a certain amount of intolerance in her
views, but in private life this intolerance disappeared
under a pleasing manner engendered by good temper
and a keen sense of humour.

Amongst the visitors to Aston Clinton I must make
mention of some gifted musicians : thus one very remarkable Sunday in 1873 stands out pre-eminently in
my memory, when Joachim, the great violinist, Piatti,
the brilliant Italian 'cellist, and their friend Zerbini gave
us a never-to-be-forgotten musical treat. We made fast
friends with the two first-named musicians, both masters
of their separate instruments, and distinguished for their
intellectual gifts. Joachim had a very searching and
thoughtful mind ; in all things he was great : straightforward, direct, severe, simple, the very best type of the
German grafted on to a Semitic stock. Piatti was a
thoroughgoing Italian, with a genuine love for art in all
its expressions : music, painting, sculpture, literature ;
he was more playful, less uncompromising than Joachim,
but they were both admirable performers. On another
occasion we were given a fine rendering of Spohr's duet
for two violins, Madame Norman Neruda being first
violin to Joachim as second. The interest of the
evening was enhanced by the presence of a very enthusiastic guest, Lord Chief Justice Cockburn, whose
beaming countenance and frequent applause testified
to his delight in good music.

We had other most interesting performances with
Sir Charles Hallé and Anna Molique at the piano, all
the artists who came to stay with us being on the
friendliest terms with one another.

The Duke of Edinburgh, then in all the glow of

youth and good spirits, brought his own beautiful violin when he was our guest, and his accompanist was Sir Arthur Sullivan, that genial composer of both light and serious music.

Those were delightful days and evenings at our Aston Clinton home, which, in its comfort and comparative simplicity, extended a cheery welcome to such honoured visitors, making a bright setting to their performances. But there were others, known and unknown to fame, whose names, as I see them in the visitors' book, recall many little incidents, some sad, some gay or humorous, but all pathetic, for do they not speak of those now passed from this world, who once combined in making it precious and fragrant to my sister and myself?

Beautiful women, clever men, kindly souls, affectionate friendly hearts, do you not all come trooping back when memory's cells are unlocked?   Were you not all at your very best under the genial, sunny welcome of my parents, and was it not the case that " evil speaking, lying and slandering, vulgar gossip and malicious tittle-tattle, could not live in the presence of my mother"? At least so wrote the late G. W. E. Russell, in some unforgettable words penned after her death.

The hospitality offered at Aston Clinton was not narrowed by artificial boundaries, such as those of race, nation, creed, or politics, and yet it had its own individual colouring, a colouring that seems almost to have faded away with the outgoing years of the last century.

CHAPTER XII

Party is the madness of the many for the gain of the few.—SWIFT.

IN what is called the "Book Room" of The Pleasaunce,
Overstrand, situated at the top of the house, there is a
collection of engravings, each one the portrait of one of
England's Prime Ministers, starting from Sir Robert
Walpole, 1715. This collection was made with very
great care by my husband, and I used to amuse him by
saying that sitting in that room was as good as having
a lesson in English history. It was further made more
interesting to me by the fact that I had known some
of the originals, and could even claim a few as my
personal friends.

As a very young child I was once walking with my
father in the Park, when he suddenly stopped, raised
his hat, and said, "Look well at that gentleman riding
on that white horse." I also remember hearing some
one call out at the same time, "There goes the great
Duke of Wellington." He had been Prime Minister
from 1828 to 1830, and again for a few months in 1834.
When I looked up I saw an old gentleman riding towards
us. I noticed his somewhat stern expression, his rather
narrow face, his hooked nose, his white beaver top-hat,
also that he returned the many salutes that greeted him

without a smile. I never saw him again, but I never forgot that little incident.

When I first came out and made my appearance in London society, it was the fashion for the Prime Minister and his wife—Lord and Lady Palmerston—to hold receptions every Saturday evening during the months when the Houses of Parliament were sitting. As I have already said, there were but few week-end country - house parties in those days, and Saturday evening being a free evening for the members of the Houses of Lords and Commons, it was the most convenient one in the week for those reunions.

They were held in Cambridge House, Piccadilly, now the Naval and Military Club. The house stands opposite to the Green Park, on rising ground, with an entrance leading through great iron gates into a courtyard and up to the front door. On those reception nights it was the fashion for a head coachman, in his wig, generally a man of stout and imposing presence, to stand near the door of the front hall; somewhat in his rear were two or more powdered footmen in very smart liveries, whilst again behind them black-coated servants with gracious manners were pointing the way to the cloak-room, and finally a functionary was visible on the stairs announcing in a clear and distinct voice each arrival by name to the patient hostess standing at the entrance of one of the drawing-rooms, receiving her guests.

In some of our great houses (that are, alas! rapidly changing owners) there are very beautiful staircases of fine and noble proportions, and the sight of the ascending and descending figures in brilliant dress with dazzling jewels often suggested to me a picture by Paolo Veronese.

There was no very marked social cleavage between Whigs and Tories in those days, although, politically, much bitter opposition. Thus the great Whig families of Devonshire and Lansdowne were of equal standing with those of Richmond or of Derby. The heads of both were generally large landed proprietors, carrying politic- ally as well as socially vast weight in their respective counties. They had had from childhood much the same sort of environment ; their sons were educated at the same schools and universities, which they left to enter the Army or Navy. A snug family living was generally kept warm for a younger son, who often found himself ministering in one of the villages where he had been known from infancy. The junior members of aristocratic families were hardly beginning in those days to add to their frequently modest incomes by taking up trade or business connections. I can remember when it was thought extraordinary for a duke's son to become a tea merchant, or for an earl's brother to go on the Stock Exchange !

To return to Cambridge House. Up the stairs we went to be received by Lady Palmerston, then an old lady, once a very fascinating woman, always a distinguished one. She was sister to the celebrated Prime Minister, Lord Melbourne, and widow of Lord Cowper. Gossip, in days gone by, had been free with her name, but I was ignorant of such tales, and only looked with a certain amount of awe upon the wife of the popular Prime Minister.

Lord Palmerston was pointed out to me by my father, and I had the honour of having three of his finger-tips extended to me. The rooms *en suite* were thronged with guests : old and young, distinguished or more or less commonplace, and members of embassies and legations, with a sprinkling of foreign visitors, who had brought their credentials to our genial Prime Minister, once Secretary of State for Foreign Affairs.

Lord Palmerston, although not a favourite at our Court, was very popular in the country, largely owing to his love of sport. He certainly understood the temper of the English people. I fear I was too young and too ignorant in those days to take an intelligent

interest in home or foreign politics ; to me the parties
at Cambridge House were attractive as brilliant social
gatherings, where I first saw the distinguished men
and women whose names were fairly familiar to my
ears, and where I was certain to meet acquaintances
and friends of the ball-room.

My parents were well acquainted with Lord John
Russell, third son of the sixth Duke of Bedford, and
raised to the peerage as Earl Russell in 1861—often
spoken of as " Johnny Russell." He was Prime
Minister for the second time in 1865, after the death
of Lord Palmerston, but only for the period of one
short year. Although I knew Lord John Russell well
by sight, I cannot recollect ever having spoken to him,
but his name was always mentioned with great regard
by my mother and with gratitude by my father for
the timely services he rendered to my uncle, Lionel de
Rothschild, when the latter was standing as M.P. for
the City of London in the 'fifties.

Our old friend, George Russell, would frequently talk
to me of his famous uncle, and spoke of his wife, Lady
Russell (an Elliot of the house of Minto by birth), as
one who had been the good angel of her husband's home
for thirty-five years.

A curious and arresting figure, and one that loomed
largely in our young lives, was that of Benjamin Disraeli.[1]
I cannot exactly recall when he first appeared on my
horizon, for he seemed always to have been a friend of
my parents, and with his most original wife was one of
our constant visitors at Grosvenor Place. He had known
my mother and her sister from old days, when as girls
they were living at home with my grandmother in their
Stanhope Street house. I believe they were not a little

---

[1] In order to avoid confusion of names, I will keep to the form of
Mr. and Mrs. Disraeli in these Reminiscences, merely noting that in
the year 1868 the title of Viscountess Beaconsfield was conferred upon
Mrs. Disraeli, her husband accepting that of the Earldom later, in 1876,
when he left the Commons.

amused by Mr. Disraeli's very unusual appearance and CHAPTER
dress, and greatly attracted by his dazzling powers of XII.
conversation, pointed by witty sallies and brilliant nonsense.   In all that he thought, spoke, and wrote there
was an Oriental touch which added to his peculiar
charm.   His pale olive skin, his dark, lustrous, flashing
eyes, and his jet-black curling hair, in his younger years,
proclaimed him to be of Eastern race.   And, indeed, he
was very different from those with whom it was becoming his lot to associate and to work, against whom
he would often have to fight, and upon whom he was
finally to impose the full strength of his will, obtaining
from them undoubted, if perhaps reluctant, respect and
admiration.   From Lady Dufferin's pen we have the
following account of Mr. Disraeli in the year 1832, as
having worn

a black velvet coat lined with satin . . . purple trousers,
with a gold band running down the outside seam, a scarlet
waistcoat and long lace ruffles, falling down to the tips of
his fingers, white gloves with several brilliant rings outside
them, and long black ringlets rippling down upon his
shoulders.

From 1837 Mr. Disraeli seems to have been accepted
as a friend by members of my family on both sides.   I
know that he frequently dined at my grandmother's
(Mrs. Montefiore's) house in Great Stanhope Street—one
of those dinner-parties, at which both Mr. Disraeli and
Mrs. Wyndham Lewis were guests, proving quite historic.
Their engagement had not yet been announced, and
my mother and her sister were quick to remark the
little intimate nods and smiles interchanged by the
two friends sitting on opposite sides of the table, and
the way they drank to one another's health as they
raised their wine-glasses to their lips.   To these young
girls Mr. Disraeli had been a joyous, fantastic, captivat-
ing acquaintance, whilst to them Mrs. Wyndham Lewis
looked and seemed very much older than the man to

whom she was about to give the unquestioning devotion
of her life; quite elderly in fact, and quite unfit for the
post she was about to fill. They thought they were
merely witnessing an amusing flirtation. When they
were told of the engagement on the morrow, their surprise was boundless. Can we not hear them saying,
"What! that old woman and our brilliant friend? Impossible!"? Perhaps they would have agreed with a
sentence taken from an analysis of husband and wife,
in a curious MS. by Mrs. Disraeli, which, according to
Messrs. Monypenny and Buckle, is still in existence, in
which she writes: "He is a genius—she is a dunce"
(which she was not).

Mr. Disraeli had been Mr. Wyndham Lewis's colleague
in the Parliamentary representation of Maidstone, and
after meeting Mrs. Wyndham Lewis for the first time, he
alluded to her in a letter as "a pretty little flirt and
rattle." In 1837 Mrs. Wyndham Lewis, as she was then,
wrote to her brother:

Mark what I say—mark what I prophesy: Mr. Disraeli
will in a very few years be one of the greatest men of his
day. His great talents, backed by his friends Lord Lyndhurst and Lord Chandos, with Wyndham's power to keep
him in Parliament, will ensure his success. They call him
my Parliamentary *protégé*.[1]

On August 27, 1839, Mr. Disraeli and Mrs. Wyndham
Lewis were married. In December of the same year he
writes to Sarah, his sister and constant correspondent:
"Last week we dined *en famille* with Mrs. Montefiore,
to meet Anthony Rothschild, who is to marry one of the
Montefiores." (That was my mother.)

In time Mrs. Disraeli became a very true friend
of my dear mother's, and I recollect that on busy
political nights, when Mr. Disraeli could not leave the
House of Commons, "Mrs. Dizzy," as we all called her,
would come and spend the evening with us at Grosvenor

[1] Monypenny and Buckle.

Place, particularly on nights when it was the fashion for
my mother and my grandmother to indulge in " high
tea " (a meal to which we children were sometimes
admitted) instead of the conventional dinner.   This requires explanation.

The foreign post in the 'forties and 'fifties came into
London at a later hour on Tuesdays and on Fridays,
and it had always been my father's custom to remain
at New Court (the banking house of his firm) in order
to receive and open letters that arrived from foreign
relatives ; thus he was seldom home on those occasions
before nine o'clock, having dined previously at his office
in the City.   So the more solemn meal was dispensed
with at Grosvenor Place, and at the cheery tea-table
we constantly found Mrs. Dizzy, in her high afternoon
frock, with her smart Victorian headgear, loquaciously
vivacious, talking without pause of her beloved " Dizzy "
and of his social success.   Of politics she used to declare
she knew nothing.

Over and over again Mr. Disraeli mentions members
of my family by name in his letters and diaries.   Although
he had never belonged to the Jewish Community in
practice, for he had been baptized as a boy, he had a
true and profound feeling for his own race, and some of
the finest passages in his novels give very marked expression to those sentiments.   From the first he was deeply
interested in the removal of the civil and political disabilities of the Jews, and foremost in supporting the
Bill which was to abolish the words of the Oath that
prevented a Jew from taking his seat in the House of
Commons.

Mr. Disraeli was constantly voting against his party
on those occasions.   It was Spencer Walpole who once
rose in the House to defend Mr. Disraeli's fine con-
sistency when dealing with this subject, although he,
Walpole, was opposed to the repeal of the Bill.   He
said : " If there is one thing more than another for
which my right honourable friend is entitled to the

respect of both sides of the House, it is for the manly and honourable way in which he has come forward in support of the Jewish race." This was a fine testimony from an opponent. And many long years afterwards, when Disraeli was recognised as one of the greatest politicians of the age, he said to my cousin, Leonard Montefiore, then upon the threshold of an anticipated political career, " You and I belong to a race which can do everything but fail."

Mr. Disraeli was supposed in his character of " Eva " in *Tancred* to have portrayed my aunt, Baroness Lionel de Rothschild. He was also supposed, in describing some scenes in his later novels, *Lothair* and *Endymion*, to have been influenced by old impressions of the Gunnersbury Park he had known so well, and of those who had peopled it.

Meanwhile Mr. Disraeli had become the fast friend of my uncle, Lionel de Rothschild, and this although they followed opposed Leaders in the House of Commons. But my uncle was far from being an advanced Liberal, nor could Mr. Disraeli have been ranked amongst the old-fashioned Tories. Besides which, his intense pride of race brought him into close and intimate touch with my family. He always maintained that Christianity was completed Judaism, and believed more in the compelling power of a common ancestry than in that of a common faith. He said to me, as he has said over and over again in his novels, " All is race, not religion— remember that."

Mr. Disraeli was a great admirer of my dear mother, as, indeed, who that knew her well was not ? I remember one special Sunday afternoon, when, walking with my mother and sister in the Park, we met Mr. and Mrs. Disraeli also on foot. We stopped first to greet one another, and then all continued walking on in the same direction, Mrs. Dizzy insisting upon her husband and my mother preceding us. With a gesture of approval, she said to us, " Don't they look nice together ? "

repeating this several times with relish. Dear, fond woman ! If foolish, and at times perhaps even ridiculous, she was a splendid wife ; one could smile at her absurdities and love her all the same, or all the better ; whilst one admired the temper and the gratitude of the man who was never ruffled by these same absurdities, ever grateful for the devotion that their perpetrator showed him. Mr. Disraeli knew what he owed her, and she never doubted this. On the night of one of his greatest triumphs, April 12, 1867, when he had made a brilliant speech on the Conservative Reform Bill that had given his Government a majority of 21, he was pressed to stay at the Carlton Club and sup with his cheering and enthusiastic supporters ; but, no ! he refused, returning to his wife, whom he would not disappoint on such an occasion, and who had a raised pie and champagne ready for him.

I remember Mrs. Disraeli telling my mother how she sat up for her husband, however late might be his return from the House, how she lighted up the rooms to receive him, and invariably gave him a hot supper !

We had the great pleasure of receiving Mr. and Mrs. Disraeli upon more than one occasion as our guests at Aston Clinton, one particular date standing out prominently in my memory. It was in May 1868, when Mr. Disraeli was Prime Minister, and the event that brought him to stay with us was no other than the opening of an Industrial Exhibition, held in the picturesque little village of Halton, in the old Manor House and grounds that had passed from the possession of the Dashwood family to that of my uncle, Lionel de Rothschild. This was one of the first of these Exhibitions, now so common in all the towns and many of the villages in the kingdom, but then a complete novelty, and as such producing a great stir and excitement in the Vale of Aylesbury.

We paid more than one visit to Hughenden Manor, the charming Buckinghamshire home of the Disraelis, about seventeen miles distant from Aston Clinton. There

were no motor-cars in those days, and a very inconvenient train service, but in a comfortable carriage, with
fleet horses, I remember how much we enjoyed that
drive on one perfect autumn day, skirting the beech
woods on the Chiltern Hills, leaving the historic seats of
Chequers and Hampden on our left, passing through the
growing and prosperous town of High Wycombe, and
finally making the slight ascent which brought us to
the gates of Hughenden. There we were affectionately
received by the great statesman, dressed as a country
squire, and by Mrs. Disraeli, both ready to do the
honours of their attractive home.

Hughenden is graphically described with a very
appreciative pen in the *Life of Benjamin Disraeli*, from
which I have already largely quoted. Our hosts showed
us with pride the beautiful woods in close proximity to
the garden, and that which they called the German
forest. There, with the help of two labourers, Mrs.
Disraeli had cut a number of cleverly planned walks
among the beeches, carefully trimming and felling the
trees in places, where views of yet more distant woods
or of the picturesque parts of the town of Wycombe
could be obtained. Over and over again " Dizzy "
bade us pause and admire the sylvan scene, as he expressed it, evidently relishing that sweet-sounding word
" sylvan." He lingered over it and repeated it more
than once. " And," he added, " this is all owing to the
cleverness of Mary Anne; she devised the walk, and she
made it with the help of her two old men of the soil."

How he loved the place! And how he tried to act
up to the character he had imposed upon himself, that
of the country gentleman! for, dressed in his velveteen
coat, his leather leggings, his soft felt hat, and carrying his little hatchet, for relieving the barks of trees
from the encroaching ivy, in one of those white hands,
which probably hitherto had never held anything heavier
than a pen, Mr. Disraeli was *the Squire* of the Hughenden
estate, the farmers' friend, and their representative in

Parliament. " I have a passion for books and for trees,"
he wrote in one of his letters quoted in his biography;
" when I come down to Hughenden I pass the first week
in sauntering about my park and examining all the
trees, and then I saunter in the library and survey the
books."

I can remember that upon one of those visits a school
feast for the village children was being given in the
Hughenden grounds. Mrs. Disraeli was receiving her
guests with much effusion, and Mr. Disraeli, ready for
the occasion, was starting the children on their races by
blowing on a penny trumpet to the delight of the onlookers.
I can remember the cheers of the assembled villagers,
and the banner bearing the words " For Church and
State " hanging above a small platform, where the prizes
to the fortunate winners of the races were presented.
A strange mixture of old-fashioned English village life,
with its Conservative colouring, and its presiding genius
a man of marked Oriental lineage and bearing.

I once heard Mr. Disraeli address his constituents at
Aylesbury, and on another occasion I attended a great
Agricultural Show with my father in the same town.
To my amazement Mr. Disraeli offered me his arm when
we went to the public luncheon, and I had the honour
of sitting next to him. He was most kind to me as
usual, but was evidently much occupied with the speech
he was going to make to the farmers later in the day.

I met Mr. and Mrs. Disraeli on one of our visits to
Ashridge; it was when the latter was getting old and
not at her best, going to sleep after dinner in the drawing-
room and waking up rather cross, and asking all manner
of random questions. The younger members of the
party rather made fun of the gallant old lady, and
of her queer wig, so often awry, her flame-coloured
dresses, her vain attempts at a somewhat youthful
appearance; but her husband never seemed cognisant
of such a state of things, and preserved his sphinx-like
immutability of countenance, and his gracious, half-

protective, half-deferential manner to his wife. After
more than thirty years of exceptionally happy married
life, at the time of his wife's death Mr. Disraeli was
able to write : " There was no care which she could not
mitigate, and no difficulty which she could not face.
She was the most cheerful and the most courageous
woman I ever knew."

There is also a well-attested story of an acquaintance
once asking Mr. Disraeli if he was not often irritated by
his wife's somewhat irrelevant talk, to which he replied,
" No, because I possess a quality of which you are
probably deficient, namely, that of gratitude."

In regard to Mrs. Disraeli's courage, it was often told
me by my mother how, on one memorable occasion,
when she had driven with her husband to the House of
Commons, her hand was shut into the door of the
carriage by an awkward young footman. The pain was
excruciating, but no sound escaped her lips, so that her
husband's equanimity might not be disturbed on the eve
of one of his great speeches.

Again I met Mr. Disraeli, as a widower, with his
devoted private secretary, Lord Rowton, at Sandringham, where I spent a Sunday with my father in the
January of 1874, and again had the honour of sitting
beside him on the first evening at dinner. I remember
that we sat exactly opposite to the Princess of Wales,
for whom Mr. Disraeli expressed profound admiration.
The Bishop of Peterborough (Dr. Magee, later Archbishop
of York) was of the party, mentioning the fact in his
Memoirs, recording that it was a strange company to
have asked him to meet—Jews and Roman Catholics,
for both were amongst the guests.

I heard the Bishop preach in the little Sandringham
parish church on the following morning ; his sermon
gave some offence to the group of young men who
accompanied H.R.H. to morning service, for he made
some scathing remark about the *jeunesse dorée* of
England. I thought his words apt and good, but those

whom the cap fitted were not too well pleased. I
was silently amused by the comments I heard later in
the day.   I watched Mr. Disraeli at church; he looked
more sphinx-like and inscrutable than ever.   After the
service he told me he had enjoyed listening to the perfect
singing of Teresa Caracciolo, whose beautiful voice was
distinctly heard above the choir in the hymns, " Art
thou weary, art thou languid ? " and " Hark, hark ! my
soul, angelic songs are swelling."   Teresa's mother,
who was also at Sandringham, had begun life as
Miss Locke ; at the age of sixteen she married Lord
Burghersh, after whose early death she became, on
her second marriage, wife of the Duca di San Arpino
(her title when I then met her); later she divorced
her Italian husband, who had become in succession
to his father Duca di San Teodoro; and she entered
upon a third experience of matrimony as Lady Walsingham, but this, alas ! did not prove as happy a
union as she had hoped.   Both husband and wife have
now passed away.   At the early age of eighteen her
daughter Teresa, a very pretty and attractive girl,
became the wife of Prince Colonna, and after his death
she astonished the Roman world, in 1920, by allying
herself with the distinguished antiquarian, Lanciani.

That afternoon at Sandringham, between tea and
dinner, the Princess of Wales, with Lord Rowton as accompanist at the piano, and with others to support her, sang
very sweetly a number of her favourite hymns.   I remember that at midnight, when I thought that the time
for well-earned repose had come, the Prince of Wales
looked at his watch and said, smiling and bowing to the
Bishop, " Sunday being over, we may resort to the
bowling-alley."   I think the Bishop was not ill-pleased
at being allowed to seek his own room, and many of us
were probably of the same opinion, whether we followed
his lead or not.

With a backward glance to the year 1868, I feel that I
cannot resist including a letter from Mrs. Disraeli to my

dear mother, which I gave Mr. Monypenny upon the occasion of his solitary visit to Aston Clinton in 1909, when he came to glean hints and suggestions for his work :

Feb. 26, 1868.

MY DEAR LADY DE ROTHSCHILD—By the time this reaches you " Dizzy " will be Prime Minister of England. Lord Stanley is to announce this at the House of Commons to-day. —Yours affectionately,   M. A. DISRAELI.

There were other notes and letters written to my parents, gracious acknowledgments for presents of game, etc., etc., but what we most prized were the two most delightful letters, both critical and complimentary, addressed to my sister and myself after the publication of a book, *The History and Literature of the Israelites,* to which I shall refer later.

The last visit that I paid with my dear mother to Hughenden Manor, in the autumn of 1872, was a very sad one. Mrs. Disraeli could no longer take pleasure in her woods or her walks ; she was slowly dying, but still full of unselfish courage. She tried to show an interest in everything, and it was pitiful to see the attempt. Mr. Disraeli, calling my mother aside, spoke with deep emotion of his wife's condition, adding, " I am the most miserable man alive." A few weeks after our visit the end came.

Strange and pathetic that my dear mother's first motor drive, taken in my car in 1909, should have been to Hughenden ! There our steps led us to the church, where we saw Mr. Disraeli's (Lord Beaconsfield's) pew, with his banner of the Garter hanging over it, and the Queen's beautiful inscription engraved on a marble tablet. Then we sought the grave of our old friend, in the quiet little country burial-ground. He lies just outside the east end of the church, his grave between those of his wife and Mrs. Brydges Willyams. The last named was Mr. Disraeli's devoted friend and benefactress, already of advanced age when she made his acquaintance, with whom for ten years he maintained an affectionate correspondence, and by whom both he and his wife were repeatedly entertained at Torquay. Mrs. Brydges Willyams, whose admiration for Mr. Disraeli was unbounded, made him her residuary legatee, only asking that she might be buried at Hughenden, in the close vicinity of her two friends.

The sexton, seeing us standing near the grave, said, " Ah ! there lies a great man, a very great man." When I told him that I had known the great man, he looked at me with some manner of respect ; but when I added, glancing towards my mother, that she had been his friend, even before his marriage in 1837, he shook his head, and evidently thought I was more imaginative than truthful !

I write the name of the Right Honourable W. E. Gladstone with some trepidation. It represents a very wonderful man, whom I only began to know long after I had arrived at years of discretion. Mr. Gladstone came upon my horizon, therefore, when I was able to recognise that he was a giant amongst men, and that he represented the side of politics which I was proud in my small way to support and further.

The reverse was the case with Mr. Disraeli, who had been known to us from our childhood, and who was first our friend and then the statesman.

My parents had met Mr. Gladstone several times at my uncle's house in Piccadilly, in the days of their many political and social reunions, and I remember my mother telling me how, in the late 'fifties, on one occasion she had been taken in to dinner by Lord Macaulay and on another by Mr. Gladstone. My aunt, who was a true admirer of our mother's intellectual qualities, would often place her by the side of a man of commanding mental power or literary ability, but, owing to her modesty, I feel she often failed to do herself justice. It was in later years that Mr. Gladstone recognised her true

worth and the ardour of her Liberal views.   When Mr.
Gladstone received her with blindfolded eyes at Dollis
Hill, shortly after his operation for cataract, he asked,
" Is this *my* Lady Rothschild ? " to the great delight
of her daughter.

But I am anticipating.

During my dear father's lifetime I cannot recollect
Mr. and Mrs. Gladstone having been our guests (certainly
not at Aston Clinton), although they may have found
themselves at one of our big London dinners, nor were
any of their immediate circle amongst our habitués.
Later in my life, after my marriage, when my husband
became Liberal Member for Brecon, a new era was opened
for me, and Mr. Gladstone loomed large and commanding on my immediate vision.   Personally, I do not think
that *I* ever made any way with him—I was one of a
crowd, and when he talked to me, as he did on various
occasions most interestingly, I felt that he was enunciat-
ing some of his favourite doctrines, quite regardless of
the identity of his listener.   There were just one or two
exceptions, which I shall record in these pages.

I cannot recall ever having had the honour of speaking
to Mr. Gladstone until the 'eighties, when he had already
passed his seventieth year ; but he had still the mental
vigour, the grasp of intellect, the power of concentra-
tion, the glow of enthusiasm, and the fascination of
speech, which would have been remarkable in a man of
fifty.   It was then that I met him at various social
gatherings.   I heard him speak in the House of Commons
more than once.   I was in the Speaker's Gallery on that
memorable night, the 8th of June 1886, when the veteran
of seventy-seven years made his great appeal for justice
to Ireland.   I can recollect his address to that crowded
House, his glance directed towards the white, eager,
expectant faces of the Irish Members and towards his
own supporters, who seemed actually clinging to every
word that he uttered.   Who could forget the passion of
those words ?—

" Ireland stands at your bar, expectant, hopeful, almost suppliant. . . . Think, I beseech you ; think well, think wisely, think, not for the moment, but for the years that are to come, before you reject this Bill."

I can still picture the uproarious scene that followed the defeat of the Bill, the frenzied delight of the Tories, the hubbub, the noise down below, the affectionate gathering round Mrs. Gladstone in our gallery (that wonderful wife had remained persistently in her seat through all the long debate), the weary and disappointed appearance of my husband when he came to fetch me (he was one of the Liberal Whips at the time) ; and I can also recollect how we were cautioned not to try to encounter the huge crowd at the big entrance of the House, and were then let out by a side door, where we found a friendly hansom for our homeward drive.

Lord Morley writes in his wonderfully interesting Life of the great statesman : " As I passed with Mr. Gladstone into his room at the House that night, he seemed for the first time to bend under the crushing weight of the burden that he had taken up."

I should also like to record here that, during the afternoon sitting of that memorable day, when my dear mother was my companion at the House, we heard Parnell plead for his country in a speech of unparalleled interest. With no apparent enthusiasm, in a cool measured tone of voice, without gestures of any sort, but with an occasional flash from his wonderful blue eyes, Mr. Parnell made, according to Lord Morley, " one of the most masterly speeches that ever fell from him. Whether agreeing with or differing from the policy, every un-prejudiced listener felt that this was the utterance of a statesman."

I shall always feel grateful for having been permitted to witness that scene, racking as it was to the nerves and exhausting to the brain.

Three times did we have the extreme pleasure of being entertained at Hawarden, and twice did our

R

mother, at our instance, when my husband was an ardent politician and supporter of Mr. Gladstone, receive the great statesman and his wife at Aston Clinton. I should like to give more than a passing allusion to those visits.

During the early days of October 1881 we were bidden, for the first time, to Hawarden. Unfortunately, on the very eve of our arrival Mr. Gladstone had been called away to some great political gathering at Leeds, and Mrs. Gladstone came to the door to meet us, full of regrets and excuses. It was a blow, I confess, but we were determined to let nothing interfere with our enjoyment, and Hawarden and the family, chiefly to my mind represented by Mrs. Gladstone and her daughter Mary, occupied us fully for the few days that we spent in that interesting spot. October is a delicious month in any place where fine timber exists, and although it was generally believed that Mr. Gladstone, with that much-quoted axe, had effectually cleared his well-wooded park, proof to the contrary was very soon made manifest to our eyes. The trees grew in fine profusion, and were beautiful in size and variety. The house was roomy and comfortable, in spite of the happy-go-lucky ways of the family. These were startlingly apparent one afternoon in particular, when my husband, much to his own astonishment, drew out from between the back and seat of a sofa standing conspicuously in the centre of the drawing-room, where he was sitting, a number of original letters from Queen Victoria. Mrs. Gladstone did not seem at all upset at this discovery, but merely said, in taking them from my husband, " Oh, William must have been disturbed whilst reading the letters and must quite have forgotten that they had been pushed into that little safety spot of the sofa." Mary laughed, and proceeded to take me upstairs, and to show me, in her own cosy room, the chest of small drawers where her hundreds of letters, neatly docketed and labelled, with the names of her correspondents, reposed in safe keeping, some of

them being destined to see the light of publicity.   From
Mary's lips I heard much of the family history of the
Gladstones, which she detailed to me during our long
walks in the park and village.   Mrs. Gladstone proved
to be a very genial, cheery hostess.   She was still
of striking appearance; her portrait and that of her
sister, Lady Lyttelton, both painted when they were
young and handsome girls, hung in the dining-room
and attracted my attention.

The details I now mention are taken from the Diary
I kept at the time.   In the year 1888 we again spent
a few days at Hawarden.   Mr. Gladstone was then out
of office and was seventy-eight years of age.   It was
the third week of November.   Upon this occasion we
were cordially received by the great statesman as well
as by his wife.   Lord Acton, whom I had never met
before, was one of the party.   I thought I had never
heard any one talk more persistently or more learnedly.
He seemed to have sounded the depths of the literature
and the history of all nations.   He and Mr. Gladstone
discussed at length the points of difference between the
Roman and Greek Churches.   We spent Sunday at
Hawarden, on which day every one found a chrysan-
themum on his or her plate at breakfast time.   In spite
of a cold and snowy morning Mr. Gladstone attended
both the 8 and 11 o'clock services.   Mrs. Gladstone went
to the latter in her small pony-chaise; my husband
drove her pony, whilst I was honoured by being allowed
to walk with Mr. Gladstone.   He talked the whole way
most interestingly, and gave me an account of some
Greek services he had attended, either in Corfu or in
Greece.   When we arrived at the church we found it was
crowded, and the congregation seemed gathered from far
and near, not merely a concourse of villagers.   I cannot
recall the subject of the sermon, but what I shall never
forget was Mr. Gladstone's reading of the First Lesson,
that last wonderful chapter of Ecclesiastes, and the
expression he gave to the words, " Or ever the silver

cord be loosed, or the golden bowl be broken." He thoroughly enjoyed it all—who more devout, more reverent ?

In the afternoon I was allowed to enter the "Temple of Peace"—Mr. Gladstone's cherished library—and he said I might sit there, provided I did not talk, as he wanted to read. He asked me what book I was holding in my hand. I told him : *The Old Documents and the New Bible,* by Paterson Smyth, and most fascinating I thought it. He wished to look at it ; of course I assented, and he gave me a volume in exchange. He soon became immersed in mine and suggested keeping it until the next morning, as he wanted to finish it. And there we both sat silently, he reading persistently and I taking stolen glances at him.

In this "Temple of Peace" were his two writing tables : the one for politics and working days, which he never touched on Sundays, and the other the "Greek" table, for the Day of Rest, when he studied his favourite Greek authors.

Mr. Gladstone and Mary attended the evening service, returning to a late supper, during which Mr. Gladstone was very chatty and quite merry, he and his sons and daughters teasing Mrs. Gladstone about all manner of subjects, Mrs. Gladstone shaking her head, winking at us, especially at Cyril, whom she had made into a kind of confidant, and not apparently understanding what she was being chaffed about. I believe in some cases she did, but she was an adept at pretending ignorance when it suited her.

In December 1895 Cyril and I found ourselves once more at Hawarden. The wonderful old couple were still alert and hospitable, but considerably aged. Mr. Gladstone seemed to have grown shorter, and he had become very deaf. Mrs. Gladstone was less stately than of yore, still with traces of her former bright looks, but less careful of her appearance. She had grown very forgetful, often inattentive to passing talk, and did not

seem to take much interest in what was said. Unlike
their old matutinal habits, neither husband nor wife
appeared at breakfast. Mary and her handsome blue-eyed
husband, Harry Drew, first curate and then rector of
Hawarden, were living in the house, with their little golden-
haired daughter, " Dossie," who was the delight and play-
thing of her grandparents, especially of Mr. Gladstone.
Lord and Lady Ripon were the only other guests, both
very pleasant. I remember Lord Ripon going to Mass
at Chester at 7 A.M. and appearing at breakfast at 9.30.
We went as before to the village church at Hawarden,
Mr. and Mrs. Gladstone driving there together. Again a
large congregation were assembled. I sat by Mr. and
Mrs. Gladstone. He was quite a study in church, for he
never took his eyes off Bible or Prayer-book, following
every word most conscientiously. When it came to the
sermon, he left his place for a high seat arranged close
to the pulpit, that is to say, he sat on a hassock placed
on a bench, and then fixed his eye in rather a terrible
fashion upon the preacher's face.

The sermon was upon the " Grain of Mustard Seed,"
and was sensible and well delivered. We had the Litany,
the Lessons and Psalms for the day, also hymns beautifully sung. After church we called at the Rectory ; then
at the Library and Hostel of St. Deiniol. There were
thirty thousand books in the former, in two large rooms
—one for theological and the other for secular works.
The Hostel was at that time capable of receiving twelve
students ; there were two or three there already, and
seven were expected. Mr. Gladstone had planned everything, and arranged most of the books himself. We
walked home in a mixture of falling snow and rain. The
cold was intense. I spent the afternoon writing and
reading, and talking for a little to Lady Ripon. Mr.
Gladstone was only at tea for a short time, as he wanted
to have some private talk with Lord Ripon in his library.
At dinner I sat next to Mr. Gladstone, but, alas ! on the
wrong side, so that I did not get his good ear. I had

therefore to shout, and the whole table listened, which made it awkward and difficult. We talked much about Mr. Morley; the three biographies that he had quoted as the best in the last century: Lockhart's *Scott*, Trevelyan's *Macaulay*, Stanley's *Dr. Arnold.* Then the fact was mentioned that Mr. Morley was studying Italian, and that he had expressed great admiration for Manzoni's " Ode to Napoleon."

Mr. Gladstone was at that time much interested in animals and in their moral qualities; he praised the study of Natural History and of Science in prefer-ence to that of modern languages, which seemed to me somewhat strange. Later in the evening he asked me to come and sit with him in his " Temple of Peace." We had the following conversation. Mr. Gladstone had just brought out and arranged a Concordance of the Psalms, a copy of which I had with me at Hawarden. In this work he had grouped certain Psalms and excerpts from Psalms under special headings, such as " The Creation," " The Messiah," " The Angels," also under " Mortality " and " Life to Come." With the aid of a Hebrew Bible and Dictionary I had tested some of these deductions, especially those dealing with a future life, and I was not quite in agreement with Mr. Gladstone. I had ventured to mention this to Mary in the afternoon, and she had said, " You must tell my father, he would be much interested," which almost sent me into a fit of alarm, but, as I said before, I suddenly found myself in the " Temple of Peace," and I was confronted by the great man, who asked me to state my objections.

" Mr. Gladstone, I think you attribute too distinct a belief in a future life, as we now picture it, to the old Hebrews. I do not see it as clearly defined in the Psalms as you do."

Mr. Gladstone : " Pardon me, the question is a very big one; shall I tell you what I think of it ? " Of course I murmured my assent.

Mr. Gladstone : " At first amongst the old nations

there was merely an idea of the survival of something connected with the body, not the actual body, but the idea of eternity was hardly understood; it was too difficult to grasp, it was only survival.   This was probably the case amongst the Hebrews, but still they did believe in some shadowy future existence, viz. Enoch, who walked with God; Elijah, who rose to heaven in a chariot of fire; David, who mentions going to his child.   Three distinct proofs.   The old Hebrew did not think with any rapture of a future life; it did not appeal to him as it does to the Christian, to whom the belief in the resurrection of the body is part of his Creed ; but we may take it for granted that the idea always existed."

Mr. Gladstone said much more to the same effect, and then burst into a wonderful rhapsody on immortality, adding : " It is far better not to try to define what eternity means, or we shall be drawn into all the difficulties of eternal punishment.   But," he continued, " I maintain that the Hebrews of old *did* believe in a future state, and that to them ' Sheol ' was not merely the grave, the pit."   I may have had my doubts, but I did not say so.

We also talked of the Book of Job, and he asked me if I could tell him the supposed date of that book as given by the Hebrew authorities.   I replied : " Late, on account of the Chaldaic Hebrew—post-exilic." Then we talked of the Apocrypha, and I ventured to say that some of the books had been written in Hebrew, others in Greek, that the whole of it had been included in and then excluded from Luther's Bible, but I believed it was now read in the Lutheran Church.   I then brought him his Concordance of the Psalms already mentioned, and asked him to write a verse in it, which he did :

Keep me as the apple of an eye ; hide me under the shadow of Thy wing.—W. E. Gladstone, Dec. 8, 1895.

I thanked him warmly; he seemed pleased, and said the Psalter was the most beautiful book that existed.

At this point Mary Drew came in, looking at her watch : " Papa, it is getting late." It was, indeed; we had begun talking at 9.15 and it was then 10.45.

" Very late, my dear; call the household for evening prayers. Where is Mamma ? "

Mary, with slight hesitation : " Mamma has sent the servants to bed, she thought it too late; she has also gone upstairs : I am afraid it was wrong."

" Wrong ! my dear, it was base ! " And I was the innocent cause of this " base " conduct. I was terrified and effected a hurried retreat. Cyril met me on the landing and, seeing my confusion, said, " What were you and the great man discussing? What could have kept you so long ? "

I left Hawarden on the following morning, and I wrote : " I shall often think of Mr. Gladstone immersed in his work, studying from eight to nine hours a day ; reverent, devout, perhaps prejudiced, but very wonderful, kindly, and always gracious to us."

Mr. and Mrs. Gladstone were our guests at Aston Clinton in 1888 and in 1890, both occasions falling in April and Easter-time.

In 1888 Mr. Gladstone was out of the strife of politics, and of him at that date Lord Morley writes in his inimitable language : " As from his youth up, so now behind the man of public action was the diligent, eager, watchful student, churchman, apologist, divine."

At that time there was a strong party in the county opposed to Mr. Gladstone's politics, in which many members of our family figured actively, but there was also a goodly number of his devoted followers and admirers in the Mid-Bucks constituency ; of these very many assembled to do him honour upon his arrival at Tring station. My husband, with an open landau, four horses and postillions, that had seen much electioneering work, was at the station to receive Mr. and Mrs. Gladstone, who had a kind of royal welcome. Besides our own small home party, including our three

selves and my dear sister, we entertained during that
week : Lord and Lady Herschell; the present Lord
and Lady Esher (at that time still Mr. and Mrs. Reggie
Brett)—*he* it was whose very aristocratic appearance
made Edmund Gurney remark, " If there were ever a
revolution in England, Reggie Brett's head would be
the first to fall "; Lord Bryce, later one of our most
successful ambassadors at Washington; Archdeacon
Wilberforce and his wife; Mrs. Dugdale, a sister of
George Trevelyan; Henry James, the much-beloved
American author; Mr. J. Pease, later a member of the
Liberal Government, now Lord Gainford; and last,
but certainly not least, George Russell, the devoted
disciple of Mr. Gladstone, and a warm friend of all
the members of his family. There may have been
others coming and going, whose names have not been
recorded.

Mr. Gladstone was not at all alarming, and made
himself most pleasant and approachable to all. Mrs.
Gladstone was very chatty, and quite ready as usual
to enter into all plans that would conduce to her
husband's enjoyment and comfort. They were both
very particular about what they called " fivé o'clocké "
—this according to the French way of alluding to
the sacred hour of afternoon tea—and all drives or
visits had to be organised to allow of this hour being
faithfully observed. Mr. Gladstone was perhaps at his
very best at that time of day. Once, when he happened
to be in rather a silent mood after " fivé o'clocké,"
I ventured to suggest that he should write out for me
the translation of a Latin hymn that he had once
composed in church, when the sermon had been displeasing or too lengthy. After thinking for a few
moments, he wrote, without hesitation, not the hymn,
which he said he had forgotten, but Mr. Canning's
" Lines on the Death of his Son "—unpublished—only
failing to remember two out of twenty lines, which he
sent me later with the following letter :

. . . The two lines which I felt were missing in Mr. Canning's beautiful verses on his son have come up in my recollection.

Let me repeat my thanks for all your kind and pleasant hospitalities—my " your " is in the plural.—Sincerely yours,

W. E. GLADSTONE.

What do I remember most clearly of that visit ? A drive to Chequers, of which historic place Mr. Gladstone had heard much. Some members of the family were absent, but I think that Bertram Astley, the eldest son of Colonel Astley, received us, the run of the fine house being at our disposal, with a tempting tea-table laid out in the long gallery, which is devoted to Oliver Cromwell's relics and memory.

Mr. Gladstone for once disregarded his favourite meal, for he was deeply interested in a parrot, whose cage stood near the table, and who could speak one or two sentences in classical Greek, which he proceeded to do to the delight of our distinguished guest. That Greek scholar was, however, struck by the wrong pronunciation of one of the words when all else in the sentence was perfect ! I believe that Mr. Gladstone answered in Greek, but fear that this did not lead to further conversation.

We visited the somewhat recently constructed but fine house at Halton belonging to my dear cousin Alfred, and a repository for some of his very beautiful pictures and *objets d'art*. The generous owner of the place was absent; this evidently gave rise to some caustic expression from the lips of Mrs. Gladstone. Her husband made no remark on the subject.

I can recall during the same week the visit of a party of men from Hazell, Watson, and Viney's Printing Works, Aylesbury, who were granted an interview by Mr. Gladstone. It was most interesting and touching to see the men clustering eagerly round their great chief, listening breathlessly to his words. He knew that they were mostly engaged in one special branch of trade, and, with extraordinary skill, he directed much of his talk to that subject—" as if," said one of the men to me afterwards, " Mr. Gladstone had begun life in a printing office, he knew so much about it." He did indeed, and he went on to talk of some of the finest printing in England and in other countries, then, by some stroke of genius, branched off into the politics of the day.

One evening between " fivé o'clocké " and dinner, Mr. and Mrs. Gladstone looked in upon a village concert at the Anthony Hall, thus giving the people of the place the opportunity of seeing them. Mrs. Gladstone was in a long trailing blue velvet gown, and her lace headdress was fastened with diamond brooches almost in the shape of a tiara, so that she had a very regal appearance. The audience rose upon their entrance; although there was no speech from the statesman, there were many bowing acknowledgments and much smiling on Mrs. Gladstone's part. I noticed that she invariably whispered to her husband what was expected of him.

A book at that moment interesting Mr. Gladstone most profoundly was one that had but lately made its appearance, *Robert Elsmere*, by Mrs. Humphry Ward. He had it with him and was reading it with care, pondering deeply over the subject of the volume, and already putting into writing some of the thoughts that it awakened in his mind. I may be pardoned for alluding to this, for I have since learned that Mr. Gladstone actually wrote to Lord Acton on that Easter Day of 1888 a letter, bearing the Aston Clinton address on the notepaper, and therefore doubly interesting to me :

" Were you here," he writes—(I wish he had been)— " I should have much to say on many things ; but I will now speak, or first speak, of what is uppermost. *Robert Elsmere* would, if a mind is like a portmanteau, be taken or tumble out first."

Then comes an account of the subject of the said book, and his views upon it, ending up with :

"Knowles" (of the *Nineteenth Century*) "has brought this book before me, and being as strong as it is strange, it cannot perish still-born. I am tossed about with doubt as to writing about it."[1]

But his doubts were seemingly removed, and his article did much to stimulate the already strongly-awakened interest in the book. Still, Mrs. Humphry Ward told us in her autobiography, *A Writer's Recollections*, "that there was never any doubt at all of the book's fate, and before Mr. Gladstone's review of it the three volumes were already in a third edition, the rush at all the libraries in full course. . . ."

Mr. Gladstone talked long and conclusively to my mother concerning the book, which he evidently considered dangerously clever.

In the Easter week of 1890 we were honoured by another visit from Mr. and Mrs. Gladstone. Unfortunately the weather was inclement. It was a late spring, the country not at its best. We tried to make up for this by a cheerful house-party, and had collected the following guests during the week : Mr. Augustine Birrell[2] and his wife, he already well known as a most fascinating writer and brilliant talker ; Lady Sophia Macnamara, an ardent Liberal ; Jane Cobden, the daughter of the great Cobden, later to become Mrs. Fisher Unwin—I can remember Mr. Gladstone telling her that Nature had broken the mould in which her father, Cobden, had been cast, so that his like could never be repeated ; Sir Richard and Lady Jebb, both friends of my husband (she was a chatty and lively American, very pleasant-looking) ; Philip Currie from the Foreign Office, later Lord Currie, our Ambassador in Rome ; Herbert

---

[1] See Morley's *Life of Gladstone*.

[2] Mr. Birrell is now one of my esteemed Norfolk neighbours, and a favourite one, being the owner of a house called "The Pightle" at Sheringham.

Paul, of the caustic, brilliant pen, and his handsome
wife, a sister of Sir Richmond Ritchie ; my cousin,
Blanche Lindsay ; Sir Schomberg Macdonnell, destined
to be one of the first victims of the Great War ; Mr.
George Russell ; my dear sister, of course ; and Alick
Yorke, who had always expressed a great wish to meet
Mr. Gladstone ; and I must not omit the name of
Mr. Frederic Harrison, the celebrated Comtist, whom I
learnt to know and to appreciate better during two
visits that I paid to Bath, the ancient and beautiful
city which he has made his home, and of which he was
given the freedom on his ninetieth birthday (1921).
He sent me the fine and inspiriting address that he
delivered on that occasion.

Mr. Gladstone had evidently lost some of his physical
strength ; he rather feared the cold, and was less anxious
for pedestrian exercise ; but in mind and spirit he was
still amazing. The political world was much occupied
at that time with the probability of a Liberal reaction,
and I felt that Mr. Gladstone was vividly alive to the
work that might await him in the next Session.

I remember my mother mentioning how delighted the
villagers had been at the prospect of seeing him again,
and how enthusiastically she heard he had been received
when driving through Tring. " Yes," responded Mr.
Gladstone, " we Liberals expect to be well received in
the villages ; there our strength will lie if the towns fail
us."

My husband, who at that time was devoted to the
art of photography, in which he excelled, made a very
careful and successful study of Mr. Gladstone with his
camera, and at one moment the great statesman was
actually seated in our conservatory with two rival
photographers immortalising his features. He took it
all quite naturally.

One evening some of our own party were amusing
themselves by playing a game, very much in vogue in
those days, called " Telegrams." It was as follows. A

subject was suggested, then the name of a place, upon which the players, with pencil and paper in hand, had to write a supposed telegram bearing upon the subject indicated, each word beginning with one of the letters of the place (generally a city or county). The papers were afterwards collected and read out ; they were unsigned as a rule, and much amusement was caused by guessing who the authors were. We chose as a subject "The Approaching Election"; the word was *BRIGHTON*. In the space of a few seconds Mr. Gladstone handed me his paper, and I read out :

Be Ready In Great Houses To Operate Nobly.

All the other telegrams have passed out of my memory, although some of them were very apt and good.

I fancy that Mr. Gladstone suffered from the cold unseasonable weather, for one evening he very wisely remained in his room, and on the day before the one settled for his departure his wife asked my mother whether he might continue as our guest for a little longer. Of course we were delighted, our principal regret being that Mrs. Gladstone could not stay with him, as her eldest son, William, then very ailing at Hawarden, urgently demanded his mother's care.

So we were left (my mother and I), with some trepidation, alone in charge of our distinguished guest, for Cyril's duties had called him to London. We saw all the Easter party drive off without Mr. Gladstone. As the day wore on he felt so unwell that, to our consternation, he sent my mother a note asking, "How can I get my wife back if I want her ? " Most perplexing. We tried to solve that difficulty by telegraphing instead for Sir Andrew Clark, a step already advised by Mrs. Gladstone before her departure. The mere idea of his physician's visit produced a reviving effect upon our guest, who said to my mother, "Oh, dear Lady Rothschild, I have dreadful twinges of conscience at having allowed you to telegraph for Sir Andrew." "Better

than some other twinges," was the prompt reply. " I
should never have expected that from you," said Mr.
Gladstone.

Sir Andrew Clark came, tranquillised our fears, and
spent a quarter of an hour at the bedside of his patient,
assuring us before leaving that Mr. Gladstone would
soon be restored to his usual health, and refusing, as
he always did, to accept a fee from one whom he so
cordially venerated and loved.

During the time that Mr. Gladstone spent in his
room, my mother and I, at his request, went alternately
to sit with him. I have a vivid picture of our guest
sitting propped up in bed, wearing a scarlet flannel
dressing-jacket, which gave a strange glow to his pallid
face and keen searching eyes.

We had a short chat, and then he said :

" I should like to read a novel; bring me anything
you consider amusing and worth reading. I trust you
entirely."

" Old or new fiction ? " I ventured to ask.

" Whatever you like, but I should say old in prefer-
ence."

" Would you care for one of Miss Edgeworth's novels? "

" Very good ! " he answered.

" And shall I bring you a French piece of fiction, one
that I think beautifully written ? "

" Yes, and welcome ! " he replied.

I returned in a few minutes with Miss Edgeworth's
Castle Rackrent, and *Monsieur de Camors* by Octave
Feuillet. Mr. Gladstone took the books, and never was
there a more grateful recipient. He read both works
with deep interest; the French author especially claimed
his pronounced admiration.

On the morrow I was again sent for and wondered
what further piece of literature might be in request.
Mr. Gladstone was, however, not in the mood for fiction.
His writing materials were beside him, his pencil in his
hand; on his bed, Bibles, Prayer-books, Glossaries, Con-

cordances. He was engaged upon his book, *The Im-pregnable Rock of Holy Scripture*, at that time.

After our first greeting, he addressed me as follows : " You are a Hebrew scholar " (which I am not). " You can tell me whether the translation of verse 3 of chapter xxiii. in Exodus is correct as given in the Authorised Version : ' Neither shalt thou countenance a poor man in his cause.' Surely the negative in that instance is wrong ? " I believed that it was right, a signal instance of the justice meted out impartially to rich and poor by the Mosaic Law. However, I dashed down to my room, looked out the passage in my Hebrew Bible, found without trouble the offensive negative and returned with my report to Mr. Gladstone, who did not take it very placidly. In fact, having made up his mind on the subject, I think he somewhat doubted my knowledge of the Hebrew language. (Later I substantiated my rendering of the verse by an appeal to the Chief Rabbi.)

Our wonderful and delightful guest departed during the week, on a brilliant April day, the sun shining down divinely for his short drive to the station, he thanking us elaborately for our care of him, and adding that he had quite enjoyed his little rest upstairs in his comfortable room.

I had the pleasure of entertaining Mr. and Mrs. Gladstone several times at Surrey House, but I will only make mention of one special evening, which stands out before all others in my memory. We intended it to be a record evening, and our guests were chosen accordingly. Amongst them were my cousins, Nathaniel de Rothschild (later Lord Rothschild) and his wife; Lord and Lady Rosebery; Frances Power Cobbe, who with her short-cut hair, her jacket and skirt, bade defiance to all regulation evening dress, her fine expressive face and her pleasant voice, not to speak of her great conversational power, making her a welcome guest; Christine Nilsson, the charming Swedish singer, then young and beautiful, came and came gladly, bringing an accom-

panist ; also Robert Browning and Alick Yorke—the Chapter
three latter were specially to contribute to the pleasures   XII.
of the evening.   My dear sister was also with us.

After dinner Mr. and Mrs. Gladstone were established
in comfortable arm-chairs, and the entertainment began
by the great vocalist singing her Swedish melodies most
divinely ; Mr. Browning followed, reading some of his
own fine poems, and reading them well; after which,
to Mr. Gladstone's immense amusement, Alick Yorke
gave an inimitable representation of various French
actors and actresses, especially Réjane, followed by
a stirring recital of " The Revenge." At the close
Nilsson sang again and again, at Mr. Gladstone's request, most beautifully.   I can see her now standing,
as she did, near an uncurtained window, the moonlight
falling full upon her golden hair and her fine intelligent
face ; it was a beautiful picture, rendered doubly attractive by the sweet powerful voice that held us all breath-
less, so that both eye and ear were charmed.   What an
evening !   Even now I can hear my guests thanking me
profusely, and I can remember the notes I received on
the morrow expressive of the pleasure that had been
given and received.

And now to turn to the following from my Diary :

Thursday, May 19, 1898. — Death of Gladstone.
What significant words !   What did they not contain ?
Over the whole world flew the message: " Gladstone
dead."

The passing away was beautiful.   How comforting
to the survivors !   How strengthening to all of his creed !
How inspiring to the world !

For the next ten days papers teemed with accounts
of his life, his character, his political career, his theology,
his literary work, his sayings, his illness, his death.
Gladstone completely filled the whole of our reading day ;
we could talk and think and write of nothing but that one
ever-absorbing subject.   He seemed to grow in proportion as he faded from our gaze.   And then the funeral

S

on Saturday, May 28, at Westminster Abbey : wonderful, striking in every detail, simple, impressive, dignified, noble. Real emotion displayed. It struck a very high note. The Princess of Wales with her supreme loveliness paid the homage that Royalty should pay to genius and character. The music was beautiful, the hymn-singing grand, every one joined in with real fervour. Pathos was present in 'the lonely and pathetic figure' of Mrs. Gladstone. After the coffin had been lowered into the vault she sat perfectly still, following it with her tearless eyes, then the Prince of Wales (Edward VII.) suddenly walked up to her and, chivalrously bending down, kissed her hand ; this touching action was followed on the part of the other pall-bearers, who added their token of respectful affection to that of H.R.H.

Cyril walked with the Peers in their procession.

Friday, 20th.—I heard the speeches in the Lords, when friends and opponents were all doing honour to the memory of one man. Lord Salisbury and Lord Rosebery, fine and academic, not a discordant or jarring note; and I felt proud that Cyril should have been in Mr. Gladstone's Administration.

Of that very remarkable and distinguished statesman, Lord Salisbury, I can say but little, for I really cannot claim to have had the honour of his acquaintance. It is true that I met him out at dinner-parties on a few rare occasions ; on one of these, at Lord and Lady Brownlow's house, I sat next to him, and we had some conversation on rather trivial matters. I felt astonished that he knew who I was and addressed me by my name. I have also attended some of the big parties at the Foreign Office when Lord Salisbury was Secretary of State for Foreign Affairs. I never went to Hatfield except as a tripper, and although I felt attracted by Lady Salisbury's bright and witty conversation, fate did not put me in her path. I know slightly both of Lord Salisbury's daughters, who have a great gift for conversation and are, I know, pleasant members of

Society.   But I should think that my husband's politics must have horrified the great Conservative leader, had he considered them or us worthy of a thought.

I heard Lord Salisbury speak several times in the House of Lords, and I enjoyed listening to him.   He seemed not so much to be making a speech as to be thinking aloud.   He spoke very slowly, distinctly, and impressively ; his voice was a low and full-toned one, getting lower when the speaker was roused or agitated. He used to bend slightly forward, and his head and eyes were seldom uplifted.   He appeared to be thinking more of evolving his words, straightening out his ideas, than of impressing his audience.   I thought his speech on Mr. Gladstone after the death of that great statesman, to whom he had always been bitterly opposed in politics, though not on Church matters, fine and touching.

Lord Salisbury had a very happy home-life, and, like his two great predecessors, proved an admirable husband to his very brilliant wife.

The first time that I can remember seeing Mr. Balfour was in the early 'eighties.   My husband and I were dining at the house of the Dowager Lady Barrington, a sister of Lady Hardwicke, one of a very musical family. Of that party the central figure was Madame Norman Neruda—Lady Hallé as she became later—the attractive and talented violinist.   When dinner was over and we had returned to the drawing-room, Augusta Barrington, the then unmarried daughter of Lady Barrington, seated herself at the piano and proceeded to play the accompaniment to Madame Neruda's solo on the violin.   We were an appreciative audience ; one of the most appreciative was Mr. Balfour.   I can see him as he then was, of slender figure, with fair hair, large brilliant eyes, and a somewhat dreamy expression of countenance.   He was lying back luxuriously in his chair, giving himself up to the charm of a beautiful rendering of a favourite piece of music.

During the evening he discoursed learnedly about

musicians and their instruments, and I liked what he said and how he said it, also his deferential manner in addressing the great artist. On one of our visits to Cambridge we met his brother, Frank Balfour, wonderfully gifted and distinguished, who came to so tragic a death on the Alps; whilst at Ashridge, at a pleasant country-house party, we first made the acquaintance of Eustace Balfour and his wife, Lady Frances. Yet another brother, Gerald, became a much-valued friend of ours. A politician perhaps by accident, but a philosopher by inclination, he and his wife, Lady Betty, a daughter of Lord Lytton, and not unlike her father in originality and literary ability, were in the habit of spending a few weeks with us year after year at Overstrand.

For me the whole family possessed a great attraction; all were refined, intellectual, original, thoroughly high-minded, of simple habits, but with fine ideals and unspoilt by the world. Certainly the world does not claim them greatly, for they are often frankly bored by the generality of human beings.

I have the recollection of two very happy visits that I paid to Mr. Balfour and his sister Alice at Whittingehame, their Scottish home in East Lothian. The last visit took place in October 1911. It came at the close of a busy week spent with Lord Provost and Lady M'Innes Shaw in Glasgow, where I was attending the meetings of the National Union of Women Workers, who were holding their Annual Conference in that city. After a most stirring time in that northern centre of industry and commerce, and a pleasant one-day visit to Roseneath, a most beautiful and romantic possession, where I had the kindest of welcomes from Princess Louise and the Duke of Argyll, I travelled on to Whittingehame and there found practically a family party. As there were no visitors besides myself, I had the opportunity of much interesting talk with Mr. Balfour (then out of office), and I found him as agreeable and as easy to get on with as ever. He was then devoted to golf by

day and to bridge after dinner, and his two nieces,
Joan and Alison Balfour (daughters of Eustace and
Frances), were always in close attendance upon him,
and ready for any amount of games both in and out of
doors.   He delighted in their society, and they had to
provide him with books of fiction, he only making the
one stipulation, before reading them, that they should
end happily.

On Sunday morning I attended the Presbyterian
service, which appealed to me in its severe simplicity.
I heard a long but clever sermon, preached by Dr.
Robertson, the friend and pastor of the Balfour family,
and I remember that he made some allusions to one of
George Eliot's novels in a way that suggested the close
acquaintance of his congregation with that writer's
works ; he spent an evening at Whittingehame during
my visit, when he was introduced to me, and we had a
long and pleasant talk which I enjoyed.   Mr. Balfour
did not play bridge on Sunday evening, so we had more
conversation than usual.   Perhaps what may be called
an unusual characteristic is the way in which Mr. Balfour
seems to take a vivid interest in the person he is conversing with ; the very poise of his head and expression of
his eyes must encourage the one with whom he is talking
to be at his or her best.   He helps one along in a delightful manner, and perhaps that is one reason why he is
such a very great favourite, especially with members of
my sex, having numerous devoted friends amongst them.
He has always believed in female suffrage, voting persistently for that measure.

Mr. Balfour was not quite young when he first became
deeply interested in politics, for which he had been well
prepared by his uncle, the late Lord Salisbury, and he
made his first great mark as Irish Secretary in 1887,
when he gained his laurels in that most difficult post.
In those days he used laughingly to tell me that I was
a Tory by instinct and one of his best supporters; he
also declared, half in joke, that Cyril was not serious

in his politics, but that on the other hand his knowledge of art and his taste in all things connected with it were indisputable. In debate Mr. Balfour is admirable: cool, restrained, of ready wit, logical, even-tempered, sarcastic and alarming to his antagonist, but perhaps less telling as an orator than many men of inferior intellect. His voice and enunciation have always been most attractive. His outward appearance never was an index to his character, and many were surprised at the strong will and determination hidden beneath a somewhat indolent and dreamy manner. Foreigners, both French and German, find great pleasure in his society. I was amused, when at Bayreuth in 1892, to see the hero-worship he had aroused amongst the members of the Wagner family, his framed photographs being displayed on the tables of their reception-rooms, and a letter of introduction from him to Frau Wagner assured us of a friendly welcome from that very exclusive "Queen of Bayreuth." Mr. Balfour, being an ardent lover of music, was an untiring frequenter of the concert-room, and in the company of a sympathetic knot of intimate friends was constantly to be seen at the various musical festivals, at home and abroad.

My cousins, both Lord and Lady Rothschild, as well as the Leo Rothschilds, were amongst his most devoted friends, and at Ascott he might have been seen week-end after week-end in full enjoyment of the ready hospitality that never failed, and of the golf and bridge parties that there awaited him.

At Tring Park the gatherings bore a more political colouring, the host being at one with his distinguished guest on most questions of the hour.

Lord Rosebery's name has already appeared in these Reminiscences, linked with the memories of childhood. Then occurs a hiatus, until the day when I can recollect my father inviting some racing friends, Sir Robert Peel and Rosebery amongst others, to stay at Aston Clinton—

it must have been in the 'sixties, before the house had
been finally enlarged.   We were not in residence at the
time, and the guests flowed over into some of the family's
rooms.   Rosebery had my sanctum, and telling me afterwards of this visit, mentioned how much struck he had
been by my choice of books, which revealed a very
theological bent of mind.

Then after a gap of years came the news, sent by
my cousin Hannah de Rothschild herself, in a letter
which seemed to radiate joy, that she was engaged to
be married to Lord Rosebery.   She was living at Mentmore in splendid loneliness at that time—1878.   From
having been immensely considered and perhaps somewhat
injudiciously treated as a child, Hannah became, from
the very outset of her married life, one of the most
devoted and unselfish of wives that ever lived.   She
furthered her husband's success in every way.   She
went cheerfully through an amount of entertaining in
London and in the country such as rarely falls to
the lot of any woman.   She was never too tired or
too bored to be of use to him socially, and was ever
mindful of his interests and amusements.   I remember
on one occasion, when she was suffering from a severe
cold, receiving a note from her asking me to call for
some special reason.   I went, and was told that I
was (at her wish) to accompany Rosebery to the East
End of London and to introduce him to the Toynbee
Hall Settlement, of which Canon Barnett was Warden
and moving spirit.   Of course I assented, and the
memory of that pleasant expedition remains as one of
those bright pictures that time cannot destroy.   As it
happened, we did not find the Warden, but in his place
the second in command, the Rev. Thory Gardiner, who
proved an excellent guide, and became, from that day
onwards, an enthusiastic admirer of Lord Rosebery.

In the year 1901 Rosebery opened a Whitechapel Art
Exhibition, held under the auspices of the Barnetts,
where he made an appropriate and graceful speech.

Rosebery has a keen sense of humour, but he has also a strong sarcastic vein, and he can strike alarm into the heart of some timid companion, for whose benefit and his own amusement he may be giving free vent to his spirit of raillery. He has been in touch with men and women of many different classes. This is not surprising considering his aristocratic birth, also his loyal support of Liberal principles, his love of literature, together with his keen interest in sport, his connection with so many of the great and wealthy ones of the earth, as well as with hosts of his less fortunate brethren.

In 1889 he played a very important and successful part in civic life as Chairman of the London County Council, and I have often heard the late George Russell speak of the splendid way in which Rosebery entertained the members of that Council at Mentmore, where he shone as a " Grand Seigneur " and also as a most kind and thoughtful host. I have vivid recollections of some very pleasant and interesting days in that beautiful place, where we were invited on two or three occasions to meet Mr. and Mrs. Gladstone, occasions that have become historic on account of their connection with great and important events, that have made milestones in our country's history. It was particularly delightful to watch the host with his distinguished guest in the relation in which they stood to one another—the younger man admiring, respectful yet responsive, grandly hospitable, the older one enthusiastically appreciative and affectionate.

Rosebery's four children, two sons and two daughters, were all born between the years of 1879 and 1883. He was passionately fond of them, and when the boys and girls were in the nursery and schoolroom they spent much time with him. Alas! they were deprived of their mother's love at an early age, for in 1890 Hannah died at Dalmeny—her Scottish home—of a virulent attack of typhoid fever.

Who that has seen and talked with Sybil, the elder

daughter, can ever forget so brilliant and original a personality, whose vitality, both physical and mental, is so phenomenal ?   She is married to Colonel Grant, who served with much distinction in the Great War. Her sister Peggy, also handsome and gifted, is the wife of the Marquis of Crewe, son of Lord Houghton, one of the Victorian poets, and himself a man of letters, now (in 1922) Leader of the House of Lords.

Dalmeny, the eldest son, was on General Allenby's Staff in Palestine, gaining golden opinions ; whilst Neil, the youngest-born, who had given rare promise of future distinction, had already, in the House of Commons, attracted the attention of his political chief, being well on the road to eminence.   But the war called him, as it called many more, and took him from home and family, as it had taken so many of our bravest and best. Once he returned from the field of battle to greet his newly-born little girl (his wife was a daughter of Lord Derby), but he could not leave the post of danger, neither he nor his friend and cousin, Evelyn Rothschild.   They had both been offered home appointments and were pressed to stay, but they heard and obeyed the inward voice calling them away from their beloved ones, and they went with those

> who suffered countless ills,
> Who battled for the true, the just,
> (Were) blown about the desert dust
> Or sealed within the iron hills.

In November 1917 the news came to England that both friends had fallen in Palestine fighting against the Turk.

Rosebery has travelled much, and seen much of interest at home and abroad.   He has visited our Overseas Dominions, as well as many foreign countries.   He was *persona grata* at all the courts, welcomed as a favoured guest by the great Bismarck, and by more than one President of the French Republic.   He was the friend of Edward VII., as well as the devoted colleague and follower of Mr. Gladstone. His career has indeed been an exceptional one. His gifts, his characteristics, his power of attraction, his wonderful oratory, all singled him out for pre-eminence. His taste for sport is very British ; three times has he been fortunate in winning the Derby, and very popular was his success in the racing world. His love of books and fine literature is very cosmopolitan, his proficiency in the French tongue unusual for an Englishman. In Scotland he had long been a supreme favourite, and it is pleasant to recall how his appearance during the celebrated Midlothian Campaign of 1880 evoked a wave of enthusiasm only second to that which was aroused by his distinguished guest of the hour—Mr. Gladstone.

But if fate reserved for him in one of her hands a laurel wreath, with the other she dealt him a cruel blow. His devoted wife died four years before he was given the crown of his political career—the Premiership of a Liberal Government, held by him for one year, from March 1894 until his resignation in June 1895.

For some years Rosebery has taken no part in the political life of this country; he has withdrawn from both parties, and has thus removed a very important and influential personality from the arena ; the close of his short Premiership shut the door too soon upon his official life, whilst later, the determined and unfortunate opposition of the House of Lords to his suggested measures of reform in that House sent him despairingly away from a place he had long adorned, never to return, thus robbing the State of his eminent services. A gifted and effective speaker, Lord Rosebery can also wield his pen with power and wonderful charm. And perhaps I may be allowed to complete this somewhat faulty and inadequate sketch with his own words, taken from one of his masterpieces, an address on Dr. Johnson, which I venture to apply to himself :

" And now we have lingered long enough . . .

round this absorbing figure, and must perforce leave him. There is a human majesty about him which commands our reverence, for we recognise in him a great intellect, a huge heart, a noble soul."

My personal knowledge of Sir Henry Campbell-Bannerman was very slight, but I remember distinctly once sitting next to him when dining at the Speaker's house, before he was Prime Minister, and being greatly entertained by his conversation. When I repeated some of that conversation to Cyril, he said that Sir Henry had been most indiscreet; perhaps that was why I thought him so amusing. At all events I found him, and so did others with whom I compared notes, a brilliant and interesting talker. An inveterate reader of romance, especially of French novels (he was a master of the French tongue), he talked to me of those he had read one summer whilst going through his annual "cure" at Marienbad, and was able to descant largely upon the plots and characters in the said novels; indeed, Sir Henry was an omnivorous reader of Italian, German, and French literature, and could discourse most pleasantly about his books.

He had a touch of Gallic wit more than of English humour, and rolled his "r's" rather like a Frenchman; his was a very good-tempered, jolly face, although plain of feature. His affection for and his devotion to his wife were really beautiful, and the more she demanded of him the more he was ready to give. We went to the first and last reception that they held at Downing Street. I shall not easily forget seeing Sir Henry as he stood beside his wife's chair; she was then already suffering from a mortal disease, and was rather a gruesome spectacle, but had insisted upon being present on such a memorable occasion, when together they welcomed their guests. He was hard at work on important and difficult measures during the very acute stages of her illness, and when he used to return wearily from the House it was not to rest, but to repair to his wife's bedside, where he often relieved the nurses of their night duties, his wife demanding his constant presence. It was a pathetic story, and the Prime Minister's attitude was a very fine and unselfish one, but it was one he could not have maintained for a much longer period. I have still by me the letter I received from him when his self-imposed task of devotion had been brought to an end, in which he thanks me warmly for writing to him " at the commencement of his time of *desolation*," and he meant what he said.

It was in the 'eighties that we made the acquaintance of Mr. Asquith, then an able young barrister, who brought a fine literary reputation with him from Balliol College. He entered the House of Commons in 1886, as member for East Fife, a constituency he represented until December 1918, when he lost his seat at the General Election. He re-entered the House, February 1920, as member for the Burgh of Paisley, on a bye-election due to the death of the sitting member, Sir John M'Callum.

I am trying to recall the impression that Mr. Asquith made upon me at that time. I can remember a somewhat spare figure, carelessly dressed, a shapely head with smooth light-brown hair, a fine forehead, rather deep-set grey eyes, a pale complexion, such as one would expect in a hard-working student, a firm mouth that could break into a pleasant smile, no special charm of bearing or manner, but a low agreeable voice and a distinctly refined enunciation. He spoke rather slowly, choosing his words deliberately, as if what he said in ordinary conversation might have found expression in public.

When Cyril cared for any one, he cared very much indeed, and to himself it was a delight to be in any way helpful to his friend ; he took the greatest pleasure in offering Mr. Asquith all the opportunities that lay in his power of meeting such men as would appreciate him and be useful to him in his career.

Mr. Asquith, when we first knew him, had been,

from the early age of twenty-five, the husband of Miss
Melland, who was the daughter of a north-country
physician, and, I believe, a connection of the Asquith
family. She was a gentle, amiable woman, with an
attractive face and figure, a true home-maker and home-
keeper, and an excellent mother. There were five young
children, four boys and a girl, to all of whom Cyril,
the child-lover, became warmly attached. It is now
well known how extraordinarily gifted these children
were, and in what an amazing way they carried off
scholarships and prizes in their school and college careers.
They certainly were a family of wonderful intellectual
distinction and moral strength. Perhaps the simple
home life that they were leading contributed not a little
to this happy result. I remember calling with my
mother upon Mrs. Asquith (they were living near
Hampstead at the time), and seeing the wife and children
awaiting and welcoming the return of husband and
father from his parliamentary or legal work. We spent
a very pleasant afternoon with them, and I appreciated
Mr. Asquith when he joined the little group more than
I had ever done before.

In 1891 Mr. Asquith lost his wife, during a holiday
that he and his family were all spending together
in the Isle of Arran. The gentle, kindly mother succumbed to a violent attack of inflammation of the
lungs. I can still refer to the words with which he
acquainted Cyril of his sad loss. The motherless
children only crept the closer into my husband's affectionate heart, and it was owing to his suggestion that
we welcomed them all on the succeeding Christmas at
Aston Clinton, my dear mother being, as usual, the
kindest and most sympathetic of hostesses.

Little Cyril Asquith, a child of about three, a
namesake of my husband's, with his quaint pale face
and his tight red curls, proved most amusing at that
early age. I remember how he requested Miss Molique
to play the piano to him, whilst he read his book,

and how upon the morning of the children's departure from Aston Clinton, when my mother was expressing her regret at having to bid him good-bye, he promptly retorted, " Then why do you not come with me ? " They were all very clever and entertaining, and they have nobly fulfilled the promises of their childhood.

In 1894, when Mr. Asquith was Secretary of State for the Home Office, he married *en secondes noces* Margot Tennant. My husband, returning from a yachting trip, received from him a cordial invitation to the wedding, which proved to be one of the great features of that year in the London social world, its description filling columns of the daily press.

And now I have the very difficult task of giving some portrait of the bride, a most original personality, whom I first met as Margot Tennant in the beautiful home of her father, Sir Charles Tennant, " The Glen," in the lowlands of Scotland. Writing of the Tennant sisters, Mrs. Alfred Lyttelton, the second wife of Alfred Lyttelton, notes in the admirable record she has given us of her husband's life : " They were all clever and full of talent; they could not only draw and play and write, but they could talk brilliantly." And talk Margot did, and does still, with brilliancy and assurance. A clever friend of mine once said to me : " Most other women seem dull to me after Margot; talking to her is like drinking champagne." When describing her sister Laura, the gifted first wife of Alfred Lyttelton, Margot used words that might be applied to herself : " The most astonishing vitality and eagerness, nerves that were almost too highly strung for everyday temper." Yes, " vital " was the term most descriptive of Margot in her young days—a dazzling, astonishing vitality. Quick and alert in the movements of her body as of her mind, with a bright, expressive face, fine eyes, curling dark hair, she was perhaps more attractive than actually pretty, although she had a beauty of her own, a beauty of swift move-

ment and change. She was an accomplished dancer.
She was a prominent member of that remarkable
and much-talked-of confraternity, " The Souls," which
came into being in the London world during the
'nineties. The men and women belonging to " The
Souls " were drawn from both political parties : they
were intimate enough to call one another by their
Christian names, but not Bohemian enough to dispense
with all the decorum that Society demanded of them.
They were all supposed to be distinguished by some
superiority of intellect or of talent or of beauty. They
all read the same books, they all discussed and criticised
their contents, they all attended the same plays, and
spent most week-ends in one another's country houses.
In a way they were actively useful in raising London
Society to a higher intellectual level. " The Souls "
were a striking if but passing phase of the social life
of that date. Margot was a bold rider across country,
as well as a good talker in country houses, so she
had many devoted friends in the hunting field as well as
intellectual admirers in the London salons. Indeed, she
often mentioned the many whom she had enslaved,
who mostly, strange to say, ended by becoming good
friends to one another.

Mr. Asquith had led a studious, self-contained life as
a young man; he had had no time for London Society
with its allurements and fascinations. Margot was
a new and delightful experience, and he was entirely
captivated and very much in love with her. He was
then rapidly taking a front place in politics. Already,
in 1893, Sir Charles Dilke had noted in his diary :

Asquith is the only new man who is any good—a bold,
strong man of great intellectual power. . . . Much more
intelligent than the ordinary run of politician.

And again, later, he remarked :

And I looked upon Asquith as one of the greatest Parlia-
mentarians I had known—much superior in that capacity

to Mr. Gladstone. His allocution on the King's death was noble, still finer the introduction of the Veto Bill in December 1907. His speech was forcible in manner, statesmanlike in argument, felicitous in epithet and phrasing.[1]

Mr. Asquith was Chancellor of the Exchequer from 1905 until the death of Sir H. Campbell-Bannerman in 1908. It was then that he succeeded to the highest post that a British politician can aspire to attain.

King Edward was spending a few weeks at Biarritz at that eventful time, and it was there that Mr. Asquith sped with the knowledge that when he returned it would be as Prime Minister of England.

When his Premiership had been announced in the Press on his return, I added my congratulations to the many that reached him, but in writing that letter my pen seemed to halt; I felt as if my husband's pen, rather than mine, should have been the one to convey our good wishes to the new Premier. Cyril's prediction in 1886 that his friend would rise to high office in the State had indeed been realised !

Owing, however, to my widowhood, and to my frequent absences from London, I have seen but little of the distinguished statesman and the members of his family during the past fourteen years. Another daughter, Elizabeth (now Princess Bibesco), and a fifth son, Anthony, both extraordinarily gifted, were added to his first family, the child friends of Cyril, of whom all are now married, whilst Raymond, the eldest, has passed from this life on the field of battle. And here I should like to add that Margot has proved an admirable stepmother, and that the little motherless children of her predecessor were from the first devoted to her, and very proud of her many gifts.

I had one pleasant glimpse of Mr. and Mrs. Asquith and the younger children when I was staying with Mr.

[1] *Life of the Right Hon. Sir Charles Dilke*, vol. ii. pp. 287, 549.

Balfour and his sister Alice at Whittingehame in the autumn of 1911, and went over to luncheon at Archerfield. The Asquiths had taken that residence with its attractive golf-course (a property in East Lothian then belonging to the late Mrs. Hamilton Ogilvy) for their holiday time, and it was there that I found my old friend, who gave me a most cordial welcome. The finger of age had left its mark, but not an unkindly one, upon him. His hair was grey, his figure had increased in bulk, his pallid complexion had changed to one of a stronger and ruddier colour, but his eyes had still their kindly glance, his lips their pleasant smile, and his voice its arresting tone. I was unfeignedly glad to see him and his wonderfully active wife, and to make friends with their quaint little son Anthony, who, seated at the piano, with all the airs of a " maestro," performed some pieces of his own composition, much to the delight of his admiring father. They seemed to be a very happy and united family party, with the cares of the State then behind them.

T

CHAPTER XIII

FURTHER TRAVELS

Spain, Tangier, and the Balearic Islands

In 1887 we had had rather a tiring political and social season, and my husband and I thought that a trip to " pastures new " would do us both good. So we determined upon spending a few weeks in Spain, our decision being partly influenced by the fact that Cyril had been studying the Spanish language most assiduously for some time. He had been an excellent pupil—so good that we were able to dispense with the services of a courier, and that on one occasion he came to the rescue of an English party who were in a very helpless condition, owing to their ignorance of the language. I only knew one word, *nada*, " nothing "—an indispensable exclamation for getting rid of the crowds of importunate beggars who in those days were a perfect plague throughout Spain. " *Nada, nada*," with a backward thrust of the hand, would send them careering away, often with a scowl and a curse, from the carriage side or from a cathedral door. Another word, the full significance of which one only learnt in the Spain of the 'eighties, was *mañana*, " to-morrow "—a splendid excuse on Spanish lips, which really might be translated into " polite procrastination " ! " The galleries will be opened *mañana*." " The work will be done *mañana*." " Your parcels shall be sent to you *mañana*," and so on.

We started from Paris one day in late September, and

274

travelling *via* Biarritz found ourselves during the early hours of the morning on Spanish soil. In pale, clear moonlight we ran over the high bare Sierras (oh, how cold it was!), and at length, on a glorious autumn day, steamed into the station of Madrid.

Spain had always seemed to me a very remote country, much farther away than Italy and far less civilised. An aroma of the Middle Ages did actually still cling to the country, the people, the Court, and the Church.

In Madrid we found ourselves comfortably lodged in a fine hotel, situated in one of the principal squares, where there was much animation and traffic. But the Spaniard is, on the whole, a graver and more silent man than the Italian; and at that time the women in Madrid were not very frequently seen in the streets, unless they were on business bent.

From ignorance of the language I felt very much at a disadvantage when anxious to learn more about the customs and habits of the people. Italian and French were no help : the Spaniards in the shops shook their heads at me when I tried to make myself understood in either of those languages. Even " hotel " was not a word in general use—it had to be " fonda " to be rightly understood by the less educated Spaniard. I can remember how difficult I found it to direct my driver on one occasion to a certain church that I wanted to visit, and how hopelessly we misunderstood one another for some time. The guttural pronunciation of some of the letters of the alphabet gives an Eastern sound to the language and prevents it from being as soft and musical as the Italian.

Guitar-playing and singing were still much the fashion all over Spain, and we were fortunate enough on a moon-light evening to see in some quiet street in Madrid a man playing his guitar, and singing under the shuttered window of some Spanish maiden. By degrees the shutter was slightly pushed back, and perhaps, as our driver told us, a flower would be flung out to the musician, but the girl would remain invisible.   And this was the practice throughout Spain.

Of course we did our sight-seeing bravely.   We spent some hours in the rightly far-famed and glorious Picture Gallery of the Prada ;   we visited some dark and un-interesting churches;   we saw the interior of the Royal Palace—the Library, the Armoury, second to none in the world, and the fine tapestry—also the celebrated stables, with their quaint assortment of carriages, old and new.

Whilst in the Royal Palace we could see from one of the windows a procession leaving the principal entrance. It consisted of an open carriage, drawn by four spirited black horses ridden by smartly equipped and powdered postillions.   In the carriage was seated the Queen Mother, with the present King of Spain, then a child, by her side.   They were surrounded by the Queen's Guard on horseback, each man a Spanish noble, all in brilliant dress.   As the carriage was about to pass into the street, through a crowd of people who had entered the courtyard, a woman, holding a written petition on a paper, walked quietly up, unrestrained, and handed it to the Queen with a curtsey.   Her Majesty received it, bending her head, and passed it on to one of her equerries. Others followed, and there was no attempt to stop them, Her Majesty always receiving petitions on these occasions. We were told that this was a weekly occurrence. Every Friday the Queen was in the habit of going to offer up prayers, in one of the oldest churches of Madrid, to the Virgin, there represented by a little black doll. This doll, so small that when I first visited the church I spent some time before I could distinguish her, was supposed to be gifted with miraculous powers, because it was said that she had once arrested a terrible visitation of the plague in the Middle Ages, when she had been brought from some distant sanctuary and carried through the streets of the city.   The churches were very dark and badly kept, and their paved floors very dirty. Often there were no seats, or but few; men and women were kneeling before the altars on bare stones. Aged people and beggars of all sorts crowded round the entrances and followed visitors as they went through the doors.

We were most kindly entertained at Madrid by our Ambassador, Sir Henry Ford, who invited Castelar, the gifted and eloquent member of the Cortes, to meet us. He was a very interesting and amusing personality and talked freely of the Spanish Court and of the Queen Mother (she was an Austrian Princess—a Hapsburg), for whose ability and great sense of duty he had an immense admiration. He said that it was due to her alone that he was not an out-and-out Republican—but he was one at heart.

Castelar most kindly escorted us to the Chamber where the Cortes sits, the Spanish House of Parliament, and gave us a graphic description of how it looked when members were present; he also accompanied Cyril on a memorable visit to Toledo, and further supplied us with all the necessary information about the Escurial, where we spent another long day, deeply interested in that place of royal but gloomy memories.

I was not permitted to leave Madrid without having been taken to see something of the great national sport, bull-fighting. "El toro" played as prominent a part as King or Queen or Castelar or any well-known individual in the programme of every visitor to Spain in those days, if not a greater one. So I accepted an invitation, under promise of being allowed to leave some time before the end. The drive to the fine arena was the best part of the performance; it happened to be such a beautiful autumn day, and the carriages, fiacres, and country carts, filled with gaily-dressed, holiday-making folk, were all bent in one direction. They were passing us, following us, or crowding us out of principal streets into by-ways. The horses and mules, with some very notable exceptions, looked thin and over-driven, most sadly so to my English eyes. The ladies all wore the national head-dress, a lace mantilla, either black or white, beautifully poised on a high comb stuck into their well-arranged hair ; a flower inserted on one side, peeping out from under the lace, gave the wearer a very coquettish look. The women of another class went mostly with uncovered heads, but their black and glossy hair was most carefully and elaborately dressed, and they never omitted the flower above the ear.

At length we arrived at the arena, and found ourselves in a huge amphitheatre, open to the sky, the national colours, red and yellow, predominating. From top to bottom the place was packed with an expectant crowd. We entered a private box on the second tier, where some Spanish friends were awaiting us. Right down below, close to the protecting rails, stood the country folk, talking, laughing, gesticulating.

Suddenly there was a sound of trumpets ; these heralded the " entrada " or entry of the procession.

First came a Master of the Ceremonies, in a Court costume, accompanied by other officials ; he stood in front of the box where the personage highest in rank was seated, made a low bow, and demanded permission to open the proceedings.

It is customary that the key which locks the door of the stalls where the bulls are shut up shall, for the time being, be entrusted to the care of the said high personage, who, at the request of the Master of the Ceremonies, flings it down, to be caught by him in his hat. This is the signal for the opening of the bull-fight. On this occasion I remember the Royal Box was empty, and I was told that the Queen Mother hated these performances, which she could not bring herself to attend, thus incurring a good deal of unpopularity. The key having been given, the procession filed in.

First came the Banderilleros, with flags, darts, and squibs ; then the Picadors, carrying lances, mounted on their doomed and wretched horses—these poor animals wearing a thick pad over the left eye to prevent them from seeing the bull when it should be charging them ; the left side of the saddle was well protected, the left legs and arms of the men who were to attack and provoke the bull being also well padded. They were followed by the men on foot, who had later to save themselves by their quickness and agility from the violence of the animal ; the poor horses were left to their horrible fate. Finally came the Toreadors, with the red " muletas," which they flourish before the eyes of the bull at the last stage, and carrying the short sword with which they give the final stroke. These again were followed by mules, dragging a kind of huge farm-cart, in which the bodies of the doomed beasts were taken out of the arena.

We were in the company of Spaniards, who lost no time in explaining every detail to us—I having been previously warned that if I could not bear to sit out the performance, I should have to leave quietly and silently, without expressing any feeling on the subject, or I should risk giving great offence.

The procession retreated and the bull took its place— a fine young creature, black and glossy, from the plains of Andalusia, seemingly ill-disposed for the part before him. Poor animal, he was baited, tormented, and finally lashed into fury. Occasionally he tried to jump the rails that shut off the crowds and thus to baffle his tormentors, but the tortured brute was pushed back by the screaming throng. I saw quite enough to know that I did not want to see any more. I hated looking at the bull fighting for its life; I hated looking at the horses left to the fury of the bull—they could not escape, and I thought the animals preferable to the men. I made a sign to one of my kind Spanish friends; he understood and helped me to leave the arena. How glad I was to rejoin my fiacre and to go for a drive on a quiet country road, where I regained my composure ! Upon the return of my husband I heard what I had

missed : seven bulls had been sacrificed ; a number of
horses had been gored, disembowelled, and mangled ; one
man had been tossed and somewhat badly hurt.

> Such the ungentle sport that oft invites
> The Spanish maid, and cheers the Spanish swain.

Thus ended my one rather imperfect experience of
a bull-fight. But a few days later, travelling south, we
found ourselves in a first-class compartment with a
number of toreadors, bound for Seville. One or two of
them proved quite friendly and conversational, and
amused my husband by their talk. They were very
smartly dressed, rather like eighteenth-century postillions, wearing their hair plaited into short pigtails, tied
with black bows of ribbon. Many of them had fine
jewels in their shirt fronts and on their fingers, given
to them by enthusiastic ladies after witnessing their
prowess in killing the bull. It is the custom of the
successful toreador to walk round the arena at the end
of the day, hat in hand, whilst the audience pelt him
with gifts, often of great value. The men were somewhat taciturn at first, but, becoming more loquacious
and at their ease, allowed us to admire their jewels, even
taking off their rings and handing them to us for our
inspection.

After spending some interesting days at Cordova
and at Seville we went on to Granada, where we had
an enchanting time, only much too short for all that we
found there of romance and of charm. All the poetry
of Spain seems to culminate in Granada, or perhaps
I should say in the Alhambra, that wonderful relic of
the days of the Moors, rising as it does above the vast
plain of the Vega, which stretches away for miles and
miles, until it fades into the distant violet haze.

My sympathies went out to the memories of the
gallant, chivalrous Moors, who quitted that beautiful
city at the cruel order of the Catholic King and Queen,
Ferdinand and Isabella, their departure robbing Spain

in the Middle Ages of some of her best and most valuable assets. The memories of hideous persecution, on so-called religious grounds, of both Moors and Jews, leave for ever a black stain on the history of that country.

Granada should be visited in May, when her gardens are fragrant with roses, and when the woods resound to the song of the nightingale; bu: even in October the magic was great. The Gitanos (gipsies) made at that time their abiding-place in the rock dwellings or caves round about Granada, and adventurous Englishmen were warned not to go alone and unprotected (particularly at late hours of the even.ng) into those parts. Some of the gipsies whom I saw looked most alarming and forbidding, whilst their women and children followed us to the very door of the hotel, begging from us in a shameless and importunate manner.

We were introduced, on the cther hand, to a stout, distinguished-looking, elderly gentleman, calling himself " King of the Gipsies," and, at the suggestion of our hotel-keeper, invited him to bring his troupe of musicians, or rather band of guitar-players and singers, into our rooms one evening. No sooner said than done, and we invited the rest of the hotel guests, mostly English people, to come and join the audience. It was a brilliant success, and even now I can recall the wonderful guitar-playing (quite unlike anything I had ever heard before), and the half-plaintive, half-wild, barbaric chants that rose and fell on our ears that evening.

I had the pleasure of visiting Spain again in 1895. This second time it was on board my dear sister's yacht, the *Garland*.

Perhaps I might make a little diversion here in favour of the yacht, which played a great part in my sister's life for a number of years. The *Garland* stands for several *Garlands*, of which the first was a sailing yacht of 190 and the last a steam yacht of 300 tons. The last *Garland* was a very complete and beautiful

boat, fitted up with every convenience and comfort,
and although she could dance and jump about enough
to satisfy the most ardent of sailors, she could also glide
smoothly and gently along over a quiet sea with a
delicious motion, or rather absence of motion.

My brother-in-law, Eliot Yorke, had been an ardent
yachtsman, and in the very early days of their married
life had introduced his wife to all the delights of
yachting. She learned to love the sea and sea-faring,
and she yachted persistently during thirty-six years
for some weeks every year. She was stopped at last
by the Great War, and in fact was actually in Kiel
Harbour on July 23, 1914, only hearing that war was
declared upon her arrival at Bergen in Norway.

The *Garland* was sold to the French Government
in 1916. Her skipper, Darby, who was in my sister's
service for many years, was a man of very remarkable
and uncommon character. Of course he took great
pride in his yacht, which was spotlessly and beautifully
kept, the admiration of all who were privileged to see
her. But, besides this, Darby was keenly jealous of the
reputation of his crew, in whose spiritual and physical
welfare he took the deepest interest. I attended more
than once his services for the men on Sunday evening,
and was much struck by his reverential manner and
speech. Moreover he, as well as my sister — " the
Missus," as she was always affectionately called on
board—was a thoroughgoing disciple of Canon Wilberforce, and no alcohol of any sort was served out to
the men. In consequence of this the *Garland* would
often steam out of harbour when other yachts might
be detained in order to allow some of their crew to
recover from a carouse on shore the previous day.
The *Garland* had the honour and privilege of taking
many pledges during her frequent cruises, and Darby
was well known and always made welcome at the
British Sailors' Institutes which abound in foreign
parts. The crew was indeed composed of exceptionally

respectable and obliging men. My sister was devoted to the *Garland,* her little " Haven of Peace " as she called it, where she could not only rest from her many committees and meetings, but also extend hospitality to her relatives and friends. It was a paradise for the nephews and nieces, for children and young people, as well as for those of maturer years.

It was on one of our early yachting expeditions that we had the pleasant experience of seeing the Poet Laureate, Alfred Tennyson, in his island home at Farringdon, Freshwater. He knew Cyril personally, and had formed a very high opinion of him, for, unlike the generality of young men of his day, Cyril loved poetry and worshipped genius. It had been in Mr. Frederick Locker's London abode that Cyril had first met the poet, and heard him read his own poems in that arresting voice of his and with that strange accent, so peculiarly his own, which no one who heard it could ever forget. On that summer's day in the 'eighties we were expected by the poet and most cordially received, but, alas ! my husband's first words of delight at seeing Mr. Tennyson were, owing to one fatal slip, displeasing to him, for Cyril said, grasping the hand of our host and with a beaming smile, " I am awfully glad to see you, Mr. Tennyson, awfully glad." " Young man," quoth the poet, " awfully is a word you should not use in such a connection; it is quite wrong ; pray never do so again ; you might as well say ' I am —— glad to see you ' " (using an expletive that we little expected to hear from such lips). This unfortunate beginning was certainly rather alarming, but it was soon forgotten when Mr. Tennyson introduced my sister and myself to his wife, a fragile and delicate-looking figure, who was reclining on a couch in the room. The poet then took us into the garden and became delightfully communicative, showing us the tree in which some hidden sightseer had spent some two or three hours, hoping to catch a glimpse of the Laureate in his walk.

What a fine impressive face and figure had Alfred
Tennyson! His picturesque mode of dress suited the
somewhat rugged outline of his features. I saw him
again at Mr. Leslie Stephen's house, under the pleasant
auspices of Annie Thackeray (Lady Ritchie), who was
staying with her widowed brother-in-law and looking
after his infant daughter. With the child in her arms
Miss Thackeray approached the poet, and, placing her
little niece unceremoniously on his knee, exclaimed,
"She shall be told later of this honour, and shall never
forget it"—an action somewhat disconcerting to Mr.
Tennyson.

On another occasion the poet honoured my mother's
house with his presence, being her guest at luncheon.
We were greatly amused by his appreciation of a very
well-cooked mayonnaise of chicken, which was immensely
to his liking, and which he commended so enthusiastically
that I thought the cook should have been summoned to
be complimented upon her work. After luncheon he
informed us that he was going to see a monster then
being shown, called the "Two-headed Nightingale,"
and proposed taking my sister with him in a hansom.
To this day she regrets not having acceded to his
request.

I wish I could have seen the Poet Laureate again ; I
have always loved his poetry, as a true mid-Victorian
should do, and am annoyed with some critics of the
present day for belittling his genius.

The *Garland* made many satisfactory voyages, some
of them in northern waters, such as the Fjords of
Norway or the Baltic Sea, others to the Adriatic and
Mediterranean. She could carry four or five passengers
comfortably, and all who went on those expeditions
enjoyed themselves thoroughly. I am not really a good
sailor, but I loved travelling, and yachting meant seeing
new countries generally under very pleasant conditions.
So when my sister suggested that we should accompany
her on a trip in the *Garland* at Easter-time in 1895

to the south of Spain and the Balearic Islands, both CHAPTER
my husband and I assented readily. XIII.

We found the yacht at Seville, where she was lying
amongst other vessels in the Guadalquivir, which, being
a river, proved an ideal anchorage for me.

> Fair is proud Seville ; let her country boast
> Her strength, her wealth, her site of ancient days.

Seville was then crowded up with visitors of many
nationalities, attracted by the Easter festival, with its
Church celebrations and its strange semi-religious, semi-
dramatic performances, as well as the inevitable bull-
fights.

The great Cathedral was so thronged with people that
it was far pleasanter to see the outside of the edifice
than the interior, but the processions, much vaunted
and advertised as they were, did not appeal to us very
strongly. As for the bull-fights, nothing would induce me
to renew my experiences of other days ; we were told a
good deal about the wild bulls that had been driven into
the town from the country-side at a very early hour of
the morning, and how some of the smartest French and
Spanish ladies had been out on horseback to see their
approach. I remember that two of the crew attended
a bull-fight on that occasion, and were so properly disgusted that they would not remain until the end of the
performance. But it was worth while revisiting Seville
without any further inducement than that of walking
through the streets and gazing at all the beautiful
specimens of Moorish and Renaissance architecture. On
Good Friday not a vehicle of any description was to be
seen, and not a woman went out of her house unless
draped in black from head to foot.

It was on that same occasion that we visited Gibraltar, a place I had always longed to see. We approached " Gib." by land from Ronda, that most
romantic and exquisite of old Moorish cities, and as we
rowed up to the Mole, after joining the yacht, we almost

felt as if we were returning to England, for from the top of a turret at our landing-place we were greeted by the sight of the British Flag and two unmistakable English Tommies acting as sentries. Indeed, more tokens of English life awaited us: on either side of the road huge advertisements met our eyes—" Guinness's Porter " and " Bass's Pale Ale " proclaiming the fact that our countrymen had made Gibraltar their own.

As we lay in the harbour at the close of the day, under a rose-tinted sky, with a glorious sunset, the view we had from the deck of the yacht was simply enchanting. Friends whom we met had given us a vivid account of Algeciras, then just growing into a very fashionable sea-bathing place, and of the cork woods, stretching up to Ronda, where the English officers from " Gib." hunted the fox in true English fashion.

This little England in a southern kingdom, standing as a sentinel at the gate of the Mediterranean, welcoming the home-coming and speeding the out-going ships, was to me very attractive.

Before leaving Gibraltar for good we determined upon having a peep at the Orient—a peep it could only be, through a chink, so to speak, through a half-open door ; but a peep was better than nothing.

We had heard more than once from travellers of experience that Tangier was to all appearance as Eastern as any town could be, more so indeed than Cairo, and only a few hours distant from Spain. It was not an opportunity to be lost. A very smooth sea tempted us to start, and the presence of an oncoming fog did not deter us from continuing our voyage when once we were off. Oh, what rejoicings when the fog lifted, and when we knew that we were close to our destination !

The first excitement was the approach of the health officers in a boat rowed by some handsome, strapping young Moors, who looked with a friendly eye upon our crew and, grinning, showed their splendid white teeth. But it was after landing that the fun really began. We

seemed to be living in a chapter of the " Arabian
Nights."

First of all, we had to pass the Customs, where two
polite and charming-mannered Orientals received us with
grave courtesy, welcoming us in very fair English, and
hoping that we should enjoy ourselves. A young Jew,
who spoke any number of languages, constituted himself
our guide, and escorted us to an hotel where mules
and drivers were soon in readiness. We mounted our
steeds, and proceeded along the narrow steep streets
that were simply teeming with a mixed population. No
one can have an idea of a crowded thoroughfare who has
not been in an Oriental city.

I remember we were struck by the numbers of Jews
living in close proximity to the Moors; synagogues,
mosques, and minarets all seemed in harmonious companionship. The Jewish women walked about unveiled,
smartly and brilliantly attired, and met our gaze with
their large, dark, unabashed eyes, whilst the Moorish
women from the towns were covered up in their white
garments, looking like bundles. Once or twice a dark
brown baby, guiltless of any clothing save a bright bead
necklace, was held up to us for our benefit, and I thought
them so fascinating that I should have liked to carry
one back to the yacht !

We were stopped on our road at one point by a truly
Eastern sight—a long train of camels with their drivers,
some of the animals lying down to be laden, others just
rising from their knees, until the whole drove disappeared in the distance.

The Moorish men we met were fine-looking creatures,
tall and graceful in their movements.

We were taken to see the Court House, where miserable offenders were tried and sentenced, and then the
Prison, which was a ghastly sight. It consisted, as
far as I could see, of a courtyard in which unhappy
captives, wearing chains on their arms or legs, were
sitting or crawling about. We did not enter the wretched

place, but were asked to look through a large gap or window in the wooden enclosure. The stench that one encountered in so doing sent one staggering backwards, but I made out, with horror, that a wretched man, painfully emaciated, hardly covered with any kind of clothing, was approaching the hole, extending his chained hands towards us. I turned away sick at heart, but my husband put something into those poor hands, as he was permitted to do. That very week two or three evil-doers had been bastinadoed to death in that prison!

During our ride through the town our guide had carried Cyril's photographic camera for him; one or two snapshots had already been taken. At some interesting spot which we came to after the episode of the prison the camera was again in request, but it was no longer on the arm of the guide—it had vanished. Where was it? Back we went to a shop where we had previously spent some time looking at Oriental wares, hoping to find it there, but, although the stately old shopkeeper remembered having seen the camera, there was no sign of it now. Loud demands from one to another: Where could it be? The shop filled with people, quite a crowd surrounded us gesticulating, chattering, and screaming. Our guide harangued the people, and told them in flowing Arabic that if the camera did not reappear in the next five or ten minutes, two or perhaps three boys who had been hanging round us all day would be bastinadoed. Before five minutes had passed the camera suddenly reappeared as if by magic, having been stolen from us by one of the said boys, as the guide hastily explained, whilst we had been in the shop on the first occasion. General rejoicing and handshaking all round!

We were also privileged to see a most beautiful and fascinating garden.

Returning to the landing, we came across a well-known figure riding a snow-white mule. This was no other than Lord Leighton, President of the Royal

Academy. A strange place to meet in. We stopped and talked. Leighton looked aged and poorly ; he told us he had been spending some time in Tangier for his health. It was the last occasion upon which I ever saw him—the genial, gifted artist, who was as good a linguist as he was a musician, besides being able to " paint a little," as Whistler once wittily remarked of him.

As we passed the gates of the city, our friends at the seat of custom politely expressed a hope that we had spent a pleasant day in Tangier, and saluted us with Oriental courtesy. And so ended a delightful visit to an Eastern city, with a peep into the life of the Orient.

After steaming up the coast of Spain, on leaving " Gib.," we thought we could not do better than visit the Balearic Islands—the name having a delightfully out-of-the-way sound. We knew that Majorca would offer us a comfortable harbour, so we made for Palma. I remember we had a good tossing on the way, but settled down peacefully on arrival, the anchorage being perfect.

Majorca has its own physiognomy; it did not recall either Spain or Italy, but it had great charm and distinction both of landscape and people—the dwellings looked so substantial and comfortable, the country so well cultivated, and the people industrious and prosperous.

Alick Yorke, whom we had met on the previous day at Malaga in attendance on Prince Henry of Battenberg (both gentlemen having lunched on board the *Garland*), had given us particular injunctions not to miss seeing Miramar, a property belonging to one of the Austrian Archdukes. We had no difficulty in obtaining the necessary permit, and were told that the Archduke had placed a hostel in his grounds at the disposal of sightseers, only wisely stipulating that no paper or string should be thrown about on the well-kept paths.

I remember that we took the skipper and mate and our own servants with us for a treat, and as the day

U

was beautiful we all found it most enjoyable. What added to the fun was the fact that we met a gay company of dancers and singers, also two Viennese artists, already established in the hostel, which was like a large comfortable barn. They were very gay and chatty, but we could not stay long talking to them, as we were really anxious to see the house and garden. We had been told that the Archduke's servants were very polite to strangers, and that as their master had gone to Palma for the day they would show us everything.

We were much amused at the ducal household, consisting of an old man, who looked rather like a *garde champêtre*, and his wife, an ancient dame in peasant clothing, with a handkerchief tied round her head. We went all over the unpretentious house, most simply furnished in true Majorcan style ; the walls of the rooms plainly whitewashed, with high stiff-backed chairs, no note of ease or comfort anywhere. But the garden with its beautiful view was fascinating, and the little R.C. chapel very attractive.

On our return to the hostel we again found the singers and musicians, who most kindly gave us a performance.

Very pleased with our expedition, we went back to our moorings, and settled ourselves for the evening, as we thought, in our comfortable saloon. But it was not to be. In the growing dusk we heard the splash of oars, a boat rowed up to the yacht's bow, and a queer, harsh voice made some—to us—unintelligible inquiries. " I believe it's a visitor for Mrs. Yorke," said the steward ; and a visitor it was—no other than the Archduke himself, the owner of Miramar, and a very clever, amusing man he proved to be, although his accent was strange and his speech difficult to understand at first. With him came a Count Carolino—a poet—his constant companion.

The Archduke spoke English, which he knew grammatically, as well as nine other languages. He was an exceedingly clever and learned man ; disliking all pomp and show, he had left Vienna and lived in the simplest manner at Miramar, reading, studying, and writing to his heart's content, besides managing his small property extremely well. We were sorry not to have seen more of him, and he gave us such a friendly invitation to return and pay him a visit. Alas, this was never to take place !

CHAPTER XIV

CRUISING ON THE " GARLAND "

GREECE AND THE ADRIATIC—MONTENEGRO—AN EXCEPTIONAL CRUISE

THE *Garland* had already taken " the Missus " on one most satisfactory trip to Greece; in fact she had found it so enjoyable that she prevailed upon us to accompany her upon a second cruise to the same romantic country. It was also carefully put before me that yachting amongst the Ionian Islands, and then through the Corinth Canal to the Piraeus and farther, would exactly suit my seafaring powers. I did not require much persuasion, and so we started, my sister and I by train, early in March 1894, to join my husband on the *Garland* at Corfu. He was recovering from a very serious fall that he had had out hunting, and hoped great things from the rest on board and change of scene.

We were joined a few days later by Spencer Lyttelton, one of the best of travellers and sailors. On that occasion I enjoyed the experience of a short voyage on one of the Austrian Lloyd steamers, which took us on a calm and beautiful night from Brindisi to Corfu, where the *Garland* was awaiting us. It was a very happy trip, particularly the Greek part of it. We had on the whole fine weather, although cold in some instances, much too cold indeed for the mountain excursions we wanted to take. Our first view of Corfu was delightful, and we were only grieved to think that the island was

292

no longer under our flag, particularly when we heard how everything was deteriorating since it had come under Greek rule.

This was the first time I had heard Greek spoken, also my first experience of not being able to read the names of streets and buildings, in fact of being very helpless and most dependent upon an excellent Greek dragoman, by name Nicolas Segilas, who had been strongly recommended to my sister by Sir Rennell Rodd, that charming compatriot of ours, who knew Greece well, and had drafted our itinerary for us. He has now (1920) returned to England from having been Ambassador in Rome, where he was a great favourite.

I remember taking a lovely drive in the island to the Olive Groves, and being specially struck with the beauty of the peasant women, whose regular features, small oval faces, and long almond-shaped eyes were true to the old Greek type, now so fast disappearing where the race is no longer pure.   In fact, in one of the villages, whilst walking up to see a fine view, we could not resist stopping a moment to gaze at a really beautiful girl who was advancing towards us ; I believe my husband addressed a few words to her in Greek and put out his hand; she smiled, looked astonished, and walked on. Two minutes afterwards some men were coming down towards us, and one was calling out some words which caused our guide to hurry us on to the top of the village street.   Upon our asking what was the matter, for our guide looked concerned, he said: " The girl, Arethusa by name, told her friend that you had addressed her, and had even offered to shake hands with her, and her friend is very indignant and wishes now to box with you." We could not help laughing, but Nicolas said it might have been serious, the customs in Corfu regarding the female sex being peculiarly severe.   When we returned on our way back, neither Arethusa nor her companions were to be seen.

During our drive we passed the entrance gates of

Achilleion, a villa residence commanding a glorious view;
it belonged to the Empress of Austria, and that ill-
fated lady was wont to stay there some weeks every
summer, studying Greek with an accomplished master of
that language.   It was sold after her death and bought
by the Kaiser !

Before leaving we made the acquaintance of our
Minister accredited to the Court of Montenegro, Mr.
Kennedy, who was spending a few days at Corfu.
He was very friendly, and begged us to pay him and
his wife a visit at Cettinje on our homeward journey,
should we return by the Adriatic and anchor at the
Bocca di Cattaro.

We had one or two rough passages, I remember, before
we passed into the tranquil waters of the Corinth Canal,
finding ourselves at last, after a most delightful and
wonderful visit to Olympia, at the Piraeus, which is, as
it were, the landing-place for Athens.

The capital of Greece is certainly not a fine town,
it is painfully modern; but of course it is a treasure-
ground for the archaeologist and the historian, whilst
the fragrance of romance is inseparable from Greek art,
Greek poetry, and Greek scenes.

We visited the wonderfully interesting sites of old
temples and the magnificent ruins in the ancient part
of the city, whilst in the Museum we learned to know
and care for archaic art.   It is a taste that grows upon
one; after some short, too short, experience I cared for the
older art more than for the Greek art of the best period.

On one of my visits to the Acropolis I was carefully
studying *Murray's Handbook*, reading it aloud to Mr.
Lyttelton as I went up step after step, my husband
and my sister having gone on rapidly in advance.
We were deep in our *Murray* when a very American
voice penetrated to our ears, and we heard the following : " I was just stepping over that cornice, Momma,
and should have had a beautiful view, when an old
crock took me by my ankle ; he was standing below

me, busy with his camera, and said it was too dangerous
a place for me to stand on. I was just angry ! I tried
to get away, but he would not let go." Well, if she
was angry we were amused, for the " old crock " was
none other than Cyril. Soon we came upon these very
American ladies, but heard nothing more amusing from
their lips.

We had one most interesting audience in the Royal
Palace, where Queen Olga of Greece, the mother of
King Constantine, a Russian Princess, well known and
much beloved by the English as well as by the Greeks,
received my sister and myself most graciously. Queen
Olga had a charming face, intelligent and sympathetic,
and very simple manners ; when I was going to kiss
her hand she drew it away rapidly and said, " Oh,
we do not do such things here."

By the bye, the only order we received before going
to the Palace was to the effect that we were not to
wear the ordinary out-of-door veil. The Queen was still
mourning the sad and untoward death of her youngest
daughter, happily married in Russia; she had been thrown
out of her carriage and had succumbed to the effects
of the accident ; her mother told us in a pathetic voice
that she was now leading a very secluded life and that
much had changed for her. She spoke warmly of Lord
Ribblesdale's young brother, the late Reggie Lister,
then at our British Legation, and one of the most
promising of the young diplomats, and also of E. F.
Benson (now a novelist of fame), who was greatly
interested in Greek archaeology. We had the pleasure
of meeting both these gentlemen in Greece, as well as
Sir Charles Walston, distinguished not only as a student
of Greek art, but also as an able writer on many
subjects not connected with art, and were even invited
to an excavation party and entertained by the learned
excavators.

(1920.—Poor Queen Olga ! What vicissitudes have
been hers since 1894 !)

But not all our travelling on this Greek trip was to be by sea; there were places inland that we were anxious to visit, and in order to ensure our comfort Nicolas provided us with a native cook (a very excellent one he proved to be) and a young manservant—a footman. On such occasions the two would go on before us, taking with them our bedding, linen, and cooking utensils from the yacht.

Two distinct inland trips remain imprinted on my memory. The one was to Megalopolis, *en route* for the picturesque heights of Bassae. We started in very indifferent weather, not suitable for such an excursion, but as we were most eager to see as much as we could of Greece, we pushed boldly on from Tripolitza (where we had spent a night) by carriage, towards the queer little countrified town of Megalopolis. We walked down a steep pass, which landed us in the principal street or roadway, where we were received by the Demark, or chief man of the place.

As there was no hotel in the town, the Demark had been asked to entertain us, which he did by offering us his house, whilst he and his whole family, plus dogs, goats, and poultry, turned into *one* room. He was bowing profoundly when he accosted us, informing us in true Eastern fashion that everything he possessed was ours !

I often thought that Nicolas led simple people we met on this trip to imagine that we were persons of great importance, for he used to chuckle with a kind of sly delight after a confab with his countrymen, who thereupon invariably looked at us with much respect and greeted us with wonderful salutations. Their financial demands were also, generally speaking, in ratio to their belief in our exalted rank ; but these were not always conceded to by our dragoman.

Meanwhile the weather was growing colder and more menacing; grey clouds were blotting out the sunshine. Our Demark tried to be hopeful about the weather,

but even he failed, and we sought comfort in our rooms.
This was somewhat difficult, there being no stove or
open fireplace, only a brazier round which we sat, con-
soling ourselves with steaming cups of very good tea.
At nightfall we packed ourselves into our small bare bedrooms as well as we could, rejoicing in our fresh clean
sheets and warm blankets that we had brought with
us. A partition wall separated the room tenanted by
my sister and her maid and myself from those occupied
on the one side by Cyril and his servant, on the other
by the Demark and his whole family, who neither
undressed that night nor took any repose. Spencer
Lyttelton, our travelling companion, lay in a miserable
little hole of a room, where a window frame, innocent of
any glass panes, was protected by a noisy, rattling,
wooden shutter.

The threatened storm did not leave us long in doubt
of its presence. It hailed, it snowed, it blew with a
vengeance. Suddenly, above the din of the elements,
I could hear a voice calling out for help, a voice that I
recognised as that of Mr. Lyttelton, then a patter of
quick feet from the other side of the partition. The
shutter had been blown open, and the icy wind was
rushing in upon the head of the unfortunate occupant
of the room. To his surprise, as he told us on the
following morning, a young girl fully dressed had come
quickly and quietly to his rescue and had attended most
effectively to his shutter, retreating as quietly as she
had entered.

None of us slept that night, and we were not sorry
when the time for our early breakfast drew near. At
our door, awaiting our orders, or rather those of Nicolas,
stood a most picturesque Greek guide, with a string
of mules, ready for a mountain expedition. We
pointed to the sky and the falling snow, and the man,
in reply to our dragoman's inquiries, gave so lurid a
description of the pass and the road that we felt impelled
to give up the romantic excursion. But I recollect

that we sought and found consolation in less arduous roads, over the classic ground of Sparta, finally joining the yacht at Gythion.

Again we were tempted to leave our ship, this time to go north to Thessaly, and if possible to penetrate into Meteora, where we should be entertained in the monastery of San Stefano. The cook and servant had again been sent on with all necessaries for the expedition.

I remember we went from Volo to Kalabaka by train and were much amused by the motley crowds at the station : Greeks, Turks, Montenegrins, and Gipsies, mostly men ; very few women were to be seen. Either going or returning *via* Volo my husband took a snap-shot of a very handsome Greek, who seemed much pleased to have his portrait taken; he told Nicolas that he would like to have a print, and when asked for his address, answered loftily, " ' The Head Shepherd of Volo ' will find me."

We left the train at Kalabaka, where, to our astonishment, we were met by an officer at the head of an armed bodyguard of soldiers, who were to accompany us to our destination. We were told that Thessaly was unsafe for travellers at that time. It was a strange experience for us, but it was all new and interesting. We rode up a steep mountain-side, passing through dirty, squalid-looking villages, where the poor miserable inhabitants turned out in crowds to see us. On arriving at the gate of the monastery, we were much amused at seeing our footman approaching with a bouquet, followed by the cook in his white attire.

One of the old monks, a venerable figure, stood at the entrance, bowing low, with his hand upon his breast. He gave us a right kindly welcome, and we were shown into very comfortable quarters. We invited the Greek officer to be our guest at dinner and found him prepared to enjoy the savoury dishes, but unable to speak in any tongue but modern Greek, of which we were all ignorant. This did not

conduce to a flow of conversation, but it made the
meal hilarious. Cyril and S. L. fired off all the Greek
they knew, the classical Greek of the ancient poets, to
the astonishment of guest and footman, who both
responded as well as they could. The venerable monk
who had received us at the gateway had also come,
upon our invitation, to the dinner-table, but he neither
ate nor spoke, only smiled upon us, bowed when my
husband drank his health, and accepted from him a
glass of wine—I think he only raised it to his lips,
without drinking.

When we were all retiring for the night Cyril was
presented with the big key that locked the outer gate
of the monastery, and asked to keep it, as a sign that
he (for that night) was the master of the place. He
promptly accepted it and put it under his pillow. This
led to a strange incident.

It was the Thursday in Holy Week (according to
the Greek Church), and there was midnight Mass in
the chapel of the monastery. In order to summon all
within the walls, a drum, or gong, was beaten just
before Mass commenced. It was a loud instrument,
and the sounds reached down into the village, where
our arrival with our guard some hours before had
made a considerable stir. The idea came to the
people that possibly, after all, we were being attacked by
brigands, and that the monks were thus summoning
aid. In order to effect our rescue a second guard was
despatched under another officer, who, climbing the
mountain-side, arrived in the early hours of the morning.
Of course they found the monastery gate barred and
locked, and some time elapsed before their loud knocking
and cries for admittance were attended to. Cyril's
slumbers were then broken in upon by our excellent
dragoman, who came in company of Officer No. 1, with
many apologies, to demand the key which he had safely
stowed away under his pillow. It was speedily produced,
the gate was unbarred, and Officer No. 2 and his

men streamed into the monastery precincts. It really was a curious episode, and occasioned much amusement on the following morning when we sat down to breakfast in company with the officers, but the poor men, who had had a sorry night's rest, did not see much fun in the incident, and had to be substantially placated by the ever ready Nicolas, who assured us he would " make it all right."

Before leaving this strange country of Meteora, we were persuaded to ride on and, from the base of a rock, see what we could of another monastery, which was perched on its summit. We were accompanied by both bodyguards and their respective officers. When we arrived at the foot of the precipice we were told that there were only two ways of entering the monastery : the one in a kind of basket or net, which was let down from the summit of the rock, 222 feet in height, by a rope and pulley, and then drawn up again with the occupant sitting or standing inside. The ascent takes three minutes. The other means of access was by ladders of wood and rope, which could be let down over the face of the cliff. At night, when not required, these ladders are pulled up, and the monks are entirely isolated from the world below.

The soldiers, nearly all of whom were barefooted, used these ladders for climbing up to the monastery, whilst, to our horror, Mr. Lyttelton insisted upon being drawn up in the net. We tried to prevent him, but without avail; it looked simply terrifying, and we were glad indeed when he returned safely from this dangerous flight and stepped out upon *terra firma*, having received warm congratulations from the monks whom he had visited.

On our return to the station at Kalabaka, the crowd of men belonging to so many nationalities reminded me of Byron's lines :

The Turk, the Greek, the Albanian, and the Moor,
Here mingled in their many-hued array . . .

The wild Albanian kirtled to his knee,
With shawl-girt head and ornamented gun,
And gold-embroider'd garments, fair to see ;
The crimson-scarféd men of Macedon ;
The Delhi with his cap of terror on,
And crooked glaive ; the lively, supple Greek . . .
The bearded Turk, that rarely deigns to speak.

I recall being much impressed by our short journey
through Thessaly to Larissa, passing over the great
plains, with their splendid screen of mountains, Ossa
and Pelion standing out snow-white amongst the rest,
and Olympus peering above the clouds, showing us his
fine snow-capped head.

Larissa itself was our first experience of what was
once an old Turkish town, with ruined mosques and
minarets ; from the roof of one of the latter we heard
the cry, " Allah is the one God and Mahomed is his
prophet," at the hour of sunset.

We had fairly good rooms in the hotel where we
spent the night, but had to take our meals in a restaurant ;
no native women being ever seen in such a public resort,
my sister and I were objects of some curiosity.

We visited the celebrated Vale of Tempe on the
following day, and were accompanied by an armed and
mounted escort. We were told that brigands always
got some mysterious notice of the approach of strangers,
and were ready to pounce down upon them and carry
them off to their fortresses ; so that I felt much
comforted by the rather untidy-looking men of our
guard, who, on very fleet horses, seemed to be well on
the look-out for danger. And what a drive we had that
day ! I remember that we were much struck by our
Turkish coachman, who, unlike the Greek drivers,
showed great kindness and mercy to his horses, never
using the whip, but talking to them and cheering them
on when they showed signs of fatigue ; and this was
not unusual on the part of the poor animals, considering
the condition of the roads, at times muddy bogs, at

others stretches of stone or rock, causing us to hold on to the sides of the carriage so as not to be flung out. Then we turned off from the road into the plains, going at foot pace, and being much interested by what we saw. We passed great flocks of sheep and of goats, also herds of oxen ; the shepherds in picturesque garb, attended by their huge and savage dogs. There were also, I recollect, encampments of rough coarse tents, from which the women emerged when they saw us approaching, gazing at us with curiosity.

The Vale of Tempe itself is a cleft or gorge between two steep walls of rock, the river Peneus flowing through the gorge. We picnicked under the shade of some elm trees, and were enchanted with the profusion and beauty of the wild flowers—indeed we could hardly tear ourselves away from so lovely a spot. But our driver pointed admonishingly to the heavens, and we felt the hour had come for return, so off we set again ; the horses, rested and refreshed, simply bounded across morass and stones, bringing us back triumphantly to the old city that, shrouded in semi-darkness, but beautifully lighted by some mysteriously hung lamps, seemed to give us a silent and gracious welcome.

We had much hoped to visit Constantinople on that trip and to see something of Turkey, but unfortunately an epidemic of smallpox in the capital made this impossible. So we contented ourselves with a glimpse of Thermopylae from the deck of the *Garland,* and with a visit to Sunium, where the beautiful Greek temple shone like alabaster in the sunshine. But it was all wonderful.

> Where'er we tread 'tis haunted, holy ground ;
> No earth of thine is lost in vulgar mould,
> But one vast realm of wonder spreads around,
> And all the Muse's tales seem truly told.

On this homeward journey we both were ill with chicken-pox, no pleasant malady. Annie started her attack in Greek waters, and convalesced during our stay outside Corfu. I became ill as we were coasting up the Adriatic, and my worst time was spent whilst anchored off Venice. Meanwhile, in spite of these untoward illnesses, we managed to see much that appealed to us.

Whilst the yacht was at Corfu I often landed with my husband (Spencer Lyttelton had left us) and saw a good deal of the Duke of Argyll, who was laid up in the hotel with an attack of gout. His daughter, Lady Mary Glyn, with her husband and son, was looking after him, and, being anxious to give him a change of companionship, she was glad to bring us as visitors to her father. What a charming man he was! so ready to be sociable, so chatty and agreeable even when suffering. He welcomed me very kindly and said I was a cheery person. He was very proud of his hands and feet, and much perturbed by the thought that the gout might spoil the shape of the latter. He told me the following little anecdote about himself.

As a youth he had travelled in Greece with his tutor, a very scholarly man, who spoke modern as well as ancient Greek. Together they visited the Senate House in Athens, where the Parliament was sitting. The Duke went up into the gallery in order to get a good view of the senators, whilst the tutor remained below. One of the Greeks, seeing that he was a stranger and that his companion was in the gallery above, " asked my tutor if he knew and could tell him what lotion or pomatum I used, to make my hair of such a beautiful golden colour—for it *was beautiful*," the Duke continued with a sigh, "like Frances's hair, only much more golden. And, fancy, the man would not believe that the colour was natural." This appeared to please him very much, and when I looked at his small golden head, which he always threw back when he was talking, I remembered my mother telling me that when young he had often been compared to a golden pheasant.   I think he had a very tender nature, for although he differed on so many points at that time from Mr. Gladstone, he spoke of him in terms of true affection, and was deeply moved at the prospect of the operation for cataract that lay before the great statesman.   His keen interest in natural history asserted itself when he bade me carefully watch and describe to him any birds that I might see in driving about the island.   Not forgetful of this behest, but anxious to bring a little fun into our daily visits, I invented a description of a fabulous bird when next I saw the Duke.   He looked at me with his piercing glance and, patting my hand, said, " I am too old a bird to be caught by that story."

The interest attached to that memorable cruise was certainly heightened by our visit to Cettinje, made at the invitation of Mr. Kennedy, our representative at the Court of Montenegro, whom we had met with his wife at Corfu.   We fortunately managed, I think very cleverly, to get this visit in between our attacks of chicken-pox.

Leaving Corfu on a perfect morning, we steamed straight for the Bocca di Cattaro, the little town lying on the shores of the Adriatic, the Bocca forming a close and safe anchorage.   After twenty-four hours of sea passage we thought a mountain expedition would be most enjoyable, particularly as it led to Cettinje, the capital of Montenegro.

The road to Cettinje winds in endless zigzags up the steep mountain-side from Cattaro, and before starting we could see the exact route that we were to take !   I was told that this miniature principality was only fifty miles in length and thirty in breadth, and that it contained between two and three hundred villages, the largest of which had only a population of something over 1000.   The country bears the name of Montenegro on account of its black pine-clothed mountains.

We studied our guide-books industriously before starting on our drive, which we were told would only take three hours, but which was not accomplished under five, although we had excellent little horses that trotted along in spite of its being a steady climb nearly the whole way. The first part was wonderfully beautiful, through the pine forests, with glimpses every now and then of the dark blue sea and the little scattered villages lying amongst the hills. Then suddenly we left trees and shade behind us, and found ourselves on a rocky path, with the most extraordinarily-shaped dark mountains rising all round us; it had quite a diabolical aspect. We stopped to rest our horses at one of the wayside inns that are common in those parts, and there we saw, and with our driver's help were able to speak to, some of the inhabitants.

The men are magnificent creatures, very fine-featured and generally over six feet high, and are always fully armed and prepared to go into battle, being surrounded by hostile people.

The women perform the part of beasts of burden, carrying huge loads of hay and straw or provender in great baskets strapped to their backs. With their bare feet in sandals, they run up and down the steep mountain-side, never taking the road, and climbing like goats from rock to rock. They are rather swarthy and hard-featured, and less good-looking than the men. They are all inured to every kind of hardship and privation, and both sexes are remarkable for patience and courage. Poor people, these qualities were terribly put to the test in the Great War!

We went on our way, arriving at Cettinje, the capital —a strange capital of a strange country. It looked to us like a straggling village, with whitewashed houses and a village green, surmounted by the one beautiful tree that the place could boast of. We were most kindly and cordially received by Mr. and Mrs. Kennedy, who, though they had had to take rooms for us in the hotel

X

close by, were really our hosts. They were determined that we should see as much as possible of this strange country, and not only of the country, but also of those who were helping to make it interesting. Soon after our arrival, the Minister for Foreign Affairs was announced. In walked a very handsome man, who astonished us by speaking French quite beautifully. Hardly had he departed when Mr. Kennedy brought us a message from the Prince, inviting us to call upon him. Cyril had been advised beforehand to bring a black coat, which he hastily donned, whilst our Minister was in regulation garb. Off we walked, arriving in about five minutes' time at the Royal residence—a most unpretentious building. Two magnificent Montenegrins received us at the door, bowing low and conducting us into the presence-chamber.

The Prince came to meet us, and entertained us most kindly and cordially. His Highness—since then His Majesty—was closely connected with the Russian Court. His Queen was a Russian Princess, and belonged, as indeed all the inhabitants of Montenegro do, to the Greek Church.

The Prince, a tall, handsome man, was in national full dress, which suited his fine martial figure and bearing. He made us all be seated, and the conversation was carried on in French. The ladies of the Court did not appear, as they attend very strictly to their religious duties during the Easter week, when they never receive guests. The Prince began instantly to tell us how much he admired the English character, and I remember he said that he wanted to visit England for three reasons : to kiss the hand of Queen Victoria, to express personally his gratitude to and admiration for Mr. Gladstone, and to place a wreath of laurels upon the grave of Tennyson, who had composed a sonnet on Montenegro. He told us how his people were all fully armed, and that, should they be attacked by any of their quarrelsome and aggressive neighbours, he could depend upon having a competent army, ready for active service, within two hours' time! He was a despot, but one of the best, adored by his people : a true Montenegrin, devoted to his strange, wild, mountain principality.

Under that one historic tree, standing on the village green, he would listen to complaints from his subjects and administer justice, without his decisions ever being questioned. We were much impressed by this splendid warrior, who was not only a great general, but an intelligent and cultivated man.

Our dinner-party was enlivened by the presence of the Austrian Secretary, a Swiss tutor of the Kennedy boys, and an exceedingly able and interesting Montenegrin engineer. We remarked that the men who were waiting upon us carried daggers stuck into their waist-bands, and were told that they all had loaded pistols on them.

We left Cettinje with regret, and never saw its ruler again. In one way his dream was realised, for he carried out his journey to England. But Mr. Gladstone was no longer there to receive him, and I think it was King Edward, and not Queen Victoria, who bade him welcome at Windsor.

Such cruises as we used to indulge in on the *Garland* were both amusing and instructive, leaving lasting impressions. Fortunately the memories of beautiful scenery, agreeable personalities, and amusing adventures are far more enduring than those of bad weather and rough seas, sea-sickness and small contretemps.

The *Garland* went on one very exceptional cruise, when I had not the honour of being a passenger, but was only an occasional guest. This was when she carried Mr. and Mrs. Gladstone, their son Henry and my husband, with " the Missus " in command, on a tour to the West of England—really an electioneering campaign. This took place in June 1889, and was recorded in *Punch* as follows :

TO THE WEST !

New Gladstonian Version

G.O.M. *sings* :

To the West, to the West, for a Whitsuntide spree,
Where Devon and Cornwall jut out to the sea,
Where the tired G.O.M., if he's willing to toil,
May hope to ingather political spoil.

Where meetings are scarce, where my generous host
My aid at political fireworks will boast,
Where the mobs will exult whilst I spout, scorning rest ;
Away, far away, to the land of the West !

To the West, to the West, where my speeches will flow
Like rivers of words, spreading wide as they go ;
Where Weymouth and Dartmouth shall stir at my call,
And Torquay and Plymouth keep rolling the ball ;

Where the steam-yacht of kind Mrs. Eliot Yorke,
The *Garland*, shall waft me away to my work,
Till Tintagel's truth I shall put to the test ;
Away, far away, to the crowds of the West !

To the West, to the West, there are votes to be won,
There's Home Rule to clear up, lots of work to be done.
I'll try it, I'll do it ; I'll never despair
Whilst I've breath to orate or a moment to spare.

Poor Pat's independence my labours shall buy,
Though Chamberlain swears that the game's all my eye.
Away, boys, away, let us hope for the best,
And fight for Home Rule in the land of the West ! [1]

The great statesman, then a venerable figure with a
most imposing presence, still retained his wonderful
gift of oratory. Mr. Gladstone had been induced to
gratify the desire of his ardent supporters, namely,
that the many who only knew him by repute, but who
gave him their devoted allegiance, should be offered

[1] By permission of the proprietors of *Punch*.

the opportunity of seeing him face to face and hearing him address an audience.

The weather was propitious for a cruise. My sister was as convinced a Liberal as was my husband ; Mrs. Gladstone was ready to fall in with their arrangements and to make things easy and comfortable for Mr. Gladstone. She was indeed a wonderful wife, ever anxious for his popularity and ever mindful of his health and well-being.

The *Garland* was escorted by the *Sunbeam*, Lord Brassey's celebrated steam yacht, and two of his guests were the late Arnold Morley and Mr. Jack Pease, now Lord Gainford, both strong supporters of Mr. Gladstone.

My mother and I had arranged a little trip to Devon and Cornwall at the same time, which would enable us, when possible, to meet the *Garland*, and also to be present at one or more of the political gatherings.

The cruise was a very successful one, and the huge audiences most enthusiastic. We met the *Garland* at Dartmouth and spent a short time on board, whilst my sister gave us some amusing experiences of life on the yacht. Mr. Gladstone had been reading with the deepest interest the *Life of Cardinal Manning*, and could hardly tear himself away from the book. He was, indeed, far more anxious to talk about the contents of the volume, and to discuss some errors he had found in it, than to prepare his political orations. But he did allow Darby, the skipper, a very advanced and uncompromising Liberal, to hold converse with him, and he knew that the crew were very proud of their distinguished passenger. Crowds assembled whenever he landed, and fortunately the fine weather allowed numbers to attend the meetings. I was only present on one occasion, at Torquay, which I believe was the least exciting of these gatherings, although the audience gave Mr. Gladstone a hearty welcome; but Cornwall nearly went mad over the advent of the great orator.

We parted company at Plymouth.

CHAPTER XV

NORWAY—BALHOLM—DENMARK

CHAPTER XV. THE last cruise that I had on the *Garland*, in July 1911, was taken partly at my request, and included one memorable and historic incident.

Since our old trips much had changed and many dear ones had left us. There were fewer home letters to be written, fewer telegrams to be sent, dates were no longer so carefully noted and attended to. In the old days my husband was chiefly consulted about the places he wished to visit, and his tastes were much considered. He had always loved the yacht, and had been a great favourite with the crew, and with Darby.

We crossed from Newcastle to Stavanger in one of the very comfortable Norwegian steamboats, arriving after thirty hours' passage at one o'clock in the morning. It was a beautiful starlight night, and the air felt deliciously fresh and cool after the cabin from which I issued ; but the best sight for me was that of two of the *Garland's* men, who stood smiling to receive us at the landing. What a heavenly row to our moorings, and what a delicious repast was prepared on board for " the Missus " and her guests ! How we revelled in the nice, clean, home-y yacht !

Norway is indeed the country *par excellence* to visit in one's floating castle. I had never before seen those northern shores ; they have a great charm of their

310

own, and the long, narrow fjords—the inland seas— offer very comfortable cruising for indifferent sailors.

We were greatly struck, I remember, by the number of German warships disporting themselves in the northern waters ; they were to be met with in every fjord, and we were constantly coming across the very trim and active members of their crews. On one occasion we saw a German sailor struggling in the sea ; he had evidently fallen overboard, and the vessel on which he had been sailing was going on its course unaware of his mishap. Our skipper despatched one of our boats to his rescue at an instant's notice. The man was helped out of the water and rowed back to his own ship. To the disgust of our men, no thanks were expressed for this act of courtesy, either by the man or his comrades !

On another occasion, upon arriving at some heights when upon a mountain excursion, we were greeted by strains of music, and saw, to our astonishment, as we entered the hotel where we were going to have luncheon, a fine naval band from one of the German warships. The men had actually climbed up the steep mountain pass carrying their heavy instruments, and, in spite of fatigue and heat, were playing some spirited tunes for their own delectation and that of the visitors. It really was rather a fine thing to have done, and an instance of the men's power of endurance and their love of music.

We prolonged that excursion, the weather being propitious, and spent the night still higher up in a fairly comfortable hotel, placed in the midst of the most glorious scenery. We were actually surrounded by snow-clad mountains, and had the further enjoyment of walking upon snow. The window in my tiny room faced the bed, and, guiltless of blind or curtain, allowed me to watch sunset and sunrise, both taking place within one hour's time, the mountains being meanwhile suffused by a rose-coloured glow.

There was a real Lapp tent, inhabited by a real Lapp

family, not far from the hotel—an object of interest to the visitors—and some tame reindeer were tethered close by.

There was a goodly medley of visitors in that little mountain hotel, including two very entertaining and lively Frenchwomen, artists, with whom I had some conversation. They happened to be ardent suffragists, had just returned from a great suffrage meeting in Sweden, and before going back to Paris they were taking a little trip in Norway. We talked of art in England and in France ; they were quite modern in their tastes, and proclaimed their allegiance to Rossetti, Watts, and, above all others, Burne-Jones. "Ah, how beautiful is his picture called ' The Golden Stairs ' ! " said the older lady of the two — a very loquacious, stout Frenchwoman. " I am so glad," I replied, " for I have it." " Indeed ! " said the lady, " and what may be the size of the engraving ? " " Oh," I answered, " there are many sizes, some very fine ones, quite large, others small and inexpensive." " But yours," said the lady, " what size is yours ? " " Oh, that does not matter much since I have the picture itself." " You have the *original* ? " screamed the lady—" the very original ? Impossible ! " " Yes, indeed." " *O je vous en félicite !* " She jumped up and shook me by the hand. " Yes," I said, much amused, " Burne-Jones painted it expressly for us." " Then you knew him—you knew the master ? " " Yes, of course; he was a very great friend of ours." " A friend ! then you belong to us, you belong to *le monde bohémien !* " I laughed. " You should read the book by Robert de la Sizeranne on your Burne-Jones ! " " I have read it, and what is more, Monsieur de la Sizeranne gave it to me." Another scream : " *Je vous en fais mes compliments. Ah ! vous êtes des nôtres,*" and so on. " *Vous appartenez au monde bohémien.*"

We had been told by our amusing old Norwegian pilot that the *Hohenzollern*, with the Kaiser on board, had recently arrived at Bergen, and that very shortly we should be in sight of the Imperial yacht.

This proved true, for after leaving Bergen and making for Balholm, most picturesquely situated on a beautiful inland fjord, we saw straight ahead of us the *Hohenzollern*. We took up our moorings at fairly close quarters, so close, indeed, that we could distinctly hear the word of command given to the crew by the captain, also the strains of our own National Anthem, stirringly played by the ship's band. This was not to do us honour, as we might have thought, but because the same tune also happened to be that of the German National Anthem.

Our vicinity to the *Hohenzollern* excited our ship's crew and passengers not a little, and we all wondered whether we should see more of her than we could do from our floating home. We were soon to be made aware that nothing would escape the attention of her Royal master.

The following, taken from my Diary, was faithfully inscribed on the evening of July 20, 1911 :

ON BOARD THE " GARLAND," *Friday, July* 20, 1911.—At 7.30 this morning appeared an envoy from the *Hohenzollern* with a parcel of English papers for my sister, and a request from the Kaiser to have a written list of the names of those on board her yacht.

At 9.30 a visit from Prince Albert of Schleswig-Holstein, who was an old friend of Geoffrey Head's (my nephew by marriage), bringing an invitation to luncheon at 1 o'clock from H.I.M.

Well, I was very jubilant, as I longed to make the Kaiser's acquaintance, and had begged of my sister not to plan an excursion for to-day.

During the morning we watched a so-called race between the rowing boats of the *Hohenzollern*—the Kaiser, steering the leading boat, passed close by our yacht and saluted. The boat which is steered by the Kaiser, be it sailing or rowing boat, is always supposed to be the winning one.

At 1 o'clock we (five in all) boarded the *Hohen-zollern*. Received by the captain of the ship, Count Platen von Hallemund, a man with nice manners, speaking English perfectly. We were taken to the upper deck, and in a few minutes the Kaiser appeared in the undress uniform of an admiral. H.I.M. is shorter than I had imagined he would be, and has a slight stoop. His face is remarkably clever, with piercing eyes. He put us at our ease at once. There were no ladies on board, but a suite of sixteen gentlemen. Each one did the Kaiser introduce to me, not only by name, but adding a little detail, such as : " This is Moltke (nephew of the great General), my Chancellor." " This is one of my Admirals." " This is a General," and so on.

The Kaiser at luncheon sat in the middle of the long table between Annie and myself. He had a raised seat, so that he towered above us all. He uses a very peculiar knife and fork, made in one, on account of his withered arm. Prince Albert of Schleswig-Holstein sat opposite him, with my two nieces, Daisy Head and Connie Flower, one on each side. A long line of sailors, most excellent waiters, stood behind our chairs. On the table were flowers and gold and silver plate ; amongst other ornaments]a model of the *Hohenzollern* in silver. The menu cards were all in German. Forty men, all sailors, played at intervals extremely well, the Kaiser having selected the pieces he wished them to play.

I found H.I.M. very easy to get on with. He not only talked but listened. We spoke of the English Royal Family, and he praised King George and Queen Mary for their love of duty and their orderly and strenuous lives. He said : " How well they have inaugurated their reign ! and what a moment to become King !—not a moment that one would choose." Then : " The Duchess of Teck (Queen Mary's mother) was a charming and most clever woman—a great friend of mine." He spoke of " Grandmamma " with affectionate respect and admiration, also of " Uncle Bertie " and of " Aunt Argyll."

Then I happened to mention my old friend, George Bunsen, and the Kaiser exclaimed at once : " Of course, I knew him well, dear man ! " I recalled a little story that M. de Bunsen had told me about H.I.M. when a child. He nodded his head and said : " Oh yes, quite true, quite true; I loved reading about naval matters, and I did send him a little book with queries about the terms in English which I wrote in the margin." He asked me if I knew Lothar, G. Bunsen's son. I replied that I did. " He is very different from his father," said the Kaiser. " I should take him for an English cleric." He spoke of Marie de Bunsen—a very clever woman and a personal friend of the late Empress Frederick. The name of Lord Haldane having been mentioned, I ventured to say that our War Minister had been much interested in seeing the manœuvres under Imperial auspices in the previous year. " I showed him everything," said H.I.M. " We have nothing to conceal, nothing to fear, why should we mind ? We want to be good friends with you in England, but your Territorials will be your difficulty; your Volunteers were excellent, full of enthusiasm; Lord Wemyss understood them well; but your Territorials!!! " " Well, your Majesty, what do you think of them ? " " I would rather not say — they are certainly not the Guards. Your Guards are splendid, but you want a soldier at the head of your War Office. Why, when my officers met Lord Haldane in the woods of Ilmenau, wearing a long grey coat, reading Goethe, they said : ' Can that be England's War Minister ? Impossible ! ' Ah, you want a soldier, and you have sent your two best soldiers out of England." " Who may they be, your Majesty ? " " The Duke of Connaught and Lord Kitchener, of course." " Did your Majesty give your views to Lord Haldane ? " " No, certainly not, he might only have called me the tyrant ruler of a benighted country. I know in England I have been called ' a damned German.' " Then H.I.M.

shouted across the table : " Albert, who is the man who
is always writing against me in England—what is his
name ? " " Leo Maxse, in the *National Review,* sir,"
answered his cousin quickly. " Yes, that is the man ;
but why should we Germans not be good friends with
England ?   Our two countries ought to march together :
the same race, the same religion, the same interests—we
should be friends.   But we do not like to have our toes
trodden upon, and we can tread back.   Some people
are too large for their shoes "—this with a look like
the Devil, which quite frightened me.   Then we talked
of conscription, which he said would never be possible
in England : it would be the ruin of any Government.

He next touched on the Insurance Bill, Old Age
Pensions, National Education, Continuation Schools,
German prisons contrasted with English ones, popular
music ; then held forth with enthusiasm about Norway
in general and Balholm in particular, the little place
where our yachts are lying.

He gave me an account of a ball he had given last
week on board, of the pretty Norwegian girls who had
attended it from far and wide.   Also of the Sunday
services he had held on the yacht.   He explained that he
brought no chaplain, but read the prayers himself ; that
he had a splendid choir amongst the sailors, and that he
selected and then preached a sermon, from some which
he had brought with him for that purpose.   I said :
" Your Majesty ought to compose your own sermons."
" No, I should be too much criticised," he replied ; " that
would not do."

He mentioned England again with affection, and said :
" You know that I unveiled Queen Victoria's statue last
year, and never did I have a better reception."

After luncheon we sat upon the upper deck listening
to the band ; coffee and cigarettes were handed round.
" I am too early-Victorian to smoke," I said, when H.I.M.
offered me cigarettes.   "Quite right," he said ; "I do not
allow my daughter to smoke ; a bad habit for ladies."

Then he asked whether we should like to go over the yacht, and he showed us everything himself, the cabins being simply but comfortably furnished. He pointed out the various photographs upon the walls, and said : " That is a family you know." It proved to be a group of the English Royal Family. He also showed me a photograph of his revered grandmother, one of the Kaiserin, one of his daughter in uniform as colonel of her regiment. He said : " My daughter did enjoy her visit to London ; she is such a good historian, and knew everything concerning the monuments and places of interest." He also showed me Mary Montagu's [1] portrait, and said, " She is a great friend of mine ; so is her father, that dear Victor."

The Kaiser was wonderfully bright and amusing, never seemed in a hurry or bored, and took endless trouble to entertain us. He had some talk with Geoffrey Head, and seemed to know all about Lloyd's Insurance (where G. works), as well as if he had been employed there himself. He looked across at our yacht, and said to G., " I see two women on board, I suppose they are the ladies' maids ? Are they comfortable ? And do they like the yachting life ? " G. assured H.I.M. that they were most happy and that they had the use of the cabin generally reserved for smokers, whilst my sister asked him to smoke elsewhere, which amused the Kaiser.

At last the moment came for leaving the *Hohenzollern* ; the Imperial launch came up alongside to take us to the *Garland*. The Kaiser stood at the gangway to bid us adieu. He kissed my sister's hand and shook mine. I wonder whether I shall ever see him again—I hope never as our conqueror.

I carried away with me as a souvenir of that memorable luncheon-party a menu card signed by the Kaiser and by all the guests who had been seated round his table.

We felt that we could not leave Norway without

[1] Lady Mary Montagu, daughter of Admiral the Hon. Victor Montagu.

visiting Christiania, and in order to do so we took
the railway from Bergen to the capital. And, indeed,
we were well repaid. A more wonderful and a more
beautiful route can hardly be imagined. It runs
across the country from sea to sea, literally climbing
up and descending steep mountain passes. The railway
carriages are most comfortable and spacious, with windows large enough to offer fine scenic views to the
travellers. There are fewer tunnels than on the famous
Alpine lines, and the snow-capped mountains, dark
pine forests, and rushing torrents combine to produce
the most attractive pictures. We were never tired of
looking out of the windows, and so acute and numerous
were the turnings on the line that we could in many
cases anticipate the route we were going to take.

A cleanly, bustling Norwegian woman came through
the carriage from time to time, armed with a duster,
and would clean and polish the panes of glass, even
giving our seats a passing kindly brush. It was dark
when we reached Christiania, where we spent a couple
of days in a very modern and comfortable hotel. The
town is not specially interesting or attractive, but one
or two pleasant incidents connected with our stay there
stand out in my memory. To begin with, we felt, as
Englishwomen, that we ought to pay our respects to
King Haakon and his Queen—no other than our own
Princess Maud. So we got into communication with the
lady-in-waiting of Her Majesty, and received a most
kind invitation to luncheon on the following day at the
country residence of the royal couple. We were told
to come in *country toilette*, which amused us very much,
as we certainly did not travel about with trains or
elegant costumes. My sister and I set off alone in a
nice little taxi, leaving my niece, Connie Flower, with
some English friends of hers, members of our Legation.
About half an hour's drive brought us to our destination;
we hardly seemed to have left the town before arriving
at the villa. A lady-in-waiting, who spoke perfect

English, received us, and ushered us into a simply but prettily furnished drawing-room, opening on to a terrace overlooking a lawn and flower-beds. In a few moments their Majesties appeared, and gave us quite a hearty welcome. King Haakon is tall and handsome, with a pleasant, open countenance. Queen Maud, at that time, looked very delicate, and was extremely slight—a great contrast to her husband ; they were followed by little Prince Olaf, a charming, natural little fellow about nine years of age, and by an equerry, who did not seem able to converse in any language but his own.

We had a most sociable meal, and were amused at the King's son throwing a peach-stone across the table at his Royal papa, who seemed much pleased at the accuracy of his son's aim. When the very lively boy had left us to play in the garden after luncheon, the King told us that Prince Olaf spoke Norwegian far better than his parents. The King had asked him who was the more fluent in that tongue—his mother or his father—and received the following reply : " You know more words, but mother has the best accent."

The King asked us many questions about our tour, and agreed with us that the inland route from Bergen was one of the most beautiful in Europe. Queen Maud had never seen it, and upon my expressing my astonishment at the fact, the King said : " Maud is so shy that she cannot bear having crowds to meet her at all the small stations ; she would have to show herself and say a few words to the people—it makes her quite ill."

" Yes, I cannot get over my shyness," said the Queen, with a pretty blush.

The King was immensely interested on hearing of our luncheon on the *Hohenzollern.* He expressed himself quite plainly about the German Emperor, and about the German warships that were always disporting themselves in the fjords of his country, and lying in his harbours. He also gave us a good idea of his own

kingdom, and of the social status of his very democratic
subjects. He gives a grand ball once yearly, and
sends out 5000 invitations. These result in a curious
concourse of guests, as one may imagine.

Before we left the Royal villa the King and Queen
intimated that they would like to come and see us on
the yacht, so they were invited with little Prince Olaf,
and came, to our great pleasure and that of the men.

I remember their being much taken by my pretty
niece, Connie Flower, and regretting that she had not
accompanied us on the previous day. The King, who
as Prince Charles of Denmark had served in the Danish
Navy, chatted with our skipper, winning his heart by
the praise he bestowed on the trim and beautiful yacht
and its smart crew. We were quite sorry when the
Royal party took their departure, Prince Olaf gravely
saluting us all to the last.

Another pleasurable reminiscence is that of a luncheon
we gave in the hotel at Christiania, our guests being
Mr. Frederic Harrison and Spencer Lyttelton, our old
friend and travelling companion. They were passengers
on one of the large steamships, bound on a Cook's trip
to Sweden and Russia. Mr. Harrison, well on in the
seventies, was as sprightly as ever, and entertained us
with much traveller's gossip, whilst Mr. Lyttelton gave
us advice and sundry hints for our homeward journey.

Before finally leaving Christiania we went to see the
old Viking boat, which is most carefully preserved, and is
well worth a visit. In shape, and in the absence of
rowlocks, the oars being inserted through holes in the
sides of the boat, it is exactly like the Norfolk fishing
boats, with which I am well acquainted. This similarity
had been already pointed out to me many years before
by Sir Alan Young, when he was staying at Cromer.

From Christiania we continued our southward route
towards Denmark, and, after some tossings in the
Cattegat, found ourselves in a harbour facing Copenhagen. There is not much of real interest to be seen

in the Danish metropolis, except a charming collection of ancient objects of art and utility, remarkably well and appropriately placed in a picturesque old royal building. But we had with us a gracious permit from Queen Alexandra to visit the villa belonging to herself and the Dowager Empress of Russia, with its Danish name " Hvidore " (White Hours), where the two devoted sisters were in the habit of spending some happy weeks every summer in close intimacy and complete freedom from State functions and Court life.

The villa lies within a few miles of Copenhagen, the entrance turning out of a village road. Here we were kindly received by the grey-haired caretaker, who had orders from England to show us everything we might wish to see. What struck me most was the note of simplicity throughout, and the atmosphere of sisterly affection which seemed to pervade the place. There were traces everywhere of the Queen and the Empress. Their portraits on one canvas greet you as you mount the stairs leading to the prettily furnished living-room. There were two small bedrooms close to one another— that of the Empress hung with an icon and pictures of saints and angels, that of the Queen with photographs of the members of her family. Each sister had offered to take the smaller room, and there was quite a dispute on the subject, said our guide, until the choice was decided by drawing lots, and our Queen drew the larger—much to the delight of the Empress. We were shown the morning-room, with its two writing-tables, "for the ladies are never separated " ; and the conservatory, opening out of the attractive and cheerful drawing-room, where we were regaled with cups of tea. Then we were taken in hand by the gardener and piloted through the garden, until we were introduced to a tunnel underground, reminding me of the tunnel in my own Norfolk garden. The similarity had also occurred to Her Majesty, for on visiting The Pleasaunce once, in my absence, the Queen had remarked to Naylor, my gardener,

Y

who was escorting her round : " Your tunnel, like mine, connects the two gardens, one on each side of the high road, but Lady Battersea is much more fortunate than I am, for she has no stairs to go down and up again, whilst I have about thirty ! " And when this remark was repeated to me, I fully agreed with it. As we emerged from the tunnel, I was struck by the fact that a delicious walk by the seashore—and a beautiful shore it is—had been very well planned for the Royal sisters, where they could stroll and sit in perfect peace and seclusion, a garden with its sweet-smelling flowers on one side, and on the other the open sea.

It was an attractive spot, and very dear, as I learnt afterwards, to Queen Alexandra. With nosegays as parting gifts we left the villa of " White Hours "— that little secluded home of peace and happiness. The very fact of its being too small to allow of the suite being quartered in the villa, and obliging them to have their rooms in a kind of glorified village inn, contributed to the sense of privacy so dearly loved by the Royal sisters.

We spent one morning at Copenhagen, visiting the largest hospital in that city ; it seemed to us rather stuffy, and not too clean or well-kept, according to our English ideas, but the patients appeared to be very kindly treated by obliging nurses, who showed us most politely over the wards. One thing struck us favourably, viz. that the patients who were well enough to leave their beds took their meals in a ward set apart for that purpose.

We did not leave Denmark without visiting one of the celebrated creameries, motoring on that day about fifty miles to our destination and fifty back again, seemingly right across Denmark, and, as it happened, arriving too late to see the place in full working order. But an obliging young member of the firm, who spoke perfect English, showed us over the great buildings, and gave us some notion of the work carried on there.

We were even admitted into the store-room, where the cheeses were stacked ready for exportation, and we could not forget the odour of that article of food for many long hours afterwards. The exquisite cleanliness of the whole place and of all the machinery is something to see and admire.

In driving along the country roads we noticed the neat little cottages, with their well-kept gardens, and their adjoining stables, where the cows spend all the long winter months. Women were working in the fields, feeding poultry and attending to their cattle; all seemed busy, also happy and contented, as far as we could judge. I can also recollect passing a charming building on the outskirts of Copenhagen, with a nice shady garden, where some old men and women were seated under the trees, looking very healthy and well-cared-for. Our driver explained that this was one of the Danish poorhouses, and that they were widely known for the comfortable existence that they provided for their inmates. Husbands and wives are not separated, and the home, seen from the window of our car, did not look like an institution.

Of course these are very superficial remarks. We had not much time at our disposal—not enough to verify our impressions; but we left Denmark with the feeling that we had been given a glimpse of a bright little country, inhabited by an industrious population.

I have laid some stress upon this cruise of 1911, as I feel it will be the last that I can ever hope to make. My sister's yacht is sold, and I fear that I shall not have the strength or the courage to quit my native shores again.

CHAPTER XVI

THE PLEASAUNCE—OVERSTRAND

A garden is a lovesome thing—God wot !
Rose plot,
Fringed pool,
Fern grot—
The veriest school
Of peace.

T. E. Brown.

CHAPTER
XVI.

THE return of a Liberal Government in 1892, after a strenuous campaign, brought with it prizes and emoluments for those who had worked well and successfully in favour of their party. None had worked harder than Cyril, none had shown more devotion to his wonderful old leader, none had received more congratulations than the member for S. Beds. I had hoped for a Government appointment of interest and weight, but it was not to be. A peerage was tendered and accepted. I was abroad at the time, but the news leaked through in various letters from England, and was finally confirmed by Cyril, who asked me to keep the offer secret for a time. I did not receive the news gratefully or with rejoicing; my heart had been set on other things, and I was not in the least eager for such advancement.

The peerage meant an end to the old Parliamentary life, so full of adventure, surprises, and incidents, and I felt inwardly that Cyril would never take the same position in the Lords that he had had in the House of Commons. Besides which, being a very consistent Radical, I hardly looked upon a peerage as promotion. However, when I returned to London, and was met at

324

seven o'clock in the morning by Cyril, I knew in a moment that I had to congratulate him and to regard the bright side of the event, if I did not wish him to be depressed and disappointed. So for the time being we amused ourselves by discussing various names for the title, some of them suggested by relatives and friends, finally choosing that of Battersea, Overstrand being tacked on by the wish of our Overstrand friends and neighbours, many of whom had given their loyal affection to my husband from the first.

I watched Cyril taking his seat in the House of Lords with much interest, and thought he looked extremely well in his robes. I also heard him second the Address in 1894 during Lord Rosebery's Premiership—on which performance both he and I received many congratulatory epistles, none kinder or pleasanter to read than the one from Sir Algernon West.

In February 1893 the Governorship of New South Wales fell vacant, owing to the resignation of Lord Jersey, and this splendid and much coveted post was offered to Cyril by Lord Ripon. The offer was not quite unexpected,. but I had always dismissed the possibility of our accepting such an appointment from my mind. On Cyril's return from his interview with Lord Ripon I knew the worst. The idea of leaving my mother for so long a term of years and going to the other end of the world appeared to me like committing a sin. Knowing Cyril's devotion to her and his oft-expressed determination of never leaving her for long, I thought, foolishly indeed, that he would agree with me in the advisability of refusing the offer. Even now I cannot bear to retrace the events of that week and of those that followed upon it. The answer had to be sent almost immediately to Lord Ripon. I had hardly time to consider the position as it ought to have been considered. Perhaps it is best not to rake up the past; suffice it to say that I spent the most miserable weeks of my life, in the face of opposing duties, and that Cyril performed one of the greatest acts of renunciation, greater than my dear mother could ever have been aware of, for her sake and mine. Were I to live my life over again I think I should act differently, for, to say the least, it is ill-judged, perhaps unpardonable, to stand in the way of a man's acceptance of an honourable and useful career.

It was greatly owing to this disappointment that Cyril henceforth made The Pleasaunce at Overstrand his chief country home and interest. One or two bad falls in the hunting field, some changes in the hunting appointments of Mid-Bucks, probably also the toll of increasing years, all conduced to his showing less eagerness for his former well-loved sport. Besides which, when he had ceased to be a member of the House of Commons, it was no longer imperative upon him to live within easy travelling distance of London. He had for years been attracted by the glorious sea air of the East Coast, especially welcome after the relaxing south-westerly breezes and moist atmosphere of Wales, and had longed to become the owner of a seaside habitation in Norfolk. We had spent a few weeks every summer at one of the hotels on that coast, and Cyril had made acquaintance with many a village that might possibly provide us with a holiday home. In the early 'eighties it was the village of Sheringham that held great attractions for us. Unspoilt and old-fashioned, its quaint and tortuous streets were backed by some beautiful woodland scenery, whilst the modern villa was still conspicuous by its absence. A small house situated in an un-get-at-able, inconvenient corner of the little town, overlooking the sea, but cramped, almost sea-locked, was offered us. Cyril thought it would bear transformation and might be turned into a marine paradise, so he instantly set his clever brains to devise the necessary improvements. A friendly architect was called in for consultation, and Cyril assured me that I should revel in such an acquisition. I felt doubtful, but kept a discreet silence. One day we heard sinister rumours that illness had broken out at Sheringham, pronounced by medical authorities to be typhoid. The following week these rumours were confirmed, and then came the sad news of more cases, some of them ending fatally. At last an epidemic was declared. The drainage had been at fault, and the very house so coveted by my husband stood actually on one of the worst spots in the town. This decided our movements as far as Sheringham was concerned; but we still clung to Norfolk, and other sites and other houses were brought to our notice.

One never-to-be-forgotten day in 1888 Lord Suffield suggested to Cyril that he should consider the purchase of two villas adjoining one another and belonging to him. They were standing on about three acres of ground in the small seaside village of Overstrand, which then numbered about thirty houses, and within two miles of Cromer. On one of my visits to Norfolk my first view of Overstrand from the cliffs had not impressed me very favourably. I had no idea then that I was looking at my future home. But after having decidedly refused to become the owner of Desdemona's Palace in Venice, and after having heard, much to my relief, that Sheringham was out of the question, I felt that Cyril, in all fairness, ought to have a free hand in the choice of his future domicile, so I acquiesced at once in his prospective purchase.

In 1888 we took possession of our new home. Anything more unlike what it is now can hardly be imagined. Very commonplace, rather uncomfortable, extremely draughty, and with little pretence at beauty, " The Cottage," as it was then called, was neither romantic nor picturesque. The two houses built in red brick had been thrown into one and stood a little way off the main road leading down to the cliff. A field lay in front of us, whilst in a narrow lane, called " The Londs," stood some of the old cobble cottages inhabited by fishermen.

I failed to see any real beauty in the place; indeed, I had not yet acquired the taste for Norfolk scenery that grows upon one so rapidly and so strongly, but I loved the fresh sea-breezes, and the possibility of sea-bathing appealed to me greatly.

There was, however, one object of romance and beauty that lent a charm to the place, and this was the ruined church, standing somewhat away from the village on rising ground, striking in appearance, rich in architectural remains, and pathetic in its decadence. The tower was still intact, a landmark to many tourists who visited the little village, whilst the roofless nave had been utilised as a burial-ground for members of the Buxton family. The church, like many others in Norfolk, was of Perpendicular design, built at the very end of the fourteenth century. It still bore some very distinctive features, such as—most curious of all and most rare in English churches—the oven in the tower, once used in baking the Communion bread. About 1859 it became apparent that the old building would have to be restored, as age was telling upon the fabric, but, with the apathy and short-sightedness so characteristic of that period in regard to beautiful churches and ancient monuments, this measure was not resorted to, and instead a small new church was built beside the old one. Thus the venerable church of St. Martin was allowed to fall into ruin, upon which the ivy growing at will soon became a warm and picturesque mantle.

In 1911 the bold project of restoring the old church was brought forward by some of the leading inhabitants of the neighbourhood, and agreed to. With this scheme I am anxious to connect the respected name of John Lester, who was for twenty years head of our household. He was a remarkable man, well read, taking the keenest interest in all branches of art ; as he was of a deeply religious nature, his devotion to his own Church was the mainspring of his life. This was evident in the enthusiasm with which, as one of the committee, he entered into the plan of restoration. I should like to record my gratitude to Lester's memory, not alone for his faithful service, but also for the good influence he exercised in the house and the village.

It was not long before we agreed that "The Cottage" at Overstrand would require much alteration in order to make it a suitable country home. As it then stood there were not sufficient rooms to house the guests whom Cyril loved to see about him, and the temporary additions that he had made proved, to say the least, most unsatisfactory. He was therefore very soon in his element, planning, altering, and rebuilding, and, as he was an adept in the art of picturesque construction, he found plenty of scope for his powers. Mr. Lutyens, now Sir Edwin Lutyens (the gifted young architect just then coming into public notice), entered fully into my husband's views; between them they evolved out of the old cottage a truly original, but certainly a very comfortable, home-y abode, which we renamed "The Pleasaunce" at Lord Morley's suggestion. This more important building demanded a more important garden, and fresh schemes for outdoor improvements and enlargements had to be considered.

My husband proved to be an ardent gardener, a scientific as well as a practical one, and his ambition was stirred at the possibilities the ground offered. Thus, after much thought and many essays, a beautiful garden enhanced the pleasure we took in our Overstrand home. Also, keenly alive to the tastes of the many young people in whose company he delighted, Cyril included a tennis-court and a cricket-ground in our domain, and these have given unqualified amusement to more than one generation. He not only joined in some of the games, but watched them with keen interest, and, having given up his old pursuits, exchanged once for all the hunter's crop for the tennis-racket and the golfer's iron.

The inhabitants of Overstrand were also considered : football as well as cricket was started, a reading-room opened for use on winter evenings, and a good lending library provided, which has indeed proved a signal blessing.

More and more did my husband love our Norfolk home ; he was never tired of adding to its beauty, its comfort, and its helpfulness, acting upon the principle of

Not what we give, but what we share,
For the gift without the giver is bare.[1]

Twenty years after we became owners of The Pleasaunce our garden was described, as it now stands, by the picturesque pen of the Hon. Mrs. Felkin (Ellen Thorneycroft Fowler) ; this description was cleverly woven into one of her works of fiction—*Ten Degrees Backward*—and she has kindly given me permission to incorporate it in these Reminiscences.

THE GARDEN OF DREAMS

I have always loved Bythesea, and I call it the place of the Two Gardens, for with two gardens it is always associated in my mind.

The first garden is the Garden of Sleep. On the very edge of the cliff stands—or rather, there stood when last I was there, and for aught I know to the contrary there is still standing to-day—the tower of a ruined church. The rest of the church fell into the sea years ago, but the tower still remains, its walls on one side running down sheer with the cliff. Such of the churchyard as the encroaching sea has not yet swallowed lies to the backward of the tower ; and all around it are fields, which in their season are clothed with scarlet and other delights, for it is the land of the poppies.

The other garden at Bythesea I called, in opposition to the Garden of Sleep, the Garden of Dreams. And a wonder-

---

[1] Lowell.

ful garden it was. It was as young as the other garden was
old, and as carefully tended as the other was neglected. It
was also situated on the edge of the cliff, and was more like
a garden out of the Arabian Nights, which had been called
into being in one night by some beneficent Djin, than a
garden in matter-of-fact England. It was a garden of
infinite variety and of constant surprises, where nothing grew
but the unexpected ; but where the unexpected flourished
in great profusion and luxuriance. It was a most inconsequent garden ; and to wander through its changing scenes
was like wandering through the exquisite inconsistencies
of a delightful dream. The dream began on a velvety
lawn, where the velvet was edged with gay flowers and still
gayer flowering shrubs, and the blue sea made an effective
background. Then it turned into a formal garden, with
paved paths between the square grass-plots, and a large
fountain in the middle lined with sky-blue tiles, as if a bit
of sky had fallen down to earth and had found earth so
fascinating that it could not tear itself away again. Then
the dream took a more serious turn, and led along sombre
cloisters veiled with creepers. But it could not keep serious
for long ; it soon floated back into the sunlight, and dipped
into a sunk garden paved with coral and amethyst, as
only pink and purple flowers were allowed to grow therein.
Then it changed into a rosery where it was always the time
of roses, and where roses red and roses white, roses pink
and roses yellow, ran riot in well-ordered confusion. Then
the dream took quite another turn, and passed into a
Japanese garden of streams and pagodas and strange bright
flowers, till the dreamer felt as if he were living on a willow-
pattern plate. But he soon came back to England again,
and found himself in an ideal fruit garden, where the pear
trees and the apple trees were woven into walls and arches
and architraves of green and gold. Then a wrought-iron
gateway led him still nearer to the heart of England, for there
lay a cricket-field surrounded by large trees ; and beyond
that again stretched the grassy alleys and shady paths of
dreamland till they culminated in the very centre of the
dream—a huge herbaceous border so glorious in its riot of
colour that the dreamer's heart leaped up, like Wordsworth's,

to behold a rainbow; but this time not a rainbow in the sky, but on the ground.

The house belonging to this wonderful garden was more or less to match. It had begun life quite as a small house, but the magic of the garden had lured it on to venture farther and farther into the enchanted ground, until finally it grew into a very large house indeed. And one could not really blame it for stretching out longing arms and pointing willing feet towards all the beauty which surrounded it : one felt that one would have done exactly the same in its place.

I had many excursions into this modern fairyland, as the châtelaine thereof was an old friend of ours who loved to share with others the joy of her Garden of Dreams ; so we went there often. It was glorious weather, and there were many interesting people there—as indeed there usually were ; choice spirits flourished in the Garden of Dreams as well as choice flowers.

My husband was never tired of pursuing his botanical studies, and, in his anxiety to make the best possible use of his knowledge, he would sacrifice a whole year's work for some novel idea. Thus friends visiting the garden from time to time would look for an accustomed feature, and would wonder where it could have strayed— or had their memories played them false ?

The water garden took the place of the original tennis-court and was doubled in size after two years' existence, when a very promising rosery was sacrificed in its favour. The first pergola proved so great an attraction, covered as it was with vines, hops, and climbing roses, that others were speedily planned and took shape in different parts of the grounds.

Upon my yearly arrivals at Overstrand from London or Aston Clinton I would expect to be greeted by some novelty, of which I was not always prepared to be an enthusiastic admirer ; thus the first impression of the clock tower and of the cloisters was an unfavourable one. Yet now I have become quite attached to the tower, and the value of the cloisters for bazaars and fêtes is incontestable. On one occasion I was startled by the sight of some masons constructing a high brick wall to the balcony of the window in my sitting-room, which would effectually have shut out the view from my seat in my favourite corner. I indignantly began to remonstrate, and, in spite of Sir Edwin Lutyens' orders, threw the bricks down on to the terrace, to the ill-concealed amusement of the workmen.

My husband not only amused himself by adding to the house and garden, but he also arranged a flat over some disused stables and carpenters' sheds as a Guest House, where numbers of friends and relatives have spent happy weeks during the summer months.

In order to give the necessary shelter that the garden requires to protect it from the blasts of the north-east wind, we planted a great quantity of trees and shrubs, importing nearly all the evergreens (yews and box) from Aston Clinton. They flourished amazingly, and it is now difficult to believe that out of the number only two deciduous trees—an ash and a sycamore—remain original denizens of the place. They stood in old days in hedgerows ; these have since then disappeared, and the trees themselves seem to have fallen in so well with the later arrivals that, as one of my witty neighbours once remarked, they look as if they would not object to leaving cards upon the newcomers !

Two fountains, set in deep basins of blue glass of a singularly beautiful colour, in mosaic pattern, add very much to the charm and originality of the garden, particularly when the fountains are in full play, and when the Eringium (sea-holly) and Echinops (globe-thistle) are in flower, their brilliant tints added to those of the fuchsia being reflected in the water. The place responded well to the loving care bestowed upon it; the flowers blossomed luxuriantly, the shrubs grew apace, the lawns became soft and velvety, as if all were grateful for the affection they awakened.

THE PLEASAUNCE

The Sea ! the white-foamed Northern Sea !
With crumbling cliffs and shelving lea ;
    With autumn fog and summer mist,
    With surf, by early sunbeam kiss'd.
The Sea that laps this strip of land
Is like a great protecting band.

The Sea ! our stronghold from the foe,
On which our guardians come and go ;
    The Sea, o'er which I fondly gaze
    In morning light or evening haze.
My garden looks across that Sea—
Invigorating sight to me !

The very flowers they seem to know
That here they must more fully blow :
    Deeper their colour, sweeter their scent,
    With added charm by ocean lent ;
And though they northward set their face,
They gleam like jewels in their case.

In the early 'nineties there came to the parish of
Overstrand as rector the Rev. Lawrence C. Carr, whose
wife is closely connected with the Buxton family. I
speedily made friends with the Rectory party, and I
am glad to say that this friendship, now of long standing,
has not grown less with the expiration of years. Mr.
Carr, who belongs to the old Evangelical school, is a most
devoted pastor, but so modest and humble-minded that
very few people recognise the amount of self-sacrificing
work that he accomplishes. He is not troubled by any
doubts in regard to the authenticity of the Scriptures,
and is not disturbed by modernism or higher criticism.
Owing to his orderly habits and methodical mind he
is always pleasant to work with, but although very
practical in matters of business, it is the spiritual side
of divine worship that appeals to him so strongly ;
he requires no aids, such as art and music can give,
to kindle or to strengthen his faith, which is unswerving.
On the other hand, his wife (great-granddaughter of Sir

Fowell and Lady Buxton), in spite of her Quaker ancestry,
has a very true feeling for what is correct and beautiful
in art, which is evident in her clever use of the brush in
her water-colour drawings, chiefly of sky and sea.   Mrs.
Carr has become a warm friend of mine, and I owe many
happy days to the fact that she is my close neighbour.

A grievous event cast a dark shadow upon the Rectory
party in 1916, when the eldest daughter, Vera, lost her
life in a cruel accident.   Young and full of promise,
deeply loved by her parents, and closely associated
with them in every event of their daily existence, her
death came, especially to her mother, as a crushing, heart-
breaking blow, from the effects of which she can never
fully recover.   The only son, Anthony, served well and
faithfully during the Great War.   One other daughter,
Violet, completes the family circle.

An account of the little gathering of friends at Overstrand should certainly contain a mention of Mrs. Wilson,
widow of the late Canon Wilson of Mitcham and mother
of Mrs. Carr, who inhabits one of the most attractive
houses in the place, " The Grange," once tenanted by
Sir John Hare, the celebrated actor, and his family ;
and it is here that from time to time during the year Mrs.
Wilson welcomes her daughter, Sister Rachel, who is well
known and much beloved in the Wantage Sisterhood.

When I first made the acquaintance of Cromer, the
whole place seemed to be dominated by the Buxton,
Gurney, and Hoare families.   I happened to be spending
a fortnight with my dear mother at the Hôtel de Paris
in the year 1877, and it was then that we received
a kindly welcome from many of them, especially Lady
Buxton, widow of Sir Edward Buxton, at Colne House.

My mother had known some of the " Friends "
intimately in her young days.   The Samuel Gurneys
had lived at one time in the near neighbourhood of
Stamford Hill, London, and there had frequently been
communications of a very pleasant nature between
the families of Gurney, Montefiore, and Rothschild.

A favourite anecdote, repeated from generation to generation, told how Hannah Mayer Rothschild (later the
Hon. Mrs. FitzRoy) had on one memorable evening
been dressed up by her youthful friends and playmates (daughters of Samuel Gurney), and introduced in
the parlour to their parents as a new addition to the
Society of Friends. The shy and blushing young girl
looked so beautiful in her becoming, if sober, garments
that there was great lament at her return to a more
worldly style of dress. My mother also gave me a
description of my introduction to Samuel Gurney at
the early age of *three*. The meeting took place at
Brighton. Mr. Gurney, then a stout, red-faced, elderly
gentleman, with a great shock of white hair, proceeded
then and there to take me up and toss me in his arms,
which I resented as a great familiarity, calling out
lustily, " Put me down, you old white bear ! " to the
consternation but silent amusement of my parents.

My father and uncles had often had business relations
with the Gurneys ; their politics were of the same colour,
and, owing to religious principles on both sides, they
suffered from the same political disabilities. My mother
had always been attracted, as I have said before, by the
earnest lives and simple tastes of the " Friends," and she
was very glad to renew, or rather to make, acquaintance
with those who gave her so cordial a welcome in Norfolk.

" It is especially as the leading Quaker family of
England," wrote Augustus Hare, " that the Gurneys of
Earlham have become celebrated," and as such he
devotes two volumes of very pleasant reading to their
history. " In their home at Earlham," he tells us,
" the Gurneys became surrounded, as all Gurneys have
been since, by troops of near relations, with whom they
lived on terms of the utmost fellowship and intimacy,
and who dropped in daily at the family dinner-hour of
three, four, and eventually five o'clock." [1]

[1] From *The Gurneys of Earlham*, published by George Allen &
Unwin, Ltd.

But both Quaker dress and Quaker language have
gone through many changes since the earlier date ; for
instance, gone are the Quaker woman's closely fitting
cap and bonnet, her full skirt, her softly clinging shawl ;
gone are the broad-brimmed hat, the high stock of
her menfolk, and gone are the pleasant " thees " and
" thous " in Quaker converse — indeed, there is now
but little distinction to the outward observer between
members of the Society of Friends and those of the
Evangelical School of the Church of England.

In 1803 Richenda Gurney gives a description of
how the day was spent at Cromer by all these happy
young people.   " Before breakfast running about in
all directions on the sands, after breakfast receiving
callers and fixing the plans for the day ; then an hour's
quiet for reading and writing.   At eleven, bathing and
enjoying the sands, then riding on horseback, or making
some pleasant excursion.   With all these and other
delightful amusements, it would be very odd if we did
not enjoy ourselves." [1]

I feel that Cromer has always been, and will doubtless
always be, a delicious playground for the many generations of children and young people who come year after
year to the beautiful sands and cliffs of the Norfolk
coast.

Generations come and go ; there may be changes in
dress and in speech, in modes of thought and in aspects
of life, but the essentials remain.   Sand-built castles
will always be dear to the hearts of children, the mystery
of the waves will always appeal to the stroller by the
shore, and sky and earth will always hold treasures for
those who know how to seek them ; whilst the sense of
pure enjoyment in man and woman will now, as in old
days, be quickened by the rush of fresh bracing air that
seems to gather all into its embrace as soon as the
coast-line is approached.

It was at Colne House that we found Lady Buxton,

[1] From *The Gurneys of Earlham.*

Z

XVI.CHAPTER XVI.

when I first made her acquaintance, surrounded by children and grandchildren, nephews and nieces, and by her three unmarried daughters, leading a useful and contented life. I remember her calling upon my mother at the Hôtel de Paris : a short, somewhat square figure in a black silk dress, with widow's cap and close bonnet, a kind of compromise between a Quaker costume and one of a more worldly style; she had white hair, a fresh complexion, a shrewd expression of countenance, and a very bright merry twinkle in her eyes. She chatted away for about twenty minutes and then begged of us to call upon her, which we did shortly after that first visit, finding her in her pleasant drawing-room, which seemed to vanish into a grove of flowers—the conservatory. The walls of the room were hung with beautiful Richmond water-colour drawings, portraits of many members of the family. Lady Buxton was surrounded by a crowd of visitors, to whom her daughters were dispensing an excellent tea ; she was most hospitably inclined, and never happier than when her rooms were filled with guests to her liking. Every Tuesday a Bible Reading was held in the Colne House drawing-room, under the auspices of one of the many Evangelical Churchmen spending a summer holiday at Cromer.

Lady Buxton, like all her family—indeed like all those brought up in the Society of Friends—was a diligent reader of the Bible, knowing long passages, even chapters, by heart. She told me how once, when her sight was rapidly failing, she had asked the housemaid, who was lighting her bedroom fire, to listen whilst she repeated the Psalms for the day, and to correct her should she put in a wrong word or make any omission. But Lady Buxton's memory did not fail her—happily for the housemaid !

Lady Buxton was much interested in my appointment as Prison Visitor to the female convicts at Aylesbury, and asked me many questions concerning them. One afternoon, when I was drinking tea at Colne House,

the table standing just under the portrait of Elizabeth
Fry, Lady Buxton, after listening to some of my prison
experiences, ejaculated, " Oh, my dear, I do hope that
Aunt Fry knows what you are doing ! " which touched
me very much—Elizabeth Fry having been the first
woman who ever found her way as a visitor and reformer
into the prison cells, to whom those who humbly
follow in her steps must be eternally grateful. It
was the fashion to celebrate the anniversary of Lady
Buxton's birth, January 11, by a tea-party given at
Colne House to all the members of her family staying
at Cromer or in the neighbourhood. A birthday cake,
ornamented with lighted candles, one for every year of
her life, was placed in the middle of the table, round
which all gathered, old and young. I, who was not of
the family, but a privileged guest, was present on one
or two of these occasions, and generally brought flowers
with me as a gift, sent specially by my mother. After
Lady Buxton's 90th birthday I received a letter from
her, in a handwriting which is almost illegible, in which
she said :

Will you tell your mother that these expressions of her
affectionate interest are very pleasant to me. Will you tell
her so with my love. I cannot see what I write.

Lady Buxton died in August 1911, in her 98th year,
leaving 128 direct descendants. She had been absolutely
blind and deaf for some time, and the birthday parties,
at her own request, had long been discontinued. Lady
Victoria Noel, for many years a complete invalid,
wife of her eldest son, Sir Fowell Buxton, was distinguished for her great moral and intellectual qualities,
and gifted with remarkable courage and powers of
endurance. Of her Lady Buxton once wrote :

I do bless God for His gift to us in our dear Victoria.
Miss Marsh calls her " that Pearl of Pearls."

CHAPTER XVII

NORFOLK — COUNTY NEIGHBOURS — HISTORIC HOUSES:
HOLKHAM — GUNTON — BLICKLING — HOUGHTON —
WOLTERTON — MANNINGTON — FELBRIGG — SAN-
DRINGHAM — THORNHAM

CHAPTER XVII. BEFORE the days of motor-cars it was somewhat difficult to call upon one's county friends and neighbours who lived beyond ten miles from one's home; thus it was a prohibitive journey from Overstrand to Holkham. Yet at Holkham lived an old friend of my parents, Lord Leicester, with his young wife, Georgiana Cavendish (whom he had married *en secondes noces*), well known to my sister and myself, the eldest daughter of Lord and Lady Chesham of Latimer, Bucks. I like to recall that it was at my old home, Aston Clinton, that Lord Leicester, a widower of three years' standing, met Miss Cavendish for the first time, and confided to my mother how greatly attracted he was by her bright looks and charming expression. Shortly after that visit the engagement was announced, and Miss Cavendish became the wife of a somewhat elderly man, with a family of ten children. She fitted into the difficult position most wonderfully, and to the very last days of her husband's life proved the most devoted of wives. Six children were added to the existing number. As unmarried girls, my sister and I spent the last week of the year 1869 with my father at Holkham, and of this visit we always retained grateful memories.

I have by me two letters written at that time by my sister to my mother, who had not accompanied us; and from these letters I will quote. (The Lady Leicester alluded to was the first wife of Lord Leicester—Miss Whitbread.)

HOLKHAM, *December* 1869.

Here we are, actually arrived at our long journey's end, which really did seem a very long way off. Our carriage was wonderful, resembling that magnificent vehicle in which we once travelled from Turin to Susa, so that Papa could take exercise and recreation in the shape of a cigar with ease and comfort.

Our grandeur excited much attention on the line, and as the Prince was expected eager eyes gazed into our carriage and looked rather disgusted at what they saw. At Cambridge we had such an excellent lunch that I could hardly believe we were in our native country, and thus reinforced toddled on in the slowest of slow trains, the aspect of the country becoming simply Siberian : large snowdrifts on either side of the train, huge white fields, treeless and hedgeless, and over all such a cold grey sky. Norfolk struck us all as being hideous, and even Buckinghamshire, the muchabused, would look comfortable after this dreary landscape.

Arrived at the station, we found grand preparations for Royalty in the shape of red cloth, and Lord Leicester, who looked as red as the cloth, but jolly and good-natured, and, thank goodness, carts of all dimensions, in which our trunk could lie without any inconvenience. We had only preceded the Royal train by half an hour, and found all the party at home in great expectation. There were only the family, but *only* ! besides Lady Dunmore and Lady Powerscourt, and the nice giantess Lady Anne, there are four younger female members and two boys; all of these made quite a considerable group, but not an alarming one, as they are very simple and good-natured. When we had begun to thaw a little, mentally and bodily, the bell rang and the great people arrived. The two little boys toddled in first with great self-possession, followed by the Princess, who looked very charming, and His Royal Highness, evidently in an excellent temper. The other ladies are Mrs.

Grey [1] and Countess Gleichen. They have had several
disappointments: Lady Sefton and the Dudleys could not
come, but the St. Albans, both unwell, will try and come
to-day. I felt sympathetic, but still very happy only to be
sympathetic and not concerned. What would our feelings
have been under a similar trial! The gentlemen are Mr.
Chaplin,[2] Mr. T. de Grey,[3] Mr. Dyke,[4] and a Mr. Macdonald.[5]
The Princess came down to dinner in a high lilac dress,
looking very pretty. She is very simple and good-natured,
and I should think up to a great deal of fun.

Mrs. Grey is charming; she is a Swede, and talks English
with a pretty little accent. I sat next to Mr. Chaplin at
dinner, and we got on very well together; he is good-natured
and sensible, if not brilliant. His guests threw him over,
so he might have come to us last week. Imagine my
horrible brass when I tell you that I actually sat down to
play last night, happily convinced that there was no one
present that would be much the worse for a false note.
A pleasant hum of conversation crowned my efforts and kept
up my nerve. We all retired early, as every one was tired
after the journey. Our bedrooms are on the ground floor,
those generally given to bachelors; they are large and
comfortable, but neither bright nor elegant, and resembling
very much the bedrooms of an old-fashioned English inn.
I have not seen the smart bedrooms yet. The house is very
large and most difficult to describe; the rooms are spacious
with high, *domed*, well-gilded ceilings; the walls are all red,
but in our bedrooms the furniture is not of a very striking
character. There are a great number of beautiful pictures
which were shown and explained to us this morning by
an old gentleman, whose white tie gives him a clerical
character, and whom I therefore suppose to be the chaplain.
I do not know what we are going to do to-day; the weather
is cold and ungenial, but still I trust somebody will go out.

The servants' apartments are not very comfortable, and
Morrell (our maid) declares that Holkham is not to be compared to Aston Clinton, which opinion may be explained by

---

[1] Lady-in-Waiting on the Princess.   [2] Viscount Chaplin.
[3] Lord Walsingham.   [4] Sir William Hart Dyke.
[5] Later Admiral Macdonald, always called " Rim " by the Prince.

the fact that she has no fireplace in her bedroom, which is really
hard in this weather. Some merciful maid gave her hospitality
last night in a warmer room.—Y^r aff.   ANNIE.

HOLKHAM, *December* 1869.

I take advantage of a few moments before breakfast to
send you a little account of our proceedings. Holkham
clocks are exactly half an hour in advance of the ordinary
time ; this funny arrangement gives one the impression of
being in another country. We had a lovely day yesterday,
very cold and very bright ; all the gentlemen went at an
early hour to business, but the ladies were lazy and would
not go out before lunch. The Princess appeared at 1 o'clock,
looking charming in a short black velvet costume. In the
afternoon, those least humane, including myself, drove to
see the gentlemen shooting ; the poor pheasants rose in the
air in such numbers that they quite blackened the sky and
tumbled about all around us. Mrs. Grey and I were soon
quite disgusted, so we walked home at my usual pace ; she
is a very nice, dear woman, and introduces an idea of
foreign *sans-gêne* and vivacity which is rather necessary here.
They are all very kind and friendly. Lady Anne is really very
clever and jolly ; her great topic, though, is theology, and she
is at present deep in Josephus ! The other four are all more
or less shy. The Princess is excessively good-natured and not
at all alarming. We were very jolly in the evening, and
danced in a long gallery. The schoolmaster, a most elegant-
looking gentleman, played the piano for us, with much
success. Their Royal Highnesses like nothing so much as
a romp ; in more loyal language, they have a great deal of
entrain. Papa was very frisky, and danced so well that
the Princess invited him to be her partner in the lancers,
and under the Royal tuition he got on very well. There was
only one waltz, but none of the ladies besides ourselves were
given to waltzing. The Prince and I had a capital dance.
We concluded with a " Tempête," which was worthy of its
name. The St. Albans appeared late last night. She is
looking very pretty, and is quite as pleasant as she looks.
The Royal babies came in to be looked at yesterday afternoon.
They are very nice little boys, rather wild, but not showing

signs of being too much spoiled ; they make very ludicrous attempts at being dignified and talk of each other as " Prince George " and " Prince Victor."

There is no shooting to-day, so I hope and trust that we shall have a good long walk ; the sea is only within two miles, and I have a great wish to pay it a visit.

I have just discovered the failing of this establishment: there is not *one* dog—nothing wagging or barking. The Princess generally brings hers among her numerous retinue, but has just lost an old favourite.—Ever y^{rs}·   ANNIE.

Thomas Coke, the first Earl of Leicester of the present creation, was born in 1754 ; he lived to the age of 88 ; and his son, the second Earl, born in 1822, was the friend of my parents, our host in 1869 and our guest at Aston Clinton in 1873. His son, the present and third Earl, Lord-Lieutenant of the county, succeeded his father in 1909, so that there have only been three owners of the vast Holkham estate during an unprecedented length of time. It is under his reign and that of his wife (the Hon. Alice White, daughter of Lord Annaly) that the interior of Holkham House has been most beautifully restored and re-decorated, and is now glowing with warmth, colour, and light. Lady Leicester played a very distinguished part in the Red Cross work of the county during the Great War. I cannot resist mentioning an historic occasion on which I met Lord and Lady Leicester in October 1919. It was on the 18th day of the month that I, as one of the Vice-Presidents of the British Red Cross Society, Norfolk Branch, and as Commandant of my Overstrand Detachment and V.A.D. Hospital, was bidden to attend the great and memorable gathering in Norwich Cathedral of the officers and members of the Norfolk Detachments of the British Red Cross Society and Order of St. John of Jerusalem, who had served in hospitals at home or overseas during the Great War. The Cathedral, thronged with nurses and commandants in uniform and members of the R.A.M.C., presented a wonderful aspect, one never to

be forgotten.　And indeed it would have been a cold-
hearted man or woman who could have remained un-
moved at such a time, for were not all hearts throbbing
with deep-felt gratitude and thankfulness to God for
the deliverance of our country from the danger and
horrors of war.

Gunton Hall in 1877 was still complete in its pristine
charm and comfort, as yet untouched by the cruel fire
that spoilt so much of the building a few years later.
It was inhabited by a very cheery party, and the
life carried on there was that of many happy country
homes of that date.　Lord Suffield, the owner, always
faultlessly attired, a courtier, the *bienvenu* at Sandringham and Marlborough House, an adept at sport of all
kinds, remained, unfortunately for his own dignity and
the happiness of others, too young in tastes and proclivities for his years.　But of that and what it entailed
my pen shall be silent.　Here I will only recall the fact
that he was a very prominent figure, and in some respects
a remarkable personality in his own county, the husband of a most devoted, unselfish wife.　Lady Suffield
was a Baring ; she had been carefully educated by her
very cultured and intellectual mother, Mrs. Baring,
who in old days had inhabited Cromer Hall, where her
distinguished son, Evelyn Baring, later Lord Cromer,
was born.

The atmosphere of Gunton, although in some ways
different from that of the home of her childhood,
did not prevent Lady Suffield from being an admirable mother to her large family of seven daughters
and two sons, by whom she was devotedly loved.
As usual, Cyril was not slow in making friends with
the younger members of the Suffield household, and
much pleasant interchange of visits was the result.
The young people all loved the Cromer beach, and
were agile and dexterous in clambering about the
sides of the cliffs, or even taking their ponies down
what seemed to be perpendicular descents.　In their

famous kitchen garden they would, for our entertainment, leap over the compact yew hedges ; they were all slightly built, very light on their feet, and adepts at cricket and most other games.

Some members of that family I may now look upon as my own personal friends, who have contributed not a little to the happiness of my days at Overstrand, especially the Dowager Lady Hastings and Mrs. Glyn, the latter my tenant and near neighbour.

With the present Lord and Lady Suffield I have many interests in common, and I can only speak in terms of admiration of the excellent public work done by the latter, in the pursuance of which she always has her husband's sympathy and advice.

A few miles beyond Gunton lies the picturesque village of Ingworth, leading to that paradise of country seats— Blickling. The owner of that paradise in the year 1877 was Constance, Marchioness of Lothian, widow of the eighth Marquis, a Talbot by birth, and eldest sister of my friends, Lady Pembroke and Lady Brownlow. I had met Lady Lothian before the year 1877 at Ashridge, but I felt that her true setting was Blickling Hall, where she formed the centre of a noble and harmonious picture.

Interesting and beautiful as Blickling Hall undoubtedly is, one of the finest of Jacobean mansions with its glorious garden and picturesque woods, its greatest charm for me lay in the fact that it was the home of the beloved châtelaine who spent the years of her widowhood there, amongst people who loved and revered her. She belonged to the class of *grandes dames*—alas, almost vanished from our midst !—keeping to the dress, manners, and language of the mid-Victorian days. Her delicate and aristocratic beauty was only heightened by the dress she habitually wore, the plain yet sweeping lines of her skirt, the lace mantilla or shady hat on her head. I cannot remember her wearing any colour, only black, until the last sad day, when I was taken into the room where she lay, draped Chapter XVII. in white, like a finely sculptured marble image, upon her bed, a great bunch of lilies upon her breast, and palm branches overhanging her pillow.

I never went down to my Norfolk home without planning when I could meet the mistress of Blickling. Many of my friends and acquaintances of diverse views and opinions shared in my admiration for Lady Lothian and enjoyed her hospitality ; thus in a letter from Lord Morley, dated October 1891, I read the following :

My visit to Blickling was very pleasant indeed, to me at least. What a charming old house it is, and though the Conservative element prevailed in the party, I liked it none the less on that account.

Lady Lothian's death, which occurred after a very short illness in October 1901, came as a fearful blow to those who knew and loved her. Widespread and sincere was the mourning. Indeed, the loss to her tenants and cottagers was a very severe one. She was conveyed to Scotland after her death, and lies beside her husband in one of the resting-places of the family ; but in the little church at Blickling, the church she loved and constantly attended, and where she placed a beautiful memorial in memory of her husband, there is a touching and appropriate inscription to her own memory—although no one who ever had the privilege of knowing her as I did will require any words to recall her gracious presence—the last sentence of which I will quote :

. . . born June 15, 1836, died October 10, 1901, at Blickling Hall, where she had lived during her widowhood of 31 years for and with her people, helping, uplifting, in- spiring, loving and beloved by all. She made the beauty of Holiness manifest.

I have visited Houghton, Wolterton, and Mannington, all closely connected with the Walpole family, and

have seen them all under most favourable circumstances,
Lady Dorothy Nevill, herself a Walpole, and a very
clever and well-informed member of that astute family,
having been with us as our cicerone on all three occasions.
Houghton Hall, the largest country house in Norfolk,
has, since my first visit, offered its welcome to a
member of my own family — Sybil Sassoon,[1] now the
wife of Lord Rocksavage, son and heir of the Marquis of
Cholmondeley.   They have a son and heir, born 1919.

Sir Robert Walpole, the great Whig statesman, laid
the first stone of the Hall in 1722.   His collection of
pictures was truly magnificent, but these were, alas !
sold in 1779 by his grandson to pay his debts, and
passed from Houghton Hall to St. Petersburg, having
been acquired by Catherine of Russia.

My first visit to Houghton was rendered rather
remarkable by the fact that we were accompanied, not
only by Lady Dorothy, but also by Princess Stéphanie,
widow of the late Crown Prince of Austria, married
for the second time to Count Lonyay, a Hungarian mag-
nate.   Princess Stéphanie, our guest with her husband
at The Pleasaunce, was the daughter of the wily old
King Leopold II. of Belgium, who, according to his own
daughter, was the cleverest and the wickedest monarch
in Europe.   I was amused at Princess Stéphanie's
paying but scant attention to some of the beautiful
carvings in marble pointed out to her by Lady Dorothy,
being far more occupied in wondering how and why a
portrait of our King George IV. could have been painted
wearing the insignia of the " Golden Fleece," an Order,
so the Princess declared, strictly reserved for Roman
Catholic subjects or Roman Catholic monarchs.   This,
as was explained to H.I.H., was accounted for by the
fact that there are two branches of the said Order, one
exclusively for members of the Roman persuasion, the
other for those belonging to the Protestant faith—a
slight difference being made in the insignia.   This hardly

[1] Sybil's grandfather was Gustave de Rothschild.

satisfied the Princess, who declared that the artist had
been grossly misinformed.

Like many other great Georgian houses, Houghton originally possessed a magnificent outer double flight of stairs upon which opened the grand hall, this being upon the first story. But George, Earl of Orford, the third Peer, who sold the pictures to Russia, was an inveterate gambler, and one evening at play, having lost all the money he possessed, declared that he had nothing more to stake. His adversary, half in joke, reminded him of the staircase. In his passion for play Lord Orford agreed to the proposal, and thus the magnificent flight of stairs was lost; but it still exists in a picture of the house as it once stood, and it is the ardent wish of the present owners to replace that splendid attribute of the old Hall.

It was the same George, third Earl of Orford, who, according to Lady Dorothy Nevill, in order to spite his family, left Houghton away to his niece Mary, Lady Cholmondeley, instead of to his cousin, Lord Walpole.

The architect of Wolterton, also in the county of Norfolk, as well as of Houghton, was Ripley, son of a carpenter employed by Sir Robert Walpole, who raised this man to the position of architect and made him comptroller of the Board of Works. Wolterton, however, did not belong to the great Sir Robert, but to his brother, Lord Walpole — both brothers, writes Lady Dorothy, building their houses simultaneously in different parts of the county, both employing the same artists from Italy, both determined upon having magnificent residences.

From Lord Walpole, owner of Wolterton, Lady Dorothy Nevill and the present Earl of Orford claim their descent. Lord Orford, Lady Dorothy's brother, walked out of the house after his father's death in 1858, owing to the unfortunate and, as he thought, unfair nature of the paternal will, never returning to it. He

thereupon took up his abode at Mannington, another
of his properties, and a most beautiful one, transferring
thither all that he could carry away from the ancestral
mansion. Wolterton was thus allowed to fall into a state
of decay, and was uninhabited, except by rats, when I
first saw it. I must add that Wolterton has now been
rebuilt and restored to much of its old magnificence
and beauty, and there Lord Orford, with his second
wife, is now living.

I have seen the fine Georgian building since its
redemption from the rule of the rats; it is indeed a
wonderful restoration, and deeply interesting. It contains some beautiful pictures, brought back from
Mannington, which is only a few miles distant from
Wolterton.

Mannington is a very curious and historically interesting house, part of it dating back to the year 1412.
I never had the privilege of meeting Lady Dorothy's
brother, Lord Orford, but was shown over Mannington,
then inhabited by a nephew and his wife, by Lady
Dorothy herself. I was much struck, not only by the
haunting beauty of the place, but also by the quaint
humour of the late owner, manifested in many ways in
the house as well as in the grounds.

To begin with, on driving up to the door one's eye
is caught by the following inscription :

Morituro Satis,

meaning, according to Lady Dorothy, " This house is
sufficient for one who has not long to live "; and by
the side of the door, fortunately in Latin, the following :

> What is worse than a tigress ?   A demon.
> What is worse than a demon ?   A woman.
> What is worse than a woman ?   Nothing.

The site of the old ruined chapel was converted by
Lord Orford into a mausoleum for himself, where his
tomb in granite bears an inscription that he composed
and placed on it during his lifetime. There are other

memorials and other epitaphs in the little grove by the Chapter
side of the ruins, some fanciful, others pathetic, all XVII.
certainly original.

There Lady Dorothy used yearly to visit her brother,
the late very learned, very cultured, and eccentric Lord
Orford, who was deeply interested in and passionately
attached to this wonderful and beautiful old place.
There he lived as a bachelor, having parted company
in early days with his wife, Lady Orford, who made
the city of Florence her home for herself and daughters,
where she was the centre of a brilliant circle, more or
less Bohemian, composed not only of Italians, but also
of many English residents.

Felbrigg being in near vicinity to Overstrand, I have
often had the pleasure of visiting that beautiful spot,
which might so easily be made a most delightful residence, even for twentieth-century demands. It is the
home of many memories, haunted by such a name as
that of Sir Simon de Felbrigg, Standard-Bearer to King
Richard II., and then later, in the reign of Henry VI.,
by that of Wymondham—the family probably taking
their name from the town of Wymondham in Norfolk.
The house is of varied architecture and of various dates.
Thus the beautiful south front, bearing the motto
" Gloria Deo in Excelsis " in large stone letters, was
built in the reign of Henry VIII., whilst the west front
is a creation of the seventeenth century.

Perhaps the most distinguished of its owners was
William Windham, born in 1750, the last of the direct
line of his family, the friend of Nelson and of Johnson.
He represented Norwich in the House of Commons for
eighteen years, and was well known as an orator and
statesman. There is a very fine portrait of him at
Felbrigg. Mr. Birkbeck tells us that during many
years of his public life Windham often longed for
peace and retirement, and once expressed the wish that
Downing Street were in Felbrigg Park.

The property passed to Admiral Lakin on the death

of Mr. Windham, who assumed the name of the late owner, but it was sold by his grandson in 1862 to Mr. Ketton of Norwich, the father of the present owner. I have always been much impressed, not only by the glorious old house, but also by its beautiful and perfect setting of park and woods. Mr. Ketton, a strong Liberal in politics, was living at Felbrigg with his two unmarried sisters when we first came to Norfolk. He told us that the mad Windham, as his predecessor had been called, had left his house and property in a state of sad confusion. The library, supposed to be the haunted room of the house, was in an extraordinary condition of chaos: unpaid bills, unanswered letters, were open to the eye of the newcomer, whilst a writing-table containing a number of unlocked drawers proved to be the receptacle of much that was historically valuable and curious. The Miss Kettons, in showing me the house, also disclosed the contents of these drawers. They comprised the title-deeds of the estate from very early days, many of them in an unreadable script, with great and imposing seals attached to them, bearing such names as would have delighted the heart of an antiquarian. Seeing the interest that I took in them, the Miss Kettons showed me some of the most famous papers, and began to explain and translate their—to me unintelligible—wording. It was then that I heard with admiration how these two ladies had set themselves to learn the old and difficult writing—some of it black-letter—so as to put order into the documents and to construct a history of the place. It was a difficult task, but the sisters worked perseveringly and admirably. They mastered the contents of the MSS., but hesitated at attempting to put the knowledge they had gained into an attractive garb. When Lady Ritchie was once visiting Felbrigg she was entreated by the sisters to make use of their discoveries, incorporating the precious documents into some consecutive account in her own fascinating and unique style. Unhappily,

Lady Ritchie felt bound to refuse this tempting offer. She was then editing her father's works, a self-imposed labour of love, demanding all her powers and time. After mentioning this fact to me, the elder sister, to my astonishment, asked if I would undertake this profoundly interesting task, promising me all the help that she and the younger Miss Ketton could give me. I foolishly demurred, and the opportunity was lost. It was not long after that date that the younger sister died, her loss proving such an overwhelming one to her lifelong companion that it left her for some time quite inconsolable. She had much changed when I next saw her, and there was no further mention made of the work she had so much wanted to see carried out. It was, indeed, not long before she joined that beloved sister. The documents were then placed carefully under lock and key in a trustworthy safe, and the ordinary visitor, unless armed with a permit, would have had much difficulty in seeing them. Finally, permission was given to a member of the Historical Society to print them privately, but I shall always regret not having attempted so interesting a piece of work.

The Miss Kettons had at least one Royal visitor, and this was no other than the beautiful and unfortunate Empress Elizabeth of Austria, who was spending a few weeks in the month of July during the 'eighties at Tucker's Hotel, Cromer. H.I.M. divided her day thus: the morning hours she spent on the sea in a rocking rowing-boat, much to the discomfort of her ladies-in-waiting, and the afternoon she dedicated to long pedestrian expeditions to the different points of interest in the neighbourhood. The Norfolk villagers grew accustomed to seeing the Empress and her ladies, accompanied by a trusted guide from Cromer, perambulating the high roads, the Empress with uncovered head, for her hat fell back on her shoulders, tied for safety by a large bow in front, whilst instead of a parasol

2 A

she invariably carried a huge fan, not only to shield her eyes from the sun but also to hide her features from the too persistent gaze of the passers-by. One fine day the Miss Kettons were informed that the Empress of Austria had strolled into their garden and was asking leave to rest under the shade of their trees. As they said to me in describing the occurrence :

" We do not have an Empress sitting under our trees every afternoon, so forth we sallied and pressed our Royal visitor to enter the house; but no, she would not cross the threshold." This would have been quite against her rule, so she only graciously and thankfully accepted the beautiful figs that were offered her by the sisters before she set out on her homeward walk.

I have often thought that if some fairy were to give me the chance of becoming the owner of one of the celebrated country seats of Norfolk I should select Felbrigg, situated as it is between the sea and the woodlands, with its glorious old house steeped in the romance of far-distant ages.

There are many other beautiful parks and interesting country houses in Norfolk that have been brought within the radius of my drives by the advent of the motor-car, but with many of these I have merely a bowing acquaintance. Sandringham, however, I would specially mention, for, although devoid of any historical or architectural interest, it appealed strongly to me through its close connection with the members of the Royal Family, even taking a romantic colouring from the personality of the young and attractive Princess of Wales. Thus I note with what pleasure I looked forward to my visit when my father and I, in the early 'seventies, had been honoured by an invitation to Sandringham from the Prince and Princess of Wales. It was then that we met Lord Beaconsfield, the Archbishop of York (Dr. Magee), and Sir Arthur Helps, amongst a number of other interesting and distinguished people.

Sandringham is a modern house, extensive, comfortable, well adapted for entertaining T.R.H.'s numerous and appreciative guests. It was purchased by King Edward, when he was Prince of Wales, in 1863, from the Hon. C. S. Cowper. The old property of Sandringham, or "Sant Dersingham," belonged for some centuries to the Cobbes, who intermarried with the Walpoles of Houghton. There the bride of the Prince of Wales and her parents from Denmark came to visit H.R.H., and to see the future habitation of the young Princess.

There is a charming account of their visit by Dean Stanley in one of his books, when he wrote of the radiantly beautiful Princess Alexandra as "The Angel of the Palace."

I can distinctly remember seeing upon arrival the five o'clock family tea-table, round which we all sat and which was spread in the inner hall, the Princess pouring out tea for the party. Then I recall H.R.H. conducting me to my bedroom, lighting my candles, opening the wardrobe and looking at my newly un-packed garments, excusing herself most charmingly for so doing by saying that she always admired our " toilettes," which greatly pleased me. I must repeat that the touching simplicity of the Princess and the ready hospitality of the Prince struck me as being very delightful, and I felt speedily at home with them. I had the privilege of having some talk with the Princess, and remember with what tender affection and devotion she spoke of her sister, Princess Dagmar, then about to be married to the Cezaréwitch. The Prince and Princess of Wales were then shortly leaving for Russia to attend the marriage ceremony at St. Petersburg.

And here I may be allowed to make a digression.

The Cezaréwitch, eventually Czar Alexander, and the Duke of Edinburgh, the handsome blue-eyed brother of the Prince of Wales, spent a day at Aston Clinton in November 1874, having been invited by my father to shoot Rose Mead and his other beautiful coverts. Eliot Yorke was in waiting on the Duke, and a small suite

attended the Russian heir to the throne. My dear mother
was not greatly impressed by either of our two Royal
guests, but we young ones were much taken with the
kind, simple manners of the Russian Prince, a tall, burly
personage, with a ruddy complexion and good-tempered
smile. I remember that he was very particular about
the right pronunciation of his title, teaching us to put
the accent on the third and not on the second syllable
of the word " Cezaréwitch "; he also told me what my
name would be in Russian. Seeing a crowd of school
children assembled near our luncheon tent, he seized
some plates heaped with cakes and other goodies, distributing them amongst the astonished boys and girls,
thus giving them a taste of the exquisite luncheon
prepared for the sportsmen, finally making them repeat
his name over and over again, until they could do it
to his entire satisfaction.

Queen Alexandra loves Sandringham dearly, and has
spent many of her happiest years there, living the
ordinary daily life of a country-house hostess, the wife
of an owner of property, taking a personal and living
interest in her village and other neighbours. I remember
that the Royal children played a great part in their
parents' lives : the older ones, after attending the first
portion of the morning service, lunched with us on the
Sunday of my visit, whilst the three Princesses appeared
towards the end of the meal, and again at tea-time,
having walked with us previously in the afternoon.
After tea, when there was a certain amount of gossip
going on amongst the elders, I suggested amusing the
Princesses by telling them a story. They clung to me
like bees upon this proposal, Princess Maud climbing on
to my lap. I proceeded partly to invent, partly to
resuscitate, one of the fairy tales of Hans Andersen that
had entertained many other children before them. I
reminded the Queen of Norway of this little episode
when I saw Her Majesty at Christiania many years
later ; she laughed and drew my attention to the

astonished gaze of her little son, Prince Olaf, when he
heard me speak of his mother's having once been seated
on my lap.   But so it was, and the Royal children asked
for more, just as other children have done and will go
on doing when they have anything told to them that
appeals to their taste and imagination.

Since those far-away days I have revisited the
gardens and the beautiful pleasure-grounds, the kennels
with Queen Alexandra's sixty dogs, the stables with old
and new favourites, and have made acquaintance with
the village club and reading-room, the boys' school for
carpentry and wood-carving, and that of the girls for
dressmaking and all manner of needlework.   The pupils
of these classes exhibited most successfully year after
year at the annual exhibition in London of the Home
Arts Association—a society in which Queen Alexandra
and other members of the Royal Family have always
taken much interest.

When I revisited Queen Alexandra during her widowhood that earlier vision of Sandringham recurred to my
memory, and the changes that I found there struck a
sad note in my heart.   But the Queen still retained much
of her beauty and charm, also her simplicity of manner
and kind thoughtfulness, graciously taking me herself into the little parish church and showing me the
touching memorials to King Edward.   I remember
how Caesar, the beloved white-haired terrier, who had
accompanied us on our walk, jumped into the car when
it came round to fetch me, and how Queen Alexandra
had to lift him forcibly out, as he evidently was preparing for a drive—my chauffeur and his companion
on the box never surmising that the active lady in a
plain walking suit, who sprang lightly into the car,
could be Queen Alexandra herself.

On one of my visits as a tripper to Sandringham, my
companions being Lady Mallet and Miss Cohen, we were
invited, owing to the showery weather, to eat the
luncheon we had brought with us in the huge ball-room.

The family were all absent, but our introduction to those in charge had been made by the agent, Mr. Beck. (Mr. Beck, with the Sandringham contingent, went bravely to the Great War; they were reported missing after a fierce battle and were never heard of again.) We were well entertained by the housekeeper and one of her allies; these good people were sorely troubled in their minds because we only drank water at our repast and refused their repeated pressing offers of wine, or at least whisky !

It was then that we heard a long description of the Christmas entertainments that the Royal Family were in the habit of giving to their household, and of the fancy-dress balls which occasioned great amusement to the givers of the fête as well as to the guests. Upon my asking the housekeeper what costume she had appeared in upon the last occasion, she exclaimed somewhat indignantly and very grandly, " I do not dress up; I leave that to the under-servants." When later I ventured to mention fancy-dress parties to Queen Alexandra, Her Majesty quite warmed to the subject and said, " Oh, it is a capital entertainment ; it means three weeks of amusing preparation, and as long after the event in talking it over, and then in being photographed in costume—why do you not give a fancy-dress dance for your household ? "   Good advice speedily acted upon !   I gave a *bal costumé* in January 1913, and its success was pronounced.

Queen Alexandra has motored more than once from Sandringham to The Pleasaunce.   Alas ! I was absent from home on two of these occasions, on one of which my absence gave rise to an amusing episode, described to me both in a letter from Miss Knollys and in conversation with the Queen, as well as in long epistles from home.   Queen Alexandra loves the *imprévu*, and enjoys making her appearance when least expected.   One fine July afternoon in the year 1911 two smart motor-cars came running through the village of Overstrand, turning in at the entrance gate of The Pleasaunce and drawing up at my door. A lady descended nimbly from the first car, and was told by the young and inexperienced footman who answered the bell that Lady Battersea was from home. " Never mind," came the unexpected answer, " I am sure Lady Battersea would not object to my seeing the house and garden." " Impossible," came the quick rejoinder; "nothing is shown in her ladyship's absence." " But I am a friend of your mistress," exclaimed the undaunted visitor. For all reply the youth prepared to shut the door, and was about to do so, when it was whispered into his astonished ear that he was denying admittance to none other than their Majesties the Queen Mother and the Dowager Empress of Russia, with their suites. Can one not imagine the feelings of the poor domestic ? He flung the doors wide open and fled ! Naylor, my head gardener, soon appeared on the scene, and Lester, the incomparable Lester, not easily flurried or perturbed, was brought back in haste from a shopping expedition in Cromer. The Royal party enjoyed themselves, probably all the more because they were able to indulge in critical observations without fear of hurting the owner's feelings. Finally, the tea-baskets were unpacked, and the afternoon meal taken on the spot that I call my outside dining-room.

When Queen Alexandra gave me her account of these proceedings, and I began making excuses for the behaviour of the poor young footman, she said most good-naturedly, " I have only told you this so that you may know what good and trustworthy servants you have."

I was honoured by another unexpected visit from Queen Alexandra and Princess Victoria on a beautiful spring afternoon in April 1921, and I need hardly say that old times were brought vividly to the memories of those assembled at the tea-table, aroused, perhaps, by the sight of portraits and photographs of those long gone to their rest.

Not very far from Sandringham are the beautiful golf-links of Brancaster, close to the village of Hunstanton, much frequented by summer visitors. And there is the fine historic estate belonging to the Le Strange family, one of the portions of the house, now used, I believe, as the Muniment Room, dating back to the reign of King John. Much sorrow and many losses have befallen that family in recent years, the whole of the older members having been removed within a short period by death.

The village of Thornham, also close by, has been rendered famous by the iron-foundry, established there and brought to great perfection by the genius of a remarkable woman, Mrs. Ames Lyde, the daughter of another distinguished and cultivated woman, Mrs. Hogg, assisted by her artistic brother-in-law, Victor Ames, a very clever draughtsman.

Mrs. Lyde, whose appearance was peculiar — she looked rather like a man masquerading in woman's clothes—had made for herself a unique reputation ; she was recognised as having very great artistic talent, and as being unmindful of many of the small conventionalities of life. Thus she walked about the village, stockingless, her feet in sandals, and sailed her boat in company with one devoted fisherman, or alone, on moonlight nights, when most people were snugly tucked up in their beds. She spoke many languages, loved all forms of art, and had a delicious villa outside Florence, where I once visited her. But she was devoted to her Norfolk home, living amongst the people, laying out her garden with their help, starting clubs for the men and boys, and social gatherings for all. She would inform her guests that they must get accustomed to sitting down to dinner on many nights without her, so busy was she with her village work. She had a warm heart and a quick brain, and whatever she undertook she did thoroughly. She became an enthusiastic Christian Scientist, or follower of the Higher Thought,

and declared that she was fully satisfied with what was
being revealed to her. Longing to see more countries,
she started with her maid, who trod closely in her footsteps, on a tour to India and Japan. She was then
suffering from some weakness of the heart; perhaps
she may not have known this, for without premonitory
illness, almost without warning, she died on her journey,
having just had time to say to her maid, " Pray see
that my little dog is properly cared for."

She was the heart and soul of the iron-work industry,
which has now passed out of her family's hands. During
the years of her supervision much good work was
executed—I possess some fine specimens, I am glad
to say—whilst the gates at one of the Sandringham
entrances, presented by the household to King Edward
and Queen Alexandra upon their accession, were designed by Mrs. Ames Lyde and the work carried out at
Thornham.

CHAPTER XVIII

LIFE AT OVERSTRAND

My days at Overstrand have not been, and are not now, merely spent in driving or motoring about the country, or in being shown interesting estates, for I have learnt to know and to appreciate Overstrand itself and its inhabitants. Our house — modest in its dimensions before it bloomed out into The Pleasaunce—stands in close neighbourhood to the dwellings of the fisher-folk; an easy walk takes me to all the doors at which I am anxious to knock, which always open very kindly to me. During the Overstrand season, however—that is to say, for about ten weeks in the summer—it would be difficult to find the owners of these houses at home in them, for the premises are systematically let to the numerous seaside visitors who have had the good sense to discover the charm of the place, which, without the ordinary attractions such as a pier, a band, and shows of all sorts, can hold its own with many a popular coast resort. During the season the inhabitants live in strange little makeshift dwellings, even in railway carriages, standing at the rear of their houses, the latter having been given over to the lodgers, and made as fit for their reception as circumstances will permit. Happily, there is much fine weather to be counted upon during the summer or early autumn season, when the daylight hours are long, and the sea able to offer the much-appreciated bath on a grand scale. Then the shore is alive with human beings, the bathers disporting

362

themselves from early morning until the late hours of a well-spent day.

The fishermen take their boats out to sea during some eight months of the year, for crab, lobster, herring, and cod fishing. These boats bear a colour of romance, for they are still built on the old Norse pattern, that is to say, without rowlocks. The oars are passed through round holes cut in the sides of the boats, and when these have to be drawn up on the beach, during a storm or an incoming tide, they are carried by the men, generally three on either side, with the oars acting as levers. I saw one of the old Viking boats, kept as a curiosity at Christiania, made on exactly the same pattern as the Norfolk fishing-boats that I have been describing. When not out at sea, the men are mostly to be found standing on the top of the gangways—which, be it said, are draped with hundreds of yards of drying fishing-nets—gazing seawards. When not on the cliff, most of them may be seen in a fisherman's hut, or look-out, given them by my husband, where they clean their lobster-pots, mend their gear, and look to their ropes. In this shelter the men keep their heavy mackintosh coats and their high sea-boots, such boots as would, I feel sure, prevent them from ever being able to save their lives in an accident at sea. They wear a picturesque garment called a slop, like the labourer's smock cut short, of a fine red-gold colour, the tint of an autumn leaf, which can be very becoming. They talk a strange lingo, somewhat difficult to under-stand, and use a number of words quite peculiar to Norfolk. They have curious appellations for some of the lanes or groups of houses. A narrow pathway with cottages on each side, close to my house, is called " The Londs "; a lane in the village is " The Loke."

Norfolk as a county always seems to me to be very self-sufficient, running away, as it were, into the great Northern Ocean. To a large extent the inhabit-ants have preserved their old habits, old customs, old manners of speech, and perhaps old prejudices.

Norwich, the Cathedral City, the metropolis of the
Eastern Counties, is both beautiful and interesting,
with an old-world romantic colour that not even the
modern innovations of electric trams and motor-cars can
destroy.   The Vikings of old are said to have landed on
the Norfolk coast, bold sea-kings as they were, and the
constant recurrence of the termination " hame " to the
names of towns and villages in Norfolk, such as Sher-
ing*ham*, Dere*ham*, Antring*ham*, Erping*ham*, Ayls*ham*,
and many others, gives countenance to this supposition ;
for is there not a genuine Scandinavian or Northern ring
about the termination " ham " (" hame—heim ") ?

The old cottages of the fisher folk in Overstrand are
built of beautiful grey cobble-stones collected from the
beach, the roofs of a dark red tile, so that they are
mostly of a picturesque aspect, often more picturesque
than strictly sanitary or even comfortable according
to modern ideas.   The windows are small, the ceilings
low, the staircases steep like ladders, alarming to the
aged or infirm.

I should like to give a detailed account of my many
Norfolk friends amongst the inhabitants of Overstrand,
but for obvious reasons this might prove difficult and
not always politic.   So I shall allow myself only a few
words, making it clear that I have met many interesting and very original characters amongst them deserving
of the pen of a Miss Mitford or a Miss Edgeworth.   I
recall one curious old couple : the husband past work but
still able to pocket some pennies from the visitors, with
whom he would pass the time of day, and for whom he
would carry camp-stools or baskets down to the beach ;
they were amused by his loquacity and pitied him for
his apparent poverty.   He turned the pennies into beer
regularly every evening, and returned often in too lively
a mood for the comfort of his poor wife.   In the winter
months, when visitors were no longer to be caught, he
betook himself to the workhouse, returning in the spring,
much to the chagrin of his wife, who was far more com-

fortable in his absence. I never saw her out of bed.
She was a very amusing old lady, who could talk by the
hour. She informed me that she had had a family of
twenty-two children; of that number she could only
account for nineteen—what had become of the remaining
three she knew not. As a friendly greeting for visitors
she would say, " Bless your bones ! " but when she
wished to be specially affectionate she varied this to
" Bless the flesh on your bones ! " At last the husband,
a very unsatisfactory member of society, became a
sore trial to her, helpless as she was ; he was often
reasoned with by more than one person, and announced
at last that if he did go to the workhouse again, nothing
less than a carriage and pair should ever take him there.
And so it befell, for my brougham, with a pair of
horses, driven by my coachman, called for the old man
at his cottage door, and deposited him, to the amazement of the master of the workhouse, at the gate of that
institution. His wife spent her few remaining years in
peace, and when dying sent for Cyril and pathetically
told him that she could not leave the world without
bidding him good-bye; she kept him sitting for some
time by her bedside, and at last clung to his hand with a
kind of agonized grasp until a few moments before her
death. I have never seen any one quite like her, nor
can I forget that low dark room, with her little truckle-
bed in one corner, with no view of either sky or earth, or
anything save a few faded photographs and samplers in
their frames.

Then I could add the picture of a poor blind woman,
bedridden and patient, lodging with a deaf inhabitant
of the village, the two friends spending thirty years
together in perfect harmony, the deaf woman outliving
the blind one, and at length marrying a poor crippled
man, for, as she said, she would have had to pay a man
to dig up her garden ! Then there was the old so-called
" butterfly man," with his one great treasure—his
brilliant design of the Prince of Wales's Feathers formed

with a collection of butterflies' wings, the man's own handiwork, of which he was justly proud. And who could put on paper any adequate account of a somewhat romantically placed dwelling actually standing in two parishes, and the home for many years of a very original tenant? In appearance, in speech, in dress, in everything was my tenant original, and since she has passed away (1921) I feel that the village is the poorer for the loss of her quaint personality.

Miss Matty was a subject of interest to all visitors, as she walked with a little mincing gait, holding up a parasol, bowing right and left from under her white lace veil. On King Edward's death she wore a white serge dress with a black veil—" Court mourning," as she called it. She was fond of telling all her numerous visitors that her home was like herself, very quaint; it was crowded with old and odd pieces of porcelain and some antique furniture, including a spinet. Amongst her callers were Mrs. Florence Barclay and Mrs. Felkin (Ellen Thorneycroft Fowler). The latter she once greeted as follows : " Oh, Mrs. Felkin, the novelist, and I do love a little friction ! "

As all visitors to Overstrand know, the name of " Cork " predominates, and many are the fancy appellations to distinguish one Cork from another. They are fishermen by profession, but are also ready to offer their services for work on the land in the winter months.

Cyril had a perfect genius for cheery and friendly intercourse with men and women in general, but was particularly interested in children and invalids. He would carry fresh milk, delicious fruit, and tempting cakes day after day to a poor consumptive youth who was dying by inches, by whom the sunshine of his presence was as much appreciated as his gifts, if not more. But much of his good work was done under cover of such secrecy that it was often unknown to me during his lifetime. Needless to say, I was always most happy to assist him when I could in his schemes for the good of the people.

The Pleasaunce bears few of the characteristics of a purely country residence—such characteristics as are inseparable from sparsely inhabited tracts of park and woodland, where neighbours may be few and far between, and where people are thrown back upon their own resources for amusement and interest. Here I have many neighbours calling in a friendly way, some well known in the great literary world, whose presence has added to the reputation of our seaside resort, and I cannot resist mentioning some of them by name. Sir Frederick Macmillan, the distinguished publisher, and his practical, clever little wife, inhabit during the summer months a charming cottage residence on the cliff, with a garden of small dimensions but infinite variety and surprises. Sir Frederick, stout of build, ruddy of countenance, cheery of speech, delightful to meet, seems born to enjoy all the good things of this life, amongst others the fine air of the Norfolk coast and the pleasant run of the golf-links. The kindly hospitality shown to me by Sir Frederick and his wife in London continues in an unbroken stream during the remainder of the year. I look upon the Macmillans as warm friends as well as valued neighbours.

Up a small lane, on rising ground, stands Carrwood House; it was built by Sir Henry Fowler, the late Lord Wolverhampton, and left to his son and daughters. The father's intellectual capacities, although in a somewhat different line, have descended to the daughters, for both Mrs. Felkin and her sister Mrs. Hamilton are clever and witty writers. In *Ten Degrees Backwards*, a novel by Mrs. Felkin, there occurs the description of my garden which I have reproduced in a previous chapter. Both sisters are vivacious talkers, very entertaining, lively, and fully interested in the things of the day. They are remarkable for their quick repartee and brilliant epigrams, which follow one another in

such swift succession that I find it difficult to give
any adequate idea of their animated conversation.
Carrwood House is a pleasant holiday home for both
families.

On the opposite side of the lane is a small but picturesque house, which was tenanted for a few years by
a writer of distinction, no other than Professor Gilbert
Murray, with his wife, Lady Mary Howard, who were
most interesting neighbours and whose departure I
regretted.

In old days, Sir George Lewis and his lively family
were located for the holiday weeks of the year in the
Danish Pavilion—a wood-and-plaster house, conveyed
bodily from the " Rue des Nations " in the Paris Exhibition and erected by them on the cliff, overlooking both
the sea and the golf-links. The ground was cleverly
converted into a garden and tennis-court, with cunning
little devices for shelter from wind and weather, and
there the Lewises received their many friends—chiefly
members of the artistic, literary, and dramatic pro-
fessions. Sir George Lewis was one of the most noted
solicitors of his day, concerned in many celebrated
cases ; he was known to be not only very clever in
extricating his clients from difficult and uncomfortable
situations, but also very discreet concerning the many
confidences that he was inevitably entrusted with. It
is a fact that he did not leave anything in writing
which, had it got into print, might have caused distress
to the families of his quondam clients.

Lady Lewis was indeed the life and soul of the family
party. Brilliantly endowed as she is with intellectual
qualities, and also with a genuine love of music and of
poetry, she is no less the capable house-mother, the
indefatigable and adroit needlewoman, quick in her
decisions, warm in her sympathy, and a true and
devoted friend.

The very attractive house called " The Grange " had
for a time been in the possession of the celebrated actor,

Sir John Hare, and his family. Much pleased with his experience of a few weeks spent at Overstrand during the summer holidays, and also owing to his friendship with Sir George and Lady Lewis, Sir John was beguiled into the purchase of the property. But he soon found that the solitude of the country during the earlier months of the year, when there was no club life with bridge and gossip to turn to, was more than he could bear, so "The Grange" became the home of Mr. Player and his family. To their generosity the village was much indebted. After a short tenancy the house was again offered for sale, and was acquired by the rector, the Rev. L. C. Carr, and let as a permanent domicile—and a very pleasant one, as I have already stated—to Mrs. Wilson, the mother of Mrs. Carr.

That which was once a small but picturesque cottage, standing in an apology for a garden in a by-way between the high road and the cliff, was owned in former days by a distinguished member of the medical profession from Norwich, Dr. Beverley. In time this cottage, with the grounds, was offered for sale, and finally became the property of the late Mr. Richardson and his wife, Victoria, Countess of Yarborough. A transformation scene under my husband's auspices soon took place. The cottage, now renamed "The Corner House," assumed a villa appearance, and the rough ground was turned into a little garden, an offshoot of The Pleasaunce. Both husband and wife had been intimate friends of ours for years, and had been specially connected with Cyril in his hunting days, for Mr. Richardson—or "Cat" Richardson, as he was familiarly called—was a noted sportsman, a matchless rider to hounds, whilst his wife was a fearless and perfect horsewoman. Apart from the pleasures of the chase, they both loved the country with its open-air life, and when in Norfolk took very warmly to golf and tennis. They soon became great favourites in the neighbourhood and gathered many friends about them. Moreover, Lady

2 B

Yarborough felt a spirit of kinship with the county, for she had owned and still owned relatives in Norfolk. Her mother, who began life as Miss Windham, daughter of Vice-Admiral William Windham of Felbrigg Hall, married in the first instance G. T. Wyndham of Cromer Hall, by whom she became the mother of two daughters. Widowed at an early age, Mrs. Wyndham married as her second husband the Earl of Listowel, who as Captain Hare had once been her unsuccessful suitor. He carried her away to his Irish property, whilst the Cromer possessions passed, as time went on, to her two elder daughters, the Miss Wyndhams, who married, the one The Macdonald, Lord of the Isles, and the other (the younger sister) Lord Alfred Paget, a prominent figure of the Victorian age. A tablet, recording the names and ancestry of the two sisters, may be seen in the church at Cromer.

Lady Listowel had a large family of sons and daughters, one of whom, Lady Victoria Hare, became at an early age the wife of the then Lord Yarborough. After some years of married life, Lord Yarborough died in 1875, and in 1881, when her son, the present Earl, came of age, " his mother felt free to marry the man of her choice." Thus writes Miss Richardson in the memoir she has compiled, called *The Life of a Great Sportsman*, being a delightful account of her brother, Maunsell Richardson, second husband of Victoria, Countess of Yarborough.

At Felbrigg Hall there are some portraits of members of the Windham family; these naturally proved of great interest to Lady Yarborough, who loved to trace a resemblance to her son, Jack Richardson, in the features of the blue-eyed, rosy-cheeked General Windham.

To the great regret of his many devoted friends, Mr. Richardson passed away in 1912. Of him I have written (at the request of his sister) a short appreciation in the book she has dedicated to his memory, and from this I will quote :

He had the qualities of a true English gentleman, and very lovable ones they are, and he carried on the best traditions of the old sporting world, such as have been known for many a day in this our country of England. He was typically English in his great love of nature, added to a keen spirit of enjoyment, and in being devoid of all conceit and self-sufficiency, whilst very generous in his estimation of others.

After Mr. Richardson's death his widow sold "The Corner House" to a lady who became widely known as a writer of fiction—Mrs. Florence Barclay. Niece of a much-read authoress of Victorian days, Miss Charlesworth, whose book *Ministering Children* had become a household word in thousands of English-speaking homes, Mrs. Barclay by her novel *The Rosary* leapt into sudden fame. The demand for the book was extraordinary. It satisfied the tastes of the many who read little besides fiction but who shrink from literature that may bear a touch of unseemliness or irreverence. Mrs. Barclay had an arresting personality, and a fine mellow voice in speaking and singing ; she played the organ for years in her husband's church. She could also look back upon a long course of Bible lectures that she gave week after week for twenty years to consistently well-attended meetings of women, proving herself a most impressive speaker. She died unexpectedly, after a very short illness, in March 1921. I should advise all who take an interest in her writings to read a memoir of her life by one of her daughters, which gives a very true and vivid account of a remarkable woman.

One fine summer's day brought Sir Edgar Speyer and his wife, a most talented violinist, on a visit to Sir George and Lady Lewis at the Danish Pavilion. Overstrand was then in holiday trim and looking its best. It so captivated the visitors that they set their hearts upon possessing a summer residence in the village. They lost no time in acquiring a few acres of ground for that purpose, where before long there rose a low-roofed, cottage-like villa of ample proportions, which had seemingly engulfed the red brick house formerly standing on part of its site, commanding a glorious view of the North Sea. There were no cobble-stones or red brick walls to be seen in its construction, nothing reminding one of Norfolk architecture, only wood and plaster, black and white, as in the Cheshire and West Country habitations. It was comfortably, nay, luxuriously, appointed within, and was given the somewhat fanciful name of "Sea Marge." A garden surrounding it, with tennis-court and croquet-ground, was speedily brought into being, and there the occupants spent many bright and happy holidays, happy for themselves, also for the villagers, to whom they always showed much generous kindness, until the Great War cast its shadow upon them, and severed their connection with this country.

About twenty-five years ago we were visited at Overstrand by the Hon. and Rev. Edward Lyttelton and his wife ; they came over from Cromer to see us, bringing their two little girls, Nora and Delia, with them. I had known Edward Lyttelton when he was an undergraduate at Cambridge, and when, in all the strength and beauty of youth, he had visited Aston Clinton for a cricket match, and had given us a taste of his singing voice, which had pleased us so much that we begged for his services at a Penny Reading in the village. He came, sang, and conquered. His success was assured, and we were asked over and over again " when the gentleman who sings a song called ' Jinny ' may be coming back to sing again at a Penny Concert ? " Unhappily, I cannot remember any coming back to Aston Clinton. Edward Lyttelton disappeared for a few years from our vision. When next I saw him he was ordained and married. His wife, Miss West, daughter of the Dean of St. Patrick's, Dublin, was strikingly handsome, and also endowed with a fine

voice and much taste for music. It was music that CHAPTER
had brought the pair together, and music naturally XVIII.
took a prominent part in their married life.

Overstrand must possess some potent charm, since
so many visitors who come but for a short holiday end
by purchasing, or trying to purchase, a small *pied-à-
terre* on this coast. Here again was a case in point.
The Lytteltons decided upon buying—and were fortunately able to do so — a piece of ground between
Overstrand and Sidestrand. Mrs. Lyttelton devoted
herself most ably to the work of supervising the
building of her house and its furnishing, and showed
a real genius in so doing, as well as in the laying out
of her garden. Both house and grounds are charming
and quaint. They are known by the Irish name of
" Grange-Gorman."

The newcomers were well received, all the residents
being delighted at having so distinguished a neighbour
as Dr. Lyttelton, who became Head Master of Eton in
1905. After his retirement from that prominent position, Dr. Lyttelton officiated in the parish of Sidestrand
in the place of the Rev. Ivo Hood, the young and gifted
husband of Sir Samuel and Lady Hoare's youngest
daughter, Christobel, the learned author of *Records of
a Norfolk Village*. Mr. Hood had left his Rectory to
join the Army, and was, alas, one of the victims of the
Great War!

Edward Lyttelton has a very engaging and original
personality. His preaching is most appealing, interesting,
and inspiring. In the Norwich and Ipswich churches, as
well as in London, he is warmly welcomed. His keen
sense of humour leads him not only to appreciate that
which is quaint and droll in others, but also to relate
stories against himself that may be original and amusing.
But to me his great charm lies in his really beautiful and
unselfish nature : this was daily evident in his untiring
devotion to his wife during her long years of great
suffering. In all things he practises what he preaches.

When we first visited Cromer Mr. Samuel Hoare (later Sir Samuel) with his wife and family lived at Cliff House, one of the largest residential houses in the town, and there Lady Hoare laid out a garden, or rather a succession of gardens, most cleverly, on the very cliff itself; in fact, she initiated the cliff gardens in this district, specially introducing the beautiful shrub called Buckthorn, which, with its orange-coloured berries, has become a great feature in the autumn and winter on the Norfolk coast.

Sir Samuel Hoare, M.P. for Norwich, was closely connected with the Buxtons; like them he began life as a Liberal in politics and an Evangelical in religion, but he ended his career as Sir Samuel Hoare, a Conservative and an advanced Churchman. He was a handsome man, of rather the grand Saxon type, sensible, straightforward, industrious, kindly, much beloved by the members of his family and popular in the county. He had been a success as a boy at Harrow and always retained a great affection for his school, where he had shone conspicuously as a cricketer. He was of a very hospitable nature, fond of the society of his neighbours and of entertaining guests in his house. From Cliff House the family eventually moved to Sidestrand and settled in a renovated and rejuvenated old building called Sidestrand Hall, standing in the centre of much of their property, with a fine view over the sea and the Overstrand village. Here the family grew up and prospered, preparing themselves to go out into the world, where each in his or her way was to gain distinction.

Lady Hoare, left a widow in 1915, has shown very remarkable pluck in her long severe bouts of illness. She has accomplished many clever things with her skilful fingers, such as beautiful tatting, an art she has revived, and the making of toy animals in velvet and soft materials, which are a delight to children and objects of admiration to adults. She is a great centre to her family, an adoring mother and grandmother. She has, indeed, reason to be proud of her sons and daughters, among them being Elma, wife of Dr. Paget, Bishop of Chester, Sister Anna Louisa, a prominent member of the Wantage Sisterhood, and her eldest son, Sir Samuel, the well-known Member of Parliament.

Lady Hoare's special interest lies in the beautiful little church at Sidestrand, which, with the exception of the tower, had been removed by Sir Samuel Hoare from its original position on the cliff, to rescue it from the encroaching sea. But the tower, in its isolation, stood for some years as a memory of the past, as a landmark to the fishermen, and as though guarding the many sleeping around it. On one tempestuous night in 1916 this tower, like its ancestor, was shattered, and in the morning light the old graveyard, familiarly known as the "Garden of Sleep," presented a pathetic aspect. Since then the gravestones have been removed by Lady Hoare, and reverently placed against the wall surrounding the village church.

Neighbours after the advent of motor-cars, but hardly neighbours prior to that period, were Mrs. Petre and her family of Westwick Hall. Later, after the marriage of the elder son, it was at Furze Hill, a comfortable abode in the country town of North Walsham, that mother and daughters made their home ; it would, indeed, be more correct to say daughter, for the Salvation Army claimed Mildred, the eldest daughter, some twenty or more years ago, and never was there a sweeter or more attractive face to be seen under the shadow of the Salvation Army bonnet than that of Mildred Duff.[1] The second daughter, Leila, like her sister devoted to great causes and personal work, has left a name that will not easily be forgotten, so closely connected as it was with that grand institution, the Y.W.C.A.

[1] The owner of Westwick Hall had to take the name of "Petre" on inheriting the estate, but the other members of the family retained the original name of Duff.

The youngest, Basilia, full of fire and energy, ready to take up rural, civic, or social duties as the case may be, is a very striking figure, and one well known not only in the country districts where she inspects and inspires the Girl Guides of Norfolk, but also in Norwich, where she made her mark as Lady Mayoress during her brother's year of Mayoralty.

Perhaps the keynote of the whole family is work for the good of others, done from the highest motives. The very wonderful mother encourages such work and, despite age and infirmities, rejoices at her children's activities.

Northrepps Hall, with its beautiful woodland scenery and its banks of luxuriant rhododendrons, is a delightful property, within easy walking distance of Overstrand.

It was at Northrepps Hall that Sir Fowell Buxton (the friend of Wilberforce) and his wife Lady Buxton (Hannah Gurney by birth), with their large and growing family, spent some years of their strenuous lives; it was there that Sir Fowell died in 1845—after having seen the Bill for the Abolition of Slavery passed in the Houses of Parliament, ten years before his death. And it was at Northrepps Hall that his loving and devoted wife ended her days, but not until 1872. I had often been told of her singular charm and attraction, and indeed this was made manifest to the eye in the beautiful water-colour portrait painted of her by the great artist Richmond, to whose brush may be attributed no less than fifty likenesses of the Gurney and Buxton family.

I regret never having seen Lady Buxton, but she died a few years before my first visit to Cromer, and I only connected her and her husband with the graves that were shown to me in the ruins of Overstrand Church.

Northrepps Hall has retained much of its old-world colour; it seems to have resisted many of the improvements, and perhaps some of the disfigurements, claimed by the requirements of modern existence. The long

drawing-room, from which you step straight into the CHAPTER
flower-beds, seems to carry with it an aroma of the past. XVIII.
I always feel as if the unrest and excitement of present-
day life must be foreign to it. I cannot resist quoting
this description of Northrepps Hall and its owners,
written by a Miss Clowes in the year 1833, that occurs
in *The Gurneys of Earlham*.[1]

"I have in my memory," she writes, "vivid visions of
Northrepps Hall, that sunny court, brilliant with flowers.
. . . There were Sunday evening meetings in the old Hall,
held in the large dining-room for the country people and
visitors ; besides the invited guests and Mr. Buxton's own
household, the Overstrand fishermen occasionally came, those
rough, weather-beaten old men, with long, floating hair ; the
stout ploughmen and the farm maidens were already
assembled. It was a simple service as conducted by the
master of the Hall without formality and with great
solemnity ; and after the chapter of the Bible was read,
his own well-digested, well-arranged, and homely remarks
were made, well adapted to his village hearers."

On Lady Buxton's eighty-first birthday she wrote
to her brother, Daniel Gurney :

I must send you a line on my birthday—81. Surely
goodness and mercy have followed me since I was born at
Bramerton, 1783.

Only a few years later, when she had attained the
ripe age of 88, she passed from this life in the quietest
and happiest manner—her death being so little expected
that she was actually preparing for the evening meal,
when, as Mr. Hare tells us, " the summons came."

Since the year 1872 Northrepps Hall has been tenanted
by members of the Gurney family, and now the occupant
is Mrs. Richard Gurney, the last remaining daughter of
Sir Edward and Lady Buxton, and granddaughter of
the Sir Fowell and Lady Buxton whom I have already
mentioned.

[1] By Augustus Hare.

CHAPTER XIX

OUR VISITORS' BOOK AT THE PLEASAUNCE

Welcome ever smiles,
And farewell goes out sighing.
SHAKESPEARE.

CHAPTER XIX. THE Visitors' Book, that precious possession, containing autographs of so many honoured and beloved friends, men and women—some, alas, who have passed away from this earth, others who are still happily with us !—lies by my side, helping my somewhat treacherous memory when it may be at fault.

To begin with (as a loyal subject of our reigning House), I will refer to the pleasant visits paid us by a truly attractive and gifted woman—Princess Louise. Her Royal Highness was one of our earliest guests (1889), when the house was little more than a cottage, and when there was no garden, but a few feet of very indifferent lawn between ourselves and the general public.

In a somewhat gossipy account of "Poppyland," written by Clement Scott in 1889 (the author of the song "The Garden of Sleep"), I find the following, which I will transcribe in part :

Cyril Flower's red cliff-side cottage, with its pretty verandah, its garden of poppies, has great fascination. . . . It is so unpretentious, so tiny, so completely under the eyes of everybody, that one is overwhelmed at the idea of a member of the Royal Family staying there, for Princess Louise actually took her tea on the wee lawn and nobody even turned their heads to look at her. That the fishermen's

378

wives hung their washing up in full view, just the same as they are doing now, and the Royal visitor bought her own stamps at the shop and strolled unattended on the sands—this seems incredible.

Again I transcribe :

The Liberal Whip, Cyril Flower, is stalking along in earnest converse with Signor Novara, the huge bass of the Italian Opera. . . . There is Mr. Flower clad in white samite, as mystic and wonderful as he can be, with a bath towel round his neck, or a camera slung on his back, or there is the grey-clothed Lord Suffield, looking affectionately at the pretty little house on the cliff . . . or laying out imaginary terraces and Queen Anne villa residences in company with the ubiquitous and popular Mr. Oddin Taylor, who, in his capacity as the County Solicitor, is generally believed to know every family secret!

The Princess brought paint-box, brushes, and sketch-books with her, also the determination to enjoy herself thoroughly in her own happy, easy way, and settled down quietly with ourselves (my dear mother being with us) in the simplest manner possible. The weather being beautiful, our guest was able to sketch in the morning and to drive in the afternoon, whilst after tea I was always bidden to read aloud, when she steadily sat and copied some designs of beautiful Italian needlework for her School of Art Embroidery in London. My niece, Dorothy Brand, just emerging from childhood, and spending the summer with her mother in the village, was pressed into the service of Her Royal Highness, and became most useful as a kind of self-constituted maid-in-waiting. This first visit was followed by others ; on one occasion we called upon Lady Buxton at Colne House, who, being of a very loyal nature, was particularly gratified with this attention from one of our Queen's daughters, and pleased that our visitor should have shown deep interest in Richmond's portraits of so many members of the Gurney and Buxton families.

There was nothing the Princess enjoyed more than giving her valuable advice concerning the laying out of gardens, or in suggesting some architectural or picturesque addition to a house. She had excellent taste and much knowledge, and naturally had much in common with my husband in such matters. She took the kindliest interest in our little home, and gave readily of her advice, often of the best, and many of her suggestions were followed to the letter.

I remember it was the Princess who opened the little Reading Room that my husband gave to the village, and that has been of such unqualified use to us in so many ways. It served as a most valuable though small Red Cross Hospital during the first two years of the Great War, until larger hospitals were more available, when it was closed, but reopened as a Y.M.C.A. Hut. There hundreds of men from local camps and billets congregated night after night, preferring its attractions to those of the public-house.

In the year 1890 Her Royal Highness, accompanied by Lord Lorne, was again our guest, in order to be present at one of the triennial Musical Festivals at Norwich ; and yet another time I was with the Princess when she gave prizes to the pupils of the girls' High School in that city—a very interesting function.

Lord Lorne and his brother, Lord Archibald Campbell, had been Cambridge friends of Cyril, whom they used jocularly to call " Flos " in old University days, and indeed long after, and it was owing to the fact of this friendship that we had the honour of meeting Her Royal Highness on a more intimate footing than we might otherwise have done, and of being associated with the Princess in many of her good works.

Once upon her homeward journey from Overstrand— I believe in the year 1900—Princess Louise asked me to accompany her as far as Ely, where we spent the night. It was upon that occasion that I was greatly

struck by her kindness of heart and promptitude of Chapter
decision, so much so that I feel tempted to record the XIX.
following.

We were walking near the Close of the Cathedral on the morning after our arrival, when the Princess, who was quicker of discernment than I was, noticed some children playing in the long grass, and saw that the movements of one boy were very peculiar. She feared that the other children were perhaps maltreating him, and, after watching them for a minute, went up to them and said she hoped they were not hurting the boy, as his legs were sticking up in such an unaccountable manner. We found, however, that he was pushing himself forwards with his hands, whilst lying on a little truck which was being dragged by the children ; they said that as the boy could not move his legs they were obliged to pull him along in that way. We then asked to be taken to the boy's mother, and the children led us to a cottage at no great distance. A very respectable-looking woman, the wife of a soldier, came speedily to the door, evidently much surprised at our procession. The identity of my companion was carefully concealed, and most of the conversation fell to me. After many questions, eliciting very straightforward answers from the poor mother, we asked if she would like the boy to be medically treated, H.R.H. thinking there was not a moment to be lost, as the child was twisting his hands by the way he used them. This suggestion the parents very willingly accepted. The boy was therefore sent by the Princess, in the first instance, to St. Bartholomew's Hospital, but was transferred later to the small Hospital for Children at Chelsea, where he was very carefully treated for some time. There he got very much better, and was able eventually to take up a trade, having recovered the perfect use of his hands.

I often had the honour of accompanying Princess Louise upon charitable and other errands, and I have invariably had occasion to remark upon her quickness of perception, her practical turn of mind, her sustained power of work, her very true feeling for art, and, indeed, her great executive ability in many of its branches. The Princess was the heart and soul of many popular and charitable movements, she had unbounded energy that often outran her health and strength, and never grudged giving time and attention to the causes with which she was connected.

Of the Princess's invariable consideration and kindness both to my husband and to myself I can only speak most gratefully. Indeed, I have had many proofs of Her Royal Highness's friendship: as a hostess at Roseneath and in Kensington Palace; as a guest at Overstrand, Aston Clinton, and Surrey House; as a travelling companion in France and in England. The last time that I was in company with both Princess Louise and her husband, then Duke of Argyll, I was their guest at Kensington Palace. I cannot refrain from mentioning that I had the honour on that visit of sleeping in the very apartment used by the Duchess of Kent and her daughter, Princess Victoria—in which room the young Queen was awakened at six o'clock in the morning on June 20, 1837, to receive the news of her accession to the throne of England from the Archbishop of Canterbury and Lord Conyngham.

It was on the occasion of the opening by Princess Louise of the "Ada Lewis Home" that I stayed with Her Royal Highness at Kensington Palace. This hostel in the New Kent Road, in which Sir Algernon West was deeply interested, was designed for working women and girls. Sir Algernon was the prime mover and instigator of the scheme. Mrs. Ada Lewis, widow of the well-known moneylender, had bequeathed £50,000 in her will for the purpose of building, starting, and endowing this hostel, and had been moved to do so by Sir Algernon's bold request for £40,000. This request, however, had remained unanswered during her lifetime, but in her will it was found that Mrs. Lewis had not only responded to

Sir Algernon's appeal, but had added £10,000 more than was asked for.

I well remember that on the evening before the interesting ceremony, after dining quietly with my hosts, Her Royal Highness and the Duke of Argyll (Princess Louise being busily engaged in knitting), I, seated between the two, was asked to read aloud the report in *The Times* of a great and important speech that had been delivered in the House of Commons on the previous night. I have forgotten the subject of the speech, I have forgotten much besides, but this little intimate picture clings, in default of many a grander one, to my memory, and seems a precious link with the days that are no more.

But to return to Overstrand. In turning over the pages of the Visitors' Book I see in rather large and uneven calligraphy, recurring year after year, a name that was well known in the social life of London during a great part of the last century, that of Lady Dorothy Nevill, a scion of the Norfolk house of Walpole. Lady Dolly, as she was familiarly called, was always devoted to the county of her birth. Hers was a remarkable personality. She was invariably true to herself. The garments that she wore suited her small, neat figure, for she never followed the fashions when they were to her disadvantage. Of course I could not have known Lady Dorothy in her youth, but my mother told me that she was a pretty, graceful girl with fair ringlets, dancing eyes, and an engaging smile that was unique. The ringlets had disappeared under a quaint little black silk cap when I first saw her, but the eyes had still their merry twinkle, and the smile had never left her. She invariably cast her head downwards, her eyes looking slyly up when she smiled. She spoke the purest, best English of two generations ago, but preserved the habit of saying " Dook " for " Duke," " yaller " for " yellow," " charot " for " chariot," and some other peculiarities of pronunciation dear to the aristocracy of that period. Her precise enunciation and careful choice of words always appealed to me, and formed a great contrast to the slovenly way of talking common to many of the present generation. She was as tidy in person as in language. Her interest in botany and in natural history never failed her, and she could be a most stimulating and agreeable companion. She had some funny little ways of her own, such as expressing by a very audible grunt her disapproval of any antipathetic subject or personage alluded to in conversation. She always talked of her political views as if she were a Tory of the Tories, but would murmur in an aside, " Your friends, the Liberals, are all horrors, but I like them, they are much the most amusing "; and, indeed, many of these " horrors " became intimate friends whom she gladly saw at her house and table. She had a passion for collections of all sorts of things, not necessarily beautiful or artistic, but quaint or possessing some historical interest. She had delicate fingers that could twist or plait coloured paper into patterns, an art that had long died out, but that had a charm of its own.

Mr. Gosse has written a very delightful sketch of dear Lady Dolly in his *Literary Impressions* (1919), which gives a truthful and intimate picture of the little lady. We loved entertaining her at Overstrand; she was one of our most constant visitors, and I have distinct visions of her on many different occasions. I can still see her walking up and down my paved garden paths, garbed in a violet silk dress of ample dimensions, with a soft-tinted and fringed shawl (at other times a tiger skin) about her shoulders, a little poke-bonnet with brilliant flowers, two veils to preserve the delicacy of her complexion, her small hands encased in black lace mittens, carrying a bright red or yellow sunshade. True to the fine manners of a past age, Lady Dorothy was always scrupulously punctual, and I would find

her seated at my breakfast-table or ready for the
morning walk or afternoon drive at any hour that
had been previously settled upon. But she showed
a modern taste in her habit of cigarette-smoking, also
perhaps in her insatiable curiosity for what was exciting
or interesting in politics, discoveries, inventions, or sales
of the day. So she grew old very slowly, perhaps
never at all (she was with me at The Pleasaunce in
1912, the year before her death), but just faded gently
away when well on in the eighties.

I am giving the following, written in 1908, as a sample
of Lady Dolly's little notes (she always declared that she
was no good with her pen):

45 CHARLES STREET, MAYFAIR, W.
December 11.

OH MY DEAR LADY BATTERSEA!—I do so want to know
something of you and where you are. I have been a great deal
about, but now am settled here for this terrible time of Xmas.

I so often think of you and all the happy days I have
spent with you, and I do hope later on I may come when the
weather is very nice.

I have no fresh news, the Govt. going on recklessly to
their ruin and ours, but I believe these creatures will get
the vote [1]—if not with this Govt., certainly with the next.
We have plenty to think about just now. I have been so
interested in the poor Amhersts' sale. My brother in 1869
sold these tapestried chairs out of Wolterton, where they had
been from the time of the Ambassador Walpole, brother of
Sir R. W. He got £229 for the twelve chairs and sofas,
to-day they went for £7000—such are the times!

I do hope to hear from you how you and your dear
mother are.—With love, yrs. affec.,   D. NEVILL.

It was Lady Dorothy Nevill who introduced us to
that very interesting Canon Jessopp, rector of Scarning
parish at the time when we knew him. He was a keen
historical student, principally of the fourteenth and
fifteenth centuries, and had an amazing knowledge

---

[1] Referring to the Suffragettes.

2 C

of Norfolk customs, habits, and speech, not only of that period but of many others. One of his works, entitled *One Generation of a Norfolk House* (that of the Walpoles), has been very widely read and deservedly appreciated, the ghost story contained in its pages adding to the interest it awakened. In spite of his literary power and his good parish work, for he was a most devoted pastor, it was impossible to secure preferment in his favour, from either the Conservative or the Liberal Prime Ministers. As he said himself, his politics did not appeal to Lord Salisbury nor his theology to Mr. Gladstone. He had a striking personality, being very tall, with fine features, brilliantly blue eyes, and a happy, pleasant smile. He looked particularly well in the evening in the dress of a Royal Chaplain, for this distinction had been granted him.

I often recall having seen Canon Jessopp and George Meredith (then our guest) sitting cosily over the fire together indulging in reminiscences of past days. By some extraordinary freak I had imagined that Canon Jessopp was a Conservative, and this error of mine was the cause of much merriment on the part of the two elderly gentlemen, who kept on ejaculating, " Fancy such a thing ! " between peals of laughter, in which I joined. I remember that I thought not only how handsome and distinguished they looked, but what a delight it was to listen to their racy talk. Canon Jessopp was a great lover of music, and when young had a charming voice. He encouraged hearty congregational singing in his church, not fancying anthems, except in cathedrals, but loving old-fashioned hymns, and getting his congregation to select and propose their favourites for successive Sundays.

I quote a few lines from one of his letters :

SCARNING RECTORY,
October 1897.

DEAR LADY BATTERSEA— . . . I had a most delightful visit. What a beautiful and wonderful place his Lordship has made ! Who shall say that there are no magicians any longer on the face of the earth ?

It was very grievous to me that I could not possibly remain at Overstrand till to-day, but even we small folk have our duties and our calls which may not be put aside : " Duties loved of love, beloved yet hated."

With a thousand thanks for a most delightful time and for the kind hopes held out that even more delightful days may possibly be in store for me, when your presence will add a new charm to what is already so charming.

George Meredith was one of our most honoured visitors. He came to The Pleasaunce in 1896—the year that he met Canon Jessopp in our house. Of him Lord Morley wrote to me :

What a joyful thing for you to have had Meredith with you. *There* is a man of radiant genius if you like. I am glad that he spoke kindly of poor me. I owe many a glorious hour to him so many years ago. Did you ever read his sonnet " To J. M." ?

I can recall George Meredith's arresting personality, his tall slim figure, which was rather shrunk and bent with rheumatism, his intellectual and really beautiful face, his delicate features, the piercing glance of his bright eyes, his full deep voice, his measured way of talking, his extraordinary and original flow of words, and his unexpected replies or retorts to the most commonplace questions or remarks. Occasionally he alarmed his interlocutors, often he silenced them, and still more often he diverted or exhilarated them. Alfred Lyttelton declared that to listen to George Meredith was one of the greatest intellectual treats a man could have, and enjoyed nothing more than meeting him as a fellow-guest.

Alas ! Mr. Meredith had two serious drawbacks against which to contend : the affliction of ever-increasing deafness, and very serious crippling lameness. But he enjoyed his daily drives in my victoria,

where I was privileged to become the recipient of many
interesting and delightful reminiscences which it amused
him to recount. Thus I heard of his early struggles to
enter upon a literary career, of his first ventures, of his
climb into fame, of his many friends, and much of his
children and grandchildren—the latter he simply adored.
They were all staying one summer in Overstrand. I
was a witness of the grandfather's love for the tiny
mites, with whom he spent many portions of the day.
He showed much pretended annoyance with the children's nurses for their lack of appreciation of the Overstrand beach. They complained that it was deplorably
dull : no Christy minstrels, no band, no amusements
of any sort. In order to relieve the situation, Cole,
his faithful valet, was requisitioned by his master to
blacken his face and serenade the nurses under their
windows, for which performance he would receive the
magnificent gratuity of £5. Cole was equal to the
occasion, but he wisely chose the shades of evening
for his adventure and so avoided the suggested disguise.

After leaving us Mr. Meredith sent me a charming
letter, in which occurred these words :

I had been promised the sweetest possible time at The
Pleasaunce—such was my experience, and I beg that you
will bear to hear of the sensibility of one of your guests whose
crippled condition taxed forbearance, and seriously advises
him to abstain from acceptance of future invitations. But
I shall have the happiest recollections of my days at Overstrand.

On one of his visits George Meredith found himself
in company with a great friend of ours, Prince Troubetzkoy, and his wife, she being no other than the somewhat celebrated American novelist, Amélie Rives, author
of *Virginia of Virginia, The Quick or the Dead?* etc.,
etc. Meredith, nothing daunted by that lady's success
with her pen, gave as his opinion that hardly any
woman had produced a first-rate novel, not even Jane

Austen, Charlotte Brontë, or George Eliot, whose names we brandished triumphantly before him. He kept to his opinion, and Princess Troubetzkoy heaved a sigh, less in conscious acquiescence as to her own shortcomings than in sorrow that so great a genius should commit such an error in judgment. Prince Troubetzkoy was in many respects a remarkable man. To begin with, he was 6 feet 7 inches in height, but so perfectly proportioned that he did not oppress one by his great size ; he had a handsome face, with a good, kind expression, and his manner and manners were perfect. Of half-Russian, half-American parentage, he had never lived in Russia, but had worked as an artist chiefly in Italy and in France. He was a fair portrait-painter, devoted to his art, as well as to literature and to music. His was a simple, childlike, and eminently pure nature. I enjoyed his society greatly.

The Hon. Emily Lawless, one of our dearly-loved visitors, was a very gifted woman, whose literary ability could rise at times to genius—*vide* two of her novels, *Grania* and *Hurrish*, both of them giving a faithful and beautiful picture of the Irish peasantry of her day. These productions are enough to place the author's name amongst those of the best writers of fiction. Cyril, one of her most ardent admirers, distributed at least a dozen copies of *Grania* amongst his friends. She had, moreover, the true poetic vein, and her verse was both noble in aspiration and striking in expression.

Stopford Brooke wrote a preface to her *Songs of the Wild Geese*, a book of poems well worth reading, but bearing a somewhat misleading title. She was one of those who actually foretold the terrible war initiated by Germany, always assuring me that England was overrun with German spies, and that we, with incredible blindness, gave our enemies every opportunity of starting a campaign of invasion. She did not live to see the verification of what she had predicted. In the same way her

prognostications of the future condition of Ireland were
only too true.

It was in her house that I once had the privilege of
meeting that interesting excommunicated priest, Father
Tyrrell, of whom I should have liked to have seen more.

Cyril actually built a room for Miss Lawless, called
the Gate House, in the garden, overlooking the sea, where
she might write in peace and meditate. She felt that
it was an ideal spot for a writer, but she never enjoyed
it, for her physical strength did not keep pace with her
mental vigour; she suffered constantly from attacks of
alarming and terrible illness, to one of which she at last
succumbed.

The following touching poem dear Emily left upon
my table after a visit she paid me at Overstrand in
1907 :

TO C. B.   A VALEDICTION

Farewell again, truest, most helpful soul !
   This world is dearer to me for thy sake ;
No jot or tittle of its varying whole
   Is worth what love and loving friendship make.
A broader summer track in life is thine,
A narrower, more shade-infested, mine,
Yet over both, methinks, the same stars shine !

Mary Cholmondeley was another visitor who had
become known to us through her clever novel *Red
Pottage*, which had brought her into instant and well-
merited fame. She, like Emily Lawless, is of a very
delicate physique, suffering cruelly from asthma, and
a seaside visit was not undertaken without alarm,
which was only too well justified. She and her handsome sister Victoria became great friends of ours, and
the more I knew of Mary the greater was my admiration
for her refined and distinguished intellect, her great
sense of humour, and her originality of outlook. She
and her sister, gifted with much social talent, gathered
a very pleasant set of friends about them, offering
merely tea and biscuits as refreshments on the evenings

of their receptions, the guests responding readily to their invitations, thus proving that simplicity of entertaining need be no bar to success when the hostesses are graced with intellect and charm.

Rhoda Broughton, an acquaintance of long standing, spent a few days with us on two occasions at Over-strand. She had a very accentuated personality quite peculiar to herself, was abrupt, quaint, clever and witty, most breezy and lively in conversation, and full of repartee. Her humorous and strongly-coloured novels gained enormous popularity in the 'seventies and 'eighties. My husband was much attracted by her amusing talk —perhaps, at that time, more than I was. This the observant and quick-witted writer was not slow in perceiving. Upon her second visit, when the loss of a dear sister had cast a shadow upon her life, which aroused in me warm sympathetic feeling, she remarked, not quite untruly either, " I feel that the more I go up in Lady Battersea's estimation, the more I go down in Lord Battersea's." But she never minded telling anecdotes against herself, and laughed as heartily as we did when she related how in coming down to Overstrand she had been attracted by the book-stall in Liverpool Street Station, where some of her own works had found a place with this inscription : " Rhoda Broughton. Soiled, but cheap."

Her magnificent courage, during the long years of illness (rheumatoid arthritis) that kept her a prisoner to her chair, was very fine. She would write by dicta-tion, and talked brilliantly to the many friends who visited her during the winter months that she spent in London ; but she deeply mourned and never quite recovered from the loss of Henry James, that versatile writer, who was one of her most constant visitors, calling upon her daily, until his last fatal illness laid him low.

I remember that the points about Miss Broughton's novels that struck me most were her constant use of the present tense, her dislike for old people and children, her love of dogs and true understanding of them, her great power in both humorous and pathetic writing. Rhoda Broughton died in June 1920.

How far have the present writers of fiction travelled from the novelists of my younger days !

Mrs. Humphry Ward, then at the height of her well-deserved fame, spent a couple of days with us at Overstrand in the long ago, and lectured at Norwich in the old Unitarian Chapel, where a great concourse of people awaited our talented guest. Of her as a writer and thinker I have spoken elsewhere, her connection with Overstrand having been of the slightest.

It is only of late years that I have had the privilege of Mrs. Belloc Lowndes' acquaintance—I may say friendship. She attracts me greatly, not only by the literary skill she displays in her novels, but also by her pleasant conversational powers and by her sympathetic nature. Of partly French parentage, she has many of the French national characteristics, and has even a slightly foreign accent in talking.

Mrs. Creighton and Mrs. Benson, eminently capable women, wives of distinguished men, have both been my guests more than once at Overstrand. I owe their acquaintance to the fact of my having served with them on the Executive Committees of the N.U.W.W. (now the National Council of Women).

Mrs. Creighton, whom I met for the first time at Bristol in 1894, was the wife of the late Dr. Creighton, then Bishop of Peterborough, later of London. She was President of our Association for two long terms of office, and one of the ablest we have ever had. Very decided in opinion, very clever in managing her committees, an adept in discussion, she has a master mind. I can see her now facing her audience, standing at the table covered with papers, reports, and accounts, erect and commanding, her face with its finely-cut features and brilliantly dark eyes alive to every movement in the room, prominent amongst all her co-workers—a truly

remarkable personality. It was not easy to dissent
from her. Many called her very autocratic, and took
exception to her rather brusque, decided manner, but
she could hardly have done the work which she did
accomplish had she been of a more yielding disposition
or many-sided nature. But she did yield on one great
question, either to the force of circumstances or to
that of argument, and, after having been an Anti-
Suffragist, became a supporter of Women's Enfranchise-
ment. Mrs Creighton is an able writer : the Life of
her husband she has given us is a masterpiece.

Mrs. Benson, sister of Henry Sidgwick, that distinguished and delightful thinker and writer, and the wife
of Dr. Benson, late Archbishop of Canterbury, was
to my mind a most attractive character. She had so
great a sense of humour that she told me she found
it almost impossible to preside over a committee, for
instead of attending to her duties she would be entertaining herself by summing up the little eccentricities
of the workers. But she could, and did, speak un-
commonly well, and when she gave an address it was
most delicately conceived and full of original thought. I
believe her Lenten addresses to the women of her Sussex
village, Horstead Keynes, where she spent the years
of her widowhood, were little models of deep religious
feeling, expressed in homely but beautiful language. She
had a warm, loving heart, and a most sympathetic
nature. She laid no claim to good looks, being short
and stout in figure, with no fine feature, but she had,
all the same, charm of manner and distinction of voice
and speech. She was a very dear woman, deeply
beloved by her children and by her friends.

Another lady writer, Mrs. Earle, sister of the twins,
Lady Lytton and Lady Loch, spent a few days with us
one summer ; her visit was appreciated by my husband
no less than by myself, she being such an accomplished
and ardent gardener, and much interested in what we
could show her at The Pleasaunce. Mrs. Earle has given

us many of her valuable horticultural experiences, as well as some good advice, in her published works, and being a convinced vegetarian and an adept in the culinary art she has interspersed her pages with most excellent recipes for tasty vegetarian dishes.

Cornelia Sorabji, an Indian lady, who sought and obtained higher education in one of our universities, a distinguished woman, an able writer and speaker, appeared one summer in her brilliant Oriental garb to astonish the people of our Norfolk village, and proved a very unusual guest. It was a matter of pride and a source of gratification to her that she had taken a degree which would allow her to practise at the bar in India, thus permitting her to approach the native women who could not have the privilege of personally consulting a legal adviser.

What pleasant yet sad memories are awakened by the sight of the signature of S. H. Butcher in our visitors' book! In the summer of 1909 that most attractive writer and talker spent a couple of days with me at The Pleasaunce. There was a pause in the coming and going of visitors during that glorious July week, and I enjoyed to the full our *tête-à-tête*, wishing that it might have been further prolonged. Our little dinners, served *al fresco*, bore quite a festive note ; even the dishes seemed to acquire a special distinction from the presence of my guest. I never saw Mr. Butcher again. He passed away at a comparatively early age, leaving a world that had lost its charm for him since death had robbed him of a beautiful and beloved wife. His dear little sprightly sister, Lady Prothero, and her interesting and cultivated husband,[1] editor of the *Quarterly Review*, have, I am glad to say, spent some days under our roof, where, in years still longer ago, we had entertained his father, Canon Prothero—then an old man, a friend of Queen Victoria—also his well-known brother, Rowland, now Lord Ernle.

[1] I grieve to have to add that Sir George Prothero died in July 1922.

Field-Marshal Lord Wolseley came and came again to our house at Overstrand, delighted with the keen air blowing across the Northern Ocean. Here he recruited after a painful operation, declaring that the sea breezes hastened his final recovery, and to our care Lady Wolseley entrusted him, with many words of loving caution. He was indeed a delightful guest; bright, chatty, and easily amused, always ready for a brisk walk during the day and a game of patience in the evening. His Liberal bias in politics and in army matters may have affected for a time his popularity in military circles, but subsequent events have proved the wisdom of his views. His alert bearing, his soldierly appearance, his bright expression, gave an index to his character, but they could hardly reveal his very distinct intellectual qualities, which led him to find his truest pleasure as years went by in a studious and literary life. He made his fame in the Egyptian War, receiving his marching orders at our house, Aston Clinton, in the September of 1883, and from that date he rose swiftly to the highest position he could hold in the Army. He had lost an eye in battle early in life, and he occasionally embarrassed people by asking which was the real eye and which was the glass one, a question which it was difficult to answer. His face was also marked with a deep scar, otherwise he showed little trace of what he had been through. We spent a fortnight with Sir Garnet, as he then was, and Lady Wolseley at the Royal Hospital, Dublin, when he was General of the Forces in Ireland, and a very pleasant time it proved to be, although, as usual, there were troubles in that unhappy land. As he grew older he suffered severely from lapse of memory, which made intercourse with him difficult and unsatisfactory. My last vision of him was standing at the small garden gate of his house, connected with Hampton Court Palace, an attractive residence granted to him and to Lady Wolseley for their lives by the King. It was there that he ended his days, quietly and peacefully, and it was there also that Lady Wolseley, in April 1920, went to her rest. She was well known for her knowledge and love of art, especially in regard to furniture and house decoration. She had a beautiful collection of Jacobean furniture, and some rare and curious specimens of figures moulded and carved in wax. Upon the last visit that I paid her, when I found her, as usual, faultlessly attired, she showed me a very touching memorial to her husband : a window in one of the rooms of her house. It had the effect of making the room into an oratory, and it was there, or close by, that she sat and worked, sorting and arranging the enormous correspondence that had been left to her by Lord Wolseley. The devoted wife always hoped that she would find a fitting chronicler of her gallant husband's career, but I do not think that before her death her wish had been gratified. The only daughter, Frances, the present bearer of the title, re-solved some years ago to lead her own life, untrammelled by custom or prejudice. She became an enthusiastic practical gardener, starting a school for young gardeners of her own sex, and gaining distinction in the line she had chosen.

It was during the visit of the Wolseleys that the celebrated Players' Company, under the able direction of Mr. Philip Comyns Carr, gave a performance of Milton's *Comus* in our gardens. The day was perfect, and the scene one never to be forgotten, Lord Wolseley remarking, " Your *Comus* was the prettiest thing of the sort I ever saw." The play was most beautifully ren-dered, and was followed by an Elizabethan masque. The large number of visitors were much gratified, and many of them returned in the evening when the per-formance was repeated, a mysterious lime-light from the cloisters being thrown upon the actors, whilst the gardens were illuminated. Sir John Hare took a deep interest in the proceedings, and, in company with Sir George Lewis, went round with the hat at the close of the play to solicit a bonus for members of the Company.

They were not a little grateful, many of them being in very poor circumstances. I could not help remarking the fact that the consistently puritanical spirit of our Rector kept him severely away from a performance of a masterpiece written by one who could surely claim to be as great a Puritan as himself—the poet Milton.

My first introduction to John Morley was in the year 1876, when I met him in the house of Lady Reay (then Mrs. Mitchell), a hostess famed for the keen interest she took in politics and literature, and for her ability in collecting as her guests the celebrities of the day. I did not at first catch the name of my neighbour at table, but was indeed greatly excited when I heard that he was no other than John Morley, a delightful talker, and one whom I found easy to converse with. I hoped to see more of him, but was not fated to do so for some time. It was only at rare intervals that I was privileged to meet the brilliant man of letters and rising politician, then rapidly coming to the front as one of the group of distinguished Radicals prominent amongst whom were Sir Charles Dilke and Mr. Chamberlain.

It was not until 1891, when we met at Overstrand, that I could claim Mr. Morley, not merely as an acquaintance, but also as a friend, and one whose friendship I have always greatly valued.

In those days our East Coast village was a very quiet and little-known seaside resort, unpretentious, but none the less fascinating and well suited as a rest-cure for a tired politician. It was also admirably fitted as a background for reading and pleasant intercourse. It was just the place where friends could be thoroughly enjoyed and appreciated.

Let me recall John Morley as he then was : rather short in stature, slenderly built, with a slight stoop such as would be common to many a student, eyes that had a bright searching glance and that could also twinkle with merriment ; features showing decided strength of

CHAPTER
XIX.

character, a noble and thoughtful brow, delicate white hands that seemed fashioned to hold the pen and to turn over the pages of a book—this is the portrait of the man as he appeared to me in the long-ago. Add to this a voice melodious, low-toned, yet clear as a bell, a worthy vehicle for his beautiful enunciation and perfect diction.

How superficial my acquaintance with Lord Morley might have remained had it not been our good fortune to have had him as a close neighbour at Overstrand! We had previously lent him our little house—then literally *the* Cottage—for an Easter holiday, when, tired with the strain of London life, he was seeking the rest and refreshment that our Norfolk coast could give him, in company with Lady Morley. I only knew him in those days through his letters, written at Overstrand to Cyril, but, as previously mentioned, we became friends as well as neighbours later on.

I feel that I cannot do better than quote the following from Lord Morley's *Recollections*, published in 1917 :

" In the summer (1891)," he writes, " I had the refreshment of three delightful months at Overstrand on the coast of Norfolk. Our new house was spacious " [this has since then been incorporated with the house bought and enlarged —I may say rebuilt—by Sir Edgar Speyer and called " Sea Marge "], " standing open to sky and sea, with a fine piece of meadow-land between us and the water, and excellent quarters for servants, who have well-earned air and space after the dingy inferno of a London basement. I started with the feel that the turmoil of the winter and spring had left my mind barren and inelastic. We had charming neighbours. The elements went on gloriously, and much helped the blessing of finding one's self alive and full of spring."

We met constantly during that happy summer, the presence of my dear mother adding to the pleasure we all took in that far too brief holiday-time.

Lord Morley was then acting as Reader for the

publishing firm of Macmillan, and much new and inter- esting literature found its way to the house where he, his wife, and her daughter were then staying. What a good, sure foundation such literature proved to be for our many pleasant chats! Although Lord Morley was credited with being a decided freethinker, I always felt in conversing with him that he had a singularly reverent mind. It was perhaps from a very keen sense of honesty and sincerity that he held aloof from express- ing sympathy with any one creed, but he was greatly moved by the fine musical services in the Abbey, which he constantly attended, often quietly sitting within its precincts before repairing to the House of Commons. Moreover, he had been a warm friend and admirer of Dean Stanley. He had also been deeply impressed by the power and humanity of Cardinal Manning, whose marked ability had shown itself conspicuously during the coal strike of the 'eighties. More than once he spoke to me in terms of deep feeling of Mr. Gladstone's real devotion to his faith, and I may state that Lord Morley's intense affection for his great leader was very beautiful. He always carried a letter from Mr. Gladstone about with him in one of his pockets. This was an answer to a birthday greeting written by Lord Morley, and one could feel in reading it that the words must have gone to the very heart of the old statesman.

It was indeed a privilege to see and talk so fre- quently and unreservedly with Lord Morley as I did that summer. I remember that one day, when he had been alluding to a friend who had impressed him by his " holiness " of thought and speech, at my mother's request I returned to his house after our walk and asked for his definition of " holiness." He looked somewhat startled and said, " I will tell you to-morrow." The next day I received an envelope directed in Lord Morley's fine handwriting. Upon opening it I saw that he had written out the definition I had asked him for, after, as he said, a sleepless night of pondering over so difficult a question. A year later, when he was looking through my commonplace-book of quotations, he came upon the said definition, and asked where I had found it, and by whom it was, having entirely forgotten that he had written it himself! I laughingly explained the circumstances, which drew from him, "Well done, John Morley, well done!" This definition, but greatly enlarged, appeared in a number of the *Nineteenth Century* at a later date.

We had some impromptu musical parties in the evenings of that summer, Mrs. Gilbey and her sisters, the Misses Coutts Fowlie, supplying the orchestra. We flung open the windows, admitting the fresh sea breezes, whilst the distant sound of the waves came to us as an accompaniment to the melodies. There, in a secluded corner of our little drawing-room, sat John Morley, with a smile upon his lips, grateful for the efforts of the somewhat timid yet audacious performers, whilst occasionally there was a tilt of his eyebrows and a somewhat sarcastic smile when our rendering of some well-known passage fell short of his expectations.

What more fitting than to end this slight sketch with two letters, the first relating to a delightful visit to Lord and Lady Tweedmouth at Guisachan, where I met Mr. Morley, after which I ventured to send him a silver paper-knife with the date of our stay and the following quotation engraved upon it :

Les grandes pensées viennent du cœur.
VAUVENARGUES.

TOMICH, BEAULY, N.B.
Sept. 26, 1895.

DEAR LADY BATTERSEA—I am infinitely pleased and moved by your gift. It will always recall how, when in spite of stoical appearances I was somewhat disposed to feel low, a truly sympathetic friend drew me on to the cheerful ground of thoughts, books, great men.

It is I who ought to send you a memento, for it was I

who gained most. I am none the less glad that you too Chapter entertain pleasant associations with Guisachan. The hand- XIX. some knife will lie on my table for the rest of my days.

It is quite true—and a profound truth it is—that great thoughts come from the heart. Only we won't forget that they may as well also pass through the brain. The first process, tho', is the most likely to be overlooked, so I like to have a standing reminder of it.

There is a deer-drive to-day. My wife has gone. But I sternly keep the faith. One of the worst things in the world is *Fear*, and you and I won't find our pleasure in fun which depends on fear. That isn't too pharisaic, is it?

With a thousand thanks, my dear lady, and every friendly wish both for you and Cyril.

We set our faces South in a day or two.—Ever yours,

JOHN MORLEY.

FLOWERMEAD,
PRINCES ROAD, WIMBLEDON PARK, S.W.
November 21, 1917.

DEAR LADY BATTERSEA—Your kind letter quite warms my heart. We have a great host of common and delightful memories, and I owe you my best thanks for finding them revived in my pages.

Overstrand and your house and company and Cyril and your mother will never fade out of my mind, so long as I have one.—Yours affectionately, MORLEY.

Amongst the many friends whom we delighted in welcoming at Overstrand were Mr. Gerald Balfour and his wife, Lady Betty, whose names have already appeared in these pages, but of whom I should like to make further mention. Less well known than his distinguished brother Arthur, less responsive to the pleasures of society, of a more serious and reserved tone of mind, Gerald Balfour is a very interesting personality. He was extremely handsome as a young man, with delicate refined features and a graceful pose of the head. I always enjoyed those summer weeks that brought him time after time to stay with us. He loved flowers, and had

2 D

CHAPTER made a study of them, appreciated the garden, proved a
XIX. devotee of golf, and used with pleasure our library of very
readable books. More than all, Mr. Balfour was truly
touched by Cyril's evident affection for him, and by
the care that he took to ensure the comfort and happiness of his guest. Humanity, as such, did not appeal
to Mr. Balfour, so that some people who met him in
our house thought him rather distant in manner, and
found him difficult in conversation. His wife, with
her pleasant, beaming face and her kindly ways, was
a less frequent guest than her husband, being greatly
occupied with her young and growing family of children.
But when she did come I found her socially very
pleasant, and I treasure her friendship. Lady Betty
has inherited from her father and grandfather her taste
for literature and talent for writing. The Life of her
father—that delightful author of prose and verse, who
wrote under the name of Owen Meredith, and was at
one time Viceroy of India and later our Ambassador
in Paris—has been well and interestingly told by his
daughter. For many years of his life Lord Lytton
had been the close friend of the late Dr. Elwin, once
editor of the *Quarterly Review*, and rector of Booton,
Norfolk—a very remarkable and uncommon man of
letters, as well as a devoted parish priest. The friendship, commencing with the father, descended to the
daughter, and for years Dr. Elwin and Lady Betty
corresponded regularly and frequently.

Of other friends and acquaintances whom we had
the pleasure of receiving during those years of cheery
social intercourse at Overstrand, I may mention Sir
Sidney Lee, of literary fame ; Mr. Choate, the entertaining and brilliant American Ambassador, and his
wife ; Frederic Myers, the poet, and my husband's old
Cambridge friend ; the Archbishop of York (Dr. Maclagan),
he of stately mien and of beneficent expression, and his
wife, Augusta Barrington, good, matter-of-fact, a great
but not a very interesting talker ; Archdeacon Wilberforce,

original, audacious, attractive, full of ideas, and his wife, a woman of the world, a perfect wife and a pleasant member of Society ; Sir Theodore Morison, whom I am proud to claim as a connection by marriage, his wife being Margaret Cohen by birth, the daughter of Arthur Cohen, first cousin of my parents.

We were fortunate in welcoming Mr. Cohen and his family more than once as our neighbours, during the summer holiday weeks, in one or other of the houses in our close vicinity. I always enjoyed the frequent walks that I took with Arthur Cohen on those occasions, when conversation seemed at its easiest, and when my companion allowed me many glimpses into his scholarly and original mind. He combined a very real love of his race, their history and traditions, with an intimate knowledge of English history and jurisprudence. He was, as we all know, a distinguished member of the Bar, a K.C. and P.C., and by the merest accident not appointed Judge in the High Court. His eldest daughter, Lucy, gifted with much personal charm, is keenly alive to the enjoyment of intellectual and cultured society. From her earliest years she has been the chosen companion of those older than herself; thus, whilst retaining the buoyancy of youth, she has acquired the tact and delicate perception so necessary for satisfactory intercourse with older and more experienced minds, and has proved to many of her elders a beloved friend as well as relative. Indeed, I cannot fail to acknowledge my debt of gratitude to her for the unceasing interest she has taken in the preparation of these Reminiscences, and for the encouragement she has never failed to give me.

While writing of distinguished legal figures, I must record that I have had the pleasure of entertaining Lord Halsbury at Overstrand, and congratulating him upon his 90th birthday, offering him upon that occasion a bouquet of roses, the number of which corresponded with the years of his life. Lord Halsbury, amongst other attainments, was a very good Hebrew scholar, and, to my surprise and amusement, once introduced a few correctly written Hebrew words in a letter to me. I endeavoured to send a worthy reply, but was later reprimanded by Lord Halsbury for having introduced vowels into one of my Hebrew words, omitting them in another. He added that he would bring the works of Gervinus and Buxtorf to confound me.

Lord and Lady Curzon were our guests on the eve of their departure for India. The newly - appointed Viceroy, being in very indifferent health at that time, had been ordered complete rest in a bracing climate before starting to take up his onerous duties in our Eastern Empire. He might have enjoyed the rest at Overstrand, but the bracing air of our coast was too keen, causing terrible bouts of sleeplessness. This, however, did not prevent him from being a most pleasant companion, whose conversation could be both amusing and sparkling, his uncommon personality being but little spoilt by a somewhat dictatorial manner and phraseology.

Mary Curzon (Miss Leiter), his beautiful wife, seemed ideally fitted by her radiant good looks for a Vice-Reine, and was much loved and admired in her some-what difficult and very exhausting rôle. Her beauty was indisputable ; her dark wavy hair, her deep blue eyes, and pale skin produced a kind of moonlight effect, whilst her welcoming smile and graceful figure added to her personal attraction. She was very proud of her husband and devoted to him.

Lord and Lady Rayleigh, both interesting visitors, came more than once to our Norfolk home, and we returned their visits. I have agreeable recollections of a somewhat old-fashioned establishment, a red brick house—Lord Rayleigh's property—set down in a fine well-timbered park, Terling by name, in the very agri-cultural county of Essex, where on certain Sundays in the summer months members of a pleasant social coterie would assemble.

Lord Rayleigh, with his great and well-earned scientific reputation, was extraordinarily modest and of gentle, unassuming manners. It was indeed difficult for the ordinary man or woman to recognise, when in company with him, that they were in the presence of one of the very greatest scientific and mathematical students of the age, if not the greatest.

" He was the last of the giants of the Victorian Era in physical science—Stokes, Thomson and Tait, Clerk Maxwell and Rayleigh," wrote Sir Oliver Lodge in the May number, 1919, of the *Proceedings of the Society for Psychical Research*.[1] " Cambridge may well be proud of its Alumni. From the days of Isaac Newton to the present day, it has magnificently upheld the flag of Mathematical Physics ; and from no University in the world have greater men in this branch of science ever emanated."

I remember how, on one of those pleasant Sunday gatherings, after a talk about the magic properties of oil cast upon troubled waters, Lord Rayleigh took me into his laboratory, where together we filled a small bath with water, which he proceeded to ruffle into waves ; then he bade me pour some oil gently from a jug standing close by and watch the effect, which was prompt and satisfactory.

Lady Rayleigh, a sister of Arthur Balfour, proved herself to be a most kindly hostess, loving her garden and her music, playing deliciously to her guests upon the fine organ in her drawing-room, leaving all scientific matters to her husband and her sister, Mrs. Sidgwick. The latter possessed powers of close and accurate observation which made her worthy of being the valued assistant of Lord Rayleigh in many of his most arduous investigations.

[1] Lord Rayleigh had been President of the Society for Psychical Research, and had given a brilliant and humorous presidential address when he first took the Chair.

At Overstrand I once had the honour of escorting the astronomer and popular writer, Sir Robert Ball, round the garden, and also of welcoming Lord Currie during the last year of his busy and many-sided life. Philip Currie, as we had known and called him for many years, belonged to a family the members of which had been friends of our parents and ourselves throughout two generations.

From the Foreign Office Philip Currie had taken ambassadorial rank, and had been successively our representative in Constantinople and in Rome. When he came with his wife to Cromer it was during the last years of their lives; he was physically a wreck, and it was sad to see him drawn about in a Bath chair and reflect that it was he who once had danced a wild " fandango " with my cousin Alfred in our little entrance-hall at Aston Clinton — both dancers being clad as ballet-girls, to the amusement of a gay little party of onlookers and fellow-guests.

I can remember a serious talk that I had with Lord Currie at Overstrand, when he, somewhat of a free-thinker, almost a scoffer in days gone by, told me that the religion of the Prophet Micah—as he expressed it— was the one that he could grasp :

What doth the Lord require of thee, but to do justly, and to love mercy, and to walk humbly with thy God ?

Lady Currie, his wife, was an author of prose and of verse, a minor poet, as she once humorously signed herself after her pseudonym " Violet Fane " in a book of her own poems which she gave to me. She had been a beauty in her youth, well known in the world of writers and in social circles as Mrs. Singleton, and had married Philip Currie after her first husband's death in somewhat late middle life. They had long been devoted to one another, and there was a strange and romantic ending to their existences. They were both dangerously ill, but not under the same roof, the CHAPTER wife in a nursing home in London, the husband in his XIX. own house in the country. On the morning of Lady Currie's death, the nurse, watching by Lord Currie's side, was endeavouring to break the sad news as considerately as she could to him, when he interposed, saying, " I know quite well that my wife is dead, I can even tell you the hour when she passed away," which he did quite accurately, adding, " I felt distinctly at the time that all was over."   And it was not long before he followed her.

Only space and time prevent me from lingering for a longer period over the many names that confront me in the visitors' book, names of friends and acquaintances who found their way, not only to the door of The Pleasaunce, but often also into the hearts of its owners. It constantly happened that those who began as acquaintances ripened into friends. There is one honoured name that has appeared of late years, that of Dr. Pollock, Bishop of Norwich, and here I may gratefully mention how deeply I prize his unfailing friendship and the pleasure that I always derive from his kindly visits. There is doubtless something about the place that encourages friendship. Moreover, I feel that many houses and gardens have their own individual character and colour where special characteristics grow and flourish. Thus I am indebted to our attractive yet comfortable little Norfolk home, with its welcoming atmosphere, for some of the most valued friends that I now possess. Glimpses of the garden with its many surprises, of the cricket ground lying in full view of the main road, seem to invite the entry of passers-by, whilst the boundless Northern Ocean redeems the feeling of cramped ownership, such as one might attribute to the garden if it lay meekly and cosily between gates and fencing, without that glorious horizon of endless ebb and flow.

If asked, I should say that the characteristics of The

CHAPTER
XIX.

Pleasaunce are homeliness grafted on to much of real beauty, and cheerfulness independent of company. It is a rare place for quiet hours devoted to study, and also a rare place for happy communion with Nature. May it long remain so !

CHAPTER XX

SOCIAL WORK

Jews' Free School—East End Visiting—Association for the Protection of Girls and Women
—Some Jewish Ministers

> The student (*or worker*) attains that which is the most compelling
> desire of every human being, a work in life which it is worth living for,
> and which is not cut short by the accident of his death.—Gilbert
> Murray.

From childhood both my sister and I had been taught
to look upon work for others in many a good cause
as a privilege and not as a hardship, nor as anything
meritorious in itself.

When we were still in the schoolroom we were taken
to the Jews' Free School, of which my father was the
honoured President, and my mother a constant visitor as
member of committee, and there introduced to the heads
of that institution. We were deeply interested in that
wonderful school and in the children, whose intellectual
capacities and love of learning were very pronounced.
We were asked to take a class and to hear the children
read, and were permitted to question them upon what
they read ; this led the way first to frequent and then
to regularly-timed visits, which, once instituted, became
unalterable fixtures, and continued long after we had
left the schoolroom. It was then that I ventured to
inquire what Bible teaching was given, and received
the somewhat amazing reply that the five Books of

CHAPTER
XX.

409

Moses were being taught in the following way : Genesis to a very young class, then Exodus to children in a more advanced section, and so on, until the final chapter of the Pentateuch had been reached. This did not seem very satisfactory, and, young as I was, I ventured to start a new system, being much encouraged by my mother and the kindly head-mistress. The only difficulty lay in the absence of the requisite books for the purpose. I believe my sister was working on the same lines with her class. We were young and ambitious, and did not fear difficulties. If there were no books at hand, why not write one ourselves, which we and others could use ? We consulted our mother and our excellent Hebrew teacher, Dr. Kalisch, and were advised to try and see what we could do. In three years' time we had accomplished what we had planned. I think we divided our task somewhat unfairly, as I chose the easier portion, namely the historical books, leaving the prophetic and other more literary chapters to my sister. When finished the work had attained two volumes ; it was published by Messrs. Longman, under the title of *The History and Literature of the Israelites*, and actually passed through two editions. Our mother, who hated all publicity, forbade our names appearing on the cover, but, urged by Mr. Longman, allowed a modest "By C. & A. de Rothschild " to be placed on the title-page. Many were the reviews following upon the publication ; in one of them the authors were alluded to as " two pious and well-meaning young men."

Our indulgent father's pride in his daughters' work induced him to send a copy to many of his friends, amongst others to Mr. Disraeli, with the result that the proud authors were, to their delight, the recipients of the following letters, which I am vain enough to select from the many I still possess, the daily arrival of which made the hour of the postman's appearance deeply exciting.

GROSVENOR GATE, 1870.

DEAR CONSTANCE — Your volume reached me in the midst of public disquietude, and I have not been able to look at it until to-day.

I have done so with much pleasure, for you describe in a style, animated and picturesque, the great story of our ancestors, and have treated with force and feeling their immortal annals. Your book is essentially narrative, and not critical, and therefore I question the propriety of introducing into it the critical element : as, for example, the comment on Jacob's blessing.

It is not competent for a writer partially to avail himself of the principles of historical criticism ; and their complete application would entirely change the whole character of your book.—Yours sincerely,   B. DISRAELI.

HUGHENDEN MANOR, 1871.

DEAR ANNIE—I thank you for your book, of which I have now read the greater part.

It is conceived in an enlightened spirit, without the introduction of disturbing criticism which would have marred the harmony of the general scheme.

You have dealt well with the prophets, and still better with the poets ; vindicating with truth and spirit the lyrical genius of the people.

It is deeply to be regretted that we have only a portion of this ancient literature, and that preserved, and sometimes rewritten, for a particular purpose. It would have been well if you had inserted in a chapter a summary of what is known to be lost ; but this, perhaps, has been done in the first volume, which I have not at hand.

It may be a question whether, instead of the conventional and conventicle title of " the Lord," it would not have been better to have used in your translations the real name of the God of Israel, which would have given more clearness and meaning to the narrative.

I wish very much that M. Renan would give us an " Étude " of Ecclesiastes and a new version.

What continues to please me very much in your work

is the style, which is lucid, vigorous, and graceful, and always sustained by adequate thought and feeling.

Remember me kindly to your fellow - labourer, and congratulating you both on the completion of a work so highly praiseworthy, believe me, sincerely yours,

B. DISRAELI.

The following letter came as a great surprise from the Bishop of Winchester, Samuel Wilberforce :

STRATTON, MICHELDEVER STATION,
January 20, 1871.

MY DEAR LADY DE ROTHSCHILD—I have just seen *The History and Literature of the Israelites*, and I ambitiously desire to possess it as a present from the authoresses, with my name written in it by them — and to stir them up to this act of remembrance and kindness, I have ventured to order my publisher to send a copy of my *Hebrew Heroes* to Grosvenor Place, which I hope they will accept from me.

You see I cannot let my separation from my late Diocese be an occasion for being forgotten by you.—I am, my dear Lady de Rothschild, ever most sincerely yours,

S. WINTON.

In one way we failed to meet the school requirements, the book being too long and too difficult for the purpose, but the remedy seemed easy. I rewrote my first volume and brought it out in a cheaper abridged edition, whilst Vol. II. was incorporated in Vol. I.

The task had really been a very delightful one to me, and I developed quite a passion for correcting proofs !

The next thing that I can remember which brought me into direct contact with young and questioning minds in the Community was a Girls' Class, instituted by my mother, and held about three evenings in the week, under the auspices of Mrs. Harris and her daughters, a family well known for their exceptionally good work, both religious and social.

The Girls' Classes were originally started in the East End of London for Jewish factory girls, and

became the forerunners of that excellent institution,
the Girls' Clubs, now so deservedly popular. They were
then held in the house of Mrs. Harris, and on the morning
of the Sabbath many of older years were admitted, who
enjoyed the religious instruction and the devotional
readings that were given there. My mother wrote a
series of addresses for these gatherings. These meetings
were not intended to supplant the services of the
Synagogue, at that time held at a very early and inconvenient hour, but many of the women and girls
were not habitual attendants at public worship, whilst
others came notwithstanding and joined their friends in
Devonshire Square.

Whilst the Saturday morning classes were held in
the East End it was obviously impossible for us to
attend them, as driving on the Sabbath Day would
have shocked all assembled there; but in after years,
when our good friend Mrs. Harris was no more, and
when her daughter Emily carried on the work in the
West Central district of London, within walking distance of my house, that difficulty vanished. Saturday
after Saturday I attended the classes, which were
unique in their way. They were composed of young
girls, old women, and a sprinkling of boys, whose sense
of enjoyment in these meetings was often greater than
their observance of discipline and punctuality.

Emily Harris did her best in this difficult and not
always satisfactory work ; but to her it was a labour of
love, and being well acquainted with the home conditions
of her pupils, she took a very living interest in them,
which they repaid with real affection. She was always
" dear Miss Em'ly " to them, and they were her " beloved
Rebeccas, Rachels, or Simeons," as the case might be.
She had a great sense of humour, and found much field
for exercising it during her association with her strangely-
assorted flock ; also a very ready pen, which was evident
in her profuse and really most original compositions in
prose and poetry.

Besides these Sabbath classes I was brought into other bonds of common interest with Emily Harris. My mother had long been a member of the Jewish Ladies' Benevolent Loan Society, an excellent charity of the day, and had only ceased to be an active member when my dear father's last illness claimed her constant attention. She suggested my taking her place, and as I was then unmarried and living at home (1875), I found no difficulty in doing so.

Let me here state very briefly what the duties were. A committee of Jewish ladies, at that time under the presidency of my mother, and assisted by a working secretary, had at their disposal a fund which they were permitted to loan out in small sums paid weekly, on application, to needy members of the Community. The status of the applicant had to be well known to the secretary, also the names of two securities who were willing to vouch for the ultimate repayment of the loan. But in order to bring a closer personal touch into the charity, before the borrowers were granted what they demanded they were visited by two members of the committee, it being the custom for the ladies always to undertake this work in pairs and in turn during the year. The poorer members of the Jewish Community were at that time mostly congregated in the East End of London, in the Whitechapel, Mile End, and Bethnal Green districts, and visiting, for the purpose of making closer acquaintance with the borrowers, meant spending a long morning or afternoon in those quarters.

As I said before, I was introduced in 1875 to the duties of the ladies' committee and entered with great zest upon them. I continued visiting in the East End until the charity was brought to a close in the early part of this century, and I remember with pleasure the opportunity those East End visits gave me of a closer and more intimate acquaintance with my co-religionists.

Emily Harris was for years my companion, until

ill-health and finally death came to sever a tie that had CHAPTER
lasted for two generations.   XX.

I should like to recall some of the striking features of those visits that have remained indelibly printed on my memory.

To begin with, in nearly every case we were most courteously received—indeed from some the greeting was affectionate. Thus I was generally called " My dear," and was often given a caressing pat on my arm, or a gentle pressure of the hand. When the children were home from school I found them wonderfully un-shy and ready to make friends; they would stand close to me, touch my dress, and stare at me with their wide-open, wondering eyes. They generally had thick, closely curling hair, dark, almost black, or else of a red golden colour. They looked very intelligent, and when questioned about their school and their studies would give (especially the older ones) very ready and good answers. The women were mostly short in stature, and, like all Eastern races, mature at a somewhat early age.

Many of the men were engaged in tailoring and shoe-making. There were families who only talked Yiddish, which would have made conversation difficult, if not impossible, had it not been for the kind offices of some of the neighbours, who would generally be called in to translate questions and answers. They all belonged to the very orthodox form of Judaism; they all had the " Mezuzah "[1] on their door-posts.

According to custom, the married women concealed their hair, not under a veil, as they would have done in the East, but under a front of false hair—" Sheitel," as it is called. They still keep a special set of cooking

---

[1] " Mezuzah "—literally in Hebrew " door-post," but also the name given to a small piece of parchment on which is inscribed the passage beginning, " Hear, O Israel " (Deut. vi. 4-9 and xi. 13-21). On the outside of the roll is written the name of God, " Shaddai." The parchment, being enclosed in a small case, is affixed in a slanting position to the upper part of the right-hand door-post, and is reverently touched by the pious as they cross the threshold.

utensils and crockery for the Passover holy days, when a great scrubbing and cleaning takes place, so that it is a pleasure to visit them at that time. An old woman, whom I found reading her Hebrew Prayer-book one Friday evening, assured me that she never looked at a book in any other language on the Sabbath, and I gathered that this was not uncommon in the days of which I am speaking.

We encountered various difficulties when visiting : we might climb the little, half-broken, rickety stair in some old house, looking for one of our cases, who perhaps happened to be living on the ground floor or in rooms at the back of the building ; and, indeed, it was some-times a morning's work to find the man or woman whose name might be on our list. Supposing we were bound for No. 39, let us say, in Flower and Dean Street, we would innocently conclude that 39 would follow upon 38 and be followed in turn by 40, but in some cases 39 would take an independent course of its own and might prove to be in close proximity to No. 2. It might occur that after a long and unsuccessful search, when piteously asking for assistance from a passer-by, I would be told, " Follow that lidy, my dear "—" lidy " being rather an imaginative description of the guide we had to follow. I suppose that at times we used to look fagged or worried, for the women would say in compassionate tones, " Poor dears ! are you very tired ? " and occasionally we might be offered a cup of coffee. Singularly hos-pitable, friendly, and unceremonious were these women —not respectful, not observers of class distinction, but with a kind of genial familiarity, originating in a strong racial fellow-feeling for their visitors.

On one occasion, learning from a *very* respectable Jewish woman that her son had been appointed Reader in one of the City synagogues, and seeing that son well dressed walking down the street, I could not help saying to his mother: " I hope your son will do more than merely read prayers in synagogue ; I hope he will

visit amongst our people, and do other spiritual and
religious work where it is so much wanted."

"But why?" said the mother in a shocked tone of
voice; "we are not like the *goyem* (Gentiles), we do not
want to be talked to or taught, we do not drink, and
we know how to bring up our children religiously and
soberly."

I did not like to argue the question, and left the
woman very indignant at my suggestion.

I do not know that my East End visiting—which
extended over thirty years—led to any marked results
as regards the poor people amongst whom I went, but
I am confident that I learned much from this experience,
and that I felt far humbler about my own powers, and
also more eager to bring a little sunshine into the lives
of those who so often lived under hard or difficult
conditions. I learnt to know many of the courts and
alleys about Commercial Road and Mile End, and would
trudge down some of the most disreputable streets,
quiet and harmless in the daytime, but warranted
dangerous at night. My wanderings would occasionally
take me to Toynbee Hall, and there I would be
kindly welcomed by the Warden, Canon Barnett, and
his wife, both doing inimitable work in the East End,
work which was to become world-famous and to bear a
lasting influence. I was fortunately enabled to do the
Barnetts some service by gaining the consent of the
Prince and Princess of Wales to open a little pleasure-
ground in Whitechapel, destined for the use of the inhabitants. A tradesman from that district with one of
his friends came to see me at Surrey House to consult
me about arrangements for the Royal visit. I found the
worthy but fussy little man in my inner hall, and I begged
him to come into my room, where, seated in solemn
conclave, we entered into the necessary details. On the
appointed day I drove with my husband to the spot,
where a large crowd had assembled, a part being roped
off for the Royal visitors, and where a chair had been

2 E

prominently placed in full view of the performance. Seeing me, my quondam visitor approached and said politely, " That chair is yours, madam ; you invited me into your drawing-room and bade me be seated when I came to your house in the West End ; now I am glad to be able to return the compliment." I felt much touched, and was delighted when my little friend, amongst others, was introduced by Canon Barnett to the Royal party.

The splendid work that has been done, and is being done, by the Hon. Lily Montagu, Basil Henriques and his wife, and other nobly inspired men and women—alas ! only too few—in the Community, was really begun by a much older generation, that of my mother and her family, and I am proud to think that my sister and I were links between the earlier workers and their successors of to-day, able to appreciate the courage and initiative of a former age, whilst giving our heartfelt admiration to the men and women now carrying on and amplifying the earlier traditions.

The Jewish Community were always known to have been well to the fore in all matters connected with education, social reform, and charitable relief, but there was one evil which they had never even attempted to touch, and the presence of which amongst them had been almost tacitly ignored. And it was this very evil that was to be brought forcibly before me. This is how it occurred.

One evening, in the year 1885, when I was sitting alone in my London drawing-room (Cyril being occupied in the country with some of his constituents), I was startled by the ringing of my front-door bell at ten o'clock at night, when I was certainly not expecting visitors. The servant announced " Miss Blanche Pigott "—a name connected in my mind with Norfolk—and forthwith there appeared, looking somewhat weary and agitated, my friend from Sheringham. Almost before I could speak she advanced, threw herself into a chair, and said : " You are astonished to see me, but I have come to you for

advice and help, for you are the *only* person in this huge
city of London to whom I can turn." And thereupon
she unfolded her tale. It ran as follows.

A certain Mrs. Herbert, the wife of a well-known
London clergyman, was conducting a Mission in a
crowded and ill-conditioned district of the Metropolis
and had asked for the assistance amongst others of
Blanche Pigott, a lady well known both in London and
Norfolk for her noble and self-sacrificing work. A
Mission-room had been opened, where a welcome was
offered and given every night to the unhappy street-
walkers who sought rest and refreshment, and who did
not always resent the words of comfort and advice that
were addressed to them. Amongst the many who came,
two girls of the Jewish Community were observed and
spoken to. They frankly stated in answer to their
questioners that they belonged to the unhappy sisterhood, and that even if they wished to abandon their
present way of living it would be impossible, for every
door would be shut against them. " Our own people
disown us," they said ; " their Law forbids them to receive
us again, and we will not enter a Christian Home, we
have no wish to join your Church, for, however bad we
may be, we will not give up our own Faith."

Mrs. Herbert was perplexed by this reply, and both
she and Miss Pigott insisted that there must surely be
some Jewish Home or shelter open to them. The girls
were just as positive that no such place existed, and that
they would be repudiated by the members of their own
families should they venture to return to them. Hardly
crediting the truth of the girls' words, Blanche, who
had a wonderfully attractive and sympathetic way with
her, extracted a half-hearted promise from them that
they would return at a stated hour on the morrow, and
then hurried post-haste to Surrey House to lay her
perplexities before me. Alas, I was hopelessly at sea
in the matter! The subject was one I had always
avoided, and I had never heard, nor, indeed, did I

believe, that any so-called rescue work had been needed
amongst the Jewish Community. I felt reluctant, even
if I had been able, to propose meeting the poor girls on
the morrow, but my friend, with her fine spirit of determination, made me ashamed of my lukewarm sympathy,
and, inspired by her, I wrote to my dear and valued
cousin, Claude Montefiore, the most generous of individuals, with the purest and noblest of minds, telling
him of our dilemma and begging him to meet Mrs.
Herbert and her " aide-de-camp " at the time appointed.
Claude knew as little about the matter as I did, but he
went accompanied by the Rev. S. Singer, one of the best
of men, and, if I remember rightly, still further accompanied by some stalwart member of the police.

They were welcomed warmly by Mrs. Herbert and
Miss Pigott, but waited fruitlessly for the advent of the
two poor Jewish girls, whom we should hardly have
expected if we had not been such novices in this work.
Mrs. Herbert expressed in no measured terms her
astonishment that the Community owned no harbour of
refuge for those of their own Faith, who were more sinned
against than sinning. My cousin and Mr. Singer came
back to me with a list of suggestions and also difficulties
that we should have to encounter if we tried to take
any steps forward in this matter. We sat long in
debate, but decided at last that Mrs. Herbert should be
invited to meet a few influential ladies of the Jewish
Faith, who would hear from her lips a plain and un-
varnished account of what she had witnessed during
the Mission week.

My sister readily offered her drawing-room, and there
we met one afternoon in the May of 1885. I well
remember that bright and sunny day, the arrival of
Mrs. Herbert amongst us, her account of what she had
witnessed; then her strong appeal for action on our
part, and for wise, non-sentimental, but helpful methods
of work.

We were novices, as I have already stated, but we

listened eagerly and were not unwilling to learn. Some
of the ladies present reddened and wept at the miserable
and unsavoury tales that they had to hear. When
Mrs. Herbert ended by saying, " And these unfortunate
creatures declare that no help is forthcoming to them
from members of their own race, that they are looked
upon as too vile even to be saved from the gutter,"
Mr. Singer, who was with us, sprang indignantly
to his feet, muttering, " This is surely untrue." I
whispered to Mrs. Herbert, " You have done well to-day ;
the work will begin forthwith ; you have sown a seed
which in time may grow into a strong plant." Little
did I dream how that prophecy was to be fulfilled.
Complete silence prevailed for a few minutes after our
eloquent speaker had left us, and then came words wrung
from the hearts of the hearers, with warm proffers of
personal help.

My dear cousin, the wife of Lord Rothschild, agreed
to become the president of the small committee which
this meeting had brought into being, and her name was
of good omen for the success of the work. I offered
myself as honorary secretary, which post—by no means
a sinecure—I held for twenty years, until my labours
were lightened by the advent of a working secretary, who
could give full time and complete attention to the task.
The post, grown into a very important one, is now filled
by Mr. S. Cohen, a man of great ability and initiative,
who holds the strings of the various branches of the
Association in his capable hands. To his name must be
added that of Miss Denhof, our lady secretary, to whom,
for her patience, tact, and love of her work, the Association is greatly indebted.

In turning over the pages of one of the first reports
of the Jewish Ladies' Society for Preventive and Rescue
Work, my eye is arrested by the names of many valued
colleagues, some now gone to their rest, such as Mrs.
Nathaniel Cohen, Mrs. D. Q. Henriques, Mrs. Lionel
Lucas, to all of whom the young and barely-fledged

Society owed a deep debt of gratitude. There are
many still with us, I am glad to say, who have aided
and witnessed the growth and expansion of the work
from its very beginning, and are able to judge of
its extraordinary development, such as our honoured
President, Lady Rothschild, Mrs. Halford, our valued
Treasurer of so many years' standing, Mrs. Hayman,
Mrs. Singer, and last, but certainly not least, my sister.

From 1886 to 1922 is a long period of years, during
which the work has grown by leaps and by bounds.
Indeed, Blanche Pigott, although rich in faith and well
endowed with imagination, could little have divined,
when she touched the door-bell of my house that summer
night in aid of two poor Jewish outcasts, what a train
of work she was setting in motion. Our committee
included before long such distinguished members of the
Community as my cousin, Claude Montefiore, Mr. A. R.
Moro, and the late Rev. S. Singer.

The Society shed its first name as years went on,
and is now known as the Jewish Association for the
Protection of Girls and Women ; it stands on a broader
foundation than it did originally, and its work is of a
less specific nature. Thus, besides the initial Home
for rescue cases, Charcroft House, there is a Hostel
attached to it for infants, who are thus not wholly
separated from their mothers ; a Lodging - house,
Sara Pyke House, for respectable working - girls ; a
Home, Highbury House, for friendless children ; a
Reformatory School for girls, Montefiore House, that,
with the members of its staff, shelters fifty inmates,
and has met with the warm approval of H.M. Chief
Inspector of Reformatories and Industrial Schools.
There is a Visiting Committee in connection with the
outside work of our Association, bringing us into touch
with those in need of instant help, advice, or warning. We are well looked upon and trusted by the
police-court Magistrates, many Jewish girls having been
placed by them " on probation " under our care. Our

employees, *and only ours,* are allowed to board the incoming ships in the docks, and to give Jewish immigrant girls such advice in Yiddish or other foreign tongues as might and would prevent them from falling a prey to the nefarious men who trade upon their ignorance. Our Association has now assumed international importance, bringing us into touch with others engaged in similar work in many parts of Europe and in America. And here it may be said that the members of our Society are honoured by the fact that their work is in harmony with, or rather a continuation of, the great movement initiated by Mrs. Josephine Butler under overpowering difficulties, and valiantly carried on by Mr. Stead, for the suppression of the White Slave Traffic.

Naturally, the work of reclamation has always gone hand in hand with that of prevention, and I can truthfully say that, although Jewish girls may be easy to touch for the moment, for they are generally emotional, excitable, and often full of real true feeling, they may be difficult to influence for any long period of time, and those who undertake this work must be prepared for many heart-breaking disappointments, and should come to it with a strong panoply of faith in God and love for His creatures, remembering how " the Talmud taught that religion was not a thing of creed, or dogma, or faith merely, but of active goodness."

I have known personally many of our Jewish ministers, and should like to mention some of them by name.

To begin with, the Chief Rabbi of my childhood and first youth, Dr. Nathan Marcus Adler. He came but little into our lives, but I can just remember that he was noted for his unflinching orthodoxy, for the keen interest that he took in the specially Jewish side of education, and also, so I was told, for his Commentaries on the Talmud and on other post-Biblical writings. I can recall his strong German accent in preaching and his very guttural tone of voice, also the fact that what he said appeared to me as if it belonged, in spirit, to a past generation.

With his son, who succeeded him as Chief Rabbi, Dr. Hermann Adler, I was on more familiar ground. He was a very clever man, who possessed a great fund of natural mother-wit, and although his orthodoxy was unimpeachable he belonged in many ways to the present generation. Thus he and his wife were able to mix socially with those of other creeds, to their own and the others' signal advantage. Unfortunately, Dr. Adler never lost his decidedly foreign pronunciation, and this, with rather a hesitating delivery, proved a drawback to his success as a preacher. But the matter of his sermons was often excellent, and he was an interesting writer. In correspondence he could be most telling, even amusing, and his speeches were often very witty, interspersed with good anecdotes taken from old Jewish writers. I recall spending a long day sitting beside him on a platform, during the interminable hours of an International Conference of Jewish workers ; in spite of some long tiresome speeches, I was kept lively and amused by Dr. Adler's comments addressed to me *sotto voce*, or quickly written on slips of paper and placed where I could read them. I consider that in the death of Dr. Adler the Jewish Community lost a very valuable religious head, not easily to be replaced.

The Rev. A. L. Green, who was for many years Reader and preacher at the Synagogue which we attended, was much liked and respected by my dear mother. His views on matters connected with public worship were far more modern than those of most of his colleagues, and I think, although greatly beloved, he was often in advance of his congregation. He was a sincerely good, earnest, hard-working man, throwing his whole soul into his efforts to raise and to help his spiritually or materially poorer co-religionists, and courageous in word and in action. He wrote regularly for the *Jewish Chronicle* under the name of "Nemo." I think he was

one of the first of his confraternity to take a deep interest CHAPTER
in the social movements amongst the Jewish people XX.
of his day. He died in 1883.

His nephew, the Rev. A. A. Green, has inherited
many of his uncle's qualities ; I have met him from
time to time in the Aylesbury Female Convict Prison,
engaged in visiting one of the unfortunate members of
his Community. I have there had occasion to note
his strong good sense, as well as the kindliness of his
heart, in dealing with those difficult and elusive cases.

The Rev. Simeon Singer was perhaps the minister
with whom I was most in sympathy, because he took
so decided and influential a part in the very difficult
work of the Jewish Association for the Protection of
Girls and Women. Mr. Singer was minister of the
New West End Synagogue, where he attracted very
large congregations, both by his preaching and by the
character that he bore.

Sir Philip Magnus, now M.P. for the London University, has been known to me both in and out of the
pulpit, and here, perhaps, I may include his wife's name,
although she is not one of the women preachers of the
day, like the Hon. Lily Montagu, but the wielder of
a pen that has made its mark both in poetry and in
prose.

The excellent work both of the Rev. Michael Adler
and of the Rev. Vivian Simmons during the long years
of the Great War was much appreciated in England
and abroad, and was helpful in familiarising those of
other creeds with Jewish practices. Both Jewish and
Christian chaplains had many pathetic, and indeed also
comical, stories to tell when they returned from their
service in foreign parts. At one time Mr. Adler was
lodging under the same roof with a Roman Catholic
priest, a Presbyterian elder, and an Anglican clergyman ;
they all were on the most friendly terms, their minor
differences showing small indeed in the face of that
great leveller, Death. Tragedy and Comedy, tears and

laughter, were, indeed, often close neighbours in those days, and it was well to be able to turn quickly and sympathetically from one to the other. There are stories in point, related by those whom one can trust; and when many incidents, even such as are connected with the Great War, so quickly pass out of mind, I feel that there can be no harm in alluding to them in these Reminiscences.

Surely the memory of Rabbi Bloch's splendid action will long survive — the Rabbi who voluntarily left a place of comparative safety in order to hold the Crucifix before the closing eyes of a Catholic soldier, whose priest had been hastily summoned by an urgent call to another part of the field, death by a bomb overtaking both the Rabbi and the dying soldier.

Then a scene in Belgium on a cold and misty afternoon in November, when both Jewish and Christian chaplains were engaged in burying the fallen. The Jewish chaplain's sad task for that day being ended, he was seeking somewhat hopelessly to find his way back to the place where he was stationed at some distance from the burial-ground. A young Highlander offered himself as guide. The tramp was a long one, the air penetratingly cold; the young Highlander turned to the chaplain and ventured to suggest a drink of whisky. But no whisky was forthcoming, so the Highlander proposed a hymn which might in its effect prove as enlivening as a glass of spirits. The Jewish chaplain agreed willingly, and chose a hymn that he thought might be suitable for members of both churches, "Lead, kindly Light," which was heartily sung and re-sung during the whole of the return march. Upon arrival the Highlander remarked that the hymn was almost as good as a glass of whisky!

Again, a chaplain of the Church of England made a somewhat doubtful attempt to cheer a wounded Jewish officer (a connection of mine), who was awaiting a serious operation, by the assurance that although the Rabbi

was engaged elsewhere, he, the chaplain, had been provided with a copy of the Jewish Burial Service, which
he was carrying with him !

Like their Christian brethren, the Jewish clergy are constantly overweighted by their duties. In fact, there are so few ministers for such a large and widely dispersed Community that they cannot even attempt to confine their labours to one district, and their energies are demanded in connection with religious and philanthropic movements throughout the country. Their salaries are often very meagre, and the tasks that await them very harrowing. They struggle bravely against these disadvantages, and deserve the confidence and warm gratitude of the Jewish Community. I learn with satisfaction that part of the Jewish War Memorial is to take the form of supplementing both their numbers and their salaries.

CHAPTER XXI

SOCIAL WORK—*continued*

TEMPERANCE WORK—THE GORDON LEAGUE—RECREATIVE EVENING SCHOOLS ASSOCIATION—NATIONAL COUNCIL OF WOMEN

WHEN we were children our parents' luncheon and dinner tables, as well as those of our relatives and friends, were usually supplied with beer and wine, which we contemplated as a matter of course. It was no uncommon occurrence for children supposed to be weakly and anaemic to be dosed by their mothers daily with port wine at eleven o'clock in the morning. Healthy men, as well as delicate men, took strong drink when they engaged in specially hard work, mental or physical, and they would have laughed to scorn the notion, now an established truth, that nerves could be stronger, muscles firmer, sight keener, staying powers greater, when the human material is not artificially warmed and stimulated by spirits or beer. Rich men drank for pleasure, and too often drank deeply, whilst amongst all classes of the population any occasion for good-fellowship or rejoicing found its celebration in very copious potations and much intemperance.

Drunkenness was constantly portrayed on the stage, causing much hilarity amongst the audience, and Dickens, our great master of fiction, made ungrudging use of his inimitable pen in the description of those

many ludicrous and often painful scenes where the
bottle plays so conspicuous a part.

But the evils of intemperance were vividly brought
home to us on the many occasions when some good and
trusted domestic would fail in his or her duties whilst
under the influence of strong drink. Strange to say,
or perhaps not strange in those days, the culprit was
constantly forgiven and reinstated, until at last the
vicious habit became of so ingrained a nature, and
the result so alarming, that it could no longer be
condoned. The unfortunate sinner, dismissed from
comfortable quarters in our service, and discredited in
character, perhaps uncertain in health, became literally
a castaway, for scanty provision then existed for the
reclamation of drunkards, and the idea of reform, or,
better still, of prevention, was only just beginning to
dawn upon the minds of doctors, ministers, and
philanthropists.

And here I would mention that I am not attempting
to give an account of the great Temperance movement
that came into birth in England during the 'fifties, but
shall only touch upon it as it affected the lives of my
sister and myself. Suffice it to say that after having
witnessed the effects of the sin of intemperance, both
amongst our servants and in our village, we were ready
to be enlisted as ardent though inexperienced workers
in the cause. The call came first to my sister in the
'seventies with irresistible force from the words and
example of the Rev. Basil Wilberforce, son of our old
friend the Bishop of Oxford, whose whole heart was
given unreservedly to a work which he felt to be one
of extreme importance, and then through my sister to
me. Our dear mother gave her full approval and
support; my husband, though not entirely convinced
as to the method, knew only too well the necessity of
some steps being taken to arrest the alarming growth
of intemperance in this country. We began by helping
to start Bands of Hope in all the villages which we could

touch in Buckinghamshire round my old home, and in Hampshire near my sister's residence. Her recent widowhood had somewhat withdrawn her from appearing in public, but she was keenly alive to the work that seemed to be calling for her assistance.

I took the pledge in 1884, and have never had cause to regret my decision or to revoke the words to which I then put my signature. I became president of various temperance societies in the counties of Buckinghamshire and of Bedfordshire, besides doing much active work in London and in other parts of the kingdom, this bringing me into personal touch with many remarkable and interesting personages.

I have never had lessons in elocution, nor had I been taught how to address an audience, and I had in early days to learn how to conquer my terrible shyness, or rather nervousness, when speaking in public. But I was gifted with a voice that could carry well, and I had no great difficulty in putting my words together, so that in time I quite enjoyed my temperance campaigns, some of which were more successful than I could have wildly hoped for. I once had the great pleasure of taking forty pledges at a single meeting.

My sister and I made up our minds during one autumn to attack some of the strongest upholders of the enemy in her own village, that of Hamble. There we were permitted to speak in a cottage belonging to a fisherman, whose wife had invited a few of their friends to meet us. The man had long been known as a constant frequenter of the public-house, if not a confirmed drunkard, and his friends were much of the same calibre. The space was limited, and the number of our audience not more than twelve all told, but we left that cottage with hopeful and grateful hearts. I can remember how all those present, besides taking the pledge, vowed themselves to the work, suggesting other houses where we might hold similar meetings. And, indeed, we had no reason to regret that autumn cam-

SOCIAL WORK   431

paign.   It was during the " Blue Ribbon " crusade, and Chapter
I can recollect one of the tradesmen in the village of   XXI.
Netley remarking that " there was not a bit of blue
left, but that which was seen in the sky "—for not
only did our first convert take the pledge with his own
family, but he became a great champion in the cause,
and in consequence the whole place changed its character.

Some years later, when I had been speaking at
Netley, in my sister's " White Rose " Coffee Tavern, to
a crowded audience, and had referred to that cottage
meeting, mentioning the fact of its owner having signed
the pledge, and of his having induced others to do so,
an elderly man sitting close to the platform asked
leave to say a few words, and rising in his place
announced in a ringing voice : " I am the man who
took the pledge on that day from Mrs. Flower, and that
was before she was a ' lady.' "

A ripple of laughter greeted this, as it has done on
other occasions when I have ventured to repeat those
words.   Indeed, I have often remarked that a strain
of humour is seldom absent from a successful temperance
gathering, creating a bond of sympathy between speaker
and audience.

I can never forget one of those great temperance
gatherings at which it was my good fortune to be
present.   I can still see the eager faces upturned
towards the platform from which Canon Wilberforce
was holding his vast audience.   I can recall the slight
nervous frame of the speaker, his sensitive, keen face,
his brilliant and far-reaching glance.   I can still hear
that wonderful voice, arresting the attention of his
hearers, as it rang out boldly, entreatingly, pathetically,
humorously, and, at the end, victoriously !   He knew
how to awaken the interest of his audience, how to
amuse, and how to convince.   I can see the people
lingering on in the hall, loath to go, and pressing forward
to receive the blue ribbon during that wonderful
crusade.

My dear mother presented me with a " blue ribbon," but, unlike those which were distributed at the close of the meetings, my " ribbon " is a strip of dark blue sapphires.

During the early 'nineties I joined the British Women's Temperance Association, a society of which the late Lady Henry Somerset became the honoured president. That lady was a brilliant and impressive speaker, and she, as well as her sister, Adeline, Duchess of Bedford, had both originally taken the pledge from me. The society was a prosperous and growing one, but, unfortunately, there came a split amongst its members with the advent of Miss Frances Willard from America, that distinguished but autocratic temperance reformer and lecturer attempting to introduce debatable innovations into its constitution. From that split resulted the birth of another society, the Women's Total Abstinence Union, of which Lady Biddulph was president for three years. My sister gave a very wholehearted support to this movement, and was herself a most popular and successful president of the society for terms of three, five, and then seven years !

The competition between the two societies did no harm to the cause, and probably increased the interest in the temperance question. At all events the work done by both was admitted as being well worthy, not only of kindly notice, but also of some abuse—a sure sign that the cause was prospering. Thus the two Women's Societies were well to the fore in the work that they were doing, and certainly did their share in the successful attack that was being made throughout England upon the drink traffic and drinking habits.

I cannot end this short account of my connection with the temperance movement without mentioning that my dear sister's unceasing efforts in the promotion of the cause have been fully recognised, both in Southampton and London, where, at meetings convened to do her honour, she has been publicly congratulated by many grateful friends and co-workers, who have always proved her staunch supporters.

In the 'eighties we made the acquaintance of Mr. Arnold White, a remarkable man, whose great idea at that time was to make widely known the condition of the unemployed dock labourers amongst men and women who might never have realised such distress. He organised free breakfasts for the dockers in the East End of London, enlisting at the same time the presence of well‑known and distinguished men and women, all of some social importance. These breakfasts became prominent features in the annals of philanthropic effort, creating a great stir at the time.

Mr. White was then a man of about thirty-five years of age, with a strong face, a quick and intelligent eye, and a voice and delivery well suited to arrest the attention of his audience. Besides his philanthropic ardour Mr. White had a gift for organisation and a wonderful driving power. He had been deeply impressed by the heroic story and tragic fate of General Gordon, and was anxious to link the name of one whom many may have thought mistaken, but whom all acknowledged to be gloriously intrepid, with a scheme which he— Arnold White—had originated, and which he hoped might prove of lasting benefit to those amongst whom he worked. His intention was to put some plan of emigration before men who could not find means of sustenance in England, suggesting how they might obtain employment in our overseas dominions, if this were impossible in the home country. On this theme he both wrote and spoke. My cousin, Ferdinand de Rothschild, who had been brought into touch with Mr. White, was very favourably impressed by him and thought the scheme was one to be considered. He introduced Mr. White to us, and at his request we organised a meeting at Surrey House for the purpose of making his views known.

My husband was in the chair at this well-attended

2 F

gathering, where H.R.H. Princess Louise was an interested member of the audience. After a few introductory words from Cyril, Mr. White gave a short sketch of General Gordon, whom he had known personally, and for whom he cherished real hero-worship. He then proceeded to place his scheme before the audience : it was that of opening halls in various parts of London on Sunday evenings, when all places of recreation were generally closed or unapproachable, and inviting the passer-by freely to enter for kindly intercourse, and for pure and healthy enjoyment. He would undertake with others to find men and women eager and able to offer their practical assistance, and he would be prepared to accept the services of all those who could provide music, vocal and instrumental, readings and recitations from good authors, or addresses on interesting subjects. Later on, useful debates might be started. Arnold White spoke well and convincingly ; his scheme, after some opposition, was finally accepted and brought into being under the name of " The Gordon League." H.R.H. Princess Louise was president, my husband chairman and treasurer, and Canon Barker, late Dean of Carlisle, a very active member of our committee.

Marchmont Hall in the West Central district of London was engaged for the Sunday evening experiments—Mr. White being director. Fortunately it was found that Sunday suited those who kindly gave their services, as well as those who were to benefit by them, better than any other evening in the week.

H.R.H. Princess Louise was often present at these Marchmont Hall gatherings, which had no political colour and kept strictly to their plan of campaign : that of offering pleasant evenings to the people, with some hope of future employment to those seeking it. I was present at some of these meetings, and took careful note both of the demeanour and the observations of the audience. Of all that was offered them, I believe

they responded most readily to simple ballad-singing—
one poor blind woman telling us how eagerly she looked
forward to each recurring Sunday, and the treat that was
in store for her.   These gatherings were carried on for
many years ; but the Gordon League embraced many
other philanthropic movements, amongst which I may
mention Mothers' Meetings for women not attached to
any special parish.   Ladies who were present at the
Sunday evening receptions were also often responsible
for the Mothers' Meetings, which took place on week
afternoons or evenings, in different parts of London.
It was then that garments of all sorts were made,
renovated, mended, finally prepared for distribution
or for sale.   Prizes were annually awarded for the best
work, whilst a pleasant relationship was established
between the workers and the organisers.

It was on one such occasion in the year 1919 that
I had the honour of accompanying Princess Louise.
After the prize-giving had taken place we were on the
point of leaving, when a rather dilapidated-looking
member of the working party walked up to me with a
smiling countenance, informing me that she had known
me in past days, for had she not once been present at
a party given at Surrey House to the Liberal Members
of the day and their wives?   I wondered in what capacity
she had attended that function, and was somewhat
astonished when she informed me—" as a guest."

In the early days Mr. White had visited us at Aston
Clinton and had there conceived a great admiration
for my dear mother, and for all her unselfish work in
the village ; so I feel drawn to conclude this brief
sketch with a letter addressed to me by him, in regard
to a beautiful little paper written by my mother called
" A Dream " :

DEVONSHIRE CLUB,
April 29, 1885.

Baron Ferdinand has given me " A Dream," which was,
I understand, written by your mother.

I do not know when or why " A Dream " was written, but I never read a more touching or pathetic and yet simple statement of what is wanted to get at the apathetic English poor.

Most of the " Dream " ought to be bodily incorporated into the Gordon League ; in fact, the League is but the fulfilment of the " Dream."—I am, yours sincerely,

ARNOLD WHITE.

" The Dream " was written for and read at the opening of the Anthony Hall, a building erected by my mother in our village (Aston Clinton) in 1884, and dedicated by her to the memory of my dear father. I may add that the Anthony Hall from the very first hour of its existence has been immensely popular in the parish, and has supplied and does supply a very great need, opening its doors to meetings and classes of all sorts, not to speak of concerts, theatricals, and entertainments without end.

During the Great War the Anthony Hall became a canteen under the auspices of the Y.M.C.A., and fully justified its popularity. Never has a building of the kind been more appreciated, and it is indeed a worthy memorial to both my parents, who so loved Aston Clinton and their happy country home.

It was in the year 1885 that the Recreative Evening Schools Association came into being. The one name most closely connected with this movement was that of the late Dr. Paton, a most remarkable man, the Principal of a Congregational College at Nottingham, and well known in that city and throughout England.

The education of the masses had, as yet, been somewhat barren in its results. Dr. Paton believed in its elevating power if properly directed, and was determined to devote himself to this object. After paying several visits to Germany in the 'seventies—where he studied the educational methods of that country, then far in advance of our own, and was most hospitably entertained by some of the great professors of the day—

Dr. Paton was impressed with the necessity of prolonging the education of children after they had left the day school, and prepared his scheme accordingly. His name became known to Princess Louise, who was speedily interested in his views, and who introduced him to us.

Dr. Paton was a man of commanding presence, with a noble head and a very gentle and winsome expression of countenance. His voice was soft, and his speech slow and very deliberate, as if he were always searching for the most appropriate words in which to clothe his ideas. He did not at first sight look or speak as a leader, but I was deeply impressed by him after one or two talks we had together, and I felt sure that there dwelt a refined and gracious spirit behind that somewhat slow manner. He had one interview with my dear mother and was greatly attracted by her personality. He said he kept her remembrance as a beautiful picture in his memory.

Closely allied to Dr. Paton, and also belonging to the same church, was Mr. Flower (no connection of my husband's), a Congregational minister of repute at Nottingham, who kindly gave up his duties in that city in order to undertake this new branch of important work for London and the country.

A committee was formed of which H.R.H. Princess Louise was our honoured president; my husband, treasurer and chairman; Dr. Paton, honorary secretary; Mr. Flower, secretary; whilst acting as members of committee were, amongst others, the late Rt. Hon. Hayes Fisher (Lord Downham), the late Rev. Freeman-Wills, a clergyman who ran a butcher's shop in the East End for the benefit of the poor, and Mr. Rawson, a clever man of business. The Princess herself took a very active part in the work, and on one occasion headed a deputation to the London School Board for the purpose of gaining permission to use the larger rooms of the board schools for Evening Continuation

Classes, this request being readily granted. The result, I may here say, fully justified the demand. There, with the help of a few devoted men and women—teachers and others—instruction of a practical and recreative character was successfully carried on.

Great hopes were built on the success of these Recreative Evening Classes, which proved ultimately to be the forerunners of many present - day educational methods. They touched a subject that Princess Louise had made so very much her own, that of art in the home in its many branches. But with singular wisdom and foresight Her Royal Highness urged that " the art side of the scheme should not hold too prominent a place in our programme." There were many who had declared that the love of beauty and the promotion of art belonged to the foolish luxuries of the upper classes. The Princess, I remember, pointed out at one of our meetings " that the idea of art teaching should creep along with the scheme rather than be pushed forward by itself and so risk attracting adverse public criticism." It was, indeed, the object of our Association, so the Princess affirmed, to put the possibility of learning good and useful trades before the pupils, thus giving them not only the opportunity for practical study, but also the means of spending happily-employed instead of dull evenings.

That the work of this Association had a sound moral influence upon those for whom it was initiated was proved by a few welcome words from a policeman to a member of our committee, to the effect that, where formerly two policemen together had been required to patrol the streets in the districts of the schools, a young girl could now walk alone there in safety.

I may also recall that two or more exhibitions of work by pupils in these evening schools were held at Surrey House, where also we gave a most successful party to the voluntary teachers and to others whose services we hoped to enlist. Princess Louise, our

President, was with us, and most graciously spoke to each CHAPTER
individual present—about 200—heartily encouraging XXI.
them in the work they were so generously undertaking
for the Association, and suggesting some new subjects
for their consideration. It interested me to gain from
our guests some account of their daily occupations. I
was greatly struck by their good-will in giving up
some of their leisure time to those classes, and by the
enthusiasm with which they met our views.

It is a pleasant memory that so much that proved
useful and delightful to the boys and girls of the 'eighties
and early 'nineties should have been initiated at Surrey
House, inspired by Dr. Paton, encouraged by Princess
Louise, and so ably steered to success by my husband
and his colleagues.

Early in the 'nineties it was my good fortune to
meet with some very remarkable women, and through
their acquaintance a new sphere of work was opened
up to me which gradually became one of absorbing
interest. I think it was a lady of the name of Miss
Fanny Calder, from Liverpool, who, furthering the
methods of the Recreative Evening Schools Association in her own city, was brought into communication
with us in London. She it was who first introduced
me to one or two of the leading spirits of an Association
destined to develop into the National Union of Women
Workers, lately (1919) rechristened the National Council
of Women of Great Britain and Ireland.

It was at Bristol in the autumn of 1892 that I met
Miss Hubbard for the first and only time in my life.
She was an old friend and disciple of Miss Ellice Hopkins,
that deeply religious and courageous woman, who
approached the question of rescue work from the unusual side of enlisting the sympathy of men in the cause.
With this aim she used to address meetings of men on
the subject, and evoked their interest and co-operation
in the task which she set before herself.

Miss Hubbard, who was gifted with much initiative

and working power, was then presiding over a small meeting of ladies, amongst whom, standing forth clearly in my remembrance of those days, were Mrs. Creighton, wife of the late Bishop of London; Mrs. Alfred Booth, of Liverpool; Miss Mary Clifford, so well known for her pioneer work as Lady Guardian in Bristol; Mrs. George Cadbury, whose husband was the originator of the justly celebrated Garden Suburb, Bournville, Birmingham; Lady Laura Ridding, the Hon. Mrs. Arthur Lyttelton, Mrs. Beale, and Miss Janes, ladies whose names were already connected with many admirable activities in the world of philanthropic effort. Miss Janes, a special friend and co-worker of Miss Hubbard, was for many years to hold a most important position in the National Union of Women Workers.

The lines on which this important and fast-growing Union was formed were undenominational, or all-denominational, and were without party bias, but the note that characterised both the Executive Committee Meetings and the Conferences was an elevated and distinctly reverent one. The aim of the Union was to focus all branches of women's work, religious, educational, scientific, philanthropic, social, and industrial, to establish a common bond of interest between workers, giving them at the annual conferences, which took place in a different city each year, opportunities of making their views widely known, and of having them debated and discussed. The result fully justified the hopes of the founders and early members. The Union spread its branches through many counties and cities of England and Scotland, touching Belfast and Dublin as well.

The first President who succeeded Miss Hubbard was Adeline, Duchess of Bedford, to be followed by Mrs. Creighton, who held her first presidency for three years. I began by joining the Union as a humble member, from which I rose to being elected on the Executive Committee. In 1899 I was appointed one of the three delegates representing Great Britain at the International Conference

held that year in London, owing to the illness of Mrs.
Booth, whose place I was asked to fill.

It was after this Conference that the Union became
affiliated to unions of the same character and with
similar aims in foreign countries, and was henceforth
named the International Union of Women Workers,
Lady Aberdeen being the first International President.
Conferences have been held at stated intervals in various
cities of Europe, such as Berlin, Rome, Stockholm,
Christiania, even once crossing the Atlantic to Canada.

In 1901 I was appointed President. There was no
election that year. How I felt about my new honours
I described in my diary at the time, and cannot resist
repeating here what I then wrote down :

" I am President of the National Union of Women
Workers. I certainly did not crave that honour. I
tried hard to escape from this, but I was talked over.
Encouraged by my husband and by my sister, I accepted
the honour, but not without fear and trembling. Never
shall I forget how women of different or opposed creeds
and churches joined in giving me their unanimous
support. I was duly appointed on October 29, after
a five hours' Council meeting, when we were all so worn
out that no one seemed at first to take note of the fact
that appeared so important a one to me. However,
before leaving the Hall, I received warm congratulations
from the members of the Executive, who all came
crowding round me, whilst dear Mrs. Arthur Lyttelton,
President for that year, gave me a charming word of
welcome in a little speech announcing my appointment
to the Assembly.

" Will they all be equally pleased with me at the
end of next year ? "

I suppose they must have been, because I continued
without opposition as President until 1903.[1] But when

---

[1] In 1902 we met at Edinburgh, and in 1903 at Cheltenham and
Gloucester ; in all three places I presided over the Conferences.

in 1919 my name, proposed by Lady Suffield, came up for election in Norwich as member of the Executive Committee for the Norwich Branch of the National Council, I was not elected, and quite right too. In that year, feeling that my time for retiring had come, I withdrew from active membership of the London Executive, but at one of the Conferences Mrs. Creighton, in a very kind little speech, proposed me as one of the Hon. Vice-Presidents, when I was duly elected and much gratified with the distinction I had received.

I feel that I cannot close this slight and somewhat sketchy account of a phase of work in which I was deeply interested without mentioning, and this very gratefully, how much I owe to the Council for having brought me into close and friendly connection with many distinguished women, whose society I found stimulating and inspiring. It also opened for me the doors of houses in some of our important provincial cities, where otherwise I might never have had the privilege of admission. It was, moreover, under the auspices of the Union that I attended a deeply interesting International Conference at Berlin in the year 1904. It was then that I read two papers—the one on Temperance Reform in England, the other on our Prison System for Women Convicts. I had very large audiences on both occasions, who listened to me most attentively, and upon their demanding that the language used should be German in preference to English, I was much pleased to be able to comply with this request.

Happy days of interesting work carried on in pleasant companionship under pleasant conditions, widening my views of life, and giving me lasting interests that supply my old age with grateful, golden memories.

CHAPTER XXII

PRISON WORK

WORK CONNECTED WITH THE FEMALE CONVICT PRISON AT AYLESBURY

IN the year 1894 Mr. Asquith, then Home Secretary in the Liberal Government, under Lord Rosebery's Premiership, appointed a committee to inquire into the condition of our prisons and penal institutions. In their report the members of that committee affirmed that hitherto the prison authorities had been disposed to regard the prisoners as a hopeless and worthless section of the community, and to consider that their own moral and legal responsibilities ended at the prison gate. There were but very few lady visitors to the women in detention, and they were working with but scanty encouragement and without fixed rules, their presence being only countenanced in a local, and hardly ever in a convict, prison.

It was then that Mr. Asquith, whose heart was set on prison reform, did me the honour to ask me whether I would agree to visit, at regular and stated intervals, the inmates of the one female convict prison for England and Wales, which was about to be removed from Woking to Aylesbury.

In that town of Bucks a local prison for men and women had stood for many years : strange to say, it had possessed some mysterious sense of repulsion for me when, as a child, I used to ride or drive past it,

perhaps because it seemed haunted by the figure of a
man—the last man who had been hanged at Aylesbury,
and hanged in public on the top of the arch, above
the prison gates.

When I received my official appointment I was told
that I should have a lady colleague, who proved to
be Adeline, Duchess of Bedford, also that Sir Algernon
West would be one of the regular prison visitors, as he
had been before at Woking.

I went for the first time to the Aylesbury Prison in
December 1894, under the chaperonage of Sir Algernon,
and I could not have had a better guide. It was a
gloomy afternoon, seemingly in keeping with my introduction to those whose lives were being spent in detention.
The big gates swung back and admitted us into the yard.
As they closed upon us, and as door after door was unlocked and re-locked, I had that sensation of remoteness
from the living world which seems to be inseparable
from prison walls. Every man we met was in uniform
and saluted stiffly; every wardress was dressed severely
in black, wearing a small poke-bonnet on her head,
carrying a big cluster of keys and a whistle attached to
a chain fastened at her waist, that rattled against her
when she walked. The wardresses seemed to me as if
they all had the same kind of bearing and expression;
they spoke in whispers and stood patiently, yet alert
to do our bidding.

When we had penetrated into the inner ward or
gallery of the prison, Sir Algernon West called out in
a loud voice: " I am a visitor from the Home Office;
has any prisoner a request to make ? "

Immediately there followed shrill ringing of bells, and
the voices of prisoners were heard asking for an interview. In turn the cell doors were unlocked, and Sir
Algernon, accompanied by the Governor and a wardress,
and followed by my wondering self, was admitted to
hear the varying requests or complaints of the women.
I saw the prisoners for the first time in their brown,

green, or blue garments, the colours denoting their prison grade (these have of late years given place to others of washing material—hence more hygienic), and wearing white caps not unlike those worn by the French peasantry. I noticed the expression on the faces, and remarked that there was nothing particularly striking or tragic about them, but to me the whole place seemed clothed in gloom and shrouded in silence. I felt that I was seeing women who had possibly not looked on the outer world for years, some of whom, having escaped capital punishment, were then undergoing what we called a life sentence.

I was allowed to speak to some very notorious criminals, amongst whom was Mrs. Maybrick, whose trial and conviction had belonged to the *causes célèbres* of her day. I can recall her only complaint at the time, namely, that she could not see to read by the gas jet with which her cell was supplied. We had many occasions for conversation later on.

My heart sank within me when we left the wards, there was such a cast-iron look about the place, such an oppressive sense of unalterable rule and method. I much doubted whether my visits would tend to the good of the convicts or the amelioration of their prison lives. My companion, on our homeward drive, was, however, most encouraging, and, on looking back, I feel very grateful at having had such an experience as that of a prison visitor for so many years of my life.

As time went on our position underwent some changes and we had added responsibilities, for the Duchess and I were appointed members of the Board of Prison Visitors, meeting monthly at Aylesbury, on which seven gentlemen were already serving. Sir Algernon West, our first chairman, was keenly alive to all matters of reform, just, yet merciful, a favourite with the authorities and thoughtful for the convicts. Lord Buckinghamshire succeeded him for a short while, was followed in his turn by Colonel Goodall, who finally retired under the stress of illness, when Adeline, Duchess of Bedford took his place. There was general agreement as to her fitness for the position, and perhaps it was as a compliment to her sex that I was asked to act as second on the Board during her chairmanship, which only ceased when the convicts were removed to Liverpool from Aylesbury.

In 1901 the Lady Visitors' Association came into existence, which provided, under the capable presidency of Adeline, Duchess of Bedford, ladies qualified to work amongst the criminal population of all our local prisons as well as the convict prison. Theirs was the task of visiting the women, sympathetically, intelligently, wisely, regularly, always working in direct co-operation with the prison authorities and, through the Duchess, with the Home Office. I believe that this Association has been of untold benefit both to the woman in her cell and to those in charge of her, its members forming that much-needed connecting link between the prison and the outer world.

I should like to mention here that the Duchess proved admirable in all her prison work, and gained, as time went on, the complete confidence of the Home Office. Her death, which occurred in the spring of 1920, after a very brief illness, was deeply mourned by her colleagues, and by many of the poor women to whom she had been an inspiration during their detention and a kind benefactress upon their release ; indeed, it will be difficult, if not impossible, ever to fill the place she once occupied. We worked harmoniously together for some considerable number of years, and had the happiness of seeing the introduction and success of many of our suggested reforms. Amongst these I may look back during the long vista of years upon the advent of a qualified nurse for the Infirmary ; of better and more suitable clothing ; decent nightdresses ; shoes to wear in the cell; hats instead of old-fashioned bonnets ; tooth-brushes when asked for ; greater variety in food ;

butter served on plates instead of on brown paper in
the hospital ward ; also strips of carpet for the patients
by the side of their beds in the winter months ; more
interesting employment ; more educational advantages ;
a better and more readable selection of books for the
prison library ; seats with backs to them in the work-
rooms and cells (oh, how rejoiced I was when I
first caught sight of a *real chair*!) ; plain glass windows
instead of frosted panes, when not overlooking a
thoroughfare, etc., etc. One can imagine with what
delight I wrote " granted " in my note-book when I was
told that my suggestions had been favourably considered.

The Duchess took special pleasure in adorning the
chapel, hitherto an ugly, barrack-like hall, and by this
means awakening the women's love for their House
of Prayer. She also originated recreative employment ;
this proved an immense boon, and much ingenuity
and inventiveness were manifested in all manner of
articles produced and sold during the year.

By Sir Algernon West's desire the women were at
length, as a reward for good behaviour, allowed to
retain in their cells the photographs of near relatives,
which were occasionally sent to them in their letters.
This is a concession deeply valued. During the Great
War I was constantly shown photographs of men in
khaki, and these portraits seemed to have had the power
of keeping the flames of loyalty and patriotism alive
in the hearts of the recipients.

I recall one incident that made a great impression
upon me at the time, and that I should not like to omit
from these Reminiscences. It occurred in 1901, a few
days after the death of Queen Victoria. I was visiting
the prison, going round with the Governor, anxious to
hear whether the women had shown any feeling on
being told of the passing away of their Queen, when I
noticed that some of the convicts had small black bows
pinned on to the front of their gowns. On asking for
an explanation, I heard that the women, wishing to

show some mark of respect to the memory of their Sovereign, had managed to pull small pieces off their boot-laces, which they wore as a sign of mourning. I was deeply moved by such an action, and ventured to recount this to King Edward VII. when he visited my mother at Aston Clinton. I am glad that I did so, for His Majesty was evidently greatly touched, and said more than once, " Did they really do so, poor creatures ? "

After years of experience I feel sure that intelligent and humane interest taken in these unhappy derelicts of humanity can and does produce some real improvement in their moral condition. Also that true consideration shown by the visitors for the increased comfort and well-being of the officers tends to bring about a happier atmosphere, affecting both those detained and those in charge of them. Humanise the officer and you humanise the prisoner. I once used these words at a large gathering in Glasgow, and received on the morrow a grateful letter from a prison warder who had heard me speak. After all, the gaoler and the captive are both human beings, moved alike by little acts of kindness, possessing hearts capable of being touched and responsive to a word of sympathy.

I was permitted, with the help of kind friends, to organise yearly concerts or entertainments within the walls of the prison, and these proved most enjoyable ; often the women were encouraged by the performers to join in the chorus of the songs, and indeed it was touching to listen to those voices, some tremulous with age, others fresh and strong in the vigour of youth. The recitations would call forth shouts of laughter at times, and at others audible sobs from those very emotional beings, and I have occasionally had to beg the performers not to select pieces that might prove too harrowing or exciting. On one occasion a glorious orchestra, most kindly sent by my cousin, Alfred de Rothschild, found a rapturous reception, which quite astonished the performers, unused to such an audience.

The women were extremely grateful for these enter- tainments and would frequently ask me on my visits, " When are we to have one of our concerts ? "

During my many years of prison-visiting I have had the opportunity given me of seeing some very celebrated female criminals, also of becoming acquainted with a number of suffragettes, and during the Great War with some of the foreign spies, amongst them being a very clever and well-known woman, Wertheim by name, whose life ended in Broadmoor.

And here I should like to say that whilst I acted as official visitor to the prison I only met with three Jewish female convicts, two of these being of German birth ; I have lost sight of the latter, but the one English-born has since married respectably and is now leading a quiet and normal life. I may add that amongst the convicts there were, at various times, a Moorish woman ; a negress who was set free before the expiration of her sentence and died in a Roman Catholic Home ; some American women, two well known as very clever criminals ; a Spaniard, more than one French woman, an Italian, and a Belgian ; in fact, I might compile a very interesting account of the various women I have met in prison, and of my experiences in connection with them.

I know that it would be impolitic on my part to mention the names of women notorious for the crimes they have committed or for their frequent attempts to evade justice ; still, I may record a few facts connected with the cases of some of the convicts whom I often saw on my visits.

One young and very good-looking woman had repeatedly asked the Governor to let her have a German book to read in her cell ; she assured him that she was proficient in that language, for her husband, to whom she stated she had been married at the early age of seventeen, had been an Austrian officer. The Governor approached me on the subject and asked me to put the

2 G

woman's professed knowledge to the test. I did so by going into her cell and addressing her in German. She looked at me in surprise, shook her head—not one word had she understood. In trying to give me a satisfactory explanation of the difficulty in which she had landed herself, she declared that she had forgotten the sound of the language but could read it with pleasure. However, we did not furnish her with German literature, and discovered later that the Austrian officer had been a pure invention of her brain in order to mislead the Governor as to her antecedents.

Another woman, an American, gave me a graphic and most thrilling account of her attempt to steal a valuable pearl necklace from a well-known sale-room : she had managed most ingeniously to have the real necklace perfectly copied and to substitute the copy for the authentic one ; she actually started to leave the place where it had been exhibited with the stolen prize in her small hand-bag. But her movements had given rise to the suspicion of an attendant; moreover, the small yellow ticket on the bogus necklace was not quite the right shade ; a messenger boy was hastily despatched to stop her on her way down the street. Very nearly did she escape, but when she attempted to enter a cab the attention of the driver was arrested by the frantic shouts of the boy in pursuit, and, as she herself expressed it, " the game was up." The woman seemed evidently to enjoy narrating the dramatic incidents of her story; indeed, her mind still clung to the remembrance of the necklace, for one day, upon seeing a string of pearls on the neck of a visitor, who had kindly taken part in one of the annual concerts that I was permitted to provide for the entertainment of the convicts, she said to me, heaving a deep sigh, " Those are just like the pearls that I so nearly got ! Was I not clever ? " " Yes," I replied, " but, happily, not quite clever enough."

One poor young woman, who had been cruelly treated

before she committed the crime which led to her arrest, had very nearly completed her own destruction when her intentions were discovered. The Governor asked me to visit her in her cell, and to form my own conclusions as to the state of her mind. It was a very moving interview, and I extorted a promise from the prisoner that she would let me come and see her again before making any further attempt on her life. She gave me her word and faithfully kept it, although, as she expressed herself, " she longed to go and have done with her troubles." I returned for a second visit and sat for some time listening to her story, but it was the last that I saw of her, for soon afterwards the condition of her mind necessitated her removal to Broadmoor, where, I believe, she ultimately died.

Another woman of very bad antecedents, who had been connected with an East End murder case, so convinced the prison authorities in Aylesbury, as well as the late Duchess of Bedford and myself, that she had been completely under the influence of drink and not even the chief offender in the crime for which she had been condemned, that we wrote and signed an appeal for mercy, twenty-four hours before the execution was to have taken place. My colleague and I awaited the result of our letter with intense anxiety, and to our relief heard from headquarters that the reprieve had been decided upon even before our appeal had been received. The capital sentence was cancelled and a life sentence substituted. At first the woman's gratitude was extreme and touching, but later she evinced some indignation at the term of her imprisonment, and became morose and sullen as well as violently disposed towards one of her visitors. This visitor had remarked to the woman that she was in all likelihood safer within prison walls than outside amongst her turbulent friends, and this so infuriated her that she seized a chair and was about to hurl it at the head of the somewhat indiscreet speaker, who was swiftly placed out of danger's way by the chaplain and warder. She was not allowed to see the woman again for some months ; however, when the prisoner heard that this same visitor had passed through a time of trouble and of sorrow, and had not been able to resume her prison duties, she asked to be allowed to send a penitent and sympathetic message, and I, the hapless visitor, felt touched by the woman's words and kindly thought, and from that time saw her frequently until death freed her from the prison cell.

I had always imagined that death in the prison would be singularly gloomy and terrible, but after visiting two convicts at the point of death my views underwent some change. One of the women had completed her sentence, but was too ill at the time to be released. I was struck by the tenderness and kindliness which surrounded both cases and which materially helped them in their last hours. I had promised the one, a Roman Catholic, through her priest, that she should have a mass said for her soul and flowers laid upon her coffin. These promises seemed to occasion a delirium of joy, for the poor woman, upon receiving my message, sent for Governor, doctor, nurse, and warders, insisting upon telling them herself that she would be treated as a free woman, and died almost rejoicing. The other case with which I had been concerned was that of a woman who died full of gratitude to doctor and nurse, saying she had experienced far greater kindness in her captivity than she would have done in the outer world.

And here I should like to state, from personal observation, that it would be a graceful and merciful action on the part of the prison visitors were they to supply, with the sanction of the authorities, some faithful copy of a beautiful or helpful picture, which, placed at the foot of the bed of any sick or dying convict, might so touch her heart that her thoughts would be led away from her dreary surroundings to a possible

realisation of such peace and forgiveness as we hope
await her.

I think I have learnt to detach the woman, in my mind, from the crime she has committed, and for which she is paying the penalty of the law; I have also recognised the extreme difficulty of giving adequate and sensible assistance to a prisoner on her release. And here I would repeat that prison-visiting offers a wide field to those who take a true living interest in their fellow-creatures. The visitor may be, and often is, saddened by what she sees, disheartened by what she fails to effect, but the conviction that she becomes a human link between the woman in her loneliness and the world of freedom encourages her in her task and in her endeavour to bring some ray of comfort, some gleam of hope, some ideal of a pure and beautiful life, even into the prison cell.

By the courtesy and help of the Home Office I gained access to some of the prisons in France—one being the great prison for men at Fresne, which no woman had ever before been allowed to enter; also to a prison in Berlin and to one in Florence. I once peeped into the courtyard of a House of Detention in Tangier, where the wretched prisoners were to be seen miserably clad in rags and with chains on their arms, as I have mentioned in a former chapter.

Perhaps I may be forgiven by any reader of these Reminiscences for closing this chapter on prison-visiting with a letter containing a sympathetic reference to the prisoners from Sir Evelyn Ruggles-Brise, Head of the Prison Commission, addressed to me from the Home Office :

PRISON COMMISSION,
HOME OFFICE, WHITEHALL, S.W.,
July 15, 1918.

DEAR LADY BATTERSEA—I very much regret that circumstances have, at least for a time, severed your connection with our convicts at Aylesbury.

For all your good and humane work, and all your generous thought and action on behalf of these unfortunate women, let me thank you most cordially on behalf of the official administration, and you may at least feel assured that all that you have done has been greatly appreciated.

The suggestions you make as to relieving the monotony of their lives at Liverpool are valuable, and I will discuss them with the Governor, whom I am seeing this week.

You may be sure that I shall leave nothing undone which can humanise and brighten their lives. . . .—Yours sincerely,   E. RUGGLES-BRISE.

It would be too difficult, nay impossible, a task for my pen to reproduce pictures of the past eight years —of the Great War that convulsed Europe, and has left its mark upon the smallest village in England. I am sincerely thankful that the greater part of my recollections take me back to a happier and more restful time.   Indeed, there are days when I am haunted by Wordsworth's lines :

> The homely beauty of the good old cause
>   Is gone ; our peace, our fearful innocence,
> And pure religion, breathing household laws.

Yet far be it from me to end on so sad a note, for does not another poet tell us that

> Hope had never lost her youth ;
> She did but look thro' dimmer eyes.

A SELECTION OF NEW BOOKS

MEMORIES OF TRAVEL. By Viscount Bryce. 8vo

A SCRAP BOOK. By George Saintsbury. Royal 16mo.

Mr. Saintsbury describes this volume as "a few notes of the voyage of life as taken by myself—notes lighter and graver—a farrago, in short."

THE GOLDEN BOUGH : A STUDY IN MAGIC AND RELIGION. By Sir James George Frazer, F.B.A., F.R.S. Abridged Edition. With Frontispiece. 8vo. 18s. net.

THE INTERPRETERS. By A. E. (George W. Russell), Author of *The Candle of Vision*, etc. Crown 8vo. 6s. net.

LATER POEMS. By W. B. Yeats. Crown 8vo. 10s. 6d. net.

PLAYS IN PROSE AND VERSE. Written for an Irish Theatre, and generally with the help of a Friend. By W. B. Yeats. Crown 8vo. 10s. 6d. net.

KRINDLESYKE. A Drama. By Wilfrid Gibson, Author of *Livelihood*, etc. Crown 8vo. 6s. net.

POEMS. By Thomas Sharp. Crown 8vo. 6s. net.

DRAMATIC LEGENDS AND OTHER POEMS. By Padraic Colum. Crown 8vo.

NEIGHBOURS HENCEFORTH. By Owen Wister, Author of *A Straight Deal; or, The Ancient Grudge*, etc. Crown 8vo. 7s. 6d. net.

A book about France, which contains a moving description of the devastation, and an exhaustive study of the problems, created by the recent war.

LONDON : MACMILLAN AND CO., Ltd.

2

A SELECTION OF NEW BOOKS

HISTORY OF THE GREAT WAR. Based on Official Documents, by direction of the Historical Section of the Committee of Imperial Defence. Vol. I. Military Operations, France and Belgium, 1914. Mons, the Retreat to the Seine, the Marne, and the Aisne, August–October 1914. Compiled by Brigadier-General J. E. EDMONDS, C.B., C.M.G. With 8 Sketches of Operations. 8vo. 21s. net.

> 34 General, Battle, and Situation Maps in separate case. 21s. net.

THE IRISH GUARDS IN THE GREAT WAR. Edited and Compiled from their Diaries and Papers by RUDYARD KIPLING. With Maps and Plans. 2 Vols. Medium 8vo.

A KIPLING ANTHOLOGY: PROSE. Fcap. 8vo. Cloth, 6s. net. Leather, 7s. 6d. net.

MAUD. A Monodrama. By ALFRED, LORD TENNYSON. With 8 full-page Plates in Colour, and numerous Illustrations in Black and White, by EDMUND J. SULLIVAN. *Ordinary Edition.* Medium 8vo. 10s. net. *Large Paper Edition*, printed on hand-made paper, with the illustrations in Black and White printed on India paper and mounted in the text. Limited to 500 copies, each copy signed by the artist. Super Royal 8vo. 30s. net.

WORKS OF FICTION

THE CATHEDRAL. By HUGH WALPOLE. Crown 8vo. 7s. 6d. net. *Large Paper Edition.* Limited to 250 copies. Demy 8vo. 18s. net.

THE ENCHANTED APRIL. By the Author of *Elizabeth and her German Garden.* With Frontispiece in Colour. Crown 8vo. 7s. 6d. net.

THE POOR MAN. By STELLA BENSON, Author of *I Pose*, etc. Crown 8vo. 6s. net.

WHO WAS JANE? A Story for Young People of all Ages. By EVELYN SHARP. With 8 full-page Illustrations in Black and White by CHARLES E. BROCK. Crown 8vo. 7s. 6d. net.

LONDON: MACMILLAN AND CO., LTD.

I

Printed in the United States
105523LV00005B/192/A

9 781428 655188

INDEX

2 H

Printed in Great Britain by R. & R. CLARK, LIMITED, Edinburgh.